Constructing Social Psychology

Creative and Critical Processes

This collection of papers by William J. McGuire reports research on the phenomenal self, revealing how we perceive ourselves and other complex stimuli selectively in terms of distinctive or atypical features, often noticing what is missing rather than what is there. The content, structure, and processing of thought systems surrounding the self and other complex stimuli are shown to function by balancing logical consistency, realistic coping, and hedonic gratification. Attitude-change and social-influence processes are described, with particular attention given to the personality correlates of persuadability, how beliefs can be immunized against persuasion, how persuasive communications affect beliefs, and how people can be persuaded by Socratic questioning that does not give them new information but rather directs their attention to selected subsets of information they already have. Also reported are findings on language and thought, psychology and history, and techniques of creative thinking in psychology and other fields.

William J. McGuire is a professor of psychology at Yale University. A Fulbright scholar and Guggenheim fellow, McGuire received the Distinguished Scientific Contributions Award from the American Psychological Association and the Distinguished Scientist Award from the Society for Experimental Social Psychology and is a William James Fellow in the American Psychological Society.

Constructing Social Psychology

Creative and Critical Processes

William J. McGuire

CAMBRIDGE
UNIVERSITY PRESS

PUBLISHED BY THE PRESS SYNDICATE OF THE UNIVERSITY OF CAMBRIDGE
The Pitt Building, Trumpington Street, Cambridge, United Kingdom

CAMBRIDGE UNIVERSITY PRESS
The Edinburgh Building, Cambridge CB2 2RU, UK   http: //www.cup.cam.ac.uk
40 West 20th Street, New York, NY 10011-4211, USA   http: //www.cup.org
10 Stamford Road, Oakleigh, Melbourne 3166, Australia

First published 1999

Printed in the United States of America

Typeface Times Roman 11/13 pt   *System* QuarkXPress™ [CS]

*A catalog record for this book is available from
the British Library.*

Library of Congress Cataloging-in-Publication Data
McGuire, William James (1925–)
    Constructing social psychology : creative and critical processes /
William J. McGuire.
       p.   cm.
    Includes bibliographical references (p. 433–42).
    ISBN 0-521-64107-1(h6.) – ISBN 0-521-64672-3 (pbk.)
    1. Social psychology – Research.   2. Social influence.   3. Attitude
change.   4. Persuasion (Psychology).   5. Thought and thinking.
6. Learning, Psychology of.   7. Self.   8. McGuire, William James
(1925) – Career in psychology.   I. Title.
HM251.M394   1999
302 – dc21   98-24906
                                                                        CIP

ISBN 0 521 64107 1 hardback
ISBN 0 521 64672 3 paperback

"In Breughel's *Icarus*, for instance: how everything turns away

... and the expensive delicate ship that must have seen

Something amazing, a boy falling out of the sky,

Had somewhere to get to and sailed calmly on."

from Musée des Beaux Arts (December, 1938)

In Mendelson, Edward (Ed.). *W. H. Auden: Collected poems*, pp. 146–7. London: Faber & Faber, copyright © 1976. Reprinted with permission.

Contents

Tables and Figures

FIGURES

Foreword

William J. McGuire is among the most original and influential thinkers of psychology's first century. He began his career at Yale University in the 1950s where he studied with Carl Hovland, completing his first research within the dominant tradition of learning theory. Even in his earliest papers, there is evidence of a master experimenter at work: aesthetic designs, meticulous analyses, and complex interactions predicted with precision, revealed that his use of learning theory was a tool to study the issues that most excited him concerning human thought and its complex functioning in social contexts.

After a postdoctoral fellowship at University of Minnesota with Leon Festinger, Bill spent the next several years at other great universities. At University of Illinois, he entered into a bet (with a colleague who was perpetually anxious about tenure) that he would not publish a paper until he was tenured. The evidence is in his curriculum vitae: Ten papers appeared in 1961, the year after he received tenure. Among the most notable of these contributions is a highly influential and counterintuitive idea concerning attitude change. Using the metaphor of medical immunization, Bill's genius was to suggest that small doses of a persuasive message would increase resistance to further attitude change instead of reducing it. His programmatic research on immunization against persuasion remains a model of a creative idea flawlessly executed. Bill demonstrated that ephemeral human thought processes can be described by the same laws previously considered to be true of physical and biological systems.

In the following decades, Bill continued his empirical research on attitudes, focusing on social influence processes and on the construction of effective persuasion campaigns. Academic psychologists deeply respect the originality of his theories and the elegance of his methods. Marketing researchers know and admire his creativity and boldness in speaking about attitude change and persuasion as it affects their discipline. During the middle years of his career, Bill continued his empirical research while writing exquisite reviews of attitude theory and research that simultaneously informed his peers and introduced novice students to the wonders of social psychology. He also wrote more popular, inspirational pieces that are read and re-read and for which he is beloved. One article stands out for its role in rejuvenating social psychology at a time when the field was considered to be in crisis regarding its identity and mission. In a paper presented at an international congress in Japan, Bill used the metaphor of the yin and yang of social psychology. Describing the opposite yet synergistic ways of conducting research Bill eloquently pointed out the many converging paths to truth. To social psychologists, the "yin and yang" paper offered new inspiration about their discipline and its future. Its appeal was the presentation of a view of what social psychology in all its richness could be, in language that was at once strong and inspirational. It remains among the most widely read papers even decades later, long after the field has emerged from its crisis.

Intellectual contributions come in many forms, and Bill is owed an enormous debt for his heroic service as editor of the *Journal of Personality and Social Psychology*, the premier publication in the field. His love of his field and the individuals who produce its work are exemplified in the sheer quantity of work he did as editor from 1965–1975 (personally handling 350 manuscripts a year for *JPSP*). He continues to review with zest, in a tradition of which he remains the best exemplar; detailed reviews (sometimes approaching the length of the manuscripts themselves) of exceptional quality, known also for their supreme charity and support, especially to young scientists.

In the late 1970s, Bill McGuire began a program of research to map the topography of the phenomenal self. He faulted the field for its reliance on reactive methods that forced research participants to respond to questions in formats fixed by the investigator. This time, his maverick strategy led him to study children of various ages who supplied him jewels of data in response to his simple query: "Tell me about yourself." The papers on self-concept showed the advances that are possible when an investigator dares to break away from the established method of a discipline and has the courage to opt for labor intensive methods. Many regard Bill's research on the self as among the most creative studies of uncensored human thought ever conducted.

There are many, many other accomplishments that mark this great and admired career. It remains a thrill for Bill's colleagues to watch him and his wife and collaborator, Claire Vernick McGuire walk to school each day, run experiments, analyze data, and write about their discoveries. At age 73, Bill remains not only active but dauntingly productive. He travels regularly to "hardship posts" in London and Paris, joking with local colleagues that his fame is an inverse function of the square of the distance from New Haven.

William McGuire's thoughts and words transformed psychological science in deep and permanent ways. His work embodies a rare confluence of experimental rigor, creativity, and aesthetics. Fortunately for us, he chose social psychology as the discipline in which to do his life's work. We are honored to have been able to persuade him to publish his writings in a single volume; they appear here with bridging sections and commentary provided by him. With great pride in the brilliance of our field as revealed in the thoughts and words of this genius who spent much of his life analyzing the thoughts and words of others, we offer you the writings of William J. McGuire.

Mahzarin R. Banaji   Reid Hastie
New Haven, Connecticut   Boulder, Colorado

1

Learning My Way

The young are less interested in what the old have to say than the old think they ought to be, but if any oldie talk does interest young people it is about how elders got into their lines of work. The Bildungsroman about one's coming of age by getting into bed and into one's profession (usually not the same thing) tends to sell, even when as lachrymose as *Werther*. I was at table with B. F. Skinner shortly after the appearance of his surprisingly popular autobiography, *Particulars of My Life* (Skinner, 1976), which he ended with his decision at age 25 not to be a novelist (a decision that readers of his *Walden Two* will regard as wise) but instead to go into psychology. When I asked him if he planned to write a sequel that would describe his life as a psychologist, Skinner said probably not, because few people outside one's field are interested in hearing about what happens to one after age 25. Apparently he changed his mind later, because two subsequent autobiographical volumes appeared, providing an account of his intellectual odyssey as psychologist. Disappointing sales may have left his publisher wishing Skinner had held to his initial resolve to end his "Life" when he began his work.

ENTERING A LIFE
IN PSYCHOLOGICAL RESEARCH

How Did You Get into This Field?

Youths' interest in how elders heard their calling probably reflects uncertainty about their own vocations, but elders' descriptions tend to be of little help. When I ask senior colleagues how they got into their specialties, a uniformly awkward account tends to emerge. Ask the world's leading bat maven how he got into bats, and he is likely to say: "It's unusual and a little embarrassing. During my third year in college I was biking across the campus and flew over the handlebars when I stopped short trying not to hit an old geezer who stepped right in front of me. He helped me up and talked while waiting to be sure I was OK. He happened to mention that he planned to hire someone to help him hang wires from the ceiling of a lab where he was studying bat navigation. I was a French lit major but I'm handy with a hammer so I took the job. It's been bats ever since." One makes the fundamental attribution error in perceiving oneself as having entered one's field by external accident while picturing everyone else as having gotten into his or hers very deliberately. Still, even if entry is largely accidental, it is not unreasonable to ask those of us who have become academic researchers to account for two career-choice decisions: How did we decide that we were intellectually and temperamentally suited to live in the house of intellect; and how did we choose our disciplinary room in this many-chambered mansion? I shall mention scattered evidence bearing on each question in my case, without assembling the pieces into a conclusive story.

Pleading guilty: "Smart, with an excuse."   My cultural milieu made it likely that, however suited I might have been for academia, I would not have discovered this suitability unless it took the form of a priestly vocation. Talented Catholic ethnics of my generation might aspire to the police force or fire department or, as farthest north, to a law degree (more as an entry into politics or the civil service than into corporate counseling with pro bono casual Fridays). In the unlikely case that one of us expressed interest in becoming a university professor his father might say it didn't seem much of a job for a man except that one got home at three o'clock every day. What changed the rules for me was History in the form of the Great Patriotic War of 1937 – 45, with all that service in the wartime military entailed – close contacts with people having different expectations and values, discovering one's skills at new tasks, and, as an end bonus, the "G.I. Bill," that license to steal 48 months of university education with tuition plus a modest living allowance provided. For 36 months I had served my time and learned to read and write; in return, a grateful nation gave me a free ride for 36 plus 12 months of higher education.

In retrospect there were prewar childhood intimations of my intellectual potential, usually exhibited on standardized objective tests more recently said to penalize us culturally deprived. Students in parochial schools (most of mine taught by Marist Brothers) took standardized tests periodically and, almost unknown to me, I did very well on these bizarre instruments. Once, when I was sent to the high school principal with companions in crime for some minor dereliction, the principal, after administering appropriate feedback (probably five blows of the strap on the palm of the hand), pulled me aside and told me to wise up and not allow my fellow perpetrators to lead me into trouble. He said that I had the highest I.Q. in the school and might amount to something if I worked a bit. Such scattered warnings that I might have "the smarts" alerted me to some corroborative symptoms, such as my doing more reading and having greater general knowledge than my companions. Fortunately, these stigmata were not accompanied by still more dangerous symptoms such as getting good grades in school; my prewar high school grades were seldom as good as average. Further to avoid giving off the stench of the intellectual, I early developed a formula that has stood me in good stead, then and ever after, from my high school relationships with fellow Catholic ethnics to current relationships with university colleagues of more intellectual castes. My formula has been to explain away any suspicious signs of brilliance by asserting, "Some people are creative but I have a good memory." Colleagues will recall that they have always been impressed by my remarkable memory.

On entering Fordham College after three years and three days of World War II army service I immediately fell into my prewar pattern of just-passing performances; but midway through my first post-army year for reasons I do not know I experienced a zestful transformation, taking a heavy load of courses and doing superbly well in all of them. The instructor in medieval history said that my paper on the relations of the Carolingians with the Byzantine Empire was a fine start to a great Ph.D. dissertation. The calculus instructor gave me extra problem sets to keep me occupied during class. On Saturdays I took all-day math and lab science courses, as I did also in summers. Suddenly I couldn't lose for winning. For the last two college years all my grades were 100% or 99%. When I was stopped in the street by the young statistics instructor who congratulated me for doing superbly well on his exam with an off-the-distribution 99% score, my reaction was a double surprise: How had he recognized an individual like me in his hundred-student class and how could I have possibly lost that one point? This stats instructor, later to become my colleague and then university president, joked that he and I were the only Fordham University graduates of our era who had not joined the FBI.

But why psychology? If not the FBI, then what? When and how did my intellectual inclinations get directed toward psychology? And compared to what? My career line was the typical zigzag path. Growing up in a laboring caste and class during the Great Depression, my early hope against hope was to get a job, nature unspecified. I may have visualized it as nocturnal home delivery of milk from a horse and wagon, the job my father was lucky to have and to hold during the Depression, and on which I sometimes joined him as helper and sharer of the camaraderie of nighttime laborers. My father and I would greet the dawn by splitting a quart of chocolate milk (probably accounted for on his daily account sheets as "spoilt by defective seal," but I did not report this in my weekly Confession, for it is written in Deuteronomy, "Thou shalt not muzzle the ox when he treadeth out the corn").

The improvement of my academic performance midway through that first post-army year, with grades leaping from just passing to near perfection, was uniform across fields and so did not indicate vocational direction. Nor did selecting a college major force me toward a career decision. Fordham then followed the Saint Ignatius Loyola *Ratio studiorum* curriculum. All students majored in philosophy during their last two college years via a sequence of seven courses – logic, epistemology, ontology, cosmology, rational psychology, ethics, and natural theology – which filled three morning hours five days a week. As in Plato's Academy and Aristotle's Lyceum, this left afternoons free for courses of the student's choice – mine usually in political science and psychology. The attraction of political science is plausibly explained as a *camino real* to law school and politics, a career line respected in my Catholic ethnic milieu as second only to the priesthood.

My inclination toward psychology is harder to explain: Whence came it and, particularly worrisome, whither did it lead? An obvious answer today, that it leads to an academic job of research and teaching in psychology, would not have entered my mind then as work suitable for a grown man. Still, there were adumbrations of my psychological interests. It may be significant that I still recall being fascinated as a 9-year-old when my best friend's oldest brother, George, then a college boy at Fordham, intoned stentoriously, "I am going to be a doctor of philosophy in psychology." (Actually, George later got a law degree and joined the FBI; his similarly bright younger brother got a degree in accounting . . . and also joined the FBI.)

My interests and efforts during my last two college years were neatly balanced between a philosophy morning major and an empirical psychology afternoon concentration. As graduation neared, Fordham College offered me a half-time appointment as instructor in philosophy, teaching courses on rational (as contrasted with empirical) psychology and on natural (as contrasted with dogmatic) theology. Simultaneously, I was admitted to Fordham's doctoral program in experimental psychology.

Two Critical Midcentury Years of Decision

The busy master's Year, 1949–1950. The two contrasting years following my undergraduate degree were the pivotal direction-determining period of my intellectual meanderings. The first of these two years, 1949–50, was my most laborious, even within a life generally characterized by Stakhanovite labor; in contrast, the following 1950–1 year was one of the few relaxed years of my adult life. Despite their contrasting levels of occupational demands both were crucial orienting years. The year after receiving my June 1949 B.A. degree from Fordham College I worked hard at the half-time teaching position in philosophy and at completing in one year an M.A. degree in psychology that, with its heavy course load and empirical thesis, usually took full-time students two or three years. A brief version of my M.A. thesis (McGuire, 1950) opens the collection in this chapter. I also worked that year as a part-time hospital attendant and I electioneered busily as the youngest precinct captain in Charlie Buckley's Congressional district, the strongest Democratic district in New York. I also engaged heavily in nonprofessional escapades that are better left unspecified.

A few months into that busy postcollege year I applied to the Fulbright program for a fellowship that would enable me to spend the following 1950–1 year in Belgium at the University of Louvain's philosophy institute to study phenomenology in relation to Thomistic philosophy, and to work in the psychology laboratory of Michotte, then quite old but still actively pursuing his ingenious, Gestalt-oriented research on the perception of physical causality. My applying for this Louvain Fulbright scholarship was much aided by Fordham's professor of philosophical psychology, Father Joseph F. Donceel, S.J., who had come to Fordham a few years earlier with a Louvain Ph.D. This application imposed on me another major task during that busy year, polishing my atrocious French sufficiently to squeeze by the Fulbright language-proficiency test. By year's end, June 1950, I had received the M.A. in experimental psychology, been awarded the Fulbright, and performed respectably in my philosophy teaching, hospital attendant job, political ward heeling, and other activities. My professional possibilities advanced on many fronts, an outcome attractive in itself but with the downside of leaving me as vocationally ambivalent at the end of this hard-work year as I had been at its beginning. Philosophy teaching had been challenging and satisfying; completing the psychology M.A. had introduced me to the pleasures of hands-on empirical research; even the politics option was left open by the Democratic clubhouse's appreciation of my effectiveness as precinct captain.

Perhaps significant is a book that was thrown on the scale that year. Browsing for my learning-theory M.A. thesis brought to my attention the volume by Hull, Hovland, Ross, Hall, Perkins, and Fitch (1940), *Mathematico-Deductive Theory of Rote Learning*, which captivated me by its elegance. The wonderfully interdisciplinary set of authors (two psychologists, three mathematicians, and a symbolic logician) began in the Euclidian tradition with a few obvious associationist basic postulates about rote memory (Ebbinghaus, 1885/1913; Robinson, 1932). From these axioms they formally deduced quantitative theorems including nonobvious, empirically testable relations (e.g., the reminiscence phenomenon and the asymmetry of the serial position effect). Foes of censorship say that no one ever lost his or her virginity to a book, but this book may have seduced me into psychology. Its elegance moved me, esthetically and intellectually, more than any professional reading since.

The Louvain year, 1950–1951. In contrast to this laborious 1949–50 M.A. year, the following year in Belgium imposed minimal external demands. Instead of being faced with incessant deadlines in multiple lines of work, I had large discretionary blocks of time to concentrate on topics of my own choosing. Just four years earlier I had left a ruined Europe on a troopship carrying three times as many soldiers as bunks, the former using the latter in three shifts over the 24-hour day. Now I was returning on a luxury liner, choosing from its late-night bars the one frequented by the young intellectuals, bantering with whom I developed a modified hylomorphic ontology – proposing that things are what they are by virtue, not of matter and form, but of being and nonbeing. I used the conceptualization to account for identity and individuality: Things differ, not by what they are, but by what they are not. The handful of Thomistic fellow travelers (most also war veterans and Fulbrighters) argued that I was deviating from orthodox Aristotelian Thomism toward Scotism and reminded me that such Duns Scotus obscurities had contributed the word *dunce* to the English language. These metaphysical speculations gave rise to my distinctiveness theory research, reported in Chapter 8 of this book.

So started a year of thinking, reading, resting, socializing, and solitary or companionable travel. I explored new ways of learning, as when a damaged American war veteran and I worked through Merleau-Ponty (my favorite phenomenologist) sentence by sentence, testing each other's translations and interpretations. I devoured novels of Hemingway and Dostoevsky. In my travels I detoured two days off my route and slept in the rough to view the Isenheim Altarpiece. I shared weeks of Spain's postwar poverty to see every El Greco opened to public view; and I worked out an ethical system. These philosophical and artistic activities overshadowed what little psychology work I did that year (attending Michotte's lectures on the two schools of Gestalt psychology, hanging out occasionally in his laboratory discussing the perception of physical causality with his technicians and doctoral students but doing no experimental work of my own). Yet, in spite (or because) of the low salience of empirical psychology relative to humanistic studies in those very rich European hours, I had, within a few months of arriving in Leuven, resolved my career ambivalence in favor of empirical psychology.

I spent December 1950 completing applications for a half-dozen fine U.S. doctoral programs, arduous then to do from abroad. At the end I was terribly conflicted between Hullian Yale and Skinnerian Harvard, but finally accepted Yale because I perceived it and Hull as more likely to be sympathetic to my axiomatic style of theorizing; but after I arrived in New Haven in September 1951, I saw little of Hull, who was sick unto death. I am grateful that the Yale admissions committee did not hold against me the out-of-date proposal in my application that I work with Hull on applying symbolic logic to learning theory, interest in which had faded from the Yale scene ten years earlier.

Yale Doctoral Studies in Experimental
Psychology, 1951–1954

In graduate school one learns more from fellow students than from faculty members. Among the dozen students who entered the Yale doctoral program in psychology with me in September 1951, I was particularly stimulated by Daniel Berlyne, Roger Shepard, and Arlo Myers. During the three years of doctoral studies at Yale my stipend, tuition, and research funding came from the Air Force Project on using training films to teach motor skills en masse. Art Lumsdaine administered these grants from Washington, D.C., with Greg Kimble directing the Yale project. Kimble left Yale a year after my arrival, and so the senior graduate student on the project, Jep Wulff, and I continued the work for the next two years with little faculty supervision. For these three colleagues I maintain a lifelong affection. The research I developed on this project included some of the earliest work on vicarious learning (McGuire, 1961e) and research on learning as a zero-sum process, such that instruction serves by selectively directing *what* the student learns rather than by increasing *how much* he or she learns (McGuire, 1961d), as well as on the deleterious effects of practice (McGuire, 1961c, 1961g).

The autonomy allowed by the remotely administered Air Force project, along with my ignorance of the culture of the great non-Catholic universities and my predilection for working alone on topics of my own choosing, all combined to make me an idiosyncratic student, but the Yale faculty were far too gracious and flexible to make an issue of this, except in flagrant cases such as the faux pas I committed in my second year at Yale, when without advice I did a program of studies on perceptual figure-reversal that I regarded as my doctoral dissertation. I used as an ambiguous stimulus a rotating kinophantiscopic shadow that observers perceive as periodically alternating between clockwise and counterclockwise rotations. I exploited the analogy between these phenomenal responses and behavioral responses, between alternating perceptual responses and the alternating strings of left-turning versus right-turning motor responses by rats in a T-maze. I manipulated the reinforcements and work inhibition for perceiving the shadow as rotating clockwise versus counterclockwise and used behavioristic principles to predict various parameters of the conditioning and extinction curves for perceiving one versus the other direction of rotation. The cycles of clockwise versus counterclockwise perceptual responses of my college-student participants duplicated many of Hull's (1943) curves for rats' cycles of left versus right motor responses in a T-maze.

When I gave Carl Hovland, my advisor of record, a manuscript presenting my theory, methods, and results in this set of perceptual experiments intended as a draft of my dissertation, he explained with some embarrassment that this is not the way it is done, that I should have had an advisory committee set up in advance, and that my committee would probably have decided that, because Yale had no specialist in this area, a perception expert from another university such as Cornell or Princeton would be needed to serve on the committee. Suitably chastened, I set up an advisory committee to authorize another, more conventional dissertation, testing a quantitative theory that analyzed paired-associate learning into three separate sets of habits (McGuire, 1961b, summarized in this chapter). Further evidence of how out-of-the-loop I was and how gracious Hovland was is that, although he served as advisor on this behavioristic dissertation research he never mentioned to me that his own interests had years ago shifted from verbal learning to attitude change and concept formation, a shift of which I became aware only when I later returned to Yale as a faculty member.

During the next year, my third and final year as a Yale graduate student, I was busy with this paired-associates learning dissertation, the Air Force mass-learning audiovisual research, and especially with my probabilogical model of the structure and operation of thought systems, a topic that reemerged as my main interest several times during subsequent decades. Because of its extensions in later work I shall leave its discussion to chapter 6, even though it was the major preoccupation of my final year of graduate studies at Yale and the following postdoctoral year at the University of Minnesota.

A Postdoctoral Year in Social Psychology at Minnesota

As the studies that follow in this chapter show, my research as a graduate student was in human learning rather than social psychology, with which I later became identified (McGuire, 1980h). The only social psychology course I took as undergraduate or graduate student was a stimulating tutorial with Leonard Doob during my final graduate year at Yale. Discussing with Leonard the readings he prescribed so interested me that, rather than go on the job market as the human-learning (behavioral, S-R) theorist I had trained to be, I decided to apply for a social psychology SSRC postdoctoral fellowship to spend the 1954–5 year with Leon Festinger and Stanley Schachter at the University of Minnesota, where I proposed to use S-R reinforcement theory to account for interpersonal behavior in small groups.

Just as three years earlier I had been a decade late in applying to the Yale Ph.D. program to work with Clark Hull in using symbolic logic to derive nonobvious predictions from behavioral theory, so again my applying for a postdoctoral fellowship to do interpersonal group dynamics work with Leon Festinger was anachronistic because Leon's interests had switched to intrapersonal cognition. This out-of-date proposal did not prove embarrassing at Minnesota any more than at Yale. It was exciting to participate instead in the early dissonance research, which was more relevant than group dynamics would have been to my main interest, namely, continuing the probabilogical theory research (McGuire, 1960 a, b, c), reported in Chapter 6 of this volume.

The papers that follow in this chapter illustrate my graduate student research on learning, including abridgments of my master's thesis (McGuire, 1950); two of my "mass learning" Air Force papers (McGuire, 1961d, 1961e); my 1954 doctoral dissertation (McGuire, 1961b); my "Order of presentation in persuasion" study (McGuire, 1957), which bridges this learning-theory work with my subsequent attitude-change work, and a polemical manifesto (McGuire, 1965a), which also links my early attachments to learning theory and to social psychology.

LEARNING THE SEQUENCE OF ITEMS IN A LIST BY ORDINAL VERSUS INTER-ITEM ASSOCIATIONS

[This section is an abridgement of McGuire, 1950, my unpublished M.A. thesis, "The relative utilization of positional associations and of inter-item associations in learning series of items in sequence," Fordham University.]

A task frequently encountered in life and more frequently in the psychological laboratory is list learning, memorizing a series of items in a prescribed order (e.g., learning the names of the U.S. presidents in chronological order or remembering a long sequence of travel instructions). Learning the order of items is usually described as involving between-item associations, as if one learned each item's order by remembering which item(s) it follows. My master's thesis tested a different possibility – namely, that one learns each item's position in the list not only by learning which item it follows but also by learning its ordinal position (e.g., one learns Millard Fillmore's position in the list of presidents not only by memorizing that he followed Zachary Taylor but also that he was 13th in the succession). Aristotle's hylomorphism theory, that all entities are constituted by matter and form, supplied my conceptual framework: List-learning involves learning the matter (the items) in a certain form (their ordering). This is an "as if" distinction rather than a real temporal segregation of the two subtasks: One does not first learn the matter and then learn its prescribed form, but always learns the matter in some specific form. My thesis pits against one another the traditional atomistic versus a more innovative holistic explanation of how one learns the second subtask, the ordering of items in a list, whether by associating each item atomistically with the preceding item(s) or more holistically by associating each item with its ordinal position in the list, thus allowing the well-mastered real number series to serve as a framework for learning the list order.

Conceptual Background

General theory. Despite their commonsense plausibility, the empirical status of each of the two proposed subtasks, learning the items and learning their prescribed ordering, has been questioned. Ebbinghaus (1913) cast doubt on the first subtask (learning the responses per se) when he failed to find that learning a first list of nonsense syllables facilitated learning a second, derived list made up of the same syllables in a different order. Robinson (1932) and Woodworth (1938) attributed Ebbinghaus's failure to find derived-list savings to his peculiar familiarity with nonsense syllables. He would already have been familiar with the syllables on any initial experimental list from their having appeared in his many earlier experiments in which he served as his own subject. Hence, learning any initial list would result in little further saving on learning the second list of the same syllables. This familiarity excuse is weak because (1) learning the first list should have benefitted even Ebbinghaus in learning the derived list by making these syllables more available; and because (2) subsequent studies (Waters, 1939; Goldstein, 1950) found that syllable-sophisticated participants show as much saving in learning the derived list as do participants unfamiliar with nonsense syllables. That first-list learning so little benefited Ebbinghaus's learning a derived list of the same syllables in a different order I attribute, not to its failure to help on the first subtask (syllable learning), but rather to its beneficial effect on this first subtask being canceled by its interference with the second subtask, learning the syllables' new order on the second list.

The present study focuses on what cues are used in mastering the second, order-learning subtask. The conventional "atomistic" stimulus-response connectionist explanation (popular since Ebbinghaus, 1913; Robinson, 1932; Hull, 1943) is that syllable order is mastered by forming intersyllabic associations such that seeing each successive syllable becomes the conditioned stimulus for evoking (saying) the subsequent syllable. My alternative "holistic" explanation is that the order is learned also by associating each syllable with its ordinal position in the list. To the extent that this holistic factor operates, then what determines the elicitation of a given syllable on an ordered list is, not which, but how many previous syllables have been presented. Suggestive support for this hypothesis can be derived from findings regarding the serial position curve, backward associations, and the spread-of-effect phenomenon (McGuire, 1950).

Specific predictions. To the extent that ordinal-position associations operate in serial learning, a first implication is that learning an ordered list of nonsense syllables will be faster if the syllables are presented numbered consecutively rather than unnumbered. A second implication (deriving from Woodworth's 1938 postulate that the U-shaped serial position learning curve reflects the relative ease of learning ordinal positions at different parts of the list) is that numbering the items on the list will flatten the serial position curve. The third, main, prediction is that when a person later learns an ordered list made up of syllables taken from two ordered lists learned earlier, the earlier list-learning will facilitate learning the later, derived list to the extent that the syllables retain the same ordinal positions on the later list as they had on the earlier lists, regardless of the extent to which they retained the same preceding syllables.

Method

Fordham University students (*N* = 32) participated individually in two sessions, two weeks apart. In the first session they learned by the usual anticipation method two ordered lists, each made up of eight consonant-vowel-consonant nonsense syllables, all with meaningful association values of about 50% (Glaze, 1928). In the second session two weeks later, participants learned two derived lists, each made up of eight nonsense syllables, four drawn from each of the participant's two first-session lists in the patterns shown in Table 1.1.

Independent Variables. The design included four main independent variables. (1) The eight syllables making up each of the two first-session ordered lists appeared numbered consecutively on one list and un-numbered on the other (order of lists counterbalanced among participants). The numbering was predicted to facilitate learning each syllable's ordinal position and thus to speed mastery of the ordered list. (2) The second independent variable was the syllables' ordinal positions, 1 to 8, predicted to produce U-shaped serial position curves that would be flatter and more symmetrical on the numbered than on the unnumbered lists. The third and fourth independent variables were the extent to which the syllables on the second-session derived lists (3) retained the same ordinal positions and (4) retained the same predecessor syllables as they had in the first session list. Table 1.1 shows that the syllables' ordinal positions on the second-session derived list become progressively more discrepant from their first-session ordinal positions as we go from Derived List I to II to III to IV; and that the extent to which each syllable follows the same preceding syllable on the derived list as it had on the earlier-learned lists is highest in Condition III, intermediate on I and II, and lowest on IV. Specific syllables were rotated around conditions among participants.

Procedure and dependent variables. Participants learned eight-syllable lists by the anticipation method. Each successive syllable was shown for three seconds in the window of a modified Lipmann memory drum for a series of trials. A trial involved presenting all eight syllables on a list in a constant order, with the participant instructed to spell out the syllable as soon as it appeared in the window and also to anticipate the

Table 1.1
Error scores on learning numbered and unnumbered initial lists and on derived lists that preserve different degrees of the initial lists' ordinal and inter-item associations.

First-session lists		Second-session derived lists (all unnumbered)			
List A (Unnumbered)	List B (Numbered)	Condition I	Condition II	Condition III	Condition IV
A1	1. B1	A1	A2	B3	B2
A2	2. B2	B2	B1	B4	A4
A3	3. B3	A3	A4	A1	A8
A4	4. B4	B4	B3	A2	A7
A5	5. B5	A5	A6	B7	B6
A6	6. B6	B6	B5	B8	B1
A7	7. B7	A7	A8	A5	A3
A8	8. B8	B8	B7	A6	B5
71.91	79.06	40.31	45.69	56.83	55.94

The scores at the bottom of each column give the mean number of failure-to-anticipate errors made by the learners in that column condition before they reached the two-perfect-trials criterion.

next syllable by spelling it out before it in turn appeared in the window. At the end of each eight-syllable trial a blank appeared in the window for three seconds to signal the start of a new trial. The list was defined as learned when the participant reached the criterion of two successive error-free trials of eight correct anticipations. The participants performed on a preliminary practice list to familiarize themselves with the procedures. The dependent variable measure, difficulty of learning the list, was the accumulated number of errors (unanticipated syllables) that the participant made before achieving two consecutive perfect trials.

Results and Discussion

How numbering the syllables affected learning the initial lists.   Two predictions had to do with the effects of numbering the syllables on learning the first-session lists. First, it was predicted that ordered lists will be learned more quickly when the syllables are numbered sequentially rather than left unnumbered. Table 1.1 shows a small, nonsignificant difference in the opposite direction. Comments volunteered by several participants suggested that numbering the nonsense syllables introduced an additional difficulty by requiring learning of four elements rather than just the three involved in learning each unnumbered three-letter syllable. A reasonable conjecture is that the time pressure imposed by the numbering could have masked its facilitating learning of the ordinal positions.

The second hypothesis, that numbering the syllables will reduce the serial position effect, was not confirmed. We found the typical serial position learning curve – U-shaped, reaching its minimum slightly to the right of the midpoint – equally pronounced for numbered and unnumbered lists. Again it can be conjectured that numbering the items sequentially facilitates learning the items' order but also increases time pressure, which was shown by Hovland (1938) to enhance the serial position effect. To test these conjectures a follow-up study should compare the serial position effect in two lists, both with its syllables numbered, but numbered consecutively on one list and randomly on the other.

Effects of preserving initial ordinal positions on learning derived lists. The main hypotheses had to do with transfer effects on learning derived lists in the second session. The mean number of errors made on learning each derived list is shown in Table 1.1. Although Ebbinghaus did not show an error saving, our naive participants showed sizable savings ($p < .01$) ranging from 21% to 44% on the four types of derived lists. It was confirmed that the derived lists were easier to learn when the ordinal positions of their syllables were kept closer to the ordinal positions that they had when they appeared initially in the first-session list, which supports the holistic learning hypothesis. Specifically, derived second-session Lists I and II (on which the syllables averaged one-half step off their positions on first-session Lists A and B) were learned with a mean of 43.00 failure-to-anticipate errors, fewer ($p < .05$) than the mean of 56.28 errors for Lists III and IV (whose syllables averaged two and a half steps from their ordinal positions in the first-session lists). The derived-list savings gave no evidence that the ordering is learned atomistically, via inter-item associations between each syllable and its predecessor. Derived List III best preserved each syllable with the same preceding syllables as on the first-session list, but more errors were made in learning this List III than in learning any of the other three derived lists. These patterns of derived-list savings support the holistic theorizing that ordering is learned by associating each syllable with its ordinal position in the overall list structure, rather than by the conventionally theorized connectionist theory of learning order by stringing syllables together so that each syllable is evoked by its preceding syllable(s).

What is needed is to repeat this experiment with two improvements. Firstly, the syllables should be numbered on all first-session lists but numbered consecutively on half the lists and randomly on the other half. Secondly, there should be more participants, quadruple the present N = 32, to allow more systematic, orthogonal variation of the derived lists as regards carrying over the syllables' ordinal positions on the first list versus carrying over the immediately preceding syllables. Incidentally, this shortage of subjects in my earliest, M.A. thesis research has characterized my other academic appointments, except for my 1958–61 years at the University of Illinois. It has been the only resource I have lacked, but it is a serious loss that reduced my productivity even though I have partly circumvented it. I advise researchers, particularly young ones dependent on their university's resources, to take subject pool resources into account when a new job is offered, a criterion that tends to make large state universities like Illinois or Ohio State more attractive than elite private universities like Yale or Stanford.

Coincidentally, a just published study (S. Chen, K. B. Swartz, and H. S. Terrace, 1997, *Psychological Science, 8,* 80–6) raised the same question as did this 1950 M.A. thesis: Are ordered lists of items learned not only, as commonly theorized, by forming inter-item associations but also by forming positional associations? This 1997 article reports results similar to the 1950 thesis: Derived lists were learned with substantial savings if and only if the items retained the ordinal positions that they had occupied in the first-learned lists. These savings occurred even if none of the inter-item associations were retained on the derived list. The 1997 researchers did not heed my admonition to increase the number of participants; on the contrary, they used only two. However, both participants, Rutherford and Franklin, were rhesus monkeys, and a mere pair of our primate cousins lend an air of authenticity to a study that the several dozen Homo sapiens in my M.A. thesis fail to provide.

A ZERO-SUM CONCEPT OF TEACHING:
INSTRUCTION AS ATTENTION-DIRECTING,
NOT ACQUISITION-ENHANCING

[Adapted from W. J. McGuire, 1961d, Some factors influencing the effectiveness of demonstrational films . . . , in A. A. Lumsdaine (Ed.), *Student responses in programmed instruction,* pp. 187–207 (Washington, DC: National Research Council).]

Teaching and learning are usually conceptualized as enhancing the amount of instructional material absorbed by the student, but here we propose the quite different notion that teaching affects *what* is learned rather than *how much* is learned. In all learning environments – laboratory, classroom, or daily life – the person is experiencing an overload of incoming information of which he or she can effectively encode only a small portion at any given moment (perhaps Miller's [1956] 7 ± 2 bits). It seems to have been evolutionarily adaptive by providing reproductive advantage for the species to operate on an information-management economy such that our senses receive far more information than we can effectively encode. The person, who is constantly receiving excessive sensory stimulation, must always selectively ignore most of the incoming information. It is postulated that effective instruction involves teaching the student, not how to absorb more information, but how to select more effectively which information to absorb.

Theory and Predictions

Most teaching situations, especially those employing realistic visual demonstrations, present more information than the learner can effectively encode, much of it irrelevant to the responses intended to be taught. The teacher should assume that the person's information-encoding capacity is always fully engaged, so that the instruction should be designed, not to increase the gross amount learned, but to redirect the student's attention selectively to the performance-enhancing information, albeit at the price of less learning of the nonemphasized material. Audiovisual teaching is a zero-sum process that should use emphasizing devices (e.g., color, captions, repetition, introductions, narration, moving camera, slow motion, closeups, and animation, etc.) to select rather than to increase what is learned. This zero-sum conceptualization implies that adding audio instruction or slow motion to an instructional video will enhance learning of the information presented both verbally and visually (or in slow motion), but at the cost of lowering learning of the other information not so emphasized.

Method

The learning task and the training film.   A training film was developed that depicted an actor performing 12 postural responses that purportedly improve performance at an eye–hand coordination task (a "pursuit rotor" tracking task that requires keeping a hinged stylus in contact with a dime-sized target disc on the periphery of a rapidly rotating turntable). The dependent-variable learning measure was the extent to which the participant, when performing the task after watching the film, adopted the 12 depicted postural responses. Two observers independently rated the participant on each of the 12 responses four times during his performance trials. The training film explained the pursuit-rotor apparatus and task, then visually demonstrated the 12 postural responses (e.g., keep the back of the hand up, hold the rod and handle of the hinged stylus in a straight line, stand with both feet equidistant from the rotor, move whole arm and shoulder, etc.). The 10-minute film had four sections, each section depicting all 12 responses.

Independent variables, design, and participants.   An among-participants $2 \times 2 \times 2$ factorial design, with an additional control (no instructional film) condition, was used. The first of the three dichotomous independent variables was across-modality repetition of the instructions: One version of the film had a minimal narration that did not mention verbally the 12 responses depicted in the film; the other version visually depicted the 12 responses and also verbally described 11 of the 12 responses in each of the film's 4 sections. The second independent variable was film speed, the regular version showing all 12 responses at normal speed and the slow-motion version showing 7 of the 12 responses at normal speed and the other 5 in slow motion, one-third of normal speed. The third independent variable was within-modality repetition of instructions, with a long version showing 4 subsections of the film (each subsection depicting all 12 responses) versus the short version, which showed only 2 of the 4 subsections.

A total of 48 participants were used, 4 participants in each of the 2 ×
2 × 2 film conditions plus 16 in the no-film (control) condition. The
participants were male students in the Yale College introductory psychology subject pool.

Results and Discussion

The dependent variable measures for testing the hypotheses are the
judges' ratings as to how well the participants adopted the 12 postural
responses depicted in the film. These scores obtained a high interrater reliability of $r = +.93$ between the total scores of the 48 participants as rated 4 times by each judge. Watching any of the 8 versions
of the instructional film sizably and significantly ($p < .001$) increased
ratings for adoption of the 12 depicted responses over the control (no-
film) group's performance, the film versus no-film overall rating
scores being 35.16 versus 20.66.

Effects of repetition. As for learning differences produced by the 3
independent variables, presenting additional within-modality repetitions (4 pictorial repetitions rather than only 2) did not increase
adoption of the 12 postural responses; but between-modality repetition (2 pictorial plus 2 narration rather than two pictorially only) did
significantly ($p < .05$) improve performance. This finding that repetition is more beneficial across than within modality is compatible
with the postulate that adding verbal to visual instructions works as
an attention-redirecting rather than as a repetition factor.

Of particular interest are the pictorial-only versus the pictorial-
plus-narration effects on the 12th response (the participant's holding
the wire out of the way with his free hand), which differed from the
other 11 items in that it was clearly depicted visually but was not
mentioned in the narration. A simple prediction is that, because it
was not mentioned in the narration, the pictorial-plus-narration participants will score no better on this 12th response than will the pictorial-
only group (whose film verbally mentioned none of the 12 responses).
In fact, participants in the pictorial-plus-narration condition did worse
($p < .05$) on this 12th response than did the pictorial-only participants,
whereas on each of the other 11 response items they did decidedly
better. This interaction effect supports the zero-sum concept of teaching: that narration serves, not as a learning-enhancing across-modality repetition factor, but as an attention-directing factor, increasing

learning of the responses depicted and mentioned, but at the expense of decreasing learning of the depicted but unmentioned responses.

Effects of slow-motion versus regular speed.   The total performance score across all 12 responses did not show a significant difference for participants who saw the slow-motion versus the regular-speed film, but the predicted interaction effect was found. The slow-motion film showed 5 of the 12 responses in slow motion and 7 at regular speed. The 5 responses in slow motion were learned better ($p < .01$) from the slow-motion than the regular-speed film; but the 7 responses shown at regular speed in both film versions were learned better in the regular-speed film. Analogously to added narration, slow motion enhances the learning of the responses depicted at the attention-attracting slow speed, but at the cost of reducing learning of the unemphasized normal-speed responses. It is a dramatic reconceptualization to regard teaching as a zero-sum process that robs Peter to pay Paul. A full exploration of this postulate that instruction gains its efficacy, not by increasing the total amount of learning, but by influencing what is learned versus what is ignored, promises to advance both basic research and effective education.

VICARIOUS LEARNING: WE LEARN FROM SEEING OTHERS REWARDED AS WELL AS FROM BEING REWARDED OURSELVES

[Adapted from McGuire, 1961e, Effects of serial position and proximity to "reward" within a demonstrational film, in A. A. Lumsdaine (Ed.), *Student response in programmed instruction,* pp. 209–216. (Washington, DC: National Research Council).]

A Cognitive Reinterpretation of the Nature of Reinforcement

Among the Air Force studies that I did as a graduate student at Yale in the early 1950s was one of the first experiments on observational (or "vicarious") learning. Vicarious learning implies that the person learns, not only by directly participating in the training procedure and experiencing his or her own responses being rewarded or punished, but also by observing another person's participation and seeing which responses of this other get rewarded or punished. Such observational learning called for a shift in the midcentury concept of reinforcement as being a strictly passive, affective automatic process to its being an active, cognitive, interpretative process.

If one can learn from watching the successes and failures of others being rewarded and punished, as well as from personally experiencing these rewards and punishments oneself, it implies that reinforcements promote learning, not only by their hedonic effect on the learner, stamping the correct or incorrect responses in or out, but also by their informational content, communicating to experiencer and observer alike which responses are correct and incorrect. The experiment reported here tested if observational learning occurs and is promoted by a variety of independent variables (e.g., proximity to reward, ordinal position in instruction, and distribution of practice) in the same way that direct participatory learning is affected by these variables. The demonstration that rewards and punishments serve cognitively, by providing information (not just motivationally, by providing hedonic reinforcement) made this study one of the earliest in the "cognitive revolution" that began in psychology in midcentury.

Method

Task and instructional materials. Participants saw a 10-minute film demonstrating how a person should perform at a pursuit-rotor tracking task that calls for maintaining contact between a hand-held stylus and a coin-sized target disk on the periphery of a rapidly rotating turntable. The film depicted and urged the learner to adopt 11 postural responses while performing at the pursuit rotor (e.g., keep the back of your hand up, keep the rod and handle of the stylus in a line, stand 12 inches away from the rotor, etc.). The 11 responses were presented and recommended visually and also in a verbal narration 4 times during the film in different circumstances.

Each of the four film segments depicted all 11 of the recommended postural responses. After the 3rd, 7th, and 11th responses a time-clock sequence provided positive or negative reinforcement by indicating the proportion of time the actor was succeeding in maintaining contact between stylus and rotating target disk. The first 2 (poor performance) depictions showed the actor as a beginner who had failed to follow the 11 instructions and so the clock sequences showed a low score being obtained; the 2 final good performance depictions showed the practiced actor after training as he later adopted the 11 recommended responses and consequently the clock sequences showed him registering a good score.

Participants and design.   The participant observers were 32 male college students, 16 serving in a control (no-film) group and 16 in an experimental group who saw the film. Then all 32 participants themselves engaged in the task and were rated on 4 occasions by 2 trained judges on the extent to which they performed each of the 11 responses demonstrated by the actor in the film.

Results and Discussion

Vicarious learning.   Strong evidence of vicarious learning was found. The maximum possible rating score for each of the 11 instructed responses was 128. The mean obtained score was 63 in the control (no film) condition, whereas after seeing the film that showed the actor being reinforced for performing the 11 responses, the mean went up to 111. The film group performed significantly higher on each of the 11 responses.

Effect of serial position.   Limited resources did not allow for constructing numerous versions of the film to counterbalance the order in which the 11 responses were depicted; as an inexpensive alternative I used analysis of covariance, adjusting the judges' rating scores on the 11 responses for observers in the experimental (film) condition for corresponding ratings of observers in the control (no-film) condition. To test how ordinal position within the film affects learning it is necessary to adjust for proximity to reward by grouping blocks of responses that are separated by the successive rewards. The three points so obtained show the typical asymmetrical U-shape serial-position curve, in that the middle block of responses were most poorly learned, the terminal block was intermediate in learning, and the initial block was best learned ($p < .05$). Hence, the serial-position effect, typically found for direct learning by participants performing the responses themselves during the learning and reinforcement trials, is here found vicariously in observers who watched an actor performing the responses. This informational interpretation of the serial position effect raises questions about its usual reactive inhibition (fatigue) interpretation.

Effect on proximity to vicarious reward. The closeness of the items within each block to the vicarious rewards in the film had a sizable learning-enhancing effect (p < .01), but it took the form, not of a simple delay of reinforcement curve (Hull, 1951), but rather of the "spread of effect" curve (Thorndyke, 1933); that is, each vicariously reinforcing clock sequence in the film augmented learning, not just of the response preceding it, but also of the response following it, suggesting that proximity to the vicarious reward sequence in the film may act as a spacing as well as a reinforcement process. Even if the efficacy of the vicarious-reward sequences does derive in part from its practice-distributing effect, there is indication also of a specifically reinforcing effect in that the reward interval's retroactive benefit to learning the preceding response is greater than its proactive benefit to learning the subsequent response. Further study (McGuire, 1961f) is needed to compare the effect of introducing film segments that provide vicarious rewards versus segments providing equal spacing without any hedonically rewarding or informational content. This study shows that independent variables like spaced practice and proximity to reward affect learning in an observer in the same way as they affect subjects who actually perform the task and receive the reinforcements. A second implication is that a reward sequence in such vicarious learning situations may operate, not only as information or hedonic reinforcement, but also as distribution of practice.

A MULTIPROCESS MODEL FOR PAIRED-ASSOCIATE LEARNING

[The following section is an adaptation of my 1954 doctoral dissertation, later published as W. J. McGuire, 1961b, A multiprocess model for paired-associate learning, *Journal of Experimental Psychology, 62,* 335–347. Rather than rush into print with this 1954 dissertation, I wandered afar like Jacob for seven years, degree in hand, as a postdoctoral student at the University of Minnesota, back to Yale as a junior faculty member, on to the University of Illinois (where I got tenure), and finally published it when I came back to my hometown as a professor at Columbia University. Now, as then, the candidate thanks his dissertation advisory committee: C. I. Hovland, chair; R. P. Abelson; and C. E. Buxton.]

The Three-Component Theory of Learning

Description of the three components.   The theory tested here gives an inclusive analysis of one of psychologists' classical learning tasks, paired-associate learning such as memorizing a French-English vocabulary list. My theory postulates that learning each stimulus-response associated pair involves establishing, not a single direct habit bond between the pair's experimenter-designated stimulus member, St, and its designated response member, Rp, but rather establishing a chain of three sets of habit associations. As an example, consider the case where the participant must learn a list of nine St → Rp paired associates, all of whose designated stimulus terms, St, are solid black circles, the nine of which differ in size, and all of whose designated response terms, Rp, are three-digit numbers. Suppose the second largest St circle has associated with it, as its designated Rp to be learned, the three-digit number "523". In learning this particular St → Rp pair, I postulate that the participant must learn three habits.

(1) The first St-discrimination habit, St → r_d, requires that whenever this second largest St circle is presented the participant must learn to discriminate and recognize it by making a distinctive labeling response, r_d. For this St, r_d may be saying to oneself, "This is the second biggest circle." This distinctive labeling response has stimulus feedback s_d, hearing oneself say, when so labeling this St, "This is the second biggest circle."

(2) The second habit to be mastered in learning this particular St → Rp pair is linking the St with its designated Rp. This calls for learning an s_d → R_a habit, namely, learning that when one hears oneself say its distinctive label s_d ("This is the second biggest circle") one should respond with R_a, the first element of the designated Rp. In the case of this St → Rp pair, the R_a would consist of saying "Five" because five is the first element of "523," the designated Rp for this second-biggest circle.

(3) The third habit to be learned is Rp integration, which involves learning to string together the elements of the Rp. For this pair it would be learning the number "523" as one of the nine Rp. This third (Rp learning) task involves establishing a set of verbal habits and

their stimuli feedbacks that strings together the "523" Rp, namely $R_5 \dashrightarrow s_5 \rightarrow R_2 \dashrightarrow s_2 \rightarrow R_3$, where R_5 is the response of saying the integer "Five" and s_5 is its stimulus feedback (i.e., hearing oneself say "five"), which becomes a conditioned stimulus for evoking the next R_2 response component (saying "two" to oneself), and so on. In representing the three sets of habits involved in learning the single St $\rightarrow$ Rp associated pair, I use a solid-shaft arrow, S $\rightarrow$ R, to indicate a habit bond in the usual form of a stimulus evoking a response, and I use a dotted-shaft arrow, r $\dashrightarrow$ s, to indicate a response's producing stimulus feedback; and I use upper-case S and R symbols to indicate publicly observable Stimuli and Responses and lower-case s and r symbols to indicate private (subvocal speech) stimuli and responses. Thus learning a single St $\rightarrow$ Rp pair involves mastering the three component habits shown in parentheses:

$$(St \rightarrow r_d) \dashrightarrow (s_d \rightarrow R_a) \dashrightarrow (s_a \rightarrow R_b \dashrightarrow s_b \rightarrow \ldots \rightarrow R_n)$$

Past evidence for each of the three component habits. Evidence for the first St $\rightarrow$ r_d set of habits, such that the learner encodes each St only partially by labeling some feature that effectively distinguishes it from the other St in the list, is found in St-predifferentiation studies. Prelearning a set of designated Rp responses to a set of St stimuli has been found to result in positive transfer to learning a different set of Rp to the same St, provided the St are related to the Rp by the same distinctive aspects on both tasks (Goss, 1953). Prelearning produces no saving if the St aspect that had been relevant in the first task is irrelevant on the new task (Hake & Ericksen, 1956); and there is negative transfer when the old aspect is present and interferes with learning the distinctive feature on the new task (Kurtz, 1955). The difficulty of learning this first labeling habit component (St $\rightarrow$ r_d) can be increased by making the St in the list more homogeneous (Goss, 1953), by increasing the number of irrelevant St aspects (Pishkin, 1960), or by making the distinguishing St aspects more subtle or complex.

The second habit link, $s_d \rightarrow R_a$, whereby the St's distinguishing label, s_d (rather than the gross St itself), evokes the first element of the pair's gross Rp, has been shown to be involved by Bugelski and Scharlock (1952) for experimentally established mediating labels, and by Russell and Storms (1955) for mediating labels provided by natural language habits. That these mediators are the St-discriminating labels is demonstrated by McAllister's (1953) finding that stimulus predifferentiation results in positive transfer, to the extent that the St-differentiating labels ($r_d \dashrightarrow s_d$) are relevant to the first element of the new Rp to be learned to the St on the second list.

Evidence for involvement of the third (Rp-integrating) habit learning is reviewed by Mandler (1954) and demonstrated in response-meaningfulness studies (Hunt, 1959; Nobel & McNeely, 1957) and response-similarity studies (Feldman & Underwood, 1957; Underwood, Runquist, & Schultz, 1959), which deal respectively with two aspects of Rp learning, integrating within-Rp components and sharpening among-Rp discriminations.

The materials used in the present study are designed to allow each erroneous instance (i.e., each failure by a participant on any trial to respond to a given St with the experimenter-designated correct Rp) to be diagnosed as regards which of the three habits in the chain failed in that instance. This allows us to plot the acquisition curve, not only of the usual H_c dependent variable (i.e., the proportion of gross St $\rightarrow$ Rp pairings correctly anticipated on a given trial), but also of H_1, H_2, and H_3, where H_1 = the proportion correct of St discriminations (i.e., correct St $\rightarrow r_d$ habits); where H_2 = the proportion correct of St with Rp pairings (i.e., correct $s_d \rightarrow R_a$ habits); and where H_3 = the proportion of Rp correctly synthesized (i.e., correct $s_a \rightarrow R_b \dashrightarrow s_b \ldots R_n$ habits). Besides indicating processes involved and sources of difficulty in paired-associate learning, these three additional dependent variables enable us to compute separately the practice curves for stimulus generalization and for intrusion errors, confusion between which has long caused controversy (Murdock, 1958, 1959; Battig, 1959; Gibson, 1959; and Runquist, 1959). Each of these H_c, H_1, H_2, and H_3 dependent variables is measured on a 0 to 1 scale, the proportion of the nine habits correct on a given trial. This proportional scaling implies that $H_c = H_1 \times H_2 \times H_3$, assuming learning the three sets of habits proceeds independently, without appreciable interaction terms, an assumption that can here be checked empirically.

Method

Materials and experimental variations. The gross stimuli and responses (i.e., the designated St $\rightarrow$ Rp paired associates used in this study) were designed to allow independent manipulations and measures of the difficulty of each of the three sets of component habits, H_1 (St $\rightarrow r_d$), H_2 ($s_d \rightarrow R_a$), and H_3 ($R_a \cdots\rightarrow s_a \rightarrow R_b \cdots\rightarrow s_b \ldots \rightarrow R_n$). The usual anticipation method was used to teach the participants a list of nine St $\rightarrow$ Rp paired associates. The St of these nine pairs were all solid black circles whose critical difference was their sizes. Two different sets of St circles were used for different groups of participants. In the easy H_1 St-discrimination condition the circles' diameters ranged from .37 to 1.49 cm in .14-cm steps; in the more difficult H_1' condition the diameters ranged from .37 to .93 in .07-cm steps.

The Rp were numbers. In the easy H_3 condition these Rp were the single-digit numbers from 1 to 9. In the harder H_3' condition the Rp were three-digit numbers, each beginning with a different integer from 1 to 9, with its second and third digit assigned randomly. In the easy one-digit H_3 condition it was assumed that mastery of the H_3 response integration task was at the asymptotic value of 1.00 from the outset of the experiment (i.e., it was assumed that all participants would be able to respond with the integers 1 to 9 perfectly from the outset).

The difficulty of learning the H_2 ($s_d \rightarrow R_a$) set of habits linking St and Rp was manipulated by the manner of assigning Rp to St. For the types of materials and the task used here it was assumed that participants would distinguish each St circle with a numerical size-indicating labeling response (e.g., by labeling the smallest circle as something like "One," the next larger in size as "Two," etc., up to the largest of the nine circles, which would be labeled as "Nine"). For the difficult H_2' condition, the numerical Rp were assigned at random as regards size of circles. In the easy H_2 condition consecutively bigger Rp numbers were assigned to progressively larger St circles. In this easier condition H_2 was assumed to have attained the asymptotic value of 1.00 from the outset of practice (i.e., it was assumed that the participant was able to perform without error from the outset on this $s_d \rightarrow R_a$ set of habits that called simply for linking 1 with "One," 2 with "Two," etc.).

Experimental design and participants. An incomplete 2^3 factorial design (one quadrant deleted) was employed. The three independent variables were the difficulties of learning the three component sets of habits, H_1, H_2, and H_3, with ease and difficulty levels on each of the three variables as defined above. Table 1.2 shows the difficulty levels on each of these three components in the six conditions, with a prime

Table 1.2

H_c *(the proportion of St → Rp pairs correctly anticipated over all 80 trials)*
in each of the 6 conditions that varied the difficulty of the 3 component sets
of habits, namely: H_1 (the Stimulus Discrimination Habits, St → r_d); H_2
(the St → Rp Linkage Habits, s_d → R_a); and H_3 (the Rp Integration Habits,
$R_a \dashrightarrow s_a → R_b \dashrightarrow s_b \ldots R_n$).

Task					H_c
Condition					
	Difficulty Level				
	H_1	H_2	H_3	Predicted H_c [a]	Obtained H_c
$H_1 H_2 H_3$	easy	easy	easy	H_1	.793
$H_1{}' H_2 H_3$	hard	easy	easy	$H_1{}'$	.635
$H_1 H_2 H_3{}'$	easy	easy	hard	$H_1 \cdot H_3{}'$	.618
$H_1{}' H_2 H_3{}'$	hard	easy	hard	$H_1{}' \cdot H_3{}'$	.491
$H_1{}' H_2{}' H_3$	hard	hard	easy	$H_1{}' \cdot H_2{}'$	.462
$H_1{}' H_2{}' H_3{}'$	hard	hard	hard	$H_1{}' \cdot H_2{}' \cdot H_3{}'$	.340

[a]These predicted H_c formulas are based on the general equation, $H_c = H_1 \cdot H_2 \cdot H_3$; and on the assumptions that there are no H_1, H_2, H_3, and H_c interactions, that H_1, H_2, H_3, and H_c are all scored on a proportion-correct scale, and that H_2 and H_3 in their easy conditions are at the asymptote of 1.00 from the outset of practice.

indicating the more difficult condition and no prime indicating the easier condition on each subscripted independent variable. The 60 participants (10 in each condition) were male students recruited from the Yale introductory psychology course.

Apparatus. A Hull memory drum with 1-inch-square windows was used to present the St → Rp pairs by the usual anticipation-then-correction method. St circles were presented in the left window and Rp numbers in the right window. Each of the 9 circle St appeared in the left window for 2 seconds alone and then for 2 seconds with its designated numerical Rp shown in the window to its right, after which both windows closed again. Then the left window immediately reopened, showing another circle St on the list for 2 seconds. The participant was instructed to try to recite the appropriate numerical Rp within the first 2-second period when only the St circle was visible in the left window, before the right window opened showing the correct Rp for that St. In each of the 80 trials the 9 St → Rp pairs came in a random order. Participants were given the usual instructions for a paired-associate task. Those in the H_3 (easy 1-digit Rp) condition were also told that the nine Rp would be the 1-digit numbers from 1 to 9; those in the H_3' (hard 3-digit Rp) condition were told that the 9 Rp would be 9 three-digit numbers, each beginning with a different integer from 1 to 9. Participants in H_2 (easy) linkage conditions were given the additional information that progressively higher Rp numbers were assigned to successively larger St circles; those in H_2' (hard) linkage conditions were informed that the magnitudes of the Rp numbers were randomly related to the sizes of the St circles. All participants were instructed to try to give some response to each St. Those in hard H_3' (three-digit) Rp conditions were told to respond to each St with at least the first digit (R_a) of Rp even if they could not remember the other two digits. As a further measure to elicit even partial responses, all participants were told that even when they could recall nothing about an Rp, they should guess. Each participant worked through 80 continuous trials on each of which all 9 St → Rp pairs were presented. The 80 trials took a total of 55 minutes.

Results and Discussion

Correct St → Rp anticipations (H_c): Group means. The manipulation of the difficulty of each of the three postulated sets of habits (H_1, H_2, and H_3) did, over the 80 trials, produce the predicted effects on H_c, in the mean proportion of St → Rp pairs correctly anticipated. The difficulty of forming the first, St-discrimination, set of H_1 habit links, St → r_d, was manipulated by using .14-cm steps between stimuli diameters in the easy conditions (H_1 _ _) and smaller .07-cm steps in the hard discrimination conditions (H_1' _ _). Evidence that such H_1 St-discrimination habits were involved in learning the St → Rp pairs can be seen by comparing the H_c proportion of correct scores in Table 1.2 for the three H_1 versus the three H_1' conditions. The mean H_c scores (i.e., the proportion of correct St → Rp anticipations over the 80 trials) is significantly higher (p < .001) for participants in task $H_1H_2H_3$ than for those in $H_1'H_2H_3$, .793 versus .635; and for those in task $H_1H_2H_3'$ than in $H_1'H_2H_3'$, .618 versus .491.

The difficulty of learning the second, H_2, set of $s_d \rightarrow R_a$ habits, linking St with Rp, was manipulated by assigning the numerical Rp to the circle St consecutively (higher numbers assigned to larger circles) in the easy conditions ($\_ H_2 \_$) and assigning them randomly in the hard conditions ($\_ H_2' \_$). Hence, the H_c scores should be higher for task $H_1'H_2H_3$ than $H_1'H_2'H_3$ and for task $H_1'H_2H_3'$ than $H_1'H_2'H_3'$. Both differences are in the predicted direction (Table 1.2), .635 versus .462 (p < .001) and .491 versus .340 (p <.01).

The difficulty of learning the third set of habit links, the H_3 chains of Rp elements, was varied by using one-digit Rp in easy response-learning conditions ($\_ \_ H_3$) and three-digit Rp in hard conditions ($\_ \_ H_3'$). Hence, higher H_c scores are predicted for task $H_1H_2H_3$ than $H_1H_2H_3'$; for task $H_1'H_2H_3$ than $H_1'H_2H_3'$; and for $H_1'H_2'H_3$ than $H_1'H_2'H_3'$. All three of these obtained H_c differences are in the predicted direction (as can be seen in Table 1.2) and are significant at the .001, .001, and .01 levels, respectively.

So far I have considered only the direction of the H_c differences between the conditions, but the theory predicts the sizes as well as directions of these H_c differences. In Table 1.2 the equation for H_c in each of the six conditions is given, based on the assumption that H_2 and H_3 in the easy condition have the value 1.00 from the outset (i.e., based on the plausible assumption that these participants could recite consecutively the numbers 1 to 9 perfectly from the outset of Trial 1). Solving for H_3' in each of the three pairs of equations in which it appears, based on these assumptions, yields the following equations and solutions:

$$H_3' = \frac{H_c \text{ in Cond. } H_1H_2H_3'}{H_c \text{ in Cond. } H_1H_2H_3} = \frac{.618}{.793} = .779$$

$$H_3' = \frac{H_c \text{ in Cond. } H_1'H_2H_3'}{H_c \text{ in Cond. } H_1'H_2H_3} = \frac{.491}{.635} = .773$$

$$H_3' = \frac{H_c \text{ in Cond. } H_1'H_2'H_3'}{H_c \text{ in Cond. } H_1'H_2'H_3} = \frac{.340}{.462} = .736$$

These three H_3' values are predicted to be equal to the extent that the learning of any one of the three postulated habits in any pair proceeds independently of the difficulty of the other two sets of habits being acquired simultaneously. The closeness of the three obtained quotients, .779, .773, and .736, suggests that there is considerable independence. The closeness of the .779 and .773 values particularly indicates that the difficulty of learning the Rp response chains (R_a $\cdots\rightarrow$ $s_a \rightarrow R_b \cdots\rightarrow s_b \rightarrow R_c$) is negligibly affected by the difficulty of concurrently learning the St discriminations (St $\rightarrow r_d$). That is, it indicates that concurrent motor and perceptual learning proceed without mutual interference. The third value, .736, is slightly lower than the other two, suggesting that learning of the hard, three-digit, response chain may be (very slightly) impeded by the difficulty of the $s_d \rightarrow R_a$ linking habits being learned concurrently. Some slight interference is plausible because both the $s_d \rightarrow R_a$ association habits and the $R_a \cdots\rightarrow s_a \rightarrow R_b$ $\cdots\rightarrow s_b \rightarrow R_c$ response (Rp) learning habits involve learning numerical responses.

The H_c learning curves. How manipulating the difficulty of the three sets of habits, H_1, H_2, and H_3, affects the acquisition curves (i.e., the growth over the 80 trials in the proportion of St $\rightarrow$ Rp pairs correctly anticipated, H_c) can be traced by plotting the group learning curves from the 10 participants in each of the 6 conditions. The 80 trials (omitting "guessing" Trial 1) were divided into 13 consecutive practice points, as follows. The first point (point "2") is the mean H_c score on Trials 2 and 3 combined; the next point (point "5") is the mean correctly anticipated on Trials 4, 5, and 6 combined; the next point, "8," is the mean on Trials 7, 8, 9, and 10; and each of the next 10 points (called 14, 21, 28, 35, 42, 49, 56, 63, 70, and 77, respectively) is the mean on successive blocks of 7 trials (e.g., point 77 is based on the means of Trials 74 through 80). More points were calculated for the earlier trials in order to detect the shape of the predicted negatively accelerated functions early in practice when changes are most rapid. The H_c acquisition curves and equations in Figure 1.1 for each of the six conditions are the best fitting exponential functions for the data points in that condition.

Each of the six lines shown in Figure 1.1 is the best fitting curve (by the least-squares deviation criterion) within the inverse exponential family $H_c = c - ae^{-bN}$, where the dependent variable H_c is the proportion of the nine St-Rp pairs anticipated correctly on any trial, c-a is the proportion of correct anticipations at the outset of practice (i.e., the Y-intercept), c is the asymptote, a is the distance traversed by the curve from its Y-intercept to its asymptote, b is the rate-of-change growth parameter, and e is the natural log base. Three-parameter exponential functions were used because a priori they are the often-obtained negatively accelerated learning curves, and because a poste-

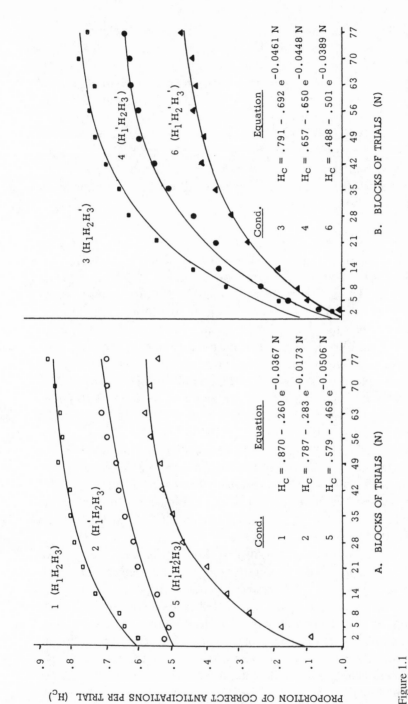

Figure 1.1
Acquisition curves for H_c, the proportion of St → Rp pairs correctly anticipated on successive blocks of the 80 trials in each of the six task conditions. (Figure 1.1A shows the curves for the three easy H_3 conditions [1-digit responses]; Figure 1.1B, for the three difficult H'_3 conditions [3-digit responses]. Lines show the obtained best-fitting exponential decay functions; the ○, □, and △ symbols show the obtained scores.)

riori they describe the data more accurately than do the best fitting two-parameter (straight-line) curves in each of the six conditions (by an amount significant at the .05 level in all cases except Cond. 2, $H_1'H_2H_3$). As a spot check, I also calculated for Cond. $H_1H_2H_3$ and $H_1'H_2H_3$ the best fitting hyperbolic and Gompertz functions, two other negatively accelerated growth functions, as alternatives to the exponential curve; but these other two growth functions were found to describe the data slightly less well than exponential functions. Cond. 3, $H_1H_2H_3'$, was the only one of the six in which the data deviated from the best-fitting exponential function by an amount that approached the .05 level. The goodness of the fit test was based on Lindquist's (1947) Case 8 with df = 10 (i.e., 13 – 3, the number of trial blocks minus the number of parameters calculated for each function). Caution should be exercised in inferring the shapes of the individual participant's curve from the Figure 1.1 group curves based on N = 10, especially because individual-difference variance in b and the b $\times$ N products are likely to be large (Sidman, 1952; Bakan, 1954).

Independent variable effects on the three parameters of the H_c learning curves. The three parameters (c, a, b) of the group learning functions shown in Figure 1.1 were interestingly affected by the difficulty level of the three independent variables, H_1, H_2, and H_3. Each of these three independent variables affected both the initial level of performance (the H_c function's Y-intercept, equal to *c-a*) and the asymptote *c* of the functions, in that, as predicted, increasing the difficulty of either the H_1, H_2, or H_3 task sizably lowers both the Y-intercept and the asymptote parameters. As regards the growth parameter *b*, increasing the difficulty of the H_1, St-discrimination task slows the rate of learning, as predicted; but the growth parameter b is affected more complexly by the difficulty of the other two sets of habits, H_2 and $H_{3.}$.

Practice curves for stimulus confusion and intrusion errors. An intrusion error is defined as responding to a given St with a Rp that is in the set of nine designated Rp but is not the response assigned to that given St. It indicates either a failure to discriminate the St correctly (an H_1, St $\rightarrow$ r_d error) or a failure to make the correct St $\rightarrow$ Rp linkage (an H_2, $s_d \rightarrow R_a$ error) or failures of both. Intrusion errors are sophisticated mistakes in that they indicate that a Rp-integration habit (H_3) has been well enough learned so that the learner is able to make a right Rp to the wrong St. When, as here, the mediating variables are scaled as proportions correct, the equation for intrusion errors, IE, is:

$$IE = H_3(1 - H_1 \cdot H_2)$$

A stimulus-generalization (confusion) error, on the other hand, involves mistaking one circle St for another, that is, giving a circle St the wrong distinctive r_d labeling response. It is measured by $1-H_1$ and so differs from IE except when both H_2 and H_3 equal 1.00. Some researchers have confused stimulus-generalization errors with intrusion errors by defining correct discrimination as having occurred only when the participant discriminates the St by using the assigned Rp, but this is too stringent a measure except in the special case where both H_2 and H_3 have been perfectly mastered at the outset of practice, as in Conditions 1 and 2 here.

Using this distinction between the two types of errors, it is possible to test hypotheses about the curves for both stimulus-confusion errors and for intrusion errors as functions of practice. In Cond. $H_1H_2H_3$ and $H_1'H_2H_3$ (the two easy H_2 and H_3 tasks with consecutively assigned one-digit Rp) the initial H_2 and H_3 levels are both assumed to be 1.00. Hence, in these two conditions $H_c = H_1 \cdot H_2 \cdot H_3$ becomes $H_c = H_1$ and the intrusion-error equation, $IE = H_3(1.00 - H_1 \cdot H_2)$, simplifies to $IE = 1.00 - H_1$. This inverse convergence of the stimulus discrimination curve and the intrusion-error curve is a special case that occurs according to the model only when initial H_2 and H_3 both equal 1.00 from the outset and there are no omissions. Figure 1.1A curves for these two conditions, $H_1H_2H_3$ and $H_1'H_2H_3$, show, as predicted, that stimulus confusion falls monotonically throughout practice.

Two other conditions, $H_1 H_2 H_3'$ and $H_1' H_2 H_3'$, use the hard three-digit responses (H_3') but simplify the St $\rightarrow$ Rp linkage learning by consistently assigning progressively higher number Rp's to larger stimulus circles, St; hence, $H_3' < 1.00$ and $H_2 = 1.00$ at the outset of practice. As predicted by the model, the obtained IE curves in both conditions are nonmonotonic, initially rising, then leveling off, and then slowly declining, in contrast to the obtained stimulus confusion curve, which falls throughout practice.

For the final two conditions, $H_1'H_2'H_3$ and $H_1'H_2'H_3'$, with random pairing of circle St and numerical Rp, the present materials yield separate values of H_3 and of $H_1 \cdot H_2$, but not of H_1 and H_2 separately. Hence, it is not possible to test the hypotheses regarding stimulus confusion with results from these two conditions, but the hypotheses regarding intrusion errors, IE, can be tested because it requires only the composite $H_1 \cdot H_2$ values. In both conditions the predicted and obtained practice curve for IE shows the predicted nonmonotonicity in the form of a brief initial rise followed by a subsequent long decline.

Hence, the present model accurately predicts the nonmonotonic shape of the intrusion error curves over diverse conditions and the monotonic fall of stimulus confusion during paired-associate learning. The results also confirm predictions about how varying the difficulty of the three hypothesized sets of component habits (H_1, H_2, and H_3) affects learning of the St $\rightarrow$ Rp pairs, H_c, as regards absolute magnitude and the shape and parameters of the acquisition curves.

My learning period. My zest for engaging in empirical research grew with these experiments on learning devised and carried out during my graduate student years, stretching from my master's thesis on list learning to this doctoral dissertation on paired-associates learning, with a batch of Air Force studies on acquiring perceptual-motor skills sandwiched in. This early experience confirmed and developed my initial belief that empirical investigation, putting questions to nature, is a powerful and exciting procedure – and also an onerous one, for these early experiences taught me that nature does not yield her secrets easily and often speaks with Delphic ambiguity.

These learning experiments show several distinctive features characterizing my style of working that became sharpened as my experience grew. My a priori theories have been atypically high in intricacy and unorthodox in content, and my derivations of testable hypotheses from these theories have tended to be unusually rigorous. I appreciated, early and explicitly, that the empirical confrontation can serve as a discovery process and not just as a test of a fixed a priori hypothesis. I tended more than typically to predict complex nonmonotonic relations, which in turn led me to use counterbalanced designs and well-scaled measures that allowed me to tease out such complex relations. Intrigued with studying the size and shape of relations, and not just predicting their simple increasing versus decreasing direction, I argued (at first implicitly and progressively more explicitly) against the excessive preoccupation with inferential statistics to the neglect of descriptive statistics. These trends can be discerned developing in the research described in subsequent chapters.

FIRST THE GOOD NEWS:
A DESIRABILITY ORDER EFFECT
IN "CONDITIONING" PERSUASIVENESS

[Adapted with permission from W. J. McGuire, 1957, Order of presentation as a factor in "conditioning" persuasiveness, in C. I. Hovland (Ed.), *The order of presentation in persuasion,* pp. 98–114 (New Haven, CT: Yale University Press, copyright © 1957). It constitutes a transition between my predoctoral learning research and my postdoctoral attitude-change research.]

Applying Learning Theory to Persuasion

Learning theory has implications for how the ordering with respect to pleasantness of a series of argumentative messages affects their overall persuasiveness. For example, in an annual report or a "state of the union" address in which the speaker has to cover a series of topics, on some arguing for pleasant positions and on others for unpleasant, is the speaker's overall persuasive impact greater when he or she presents the good news first or saves it for last? In these cases where the source attribution remains the same for a series of persuasive messages on different topics, each message presentation can be considered a conditioning trial, with the source being the stimulus to which the agreement response is being conditioned (or extinguished). Being persuaded to the source's position depends on a chain of mediating responses (e.g., attending to the message, comprehending its contents, accepting its conclusions, etc.). Conditions that interfere with these mediators tend to reduce persuasive impact. An acquisition trial occurs when the source's message evokes the chain of mediating responses leading to agreement and the agreement is rewarded; an extinction trial occurs when the agreement response is evoked but is not rewarded (or, a fortiori, is punished). Hence a source's earlier messages may either augment or reduce agreement with his or her later messages, depending upon whether agreement with the earlier messages was rewarded or punished.

   To test this analysis participants were asked to read a series of messages attributed to a single source, each message arguing that some future eventuality was likely to occur. Half of the eventualities were pleasant and half unpleasant. Agreeing that a pleasant eventuality would occur was defined as positively reinforced; agreeing that an unpleasant eventuality would occur, as negatively reinforced. This implies an order effect such that when messages arguing for the likelihood of pleasant eventualities are presented first and the undesirable ones later, a greater total amount of agreement will be evoked than when the set of messages comes in the reverse undesirable-then-desirable order. When the earlier messages argued for the likelihood of desirable (undesirable) events, the mediating responses of attending to and comprehending the message contents would have been rewarded (punished) and so would have increased (decreased) attention to that source's later messages arguing about other events.

Method

General procedure. The participants were 92 psychology students who served in 3 sessions at one-week intervals. In the first session precommunication attitudes regarding the likelihood of occurrence were measured on a wide variety of academic eventualities, some desirable to the students (e.g., more financial aid to college students) and some undesirable (e.g., more early-morning classes to reduce the classroom shortage). A week later, in a second session, each participant was presented with 4 persuasive communications that argued for the high likelihood of occurrence of 4 of 8 critical eventualities (two desirable and two undesirable), and then the immediate postcommunication likelihood attitudes were measured on the likelihood of all eight eventualities. These attitudes were measured again in a third session a week later to determine the persistence of any immediate attitude change induced in the second session.

The persuasive communications. The persuasive communication on each of the eight critical eventualities was the printed reply of a fictitious "Dr. Harold Wilson" to a question at a press conference, purportedly on the occasion of his election as president of the "National Association of University Administrators." Each communication consisted of an interviewer's question on the likelihood of one of the eight academic eventualities, followed by Dr. Wilson's 150 - to 200 - word reply, presenting evidence that the eventuality was likely to occur. Participants were allowed two minutes to read each communication. Each participant was presented with four of the eight messages, ordered either with the two messages arguing for the likelihood of desirable eventualities first followed by two arguing for the likelihood of undesirable eventualities; or in the reverse order. The other four issues served as no-communication controls for that participant.

Design and independent variables.   A before-after design was used to measure the immediate persuasive impact of the communication (attitude change from first to second session) and to measure the persistence of this initial persuasive impact (attitude change from second to third session). The crucial among-participant independent variable was the order of the four persuasive communications: For half the participants the two messages arguing for the likelihood of two desirable eventualities came before the two undesirable (the DD,UU group), and for the other half the undesirable eventualities came first (the UU,DD group). Two hypothesized mediating variables were also measured at the end of the second session, the judged fairness of Dr. Wilson and recall of the arguments he used in the persuasive communication.

Results and Discussion

The effect of desirability order on attitude change.   Strong support was obtained for the basic prediction that the total persuasive impact across the four messages would be greater when the four came in the DD,UU order than in the UU,DD order. The events' likelihood ratings immediately after the four communications in the second session are higher in the DD,UU than the UU,DD condition for seven of the eight items ($p = .07$ by a sign test). A more sensitive ANOVA test, taking into account the size of these differences, yields a $p < .01$ for this order effect. A before-after test, controlling for a "ceiling" effect by analysis of covariance yields an order effect significant on the .001 level. An "efficiency-index" adjustment for ceiling effects (Hovland, Lumsdaine, & Sheffield, 1949) also yields a significant order effect, as does an arcsine transformation (appropriate if responses on our 0 to 100 likelihood scale produce probability-type distributions). The third session scores indicate that a significant amount of the immediately induced attitude change dissipates during the ensuing week but the remaining changes are still sizable and significant.

Effects of order on the hypothesized mediators. It was hypothesized that the order variable would have its effect on attitude change through mediation of the attention and comprehension responses. In the DD,UU order the earlier messages supported desirable positions, and so attention to and comprehension of messages from Dr. Wilson would be reinforced by acceptance of their desirable position. On the other hand, in the UU,DD order, accepting the earlier messages supporting undesirable positions would be punishing, thus reducing attention to Dr. Wilson's later messages. This attention-mediator explanation was tested by a seven-item multiple-choice recognition test on the communication arguments, answered by the participant in the second session after reading all four messages. This explanation is supported in that among the 46 participants in the DD,UU group, 23 made perfect scores on this recall test, whereas in the UU,DD group only 14 of the 46 participants received perfect scores, a difference significant at the .06 level by a chi-square test. Over the 92 participants there was a correlation of +.53 ($p < .01$) between recall and attitude change.

The order effect on attitude change might alternatively be mediated by perceived source credibility: in the DD,UU condition the pleasant contents of the earlier messages might have given a more favorable first impression of the source than did the UU,DD condition. This alternative explanation is not supported in that Dr. Wilson's judged fairness was almost identical in the two order conditions. A third, wishful-thinking, explanation is that the judged desirabilities and likelihoods of eventualities would tend to be positively correlated at the outset, and so participants in the DD,UU order would have had more agreement with the initial (desirable) positions and hence would have become habituated to agreeing with the source's later messages, indicating a contiguity rather than reinforcement mechanism. On the contrary, it happened that the four undesirable eventualities in the control condition were rated as being slightly more likely and showed slightly more attitude change than the four desirable items. Deserving of further study is how (and by what processes) the persuasive impact of messages is affected by other internal rewards besides the one used here (the desirability of the position adopted), for example, rewarding the participants' need for cognition, or their need to identify with a high-prestige communicator, or to conform to the norms of a positive reference group.

LEARNING THEORY
AND SOCIAL PSYCHOLOGY

[Adapted with permission from W. J. McGuire, 1965a, Learning theory and social psychology: Discussion of W. N. Schoenfeld's paper, in O. Klineberg & R. Christie (Eds.), *Perspectives in social psychology*, pp. 135–140 (New York: Holt, Rinehart, and Winston, copyright © 1965; 1993), originating in a talk at the October 1961 opening ceremonies of the Columbia University Department of Social Psychology, whose life span coincided with my own 1961–1967 stay at Columbia. This six-year stay at Columbia was my most enjoyable academic appointment, with its fine graduate students and its New York City location. Most speakers at these 1961 inaugural ceremonies recommended that our new splinter department be devoted to turning out consumer goods, so I characteristically took an adversarial stand against the politically correct consensus by extolling the merits of basic research.]

When I read the advanced text of his talk that Professor Schoenfeld so kindly made available to me, I suspected that the Italian maxim with which he ended, *amare e non essere amato, è tempo perduto*, might be of crucial significance, so I asked my neighbor who boasts an Italian name for a translation. The neighbor's Italian was not much better than mine, but after puzzling over it he said, "I am not sure what all the words mean but I think he's being friendly," so I pursued the matter no further. Let me play my own Italian card. Browning wrote that a postmortem would reveal, engraved on his heart, the word "Italy." A similar morbid scrutiny of Schoenfeld and me might disclose on our respective hearts the words "Skinner" and "Hull," which is a very large or very small difference, depending on one's point of view. To insiders, the difference means we are in opposite camps; to outsiders, we are as alike as two peas in a pod. All cats look alike – unless you're a cat. In discussing Schoenfeld's paper I am torn between pointing out the tactical disagreements that he and I would find interesting versus indicating the broader area of strategic agreement between us regarding what social psychologists should be doing.

As learning theorists, the two of us might paraphrase Kronecker on the integers by saying, "God created the reflex arc; the rest was mapped out by learning theorists," the rest consisting of a set of propositions specifying the relations among observable variables in the environment and those in the organism's behavior. Where Schoenfeld and I differ tactically is in regard to what kinds of new propositions are most needed currently. He has stressed our need to define responses and stimuli in the domain of social behavior. I am willing to use communications (especially spoken words) as the familiar Hullian stimulus-producing, mediating responses, conveniently overt interpersonal observable behaviors, not simply covert intrapersonal constructs like "subvocal thoughts." As a Hullian my priority is to elaborate a theoretical superstructure of mediating constructs and to state relations between the observable dependent and independent variables indirectly but economically, via chains of mediating constructs or intervening variables.

These differences involve tactical priorities rather than ultimate goals and are based to a large extent on differing appraisals of the current state of psychology, Schoenfeld judging that we are waiting for our Tycho Brahe and I that we await our Kepler. I do not think there is a major difference between us regarding the ultimate aim of "social" or any other area of psychology: It is to create a precise description of the determinants of human behavior, parsimonious in its postulated relations, inclusive in its scope, consisting of empirically tied propositions and a theoretical superstructure of higher-order postulates that are a joy to the eye of the beholder and, for the student of the person, a creative tool that leaves "aim now known, and hand at work, now never wrong."

This austere program puts the behavioral theorist at odds with some other social psychologists. They say: "Your laws are very elegant and perhaps adequate to describe a rat's learning a T-maze, but account poorly for the rather more complex behavior of people conducting themselves in complex human environments. To describe a pretzel-shaped universe might one not need pretzel-shaped hypotheses?" That the complexity of social behavior requires special theories is terribly plausible – but terribly wrong. I can forgive Plato's calling God a geometrician and Jacobi's saying He or She is an arithmetician, but it seems sacrilegious to call the First Cause a pretzel bender. Paradoxically, behavior often becomes more describable as it becomes more complex. The individual electron's movements elude our most complex formulations, but the motions of the galactic worlds can be described by laws spare, precise, and elegant. Simple postulates may suffice to describe much of people's complex social behavior.

Schoenfeld, like many of the other participants in this symposium, was kind enough to suggest to us social psychologists, in the last part of his talk, a number of problems for future research. Personally, I have problems enough of my own and my research has been programmed for the next seven years. Also, we might quibble about some of his suggestions. He regrets that we have failed to follow up some studies like Daniel's and Humphrey's on cooperative problem solving; however, rich contributions to the topic have been made in the past five years (particularly in experiments on the effects of confounding group members' rewards and feedback) by Seymour Rosenberg, Robert Hall, Sidowski, Burke, Suppes and Atkinson, De Soto, and others. Schoenfeld may mean that these researchers are mostly experimental rather than social psychologists, but this union-local issue is trivial: As the Hapsburgs said (perhaps not often enough), we are all poor sinners.

But aside from such quibbles, I can say of the Schoenfeld-suggested problems that they do represent the general type of work I myself would like to see done by social psychologists. His suggestions for research differ from suggestions made by other participants in this symposium, preoccupied with the Berlin wall, the urban blight, the population bomb, and the plight of Blacks in the South. Such action-oriented research strikes me as bad strategy. Approaching research from the perspective of application rather than theory is as inelegant and inefficient as trying to push a strand of cooked spaghetti across the table from the back end. To such work assignments my response is that I have not come here to turn out consumer goods.

What do I hope to turn out? Let me explain with a parable adapted from Stephen Spender. When an undergraduate enquirer says she or he is drawn to social psychology because it might reveal ways to reduce international tensions before we blow ourselves up, I say gently: "You have a good heart. I admire you but have little to offer you. Perhaps you should speak to one of my colleagues here, or have you thought of law or the ministry?" Rarely do I get that other kind of student who says, "I've got a hunch that a social psychologist might get a neat perspective on social conflict by using a little graph theory and difference equations," and to this one I say, "Welcome home." I feel our social psychological research should begin with hypotheses derived from basic theory, ideally but not necessarily specifying quantitatively precise relations, rather than with hypotheses selected for their relevance to social action at the cost of theory relevance.

Some might object that I am calling for science for science's sake and that such an enterprise may satisfy the social psychologists themselves who will feel "the roll, the rise, the carol, the creation," but what does it offer to the rest of the public that justifies the expenditure required? I say it offers a joy in the work itself, work that can be of such intrinsic excellence that, like the unraveling of the hemoglobin molecule or Kronecker's solution of the general equation of the fifth degree, the contemplation of the work itself shakes us like a banner. Observers would not ask, "What is it good for?" but rather contemplate it with a feeling of elation and reverence, with a pride in their species derived from sharing humanity with those who have created such excellence.

Bolyai shrieked when he grasped the internal consistency of a non-Euclidian geometry. What does this have to do with socially pressing problems like school integration? Among other things, this: that although imposed partition of the student body on the bases of sex or religion or color or class should be opposed, the social psychologist is obligated to do more than make a career of such social-action advocacy. Indeed, although I personally (at the risk of being called a utopian socialist) work for the day when we poor kids may sit in your rich-kid schools, I feel that social psychologists' first 60 hours of work a week are owed to creating an elegant theoretical model to account for social behavior. Then, when the day dawns on which students find a more open school society in which rich sit side by side with poor, both will find that we social psychologists have been producing something that makes school worth coming to – something to shriek about.

2

Immunization against Persuasion

The studies reported in chapter 1 illustrate work done during my graduate student years in experimental psychology at Fordham and Yale and while switching from experimental to social psychology during a postdoctoral year at the University of Minnesota. The immunization studies reported here in chapter 2 illustrate work done during my next shimmy up the greasy academic pole as an up-or-out non-tenured faculty member at Yale and Illinois. After my postdoc year at the University of Minnesota's Laboratory for Research in Social Relations (where I enjoyed working with Leon Festinger, Stan Schachter, Hank Riecken, May Brodbeck, Herb McCloskey, Andy Papandreou, John Darley, Sr., and others) I spent the 1955 summer months at the University of Michigan in the SSRC Advanced Workshop for Mathematics in the Social Sciences. I then returned to Yale as an instructor, now accompanied by my wife (and later collaborator) Claire, whom I had met during my graduate student years at Yale. Our first collaboration produced three children, Jim, Anne, and Steve, in two and a half years.

WISDOM FROM AND FOR THE EARLY
FACULTY YEARS

Life as a Nontenured Faculty Member

The Yale Department of Psychology to which I returned had a cast of characters notably different from the players I had left just a year before. The change was confined to the untenured ranks, but that is what mattered to a junior faculty member in those days, when untenured and tenured tiers were less interactive than now. Newly arrived in New Haven that September 1955 was a batch of recent social psychology Ph.D.s: A. R. "Bob" Cohen, Irv Sarnoff, Milt Rosenberg, Jack

Brehm, Justin Aronfreed, and Bill Dember, all from the University of Michigan (or one step removed), all bright and friendly, collaborative in their own work styles but respecting my more solitary way of working, all of us highly supportive of one another. Never, before or since, has Yale psychology absorbed all at once such an infusion of new blood – young blood to be sure, but youth is a fault that time tends to cure. None of us was destined to stay at Yale in those days of out rather than up. I, knowing only the Yale system, accepted it as natural law that my Yale redux was a good place to leave from, and so I worked away without completely unpacking, waiting for the offer I could not refuse. You can't go home again, or perhaps shouldn't so soon and in so different a role as was my second coming to Yale. My senior colleagues probably found my role switch more difficult to handle than I did. Carl Hovland once complained that when I was a grad student I had acted like a faculty member, and now that I was a faculty member I acted like a graduate student – perhaps the most overtly hostile comment the gentle Carl ever made.

Within three years of my return to Yale, after brief flirtations with suitors such as Dartmouth, Clark, and Iowa, I received the nonrefusable offer from the University of Illinois: a joint appointment in Charlie Osgood's Communication Research Institute (which gave me a reduced teaching load and good colleagues like Charlie, Perc Tannenbaum, and George Gerbner); and in the psychology department (which put me in a fine social psychology group with Harry Triandis, Ivan Steiner, Fred Fiedler, and Don Dulany). Among my graduate student collaborators at Illinois were Dimitri Papageorgis, Bill Watts (who later moved with me to Columbia University), and Lynn Anderson. I never had better working conditions than during my three years at Illinois, and not just because Champaign-Urbana provided so few distractions from work. My experience leads me to suggest to young faculty recruits who have offers from both a large state university like Illinois or Minnesota and from a private elite university like Yale or Columbia that they consider that large state universities may be more generous than the elite ivy league schools in supporting the research of their young faculty. The large state universities also have greater depth and breadth of expertise across the psychology spectrum. At Illinois, when my research on personality correlates of persuadability called for factor analyses, I sought and received help from five or six world-class experts on the topic (Tucker, R. B. Cattell, Humphreys, Kaiser, Kappauf, Cronbach, etc.); but when I shifted to Columbia

University I myself was the university expert on factor analysis, teaching a graduate course on it and being a major consultant on multivariate analysis. By moving from Illinois to Columbia I achieved the legendary feat of raising the average sophistication in multivariate analysis at both places.

My frequent changes of universities during the first fifteen years after my Ph.D. (Minnesota, Yale, Illinois, Columbia, UCSD, Yale) might be interpreted as a tactic for speeding up my ascent through the academic ranks, but actually each of my new appointments was at rank and salary similar to those I had left. Perhaps conventional wisdom is correct and my not moving up when I moved in reflects my being a poor negotiator; or perhaps I turned down mega-offers because I did not want to join an institution that was willing to buy someone like me at so high a price.

One's Place at the Trough:
On Getting Research Grants

If I have been unpushing for rank and salary, I showed no reluctance to shoulder my way as vigorously as my more aggressive colleagues to get on board the research-grant gravy train even in my assistant professor days. Just after my 1958 arrival at Illinois the National Science Foundation set up a social science division to fund basic research in psychology and related fields. I applied to NSF for two years' support of research on immunizing people against persuasion that I had started during my first Illinois year, and my proposal was approved for 1959–61 at the funding level requested, supporting the immunization against persuasion research reported in this chapter. In the grant's second year (my last at Illinois, as it turned out, and the year in which I received tenure) I applied to NSF for a three-year follow-up grant, "Correlates of Persuadability and of Immunizability against Persuasion," to support research on my personality-persuadability axiomatic theory (McGuire, 1968b; see chapter 3 in this volume). This proposal was funded for the 1961–4 period as requested and the grant transferred with me when I moved from Illinois to Columbia.

Since my first grant in 1959 up to the present my research has been continuously funded (current funding being approved to 1999), a stretch of continuous funding unfortunately rare for psychologists. For the first half of these 40 years of continuous support the funding came from the National Science Foundation; for the second half, from the National Institutes of Mental Health. Without this support much of the research reported in this volume would not have been possible. I am grateful to these sponsoring agencies, to the peer reviewers, and to the taxpayers. The latter might not have approved this use of their money had they (rather than my peer reviewers) determined how it was to be spent. I shall not claim that the public received their money's worth but only that had these funds not supported my research they might have been put to worse uses.

ALTERNATIVE APPROACHES TO INDUCING RESISTANCE TO PERSUASION

[Adapted with permission from McGuire, 1964b, Inducing resistance to persuasion: Some contemporary approaches, in L. Berkowitz (Ed.), *Advances in experimental social psychology*, Vol. 1, pp. 191–229 (New York: Academic Press, copyright © 1964).]

I began working on ways of inducing resistance to persuasion under the impression that, although much research was being done on how to make communications more persuasive, little was being done on ways of producing resistance to persuasion. Later I realized that many people were investigating resistance to persuasion but were – like M. Jourdain speaking prose – unaware of it. I became increasingly aware that resistance to persuasion is not necessarily healthy. It may seem more romantically appealing to resist arguments, but susceptibility to persuasion is correlated with the ability to learn; and ignoring others' opinions can be maladaptive. At an extreme of resistance, a catatonic schizophrenic tends to be impervious to propaganda; also, some resistance-inducing pretreatments can be unhealthy, such as teaching a person to ignore or perceptually distort information in order to defend preconceptions. I shall first briefly review four general approaches to inducing resistance to persuasion (commitment, anchoring, inducing resistant cognitive states, and resistance training), mentioning variations on each approach. The last two-thirds of the chapter describes my own research that uses a fifth approach, inoculation.

Commitment Approaches

Commitment approaches to inducing resistance to persuasion involve having the believer take some hard-to-revoke step on the basis of a belief, which makes changing the belief seem dangerous, costly, or embarrassing to the believer. Such approaches can be classified into subtypes by the nature of the committing behavior or by the way of eliciting it. Four subtypes are described below in order of increasing externality of the commitment.

Private decisions.   The most subjective kind of commitment is having the person make a private decision that he or she holds the belief, without overtly expressing the decision. Bennett's (1955) participants, asked to come to a private (or at least anonymous) decision, tended to hold more tenaciously to this decision than those not so requested. Lewin (1951, 1958) felt that decision-making, even of the anonymous sort, will have a "freezing" effect that makes the believer resistant to counterpressure. However, such private decision-making is not found to confer resistance in some primacy-recency studies (Hovland & Mandell, 1957; N. H. Anderson, 1959), nor in some before-after versus after-only studies (Lana, 1959; Hicks & Spaner, 1962).

Public announcement of one's belief.   One's being publicly identified with one's belief should be more committing than such private decision-making (Lewin, 1958) and so confer more resistance to subsequent persuasive attacks. There is some confirmatory evidence (Deutsch & Gerard, 1955; Hovland et al., 1957; Cohen et al., 1959), but Bennett (1955) found private decision-making to be as committing as publicly identified decisions. Fisher et al. (1956) report that when public decisions are required, the beliefs that people announce are adjusted toward the expected attacks.

Active participation on the basis of one's belief.   Going beyond simply stating one's belief publicly to taking further action on the basis of it (e.g., writing an essay in support of it) may be more committing still, as in McGuire's studies on the efficacy of active participation, reported later in this chapter. Many "overt compliance" studies (Kelman, 1953; King & Janis, 1956; Festinger, 1957; Cohen et al., 1958) investigate conditions under which compliant actions have the greatest committing effect (e.g., when they are elicited with the least pressure; with many alternatives available, and with minimum justification; see the chapter 4 discussion of dissonance theory). The use of belief-defensive essays as the form of active participation leaves an unfortunate theoretical ambiguity: Is the increased resistance due to acting overtly on the basis of the belief or to the self-indoctrination and rehearsal of one's position? Fortunately, some "forced compliance" studies have used forms of active participation other than essay writing (as discussed in chapter 4).

External commitment. An "external commitment" approach (Rosenbaum & Franc, 1960; Rosenbaum & Zimmerman, 1959) involves telling the person that someone else thinks the person holds a specified belief, thus making the person more resistant to attacks on it, perhaps by a "self-labeling" process.

Anchoring the Belief to Other Cognitions

A second, "anchoring," family of approaches to inducing resistance to persuasion involves making explicit the belief's ties to other cognitions, thus enhancing its resistance to change by increasing the person's awareness that changing it would require also either changing the linked cognitions or enduring inconsistency. Three anchoring approaches will be described, differing in the type of cognitions to which the target belief is linked.

Linking to accepted values. Instrumentality $\times$ value theorists (Feather, 1982) argue that a belief is held firmly to the extent that it is perceived as instrumental to the attainment of valenced goals (Carlson, 1956; Rosenberg, 1956; Zajonc, 1960). It would follow that any pretreatment raising the believer's awareness that a belief is linked to valued goals (or raising the evaluation of goals to the attainment of which the belief is perceived as instrumental) will enhance the belief's resistance to persuasion.

Linking to other beliefs. An alternative type of anchoring involves linking the target belief to other beliefs in the person's cognitive system, thus enhancing the person's awareness that changing the belief would introduce uncomfortable imbalances into his or her cognitive system (Abelson & Rosenberg, 1958; Harary, 1959). For example, McGuire's "Socratic questioning" studies suggest that asking questions that remind the person of related beliefs which he or she already possesses enhances resistance to subsequent inconsistency-increasing attacks (McGuire, 1960b; and see chapter 6 in this volume).

Linking to valenced sources and reference groups. It has been shown that if a person is made to see that a belief is shared by valued others, then the belief becomes more resistant to subsequent attacks. Endorsements, even by anonymous individuals and groups, confers resistance (Schachter & Hall, 1952; Bennett, 1955), and so a fortiori does endorsement by positively valenced reference groups (Kelley & Woodruff, 1956; Newcomb, 1961) and by highly regarded, specific individuals (Kelman & Hovland, 1953; Tannenbaum, 1956). Each of these anchoring approaches can be utilized by establishing new links or by making existing links more salient, and can be brought about by procedures such as Socratic questioning (McGuire, 1960c), or directed thinking (see chapter 6), or enhancing the salience of relevant reference groups (Charters & Newcomb, 1958).

Inducing Resistant States

To the extent that specified personality, motivational, emotional, or ideological states are correlated with resistance to social influence, inducing such states in believers should enhance resistance to persuasion. However, few states have proved to be generally effective in predisposing the person to resist persuasion (McGuire, 1968b). The possibilities and problems can be illustrated by considering four such purportedly resistance-conferring states – namely, anxiety, aggression, self-esteem, and ideological preconditioning.

Inducing anxiety about the issue.   Much research has been done on the use of fear-arousing appeals in persuasion, often on the assumption that when anxiety is attached to a given issue a person is subsequently inclined to avoid the topic, thus sheltering the belief from attacks. Nunnally and Bobren (1959) found that people are less willing to receive further information on a topic after reading an anxiety-arousing message on it; but Janis and Feshbach (1953) suggest that the greater the prior anxiety arousal, the *less* is the resistance to a subsequent attack on the issue. Other studies (e.g., Berkowitz & Cottingham, 1960; Janis, 1967) make clear that the effects of fear appeals are quite complex.

Inducing aggressiveness.   It has been proposed that a person becomes more resistant to social influence attempts when angered, but

Weiss and Fine (1956) report that induced aggression decreases susceptibility to arguments for benevolent positions while increasing susceptibility to arguments for misanthropic positions. Because chronic hostility may be associated (at least in males) with resistance to persuasion, this variable deserves further study (Janis & Field, 1959; Linton & Graham, 1959).

Raising self-esteem.   Although it has been reported that a success experience enhances a believer's resistance to subsequent social influence attempts (Kelman, 1950; Samelson, 1957), even when the success and the influence attempts are on quite different topics, the relation is complicated by the possible nonmonotonic relation between self-esteem and persuasibility (McGuire, 1968b and chapter 3 of this volume; Rhodes & Wood, 1992).

Ideological preconditioning.   Brainwashing studies suggest that "ideological preconditioning" (i.e., giving the person a broad integrated ideology) increases resistance to persuasive attacks. The ideology can be cultural (e.g., adherence to a specific religious creed) or more personal (e.g., esprit de corps, or the conviction that one has secret resources of which the indoctrinator is unaware). Evidence is anecdotal and tenuous (e.g., U.S. Senate, 1956 reports that Westerners' resistance to indoctrination attempts by the Chinese Communists in the early 1950s was greater in clergymen than businessmen, in those who identified with their parents than in those who rejected them, and in marines than in army personnel). Further study is needed to identify both the states that enhance resistance and the ways of inducing these states.

Prior Training in Resisting Persuasive Attempts

General education.   It has been proposed that general education makes people more resistant to persuasion, but empirical research findings are quite ambiguous. Weitzenhoffer (1953) finds no simple relation between intelligence and suggestibility. The more intelligent (or better educated) have been found to be more resistant to conformity pressures from peers (Crutchfield, 1955; Stukát, 1958); but they may be less resistant to mass-media pressures (Hovland et al., 1949; Janis & Rife, 1959).

Avoidance and distortion.   Training in evasion skills, like selective avoidance or perceptual distortion of belief-discrepant information, may be effective although unhealthy. Perceptual distortion has been shown to facilitate resistance to persuasion (Kendall & Wolf, 1949; Cooper & Dinerman, 1951; Kelley, 1957; Cantril, 1958). However, training in such evasiveness may require considerable time, ingenuity, and have undesirable side effects. Many attacking messages will not be sufficiently indexed to allow avoidance or distortion.

Training in critical skills.   A healthier type of pretraining, enhancing people's critical capacities to recognize persuasive attempts and to detect flaws in the attacking arguments, has been shown to increase resistance to persuasion (Biddle, 1932; Collier, 1944; Allport & Lepkin, 1945; Citron & Harding, 1950). Techniques can be as simple as warning the believer to be critical just before the attack (Das et al., 1955; Luchins, 1957) or urging them to be accurate (Neuberg & Fisk, 1987) or to be objective (Monteith, 1993). McGuire's (1964b), inoculation theory research, described in the rest of this chapter, probes more deeply into the immunizing effectiveness of such prior training and warnings.

THEORIZING BEHIND THE INOCULATION APPROACH

Use of Cultural Truisms

My research program on inducing resistance to persuasion (McGuire 1961a, 1961h, 1961i, 1961j, 1962a, 1962d, 1963b, 1964b, 1964c, 1965b, 1965d, 1970a) leans heavily on the analogy of the biological inoculation process where persons are made resistant to strong doses of the attacking virus by preexposure to a weakened dose of the pathogen, not so strong as to overwhelm defenses but strong enough to stimulate them so the person will be better prepared to fight off later massive exposures to attacking materials. This approach contrasts with supportive prevention, which bolsters health by positive measures (e.g., providing for adequate rest, good diet, hygiene, exercise, etc.). Inoculation is likely to be superior to supportive prevention to the extent that the organism has been brought up in a germ-free environment and so left in a "paper tiger" state of appearing to be vigorously healthy but being highly vulnerable when suddenly exposed to massive doses of the unac-customed disease virus. The studies reported here are based on the anal-ogy that a person's beliefs tend to be maintained in a "germ-free" ideo-logical environment and so appear to be strong but actually prove highly vulnerable when suddenly exposed to massive attacks. Cultural truisms that are so widely accepted as to seem beyond attack are partic-ularly likely to show paper-tiger pseudostrength. Pretesting indicated that cultural truisms are common in the domain of health beliefs for col-lege students, a majority of whom checked "15" on a 15-point scale to indicate their complete agreement with propositions like: "It's a good idea to brush your teeth after every meal if at all possible"; "Mental ill-ness is not contagious"; "The effects of penicillin have, almost without exception, been beneficial"; "Children should get a yearly chest x-ray to detect signs of TB at an early stage."

Basic Assumptions and Relevant Variables

Underlying assumptions. Inoculation theory assumes that pretreat-ments to make truisms resistant to subsequent persuasive attacks must overcome two deficiencies: the believer's being unpracticed in de-fending the belief because it has seldom been attacked and the be-liever's being unmotivated to develop a defense because the belief seems unassailable. For a pre-attack treatment to motivate the person to acquire resistance-conferring material it should be threatening rather than reassuring (e.g., by preexposing the believer to weakened forms of attacking arguments). However, motivation alone is insuffi-cient, because lack of prior practice will have left the believer unable to act on this motivation unless given guidance and time to develop defensive material. These assumptions yield a number of predictions, including the following about the relative immunizing effectiveness of three types of prior defenses.

The defensive pretreatment variables. One pertinent independent variable, the threateningness of the prior defenses, contrasts supportive versus refutational defenses. The low-threatening supportive defenses give the believer arguments in support of the truism. The high-threat-ening refutational defenses mention several arguments attacking the belief (which is threatening enough to stimulate the person's defenses) and then refutes these attacks (weakening them so they will just stimulate without overwhelming belief in the truism). Two types of refutational defenses were used, refutational-same versus refutational-different, as described below. A second immunizing variable is the amount of unguided, active participation that the defense requires of the believer. In relatively passive conditions the believer read a defensive essay and in active conditions the believer wrote such an essay. This reading-versus-writing variable was relevant to both of the theorized difficulties in immunizing cultural truisms, the believer's lack of practice and lack of motivation in defending it. A third major independent variable is the interval (ranging from a few minutes to a week) between the defense and the attack; interactions were predicted between this time interval and other independent variables.

GENERAL EXPERIMENTAL PROCEDURE

The basic procedure typically involved a defensive followed by an attacking session. The participants, college students fulfilling a requirement of an introductory psychology course, were told that we were studying verbal skills. The issues defended and attacked were pre-identified health truisms (e.g., the desirability of frequent tooth brushing, of annual chest x-rays, etc.).

The First (Defensive) Session

Participants were told that the study was investigating the relation between reading and writing skills. In the first of the two 50-minute sessions the participants served in four (2 × 2) defensive conditions, active-refutational, passive-refutational, active-supportive, and passive-supportive, each of these defenses dealing with a different health truism.

An active-refutational defense task consisted of a sheet of paper on which an initial paragraph stated a truism (e.g., "Everyone should brush his or her teeth after every meal if at all possible") and two one-sentence arguments against this truism (e.g., "Overly frequent brushing can damage the gums and expose tooth surfaces that are vulnerable to decay"). The participant was instructed to use the rest of the sheet to write two paragraphs, each refuting one of the two arguments against the truism. The passive-refutational defenses had a similar first paragraph stating the truism and the two arguments against it, followed by two already prepared paragraphs, each refuting one of the attacking arguments. The two (active and passive) supportive defenses were analogous in format to these two refutationals, except that instead of first citing two arguments against the truism they cited two arguments supporting it. In the active-supportive condition the participant was asked to write two paragraphs, each developing one of these supportive arguments; in the passive-supportive condition participants were asked to read two already prepared supportive paragraphs. There were two variants of the refutational defenses: a refutational-same defense that refuted the same two truism-attacking arguments as would be used in the second-session strong attacks on the truisms; and a refutational-different defense that refuted two truism-attacking arguments different from the two to be used in the second-session strong attacks.

The Second (Attack) Session

An interval varied from a few minutes to a week intervened between the defensive first session and the second 50-minute session devoted to strong attacks on the truisms and the administration of a post-attack opinionnaire to measure how much the attacks weakened beliefs in the truisms and how much the prior defenses protected the beliefs from weakening by these attacks. Each attack was in the form of a three-paragraph essay: Its introductory paragraph stated the truism, remarked that there was some question about its validity, and mentioned two attacking arguments. Each of its next two paragraphs developed in detail one of these two attacking arguments. After reading all the attacking messages the participant completed an opinionnaire measuring beliefs on four defended-and-attacked truisms, and on control truisms including a "defense-only" truism, an "attack-only" truism, and a "neither-defense-nor-attack" truism. The specific health truisms were rotated around defense and attack conditions across participants.

These opinionnaire measures of the truisms were explained to the participants as needed to determine if one's feelings about the topics affect one's performance on the reading and writing tests. They included four scattered attitude statements on each truism, and participants were asked to use a 1- to 15-point scale to indicate agreement with each statement. The wording of statements was counterbalanced, but for simplicity in reporting the results below, the scale is reversed where necessary so that the "15" score always represents complete acceptance of the truism and a "1" score, complete rejection of it.

After they completed the opinionnaire, participants' perceptions of the experiment were probed, the true purpose of the experiment was revealed, and the various deceits used and the reasons for their employment were explained. Three months later a follow-up letter was sent to the participants, reminding them that the argumentative material dealt with in this experiment had been selected, not for its truth, but solely for research purposes. More detailed methods information can be found in the individual publications cited below.

EFFICACY OF SUPPORTIVE VERSUS
REFUTATIONAL DEFENSES

Six studies were done to test theoretical implications regarding the immunizing efficacy of various types of supportive versus refutational defenses. The first showed that defenses presenting arguments supporting the truism are less effective in conferring resistance to subsequent strong attack than are the more threatening refutational-same defenses. The second study demonstrated that refutational-different defenses are almost as effective as refutational-same defenses, indicating that the immunizing efficacy of the prior refutational defense is due to the threatening mention of the attacking arguments as well as to the reassuring, evidence-providing refutations of them. The third study illustrated that providing motivation by adding a threatening refutational defense to a supportive defense gives the latter an efficacy it lacks when used alone. A fourth study demonstrated that a prior threat (forewarning of the impending attack) enhances the defenses' immunizing effectiveness, especially that of the otherwise nonthreatening supportive defenses. A fifth study showed that providing prior reassurance about the truism (by prior mention that one's peers also agree with it) decreases the immunizing efficacy of the defenses. A sixth study manipulated orthogonally the number of attacking arguments mentioned and the number refuted in the defenses; it confirmed that the immunizing efficacy of the refutational defense derives from the threatening mention of the attacking arguments as well as from the substantive refutations of these arguments. The six studies are summarized below.

Supportive versus Refutational-Same Defenses

Experimental conditions. In McGuire and Papageorgis (1961i), 130 students in a first-year English course read a defensive essay on one truism and wrote a defensive essay on another. Two days later the participant read messages attacking these two truisms and also a third, nondefended truism. A fourth truism served as a control on which the participant received neither defense nor attack. The specific truisms were rotated around conditions among participants. After the attacks participants filled out an opinionnaire measuring their beliefs on the four truisms.

For 66 of the participants both the active and the passive defensive essays were supportive, first mentioning four supportive arguments and then presenting a paragraph substantiating each (in the passive reading condition), or then asking the student to write a paragraph to develop each supportive argument (in the active writing condition). For the other 64 participants both defensive essays were refutational, first mentioning four arguments against the truism and then presenting a paragraph refuting each (in the passive reading condition), or then calling upon the student to write a paragraph refuting each attacking argument (in the active writing condition). Participants in the passive condition were allowed five minutes to read each of the 1,000-word essays; the active-condition participants were allowed 20 minutes to write each essay. The attacks two days later consisted of 1,000-word essays to be read, the first paragraph of each mentioning the truism-attacking arguments that had appeared in the first session refutational-same defense, and each of the following paragraphs refuting one of these truism-attacking arguments.

Results: Immunizing effects. As Table 2.1 shows, the more threatening refutational defenses confer more resistance to the subsequent attacks than do the supportive defenses. The attacks, when not preceded by a defense, reduced adherence to the truisms substantially, from 12.62 to 6.64 on the 15-point scale ($p < .001$). The attacks, when preceded by refutational defenses, reduced the mean belief score only to 10.33, which is significantly ($p < .001$) higher than the 6.64 level in the attack-only condition and so shows the immunizing efficacy of the refutational defenses. In the supportive defense conditions, the mean

Table 2.1

Mean belief levels after attacks[a] preceded by supportive versus refutational-same defenses[b,c]

Type of participation	Refutational defense; then attack	Supportive defense; then attack	Mean[d]	Refute minus support
Passive reading	11.51	7.47	9.58	+4.04
	(35)[d]	(32)	(67)	
Reading and underlining	11.13	7.63	9.35	+3.50
	(31)	(32)	(63)	
Writing from outline	9.19	7.94	8.56	+1.25
	(31)	(32)	(63)	
Writing without guidance	9.46	6.53	8.06	+2.93
	(35)	(32)	(67)	
Weighted mean	10.33	7.39	8.88	+2.94
(Number of scores)	(132)	(128)	(260)	

[a]Control levels: after neither attack nor defense = 12.62 (N = 130); after attack only (with no prior defense) = 6.64 (N = 130).
[b]15.00 indicates complete adherence to the attacked truism; 1.00 indicates complete rejection of the truism.
[c]Data from McGuire and Papageorgis, 1961i.
[d]Figures given in parentheses are numbers of scores on which the mean in that cell is based.

belief score after the attacks was 7.39, much lower (p < .001) than in the refutational-defense condition and only slightly (p = .16) higher than the 6.64 level in the no-defense, attack-only condition. Hence the supportive defense confers much less resistance than the refutational; indeed, it hardly confers any at all.

Results: Direct strengthening effect. The participants' beliefs in the truisms were measured not only at the end of the second (attacking) session, but also at the end of the first session, after the defenses but before the attacks. Although the second-session attitude showed that refutational defense conferred much more resistance to subsequent attacks than did the supportive defense in all four participation conditions (see Table 2.1), these first-session attitudes showed that the supportive defenses were slightly superior in producing a direct strengthening effect. This type of reversal was found often in the present series of experiments: The types of defenses that left the beliefs seemingly strongest prior to the attack paradoxically conferred the least resistance to the subsequent attacks. This "paper tiger" strength immediately after the defenses is in accord with inoculation theory and shows that the immunizing effectiveness of a defense is not a direct function of its apparent strengthening effect.

Refutational-Same versus Refutational-Different Defenses

Hypotheses. A follow-up experiment by Papageorgis and McGuire (1961j) compared the resistance-conferring efficacy of the refutational defense when the later attacks used arguments different from versus the same as the arguments mentioned and refuted in the defense. Inoculation theory implies that the refutational defenses derive immunizing efficacy from the motivation-stimulating, threatening mention of arguments against the truism, and hence their resistance-conferral should be manifested even against attacks using different arguments. On the other hand, insofar as the refutational defense gains its effectiveness from the useful refutational material (rather than from the threatening mention of the attacking arguments), then the refutational defenses should confer more resistance to attacks by the same arguments as had been refuted.

Procedure. This study, being designed to distinguish between these two explanations, employed only refutational defenses and only passive (reading) conditions. The refutational defense on each truism mentioned four arguments attacking it and then refuted two of the four attacking arguments. The strong attacking message on each truism in the second session had two attacking arguments. For the refutational-same defensive condition these second-session attacks used the same two attacking arguments as had been refuted in the defenses; for the refutational-different conditions, the attacks used different arguments from those which had been refuted in the defenses. A total of 73 summer school college students served in the defensive and attacking sessions, which were separated by a one-week interval.

Results. Once again the attacks proved very damaging to the truisms when they had not been preceded by a defense. In the attack-only condition, the mean belief went down (p <.001) to 5.73 on the 15-point scale as compared to a mean of 13.23 in the neither-defense-nor-attack control condition. Both types of refutational defenses, same and different, conferred substantial resistance to the attack. After an attack preceded by the refutational-same defense, the mean belief level was 9.24, not significantly higher than the 8.70 after an attack preceded by the refutational-different defense. That the refutational-different defense was so effective supports the inoculation theory prediction that the refutational defenses confer resistance by their threatening preexposure to attacking arguments (in addition to any enhanced resistance provided by the useful and reassuring attack-refuting material).

Further to identify mechanisms underlying the resistance-conferral by the refutational defense, two mediational variables were measured at the end of the second (attacking) session. One of these was a semantic-differential scale designed to measure the perceived quality and credibility of the arguments used in the attack. The attacking arguments were seen as significantly (p < .05) less credible when preceded by a refutational-same or refutational-different defense than when not preceded by any defense. A second mediational variable, cognitive elaboration, was measured by asking the person to write down as many arguments as he or she could in support of the truism. The inoculation theory prediction was that the motivational stimulation from the threatening refutational defense would result in the believer's generating and accumulating more material supporting the truism during the week following the refutational defense. We did find that there was a slight tendency (p = .10) for the participants who had received the refutational defense to think up more supportive arguments than those who had received no defense.

Efficacy of Combinational Effects

Hypotheses and method.   A third experiment (McGuire, 1961a) used passive (reading) defenses to compare the immunizing efficacy of combinations of supportive plus refutational defenses versus single defenses. Inoculation theory attributes the ineffectiveness of the supportive defense to the overconfident believer's lack of motivation during the defensive session to assimilate or generate truism-supporting arguments because they seem to belabor the obvious. A refutational defense should supply some needed motivation by its threatening mention of arguments against the truism. A combinatory prediction follows that the supportive and refutational defenses used together would confer more resistance than the sum of their individual effects. A further interaction prediction is that this "whole greater than the sum of its parts" effect would be more pronounced when the supportive defense is added to refutational-different than to refutational-same defenses. Participants were 162 introductory psychology students who received single defenses (supportive only, refutational-same only, and refutational-different only), or double defenses (supportive-plus-refutational-same and supportive-plus-refutational-different) on different truisms. The attacking session came 10 minutes after the defensive.

Results. Both the main and interactional combinatory predictions were confirmed. When used alone, neither the refutational-different nor the supportive defenses conferred significant resistance to the immediate attacks. When used in combination, they produced considerably more (p < .01) resistance. The interaction prediction was also confirmed: Adding supportive defenses to the refutational-different defenses increased their immunizing efficacy significantly more than did adding supportive to refutational-same defenses (McGuire, 1961a).

Efficacy of Added Extrinsic Threats and Reassurances

Theory. Inoculation theory implies that prior defenses have low effectiveness in making truisms resistant to persuasive attack because the overconfident believer is unmotivated to assimilate the defensive material. This motivational deficit would be especially pronounced for the supportive defenses in that the refutational defenses do contain some intrinsic motivating threat, namely, mention of attacking arguments. Therefore, when an extrinsic threat to the truism (e.g., a forewarning that it will be attacked) is received by the believer before the defense, it is predicted to increase his or her motivation to assimilate the defensive material, thus enhancing its immunizing efficacy, and especially so for supportive defenses. Conversely, a pre-defense reassurance that the truism is indeed beyond controversy (e.g., a report that everyone agrees with it) should decrease the effectiveness of the defenses (especially of the supportive defenses) by diminishing whatever motivation there had been to assimilate these defenses. To test these predictions two experiments were carried out, one manipulating extrinsic threats and the other, extrinsic reassurance.

Extrinsic threat manipulation.   McGuire and Papageorgis (1962d) gave each of 96 participants a supportive, a refutational-same, and a refutational-different defense on three truisms and no-defense on a fourth. All were passive reading defenses. Then the participants were given four attacking messages, one aimed at each of the truisms. Finally, the participants' attitudes on each truism were measured. Half of the 96 participants served in a no-forewarning condition in that the experiment was introduced in the usual way, as a verbal skills test dealing with health topics, with no mention made of the fact that the truisms would be attacked in later reading passages. The other 48 participants served in a "forewarned" condition in that they were told that we were studying how persuaded they would be later by reading attacks on their health beliefs after first reading defenses of some of these beliefs.

Results.   The forewarning of attack did enhance the immunizing effectiveness of the defenses: After defenses and attacks in the forewarning condition, the mean belief level was 11.67 versus 10.93 in the no-forewarning condition, a difference significant above the .05 level. Also confirmed ($p < .05$) was the interaction prediction that threatening forewarnings enhance the immunizing efficacy more for the supportive than the refutational defense. That the forewarning worked by enhancing the immunizing efficacy of the defenses (rather than by itself directly reducing the attack's persuasiveness) is supported by the finding that in the no-defense condition the attack was equally effective when forewarned as when not forewarned.

Extrinsic reassurance manipulation.   In another extrinsic motivation study (Anderson & McGuire, 1965d), 96 participants received a pattern of defenses and attacks similar to that in the forewarning study just described. The major difference was that prior to the defenses the participants received, not threatening forewarnings, but reassuring consensus feedback. This was done by asking the participants at the outset of the group-administered defensive session to give their attitudes on a series of health truisms, including the four crucial ones on which defenses and attacks were to come. Then 48 participants were given feedback which indicated that the other participants had agreed almost unanimously with their own initial attitudes that the four crucial beliefs were true beyond a doubt. The other 48 "no-reassurance" participants received consensus feedback, not on the crucial truisms but on four filler truisms. Then the participants received the three defenses, followed by the attacks and the attitude measures, as in the preceding study.

Results. The final attitude levels after defenses and attacks were 10.63 in the reassurance condition and 11.53 in the no-reassurance condition, a difference significant at the .05 level, confirming the inoculation theory prediction that hearing reassuring consensus about the truisms prior to the defenses actually lessens the defenses' immunizing effectiveness. That the reassurance works by increasing the immunizing efficacy of the defenses (rather than by directly weakening the attacks' persuasive impact) is shown by the fact that the reassurance manipulation makes no difference in the no-defense attack-only conditions. As regards the interaction prediction, the reassurance did reduce the effectiveness of the supportive defenses slightly more than that of the refutational defenses, but this trend is significant only at the .20 level.

Independent Manipulation of Threat and Reassurance

Theory and method. A sixth experiment (McGuire, 1964b) investigated further whether the immunizing efficacy of the refutational defense derives, as inoculation theory predicts, from their threatening components (the mention of attacking arguments) as well as from their reassuring and evidence-providing components (the refutations of those arguments). We used a 2 × 2 design: low versus high threat (mentioning two versus mentioning four attacking arguments in the first paragraph) × low versus high reassurance (then refuting zero versus refuting two of the attacking arguments). A total of 288 participants served in this study whose defensive and attacking sessions were separated by two days. All the defenses were of the passive-reading type.

Results. It was found that both the threatening and the reassuring components of the refutational defenses contributed to resistance to the attack. As regards reassurance, agreement with the truisms after both defenses and attacks was greater in the high versus the low reassurance condition (after refuting two versus zero attacking arguments), 10.75 versus 10.23, a difference significant at the .05 level. As regards the threat variable, agreement with the truisms after both defense and attack was greater in the high versus low threat condition (mentioning four versus two attacking arguments), 11.02 versus 10.14, a difference significant at the .01 level. These results confirm the inoculation theory prediction that the refutational defenses gain their immunizing efficacy from their threatening mentions of attacking arguments as well as from their reassuring refutations of attacking arguments.

EFFICACY OF ACTIVE PARTICIPATION IN THE DEFENSE

A second series of immunization theory hypotheses dealt with the resistance-conferring effects of requiring the believer to participate actively in the prior defense of the truisms. We theorized that because truisms have been maintained in an ideologically "germ-free" environment, they will exhibit a practice deficit (because the believer will have had little experience in defending the truism) and a motivational deficit (because the believer will regard these truisms as not needing defense because they seem so obvious as to be beyond question). Because of the practice deficit, active writing defenses will be less immunizing than passive reading defenses because lack of practice in defending cultural truisms will result in the believer's being unable to evoke much defensive material. However, as regards the motivational deficit in defending cultural truisms, the active-writing condition should be less handicapping because believers' poor performances at the essay-writing task will sensitize them to how inadequately based is their confidence in the truism, thus providing motivation to accumulate any defensive material. This theoretical analysis asserts that two mediators (practice deficit and motivation deficit) affect oppositely how the participation variable (reading vs. writing refutational defenses) affects conferred resistance, which leads to a number of interaction predictions tested in this research program.

Immunizing Effects of Requiring Participation

Theory and method. McGuire and Papageorgis (1961i) tested active-participation's effect on conferred resistance by varying participation over four levels. (1) Those in the high active participation, "unguided writing," condition were given a sheet of paper headed by a statement of the truism and were told that they had 20 minutes to write an essay defending the truism, giving arguments supporting the truism (if they were in the active-supportive defense condition) or mentioning and then refuting arguments attacking the belief (if they were in the active-refutational defense condition). (2) The slightly less active "guided writing" condition prescribed the same defensive-essay writing tasks, except that the sheet was not blank but contained four one-sentence statements of truism-defending arguments (either supportive or refutational) as hints to guide writing the defensive essay. (3) Much less active was the "reading and underlining condition," in which each participant was given 5 minutes to read a printed, defensive essay about 1,000 words long whose four paragraphs developed four arguments (all supportive or all refutational) defending the truism; the participants in this third condition had a further participation task of underlining in each paragraph the shortest passage that contained the gist of the paragraph. (4) The most passive condition was the same as the preceding reading-and-underlining condition, except that the underlining task was omitted.

In the first session each of the 130 participants spent 20 minutes writing a defense of one truism and 5 minutes reading a defense of another. In the second session two days later, each received attacks on the two defended truisms and also on a third, undefended truism (the latter yielding a no-defense attack-only control score), and received no attack on a fourth truism (yielding a neither-defense-nor-attack control score). The four specific truisms were rotated around these four conditions among participants. Beliefs on all four truisms were measured at the end of each session. The active-participation requirement was predicted to have the net effect of reducing the defenses' immunizing effectiveness, especially for the supportive defense (because with the refutational defense even the passive condition provides some threat motivation).

Results. Table 2.1 shows that, as predicted, the amount of resistance conferred went monotonically down across the four participation levels, from a post-attack level of 9.58 after the "passive reading" defense to a 8.06 level after the "writing without guidance" defense. The superiority of passive reading over active writing defenses ($p < .001$) showed up both as regards the direct strengthening effect of the defenses (at the end of the first session) and as regards the attack-resistance conferred (at the end of the second session). This superiority of the reading defense obtained even though the time allowance of 20 minutes for the writing defenses was quadruple that allowed for the reading defenses. Also found was the predicted interaction effect such that the superiority of reading over writing was less for the supportive defense (7.56 vs. 7.23) than for the refutational-same defense (11.33 vs. 9.33). Subsequent studies (McGuire, 1964b) reconfirmed both main and interaction effects.

Active and Passive Defense Combination and Permutation Effects

Theory. In the case of refutational defenses, inoculation theory has interactional implications regarding the efficacy of using double defenses, active plus passive (i.e., having the participant both read and write a refutational essay defending the truism), as compared with the efficacy of using just one of these defense modalities. The refutational-same defense is theorized above to owe its efficacy both to the mildly threatening mention of attacking arguments (which motivates the otherwise overconfident believer in the truism to bolster his or her belief) and to the reassuring, evidence-providing refutations of these attacking arguments (which helps the believer to discount the subsequent attacks, especially when they employ the same antitruism arguments as had been refuted in the defense). This refutational material is less useful for the refutational-different than for the refutational-same defenses. Hence, the refutational-same defense derives its efficacy from both components, the threat-providing mention and the evidence-providing refutation of attacking arguments, whereas the refutational-different defense derives its efficacy mainly from the first (threat) component. This implies two interaction predictions. (1) In single-defense conditions the active defenses more effectively supply the motivating threat component and the passive defenses better supply the evidence-providing refutational material. Hence, for refutational-same defenses, the passive defense will be superior to the active; but for the refutational-different defenses, the active will be superior to the passive. (2) A second interaction prediction, derived by similar reasoning, is that the superiority of the double (active plus passive) defense over the single defense (active or passive) in conferring resistance will be greater for the refutational-same than for refutational-different defenses.

Method. To test these hypotheses within a 3×2 design, we used six refutational-defense conditions: active only versus passive only versus active-plus-passive, each of these three coming in refutational-same versus refutational-different variants. The second "attack" session two days later presented the attacks and then measured beliefs on the truisms. There were also attack-only and neither-defense-nor-attack control conditions. The 168 college students served in four different conditions. Further details of method can be found in McGuire (1961h).

Results. The single-defense interaction prediction was confirmed ($p < .05$), in that passive reading confers more resistance than the active writing for the refutational-same defense while the reverse is true for the refutational-different defense. The interaction prediction regarding the single versus double defense is also confirmed ($p < .01$): For the refutational-same condition, the double defense is sizably superior to the single; but for the refutational-different defense, the double is only slightly superior to the single defense. A further order effect predicted in the double-defense conditions (active plus passive) was not confirmed. The several nonconfirmations of order effects in this and other studies of this research program are discussed more fully in McGuire (1961a, 1961h).

PERSISTENCE OF THE INDUCED RESISTANCE

Theory

Assumptions underlying persistence predictions. Inoculation theory assumes that the immunizing efficacy of prior defenses derives from their mention of attacking arguments (which serves to motivate the believer to assimilate bolstering material) and from their providing belief-bolstering material (via their refutation of the attacking arguments). In the case of active writing defenses of truisms the second mechanism is largely inoperative with both supportive and refutational defenses because little defensive material is presented and the unpracticed believer is unable to retrieve much defensive material from his or her own memory, even when motivated by the active defense's revelation of the truism's vulnerability. In passive reading defenses, however, the mechanisms underlying the three types of defenses differ: With these, the efficacy of the refutational-different defense derives primarily from the first, motivating, mechanism; whereas the efficacy of the supportive defense derives primarily from the second, bolstering, mechanism; and the efficacy of the refutational-same defense, from both mechanisms.

This theoretical analysis yields predictions about the time trends for resistance conferred by the various kinds of defenses. The first resistance-conferring mechanisms, the motivating threat, is predicted (see chapter 3 for derivation) to produce a nonmonotonic inverted-U time trend as the result of two opposite mediators: Once threatened, the hitherto overconfident believer only gradually accumulates belief-bolstering material; but as time continues to pass and the threat recedes, the motivation to accumulate defensive material will itself decay. Again, there is an analogy in biological inoculation where usually a few days or weeks must pass between administration of the weakened pathogen before resistance builds up to its full strength, beyond which time the conferred resistance tends to decay gradually so that periodic booster shots are needed. The second resistance-conferring mechanism, provision of belief-bolstering material via the defense, should show up as a monotonic decay with time passage, as in classical forgetting curves.

The active-writing defenses confer resistance only via the first mechanism (the motivating effect of revealing the vulnerability of the truism), and this mechanism's time trend is a nonmonotonic inverted-U function. Therefore this trend (including an initial delayed-action immunizing effect) is predicted for all three types of defense (supportive, refutational-same, and refutational-different defenses) in the active writing condition.

In the passive reading condition, the mechanisms of resistance conferral are more complicated. Such resistance as the supportive defense confers in the passive (reading) condition stems from the second mechanism (retention of the truism-bolstering material that it contains), so a progressive temporal decay typical "forgetting" curve is predicted. The passive (reading) refutational-different defense derives its efficacy almost entirely from the second (motivating threat) mechanism, so that its time trend will show the same nonmonotonic, inverted-U function as do all three types of active defense. The passive (reading) refutational-same defense confers resistance via both mechanisms, and so its time trend will be a composite showing little decline at first when the "forgetting" trend of the second mechanism is still being largely offset by the delayed-action trend of the first mechanism, after which there is a much faster fall-off as both underlying mechanisms decay rapidly.

Selecting the time parameters. To test hypotheses about time trends, especially when nonmonotonic trends are predicted, it is necessary to set the time parameters at theoretically critical points. Unfortunately, the scaling of most social science variables is ordinal at best, thus inadequate for specifying such time parameters. In anticipation of this problem the intervals between defenses and attacks were varied from a few minutes to a week across the earlier studies to explore these time parameters. The across-studies exploratory effects were very similar to the within-study effects (compare Figure 2.1A and Figure 2.1B).

Persistence of Passively Conferred Resistance

Method. To test predictions about the differential decay rates of the resistance conferred by the supportive, refutational-same, and refutational-different defenses in the passive reading conditions, 160 participants served in all three defense conditions, plus a no-defense control condition. Attacks came either immediately, two days, or a week after the defense. McGuire (1962a) provides further details of the design, analyses, and other aspects of the procedure.

Results. The persistence of the resistance conferred by the three types of passive defense is shown by the post-attack belief scores in Figure 2.1B. As predicted, such small resistance as the supportive defense confers against immediate attacks has decayed ($p < .05$) almost completely within two days. At both the two- and the seven-day intervals, the level to which the attack reduced the belief after a supportive defense is no higher than the level in the no-defense, attack-only condition. For the refutational-same defense the conferred resistance, as predicted, decays at a much slower rate. This predicted interaction between the time (immediate vs. two-day) $\times$ type of defense (supportive vs. refutational-same) is significant at the .01 level and is in the direction opposite to a simple regression artifact. The predicted

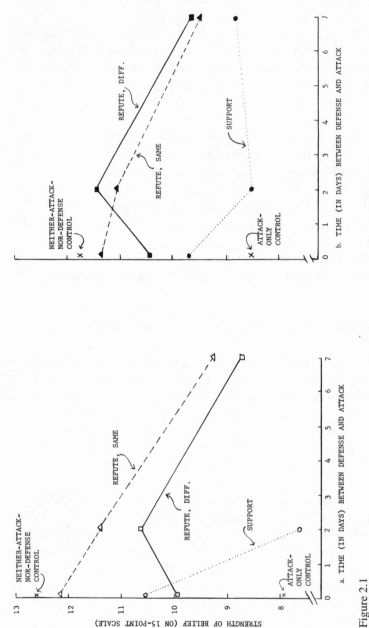

Figure 2.1

Persistence of the resistance to persuasion conferred by supportive, refutational-same, and refutational-different defenses of the passive (reading) type. The figure on the left is based on across-experimental data: zero-interval from McGuire, 1961a; 2-day from McGuire and Papageorgis, 1961i and McGuire, 1961h; 7-day from Papageorgis and McGuire, 1971j. The figure on the right is based on data from the preplanned experiment (McGuire, 1962a).

nonmonotonic effect in the refutational-different condition is also confirmed. Resistance to attacks two days later is greater than to immediate attacks, this predicted delayed-action effect being significant at the .05 level. As predicted, there is greater ($p < .05$) persistence during the first two days of the resistance conferred by the refutational-different than by the refutational-same defense. All the defenses in this study were in the passive (reading) condition.

Persistence of Actively Conferred Resistance

Method. Another experiment tested the relative persistence of resistance conferred by active versus passive (reading vs. writing) defenses in a $2 \times 2 \times 3$ design. Each of the 72 participants received an active and a passive defense of a first and second truism one week prior to the attacks, and an active and passive defense of a third and fourth truism immediately prior to the attacks. One-third of the participants received supportive defenses; one-third, refutational-same; and one-third, refutational-different defenses. The specific truisms were rotated around the defensive conditions among participants. In the second session, immediately after or one week after the defenses, all four truisms were subjected to the usual type of attacks and then the final belief levels on the truisms were measured.

Results. In the active (writing) condition it was found, as predicted, that all three types of defense (supportive, refutational-same, and refutational-different) showed delayed action effects in the form of greater ($p < .05$) resistance to attacks one week later than to immediate attacks. Persistence was greater ($p < .01$) for actively conferred than for passively conferred resistance, due primarily to the results in the supportive and refutational-same defenses. As predicted, the refutational-different defense shows similar delayed-action resistance whether actively or passively conferred.

CONCLUSIONS AND FUTURE WORK NEEDED

Some Neglected Relations

The strategy used in this immunization-against-persuasion research program started with postulates based on a biological inoculation analogy, from which a wide range of predictions were derived for testing programmatically. The accumulating knowledge derived from the successive experiments clarified parameters left undefined in the theory and thus allowed the testing of progressively more elegant and complex derivations. Space limits here allow only selective reports of the findings. One's grant applications usually propose some lines of research that never get done because the results of earlier studies draw one's efforts into new directions. Some of these proposed lines that were deferred will be mentioned here as still worth pursuing.

Immunizing Controversial Beliefs

My published research on immunization against persuasion focused on cultural truisms as the beliefs to be made resistant. The guiding analogy with biological vaccination limps least when applied to overprotected cultural truisms that would have been maintained in an ideological aseptic environment. Like the physical health of a person brought up in a germ-free environment, such overprotected beliefs tend to be "paper tigers," appearing strong but proving vulnerable when exposed to attacking material. My strategy was to focus at the start on cultural truisms as the domain where our theory was especially promising, leaving until later the exploration of its limits in less hospitable domains. I did carry out prestudies with controversial beliefs, testing predicted interaction effects between the defense variables and the controversial-versus-truism belief variable (e.g., predictions that the immunizing superiority of refutational over supportive, and of passive over active defenses would be less sizable with controversial issues than with truisms; whereas the superiority of refutational-same over refutational-different defenses would be greater with controversial issues than with truisms; and that delayed-action effects would be greater with truisms than with controversial beliefs). Exploratory work showed some trends in this direction, but results with truisms versus controversial beliefs were more remarkable for the similarity than for the differences of effect directions and sizes.

Other Lines of Proposed Research

Several other lines of immunization work were carried out only through early exploratory stages – for example, that on bidirectional immunization: When a person holds a moderate belief on some issue such as affirmative action programs, how do defenses designed to develop resistance to attacks from one direction affect the belief's resistance to attacks from the other direction? How do personality and abilities variables affect the comparative resistance conferred by various types of prior defenses? With my students I did carry out a considerable amount of the proposed personality-and-persuasibility research (see chapter 3), but we tended to use attitude change, rather than immunization against attitude change, as our dependent variable.

3

Attitude-Change Studies

My immunization-against-persuasion research at the University of Illinois in the late 1950s, described in the preceding chapter, was followed by a half-dozen years at Columbia University (including a year at the Center for Advanced Study in the Behavioral Sciences) when my research focused on communication variables that increased persuasive impact rather than on those that induced resistance to persuasion. I have retained interest in attitude change ever since and have been often called upon to write handbook chapters and other reviews of work on this topic (see chapter 4 in this volume). Indeed, for a decade after my own empirical research moved to other topics, I was probably regarded as the "world's greatest authority" on the subject, until this numero uno title passed to Richard Petty and John Cacciopo, and to Alice Eagly and Shelly Chaiken.

The usual "persuasive communication" research paradigm involves presenting a persuasive communication from an external source that argues against the audience's initial attitude, to test whether some communication variable (e.g., source attractiveness, message style, etc.) has a theorized effect on how much attitude change is produced on the issue explicitly argued in the message. My own approach, going back to my graduate student days, has differed from this conventional approach in two main regards. Firstly, I have been interested in internally induced attitude change, that is, in changing attitudes, not by presenting new information from an external source but rather by using Socratic questioning or directed-thinking tasks to make more salient information already virtually present in the target person's own cognitive arena. A second distinctive feature is that I have been interested in persuasive impact, not so much on the explicit target issue, but on related issues not explicitly mentioned in the persuasive message. I have been led into these two aberrant approaches because the main purpose behind my research has been, not to study attitude change per se, but to use attitude change as a tool for studying a more basic interest: the structure and functioning of thought systems, as discussed in chapter 6.

Chapter 3 describes two lines of my attitude change research at Columbia during the early 1960s that fall within the more conventional social-influence paradigm: (1) work on anticipatory attitude change produced by forewarning of persuasive attack; and (2) work on how the target person's personality characteristics are related to her or his influenceability.

FOREWARNING-INDUCED ANTICIPATORY ATTITUDE CHANGE

Three aspects of anticipatory attitude change will be discussed: (1) how forewarning of an impending persuasive attack itself affects the target person's attitude; (2) how forewarning affects the impact of the attack when it comes; and (3), more generally, how performance of participants in research is affected by researcher deceptions about the true purpose of the experimental manipulations. The latter issue reflects ethical and validity "crises" in experimental social psychology (see chapter 11 in this volume) arising when attitude-change researchers, to avoid guinea-pig reactions, routinely misinform participants (e.g., by claiming that the persuasive messages are a reading comprehension test).

Theory

Most researchers assume that if an audience is forewarned that an impending message has been designed to change their attitudes, this revelation will reduce the persuasive impact of the message when it comes (e.g., by raising defenses or by lowering trust in the source's objectivity, etc.). My alternative ego-defensive analysis predicts the opposite, that forewarning will increase the persuasive impact. People do not like to appear gullible to themselves or others, and so when forewarned of an impending persuasive communication they resort to anticipatory yielding to avoid appearing gullible and losing self-esteem, saying in effect, "Not to worry, I already hold the position that this message is going to argue." Hence, it is predicted that the forewarning of persuasive intent, aside from any weakening of the impact of the later persuasive message, will itself change the attitude.

[Adapted with permission from W. J. McGuire and S. Millman, 1965c, Anticipatory belief lowering following forewarning of a persuasive

attitude, *Journal of Personality and Social Psychology, 2,* pp. 471– 9.
Copyright © 1965 by The American Psychological Association]

Ego-defensive theory implies that forewarning of an impending attack will cause anticipatory attitude change toward the position that
the audience expects to be advocated. Such anticipatory change protects the audience from feeling or appearing gullible by allowing
them to claim that their postcommunication agreement is due, not to
the message's having persuaded them, but to their already having
been in agreement with the message's position. Besides this main effect prediction the ego-defensive analysis implies three further interaction predictions. (1) This anticipatory attitude-lowering will be
more pronounced when the issue is an emotional rather than a techni-
cally factual issue (because yielding on the emotional issue would be
more damaging to self-esteem than yielding on a factual issue, which
could be interpreted as a commendable openness to evidence). (2) Anticipatory change will be more pronounced when the source is expected to be highly persuasive (because the more effective the source
is perceived as being, the more one expects to be persuaded). (3)
There will be greater anticipatory attitude-lowering when the target
person's initial position on the issue is unknown, leaving him or her
free to claim any initial position.

Method

Design and participants.   The study included four two-level independent variables in a $2 \times 2 \times 2 \times 2$ design: warning versus no
warning, $\times$ attack versus no attack, $\times$ emotional versus technical issues, $\times$ high- versus low-credibility sources. The first three were
within-participant variables. Hence, each participant served in eight
conditions, on a different issue in each condition, so that the design
required eight issues (four technical and four emotional), systematically rotated around the experimental conditions from participant
to participant. The fourth variable (source credibility) was the only
between-participant manipulation of theoretical interest. The 96 participants were students taking an educational-methods course.

General procedures.   During a 75-minute session participants worked
through counterbalanced booklets in which they were told that they
would be reading passages written by skilled experts who were arguing

for their points of view. The students were instructed to read each persuasive passage carefully and then to report their own attitudes on the issues discussed. They were told that we were pretesting persuasive passages on various topics, four of the topics then named as examples. The listing of these four to-be-attacked issues constituted the "forewarning of attack" condition; for any one participant four additional issues went unmentioned and constituted issues that were in the "no-forewarning" condition. The four explicitly listed issues and the four unmentioned ones both included two technical and two emotional issues.

Participants in the high source-credibility condition were then told the passages came from editors of learned journals in the areas discussed who wrote the persuasive passages as chairmen of presidential advisory committees. The other half of the participants (in the low source-credibility condition) were told that the authors of the passages were white-collar criminals, and the passages were taken from the skillful defense testimony they gave during a trial in which they were convicted of serious crimes.

The participant then read persuasive messages on four different issues, each about 650 words long and preceded by a short description of its high- or low-credible source. Four minutes were allowed for reading each of the persuasive messages and for picking out and underlining the most important passage in each of its three paragraphs (this underlining task being used to enhance and monitor attention to the passages). The four persuasive messages received by any one participant included two on forewarned issues (one technical and one emotional) and two on issues that had not been mentioned in advance (again one technical and one emotional). The participants were then asked to fill out an opinionnaire designed to measure their own attitudes on all eight issues, experimental and control, their responses on this opinionnaire providing the dependent-variable scores.

Materials. The eight crucial issues included four emotional issues (e.g., the high likelihood of further Communist takeovers in Latin America) and four technical issues (e.g., the usefulness of the earth sciences in finding oil deposits). Each of the eight messages took a position that a prestudy had shown to be on the side opposite to the initial beliefs of most students in the participants' population. Hence, almost all of the participants could anticipate receiving persuasive messages arguing for the side opposite to their own initial positions on each of the forewarned issues.

The final opinionnaire that furnished the dependent-variable scores (attitudes on the eight issues) contained 50 items, 6 items measuring attitudes on each of the 8 issues plus 2 repeated items to allow a reliability check. The participants were asked to indicate their agreement with each statement on a 1 to 15 scale. The six statements dealing with each issue were counterbalanced for acquiescence, but as reported here are scored so that the lower the numerical value on this 1 to 15 scale, the more effective the warning or the attack was in reducing the participants' initial attitude.

Results

Main effects of warning. Our basic main-effect prediction is that warning will produce an anticipatory lowering of the attitudes prior to the actual attacks. This prediction of an anticipatory belief change is confirmed by the scores in the "warning, no-attack" row of Table 3.1 versus in the "no-warning, no-attack" row. The difference between the respective means, 9.10 versus 9.54, is significant at the .05 level, using the residual within-participants variance as the error term. The warning's effect on the impact of the actual attack is negligible: The mean attitude level in the "warning and attack" row is 7.78, almost identical with the 7.77 mean in the "no-warning and attack" row. Hence, as predicted, the warning itself and the actual attack each reduces the attitude, but the two effects are not additive. The attack, whether or not preceded by a warning, reduces the attitude by 1.78 points.

Interaction with type of issue. Ego-defensive theory predicts that forewarning of attack will produce more anticipatory lowering on emotional than on technical issues, but the attacks themselves will produce more change on technical than on emotional issues. Both issues' predictions were supported. The "warning but no-attack" row of Table 3.1 shows that the attitude levels on the emotional issues go down to 8.68; whereas on the technical issues they go down only to 9.52 ($p < .01$ for the difference). The direction of this issue effect, as predicted, reversed as regards the impact of the actual attacks. As seen in both "no-warning, attack" and "warning, attack" rows in Table 3.1, the attacks reduce the attitude levels on the technical issues more ($p < .01$) than on the emotional issues. Because the issue effect re-

Table 3.1
Pre- and post-attack attitude levels in forewarned and nonforewarned conditions as affected by type of issue and source credibility

Type of issue	Emotional		Technical		
	High-credible source	Low-credible source	High-credible source	Low-credible source	
Persuasive					Mean
No warning, no attack	9.29	9.53	9.79	9.55	9.54
Warning, no attack	8.60	8.76	9.66	9.39	9.10
No warning, attack	7.87	8.73	6.83	7.67	7.77
Warning, attack	7.71	8.48	7.00	7.94	7.78

Note: Scores are the means on a 15-point scale, with the attacks aimed at lowering the mean. Each cell mean is based on 48 participants.
Source: McGuire & Millman, 1965c.

verses between the warning and the attack, the warnings reduce the emotional attitudes 66% of the distance that the subsequent attacks reduce them, whereas the warnings reduce the technical attitudes only 6% of the distance that the subsequent attacks reduce them, a difference significant at the .001 level.

Interaction with type of source. According to ego-defensive theory, both the warning and the actual attacks should be more effective in reducing attitudes when the attacks are attributed in advance to high- rather than low-credible sources. The results in the "warning, no attack" row of Table 3.1 do not support this predicted source effect: The warnings reduced the attitudes about equally whether the messages were described as coming from high- or low-credible sources. Our manipulation here may have had two mutually canceling effects: The target person may have felt less likely to be persuaded by the low-reputable source (which would tend to reduce anticipatory change) but have felt also that it would be more humiliating if he or she were persuaded by this disreputable source (which would tend to enhance anticipatory change). A study should be done that varies orthogonally these two components of source valence. The prediction about the effect of this source variable on the persuasive impact of actual attacks can be tested most appropriately in terms of source effects in the data in the "no-warning, attack" row of Table 3.1 (or in the almost identical "warning, attack" row). As expected, when the attacks were attributed to high-credible sources they reduced the attitudes to 7.35, and when attributed to low-credible sources, only to 8.20, a $p < .05$ difference in the predicted direction.

SUSPICIOUSNESS OF EXPERIMENTER'S INTENT AS A THEORETICAL VARIABLE

In most persuasion studies, including those reported in this volume, the experimenter routinely disguises the attitude-change intent of the communication (e.g., by representing it as a reading comprehension test) out of fear that the participants will become atypically resistant or otherwise unrepresentative, thus making it hazardous to generalize the obtained relations. The McGuire and Millman (1965c) experiment just described, rather than hiding the persuasive intent of the messages, takes the opposite tack of deliberately raising awareness of persuasive intent as an interesting independent variable in its own right. Many research artifacts have this dual aspect, being an incidental annoyance in research on other topics but serving also as independent variables of interest in their own right. There are five steps discernable in the life cycle of research on such artifactual variables as suspiciousness of experimenter's intent, acquiescence, and social desirability, as they progress from being viewed as a misleading contaminant to being studied as interesting in themselves.

[Adapted with permission from W. J. McGuire, 1969c, Suspiciousness of experimenter's intent, in R. Rosenthal and R. Rosnow (Eds.), *Artifact in behavioral research,* pp. 12–57 (New York: Academic Press, copyright © 1969).]

It is a wise experimenter who knows his artifact from his main effect; and wiser still is the researcher who realizes that today's artifact will be tomorrow's interesting independent variable. Indeed, even at a given moment one researcher's artifact may be another's theory-relevant variable, as is illustrated by the variable studied here, suspiciousness of the experimenter's manipulatory intent, and related concepts such as guinea-pig reactions, placebos, faking good, and awareness. Psychologists, particularly in social psychology and personality, tend to adopt a Minsk–Pinsk deviousness in deliberately trying to mislead the participants about the purpose of the experiment by noninforming or misinforming. This is done even when studying nonsensitive issues such as the serial position effect in verbal learning, notwithstanding that experimenters from Ebbinghaus to Banaji have managed to obtain useful results even while serving as participants in their own experiments.

Five Stages in the Life of an Artifact

Interest in research artifacts tends to evolve through five stages, starting with ignoring, followed by three coping stages (detecting and rejecting, estimating and adjusting, and reducing or preventing), and finally an exploiting stage. The suspiciousness-of-persuasive-intent artifact reaches this fifth stage with the McGuire and Millman (1965c) forewarning-of-attack study described above.

The ignoring stage. Once the existence of an artifact becomes known, ameliorating steps can be taken easily, but there is resistance to recognizing its existence because coping with it upsets familiar routines. An artifact often has to be rediscovered several times and given catchy labels before it becomes a sufficiently public scandal so that some bright young people seize upon it as a device to pry their elders out of their ruts and find a place in the sun for themselves. Like much else that disturbs and advances a field of knowledge, the discovery of artifacts is the work of associate professors.

The acquiescence-response bias illustrates the difficulty of the recognition process. Despite its prevalence and seriousness, it took several rediscoveries to concentrate the field's attention. Demonstrations by Lorge (1937) and Lentz (1938) of an acquiescence response set in personality tests seems to have stirred up little interest for a decade. Cronbach (1941, 1942, 1946, 1950) deserves a "father of the acquiescence response set" title for demonstrating the problems it causes in abilities tests, where it is more dangerous and manageable than in personality research. A decade or two later acquiescence or yea-saying had become a personality variable of interest in its own right, growing out of research on authoritarianism and dogmatism (Adorno et al., 1950; Rokeach, 1960; Christie & Jahoda, 1954). The "faking good" (later "social desirability") artifact followed a similar trajectory a bit later.

The detecting and rejecting mode of coping.   Once an artifact like acquiescence or social desirability is recognized as a danger, researchers in the area devise a succession of modes of coping to mitigate its distorting effects, the most primitive being the "detect-and-reject" mode, which involves building in a "catch" scale that detects respondents in whom it operates beyond some (arbitrarily set) tolerable level, so that data from such respondents can be rejected. This procedure has the drawbacks that it loses data (nonrandomly) from the rejected respondents and fails to reduce the lesser bias in the retained data, leaving it far short of an ideal solution; but research is the art of the possible.

This detection and rejection mode of coping includes a variety of tactics, such as response counts, catch scales, and discrepancy scores. The simple response count procedure involves counting the number of responses in a certain category (e.g., the number of "?" responses, to detect a noncommittal response style) and rejecting respondents who use more than some arbitrarily set level of "?" responses. The catch-scale procedure is illustrated by the MMPI Lie scale made up of a set of items, agreement with which is highly improbable (e.g., "I have never been angry"). Another detection-and-rejection tactic is to use a discrepancy score (e.g., if a schizophrenia measure is made up of obvious and subtle items, respondents can be rejected as too concealing if the discrepancy between the subtle and the obvious schizophrenia subscores exceeds a certain preset amount).

The estimating and correcting mode of coping.   This tactic is more sophisticated than the detection-and-rejection procedures just considered in that it retains all the data: Each person's use of the response bias is measured and then his or her raw score is corrected for use of the response bias. A classic example of such an adjustment tactic is the K scale of the MMPI, used to adjust several of the old MMPI's pathology scores for suppression. A familiar example is the opinion survey tactic of dividing "don't know" respondents in the same ratio as the choosers. A basic problem with this correction tactic is that, unless the basic scale correlates at least .70 with the criterion, it is better to develop a new scale than to try to correct the old one (Norman, 1961).

The reduction or prevention mode. Because of the costliness and indifferent success of the correction modes, it is probably more efficient to take the reduction or prevention approach. One of the many prevention tactics is to use counterbalanced scales, such as avoiding the acquiescence artifact by keying items so that "yes" and "no" responses equally often indicate possession of the characteristic to be measured. A second reduction tactic is the use of ipsatizing procedures. A priori ipsatizing, as in the use of forced-choice items, is inferior to a posteriori ipsatizing such as pattern analysis. Other reduction approaches include anonymous administration, or explicit instructions to avoid the artifact, or using subtly worded items or other disguising procedures, or shortening the measure, all of which have been shown to reduce response-bias artifacts (McGuire, 1969c).

The exploitation stage. The final stage in the career of an artifact is when it comes into its own, giving rise to a new line of research. Rosenthal (1969) manipulated experimenter's expectation about the results, developing it from being a worrisome contamination to becoming itself a topic of interest (e.g., leading to research programs on the Pygmalian effect, nonverbal communication, or social influence). The social desirability and acquiescence artifacts also become individual difference variables of interest. For the suspiciousness artifact to enter this exploitation stage a necessary preliminary is to gain experimental control over it so that the experimenter is able to manipulate it. I shall consider a dozen procedures by which the extent of the participant's suspiciousness of the experimenter's intent can be manipulated, taking my examples from attitude-change studies; but the suspiciousness variable enters many areas of research.

Variables That Manipulate Suspicion of Persuasive Intent

Researchers routinely mislead participants in attitude-change studies as to the studies' purpose (e.g., by representing the persuasive message as a reading comprehension test). In addition, a dozen popular attitude-change variables can be used incidentally to manipulate the participant's suspiciousness of the communication's persuasive intent. These include four source variables: using procedures that lead the participants to perceive that the source will benefit from the audience's acceptance of the position argued; depicting the source as making a presentation to an audience rather than being inadvertently overheard; representing the source's presentation as having occurred in the context of a debate rather than a noncontroversial presentation; and placing the source's presentation as coming after the audience has been exposed to the opposition side. Four message variables are likely to enhance suspicions of persuasive intent: drawing the conclusion explicitly rather than leaving it for the participant's own inferring; ignoring familiar opposition arguments rather than taking them into consideration; advocating extreme rather than moderate positions; and using a dynamic rather than a subdued delivery style. Another four experimental procedures in attitude-change research that also may arouse suspicion of persuasive intent are: depicting the procedure as a psychological experiment; using an attitude pretest; giving an explicit warning that the experiment deals with persuasibility; and having the speaker emit suspicion-arousing nonverbal cues (e.g., visual ones like self-grooming or vocalic ones like pauses).

The obtained results of research manipulating these dozen suspicion-arousing variables have yielded complex findings that suspiciousness may raise, lower, or leave unaffected the persuasive impact; results on the implied interaction effects are similarly equivocal. Why suspicion can either reduce or enhance attitude-change impact becomes more understandable when one considers the variety of explanatory processes that may mediate suspiciousness effects.

Theoretical Housings for Suspiciousness Effects

The suspiciousness variable is best perceived, not as a troublesome artifact, but as a theoretically interesting source of new insights. That many variables, including the 12 named above, can be used to manipulate suspiciousness of experimenter's persuasive intent suggests that the variable is a complex one, raising questions about what raises suspiciousness, what aspects of the experiment the participant is suspicious about, and what dependent variables are affected via which mediator.

Diverse mediators of suspiciousness effects. Suspiciousness of persuasive intent could affect opinion change via many routes, some of which tend to reduce and others to enhance persuasive impact; and still others can operate in either direction, depending on interaction variables. Suspiciousness could reduce the persuasive communication's impact by motivating the believer: (1) to assemble arguments defending her or his own position; (2) to rehearse a defense; (3) to demonstrate ability to stand up for her or his own beliefs; and (4) to distrust the arguments presented. On the other hand, suspiciousness could enhance persuasive impact by: (5) clarifying to participants what is demanded of them; (6) informing the participants how they can ingratiate themselves with the source; (7) making the point of the message clearer; (8) making the participant aware that an informed source holds a discrepant view on the issue; and (9) causing anticipatory belief lowering to avoid appearing gullible, as in the McGuire and Millman (1965c) study described earlier in this chapter.

Two further mechanisms, (10) set and (11) distraction, operate more complexly, either enhancing or diminishing persuasive impact of the suspicious message, depending on interaction variables. As regards (10) set, suspicion of an impending persuasive attack could induce a preparatory set that would influence the way in which the person perceives the message, resulting in either assimilation or contrast. Social judgment theory (Sherif, Sherif, & Nebergall, 1965) predicts assimilation (along with increased opinion change) when the message is only slightly discrepant from the expectation or from the initial belief; with increasing discrepancy, a contrast perceptual effect (and a lessened or even opposite opinion change) becomes more likely. In the present case we are dealing, not with the participant's own position as the reference point, but with her or his suspicion-aroused opinion of what position the message will support. There is some weak evidence (Ewing, 1942) that a participant who suspects she or he is about to hear a quite discrepant communication tends to perceive it as more discrepant from her or his own position than it actually is, but overall an assimilation tendency seems hedonically likely, with people tending to distort information toward, rather than away from, their own position.

As regards (11), the distraction mechanism, Allyn and Festinger (1961) manipulated suspiciousness of persuasive intent by disguising the communication as a test of the participant's ability to judge the speaker's personality in one condition and in the other condition revealing its persuasive intent; but Festinger and Maccoby (1964) argued that the judgment task enhanced persuasion by acting as a distraction that inhibited counterarguing, rather than as a suspicion reducer. The original relation was very small; seldom has such a slight effect been made to bear so heavy a burden of explanation. Festinger and Maccoby (1964) reported that distracted audiences show more attitude change, but Freedman and Sears (1965) found little evidence for the distraction effect beyond the effect of warning. McGuire (1966b) has conjectured that any effect obtained in the Festinger and Maccoby study could have been due to hedonic facilitation (Dabbs & Janis, 1965; Janis, Kaye, & Kirschner, 1965) in that the distracting film was pleasantly amusing. Rosenblatt and Hicks (1966) suggest a resolution of these conflicting mediator effects in the form of a non-monotonic relation between distraction and persuasive effectiveness, with maximum impact occurring with a moderate amount of distraction, too low to interfere with absorbing the argument but high enough to interfere with counterarguing.

Interaction predictions. These diverse theoretical housings for the suspiciousness-of-persuasive-intent variable yield many interaction predictions, including timing, individual-difference, and other variables. Timing manipulations can include both the interval between the suspicion-arousing manipulation (e.g., warning) and the attack and also the interval between the attack and the measurements of attitude-change effect. A number of studies have indicated that the warning is more effective if it precedes the attack by a substantial interval (McGuire, 1964b; Freedman & Sears, 1965). A longer interval between the persuasive attack should increase the effect of the suspiciousness manipulation by allowing fuller overcoming of the primacy effect, cognitive inertia, practice deficit, and operation of the sleeper effect, as explained more fully in McGuire (1969c). Suspiciousness is predicted to interact also with individual difference variables in ability, motivation, and demographics (e.g., men tend to be more suspicious than women [Stricker, 1967]). People differ, not only in how easily their suspicions are aroused but in how they react to suspiciousness.

Ethical Dimensions of the Suspiciousness Issues

Experimenter deception and the suspiciousness it arouses raise ethical as well as methodological and theoretical concerns (Kelman, 1965, 1967). Deception goes beyond passively leaving the participant uninformed about aspects of the experiment to actively misinforming him or her. Deception is often used because the experimenter fears that the participants, if not given some explanation, will generate their own to account for what is involved, which may be correct or incorrect but in either case could contaminate the results in complex ways that reduce their generalizability. Paradoxically, deception is sometimes employed to circumvent other ethical concerns such as harmful manipulations, as when Milgram (1963, 1965) deceived participants into thinking that they were hurting another person rather than allowing them to do so.

Deception is intrinsically distasteful, especially for scientists whose occupational imperative is to correct misconceptions. Most researchers feel at least a slight moral revulsion, aesthetic strain, or embarrassment when deceiving a participant in order to create an experimental situation, even in the service of discovering a more enduring truth; and most of us feel obliged to give an immediate postexperimental explanation to remove the deception, although we realize this risks later participants' learning about the experiment's true purpose (Zemach & Rokeach, 1966). To avoid the use of deception some researchers have resorted to "role-playing" or "vignette" experiments, even at the risk that invalid results of these poor substitutes may deceive the public who use the research, ironically causing more overall deception than would have resulted from doing more valid experiments entailing some deception of participants. Related ethical issues are discussed in chapter 11 of this volume.

PERSONALITY AND PERSUASIBILITY

The preceding sections describe my research on anticipatory belief lowering induced by suspiciousness of persuasive intent, which provoked rich and diverse studies of warning and distraction, anticipatory change, snap-back; artifacts like suspiciousness of experimenter intent; simulated experiments; and ethical issues such as deception and informed consent. These anticipatory change predictions were guided by a simplistic ego-defensive guiding-idea theory. In contrast, the rest of this chapter will describe another of my early programs of attitude-change research, on personality correlates of persuadability, that used a more sophisticated axiomatic theorizing.

[Adapted with permission from W. J. McGuire, 1968a, Personality and attitude change: An information-processing theory, in A. G. Greenwald, T. C. Brock, and T. M. Ostrom (Eds.), *Psychological foundations of attitudes,* pp. 171–196. New York: Academic Press, copyright © 1968). See also my 1960 NSF proposal on "Correlates of persuasibility . . ." and McGuire, 1968b.]

Developing an Axiomatic Theory

Axiomatic theories, Euclid's geometry being a classical example, begin by postulating a series of relations among key variables in a topic area. The postulates may be derived from diverse sources such as commonsense observations, analyses of the results of experiments, creative inspiration (perhaps based on analogy), and functional analysis. Because one can start with any set of postulates and add others indefinitely, such theories are potentially nonparsimonious, inelegant, and unfalsifiable. Any empirical embarrassment the theory encounters can be removed by the addition of new postulates. Some weeding out can be done of postulates with low independence from other postulates, poor empirical track record, or other shortcomings.

My research on individual differences in influenceability derives from an axiomatic theory developed by means of a functional (adaptivity, evolutionary) analysis. I began with the functional assumption that a moderate, discriminating openness to useful information and to guidance from other people is optimal for survival. I added the postulate that this optimal moderate level varies adaptively with dispositional and situational variables. A further assumption is that an economical, flexible way for maintaining such a "golden mean" of openness to influence is for one's openness level to be the resultant of two opposed mediators, each of whose contributions to the variance in influenceability is moderated by specifiable situational and dispositional variables. The theory can handle a wide range of individual-difference independent variables (personality, ability, mood, demographics, etc.) and a broad spectrum of dependent variables (suggestibility, conformity, persuadability, etc.).

The Messiness of Empirical Findings
on Personality–Persuadability Relations

Susceptibility to social influence is the first individual-difference variable to have received careful empirical study in psychology, interest developing out of the late-nineteenth-century hysteria controversy between the schools of Nancy (Liébéault and Bernheim) and Paris (Charcot and Janet) over the generality of suggestibility. Binet, for example, in Charcot's Paris-Salpètrière school, studied individual differences in suggestibility before he turned to the measurement of individual differences in intelligence for which he later became better known.

During the century since, the findings on personality–influenceability relations (McGuire, 1968a, 1968b) have become increasingly puzzling, as can be illustrated even by considering the single personality variable of self-esteem, it and anxiety being the two most popularly studied personality characteristics. In the 1950s the answer regarding the relations between self-esteem and influenceability seemed simple, if ambiguous: Janis (1954) found a negative relation and McGuire and Ryan (1955, unpublished) a positive relation between self-esteem and influenceability. By the 1960s the answer regarding this relation seemed more complex but no less ambiguous. Cox and Bauer (1964) found an inverted-U nonmonotonic relation between influenceability and attitude change, and Silverman (1964) found a nonmonotonic relation of upright-U shape. Out of this nettle, confusion, our theory plucks the flower, truth. To save such complex appearances a complex theory is needed. Even the elaborate theory described here is only an abridgment of the longer story I tell elsewhere (McGuire, 1968a), and even that fuller theory fails to handle the Silverman (1964) upright-U relation (but the latter has not replicated well; see Silverman, Ford, and Morganti, 1966).

Postulates of My Axiomatic Theory

My theory to account for individual-difference variables' relations to influenceability is historically related to the classic "information-processing" (or "learning theory") approach, which predicts that how any communication independent variable (e.g., age or self-esteem) will affect influenceability depends on how it affects each of a dozen or so mediating steps (attention, learning, acceptance, etc., as listed in

Table 5.1). Typically, when students are asked how some ability or personality variable (e.g., intelligence or anxiety) will be related to persuadability, they tend to think of the mediating role of the dynamic mediators (like yielding to the arguments), unwisely overlooking the cognitive mediators (like comprehending the arguments). Thus students tend to predict that intelligence will be negatively related to persuadability on the plausible supposition that intelligence reduces yielding (because the more intelligent person has more information supporting his or her own belief, is better able to refute the attacking arguments, is more willing to hold a discrepant position, etc., all of which factors make the more intelligent person more resistant to influence). With more sophistication, students broaden their analysis to take into account that persuadability increases with comprehension ability, via which mediator intelligence tends to make the person more susceptible to persuasion. My six-postulate axiomatic theory described here is built on this type of analysis.

Postulate I: Multiple mediation. The theory's first postulate makes explicit the commonsense essence of the information-processing approach: that self-esteem (or any individual-difference characteristic and, indeed, any other independent variable in the communication situation) will be related to influenceability via its impact on each of a dozen or more mediational steps (attention, comprehension, yielding, etc., as depicted in Table 5.1). This fairly obvious proposition deserves explicit mention because most conventional thinking about personality–influenceability relations neglects the mediational roles of steps other than yielding. Failure to take into consideration the mediational role of reception steps (e.g., attention and comprehension) can leave one puzzled by such findings as that the better-educated U.S. army personnel in World War II tended to be more influenced by the "Why We Fight" propaganda films than were the poorer-educated (Hovland, Lumsdaine, & Sheffield, 1949). The present axiomatic theory clarifies that even these flagrant propaganda films had sufficient subtlety so that the superior encoding capacity of the better-educated soldiers increased their influenceability more than their superior critical ability reduced it. Postulate I calls attention to the fact that to predict how characteristics like age, education level, intelligence, sex, self-esteem, and anxiety are related to influenceability one must consider their impact on each of the chain of mediators, comprehension as well as yielding, depicted in Table 5.1.

Postulate II: Compensatory relations.   In contrast to the obviousness of the first postulate is the seeming presumptuousness of Postulate II. It asserts that not only education but most individual-difference variables are related to influenceability in opposite directions via the two mediators, comprehension and yielding. Any characteristic that makes a person vulnerable to social influence through some of the mediators tends to protect him or her from influence via other mediators. This compensatory principle is a basic postulate in the theory, and so in strict logic its validity need not be directly demonstrated as long as it yields useful confirmed predictions. However, I have elsewhere (McGuire, 1968a) directly defended its plausibility on several grounds; my fall-back position is that, whatever its universality, my theory deals only with individual-difference variables that do have such compensatory relations. I hypothesize further that most of the popular individual-difference characteristics do have such compensatory effects (e.g., anxiety is negatively related to influenceability via the reception mediator and positively related via the yielding mediator; self-esteem is positively related via reception and negatively via yielding).

Postulate III: Nonmonotonic overall relations.   One corollary derivable from this compensatory principle is that the overall relation between an individual-difference variable and influenceability will tend to be nonmonotonic, with maximum influenceability exhibited by those who are at an intermediate level of the individual-difference characteristic. Such an inverted-U relation follows algebraically from the compensatory postulate under a wide range of parametric conditions. This type of model has appeared in many areas (e.g., its manifestation in the verbal learning area is dealt with in chapter 1 of this volume and in McGuire [1961b]. Its algebraic specifications and its empirical support in the personality-influenceability area have been described more fully elsewhere (McGuire, 1968a) and are expressed graphically in Figure 3.1.

Postulate IV: Acute × chronic interactions.   My theory assumes an interaction effect on influenceability between a person's chronic ver-

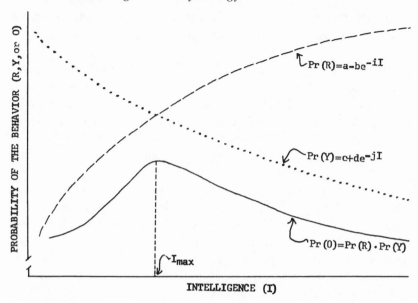

Figure 3.1
Postulate II. Nonmonotonic relation between audience intelligence (I) and probability of opinion change, Pr(O), as mediated by compensatory trends in probabilities of message reception, Pr(R), and of yielding to the argument, Pr(Y).

sus acute variations on personality characteristics. For example, an experimental manipulation of acute anxiety will have an effect on influenceability that depends upon the person's chronic anxiety level. The overall inverted-U relation implies that raising the person's acute anxiety by some fear induction (or raising self-esteem by providing a success experience) will increase the person's influenceability if he or she is chronically low on the personality variable, far to the left of the inflection point; but it will tend to decrease his or her influenceability if he or she is chronically high on the trait, near or to the right of the inflection point.

Postulate V: Confounded variables. The preceding acute-chronic interaction postulate does not fully portray the differences between acute versus chronic variations in a personality characteristic. As discussed in McGuire (1968a), chronic versus acute variations in anxiety (or self-esteem, etc.) are substantively as well as methodologically different. The person's natural, chronic level on a personality trait tends to become embedded in a syndrome of relevant traits that help him or her to cope with problems associated with chronically operating at this level on the trait. For example, if a person is chronically low on self-esteem, this trait will tend to have become embedded in a coping syndrome that includes variables such as withdrawal and low aspiration level, which will protect the person from experiencing painful failure. An experimental manipulation of the characteristic constitutes a "purer" manifestation of the trait before it becomes embedded in compensatory coping traits. Each mode of variation, the chronic and the acute, has its uses in research if it is recognized for what it is. Unfortunately researchers tend to theorize in terms of the pure, acutely manipulated meaning of a characteristic but then test it in terms of the confounded chronic variations, where the trait has become embedded in a syndrome of coping styles that distort its theorized pure relation to persuadability.

Postulate VI: The situational-weighting postulate. A theory that predicts nonmonotonic relations can, particularly when its parameters are unspecified, be a refuge of scoundrels, because it can account for almost any obtained relation when the independent variable trait is varied over a range whose location relative to the inflection point of maximum influenceability is unclear. Postulate VI ties down the relation somewhat by predicting a wealth of interaction effects on influenceability between the personality variable and other variables in the influence situation (e.g., source credibility, message complexity, etc.), depending on the contribution to the variance by the reception versus yielding mediators. Consider that self-esteem is positively related to influenceability by its enhancing comprehension but negatively related by its reducing the yielding. In a repetitive hard-sell suggestion situation like "Drink Coca-Cola" campaigns, almost all American adults will comprehend the message fully, so that little interpersonal variance in its impact will be contributed by the comprehension mediator but considerable by the yielding mediator. Hence, the inflection point for maximum impact will occur at very low levels of self-esteem. In contrast, if the persuasive situation is a technical treatise by an academic economist arguing for a change in the method of calculating the cost-of-living index, most of the covariance between self-esteem and influenceability will be mediated by the comprehension mediator rather than by the yielding mediator, and consequently the inflection point for maximum influenceability will occur at a high level of self-esteem. A fuller discussion of these complexities can be found in McGuire (1968b).

General Strategy for Testing the Theory

The systems theory described above postulates that most individual-difference characteristics over their whole range will exhibit nonmonotonic, inverted-U relations to influenceability. There will be a whole family of these inverted-U functions such that the vertical and horizontal displacement of the inflection point (the intermediate level of the personality characteristic at which maximal influenceability occurs) will vary from situation to situation as predictable from the amount of variance contributed by the comprehension and the yielding mediators. Predictions from the theory can be tested in terms of within and between experimental comparisons from research already reported in the literature, as demonstrated in McGuire (1968a, 1968b).

The theory generates many new predictions in the form of main, mediational, and interactional relations regarding how influenceability in various situations is related to a wide range of personality, ability, and other individual-difference variables. Derivations from this axiomatic theory have been tested programmatically by students who have worked with me on their dissertation and predissertation research at Columbia University in the 1960s, including Susan Millman (1968) on anxiety effects, Richard Nisbett and Andrew Gordon (1967) and Miriam Zellner (1970) on self-esteem effects, and Stanley Lehmann (1970) on anxiety × self-esteem effects on influenceability. However, adequate testing of such a systems theory requires an integrated program of research, designed within a perspectivist approach, as described in chapter 12. Such a program could systematically test a wide range of implications, with priority given to crucial predictions such as the nonmonotonic, inverted-U postulate that maximum influenceability tends to occur at intermediate ranges of most individual-difference variables. An interim substitute for the preplanned program is to do systematic meta-analyses of uncoordinated individual studies, as illustrated by Rhodes and Wood (1992) for self-esteem's relation to influenceability. Such among-experiments comparisons provide some suggestive results but leave in doubt such crucial issues as the nonmonotonicity of the overall relation. A more adequate exploitation of this systems theory awaits more programmatic planning of a series of interrelated studies, each with an inclusive experimental design and a wide variety of individual-difference variables.

4

Integrative Reviews
of Social Influence Processes

A researcher's early publications tend to categorize her or him under some topical rubric, in my case "attitude change." With continued publication one becomes recognized as a maven in the area and is asked to write reviews of its topics (such as those in this chapter), to apply basic research to the solution of practical problems (as illustrated in chapter 5), and to evaluate the relevant research of others, including manuscripts submitted to journals and research proposals submitted to granting agencies. I paid my dues in doing such reviewing even though it preempted a vast amount of time that could have been used for carrying out and reporting my own experiments. My reviews of manuscripts and proposals have yielded thousands of detailed letters to researchers about their work, perhaps improving that or subsequent work, or perhaps ending up discarded like the thousand lost golf balls or, Bartelby-like, the dead letters sent to dearest him who lives, alas, away.

ON PAYING ONE'S DUES AS REVIEWER

This review work generated a vast amount of prose that does not appear in print and yet deserves mention here because it constitutes my main pedagogic contribution. There were periods in my life when my manuscript and proposal reviewing reached awesome levels, especially during the decade from 1965 to 1975, during part of which I was editor of the *Journal of Personality and Social Psychology* (which received 650 manuscripts per year, 350 of which I reviewed personally with long, detailed letters to the authors) and at the same time I was also consulting editor to five other journals. (Over the years I have been consulting editor on over 15 journals, including most of the English-language social psychology journals published in North America and Europe, as well as journals in other disciplines.)

In that same 1965–75 decade I was also on the review panels of most of the major U.S. granting agencies, governmental and private, in the social sciences, such as the National Science Foundation, the National Institutes of Mental Health (and a half-dozen other National Health Institutes), the Social Science Research Council, and the National Research Council. Serving on some of these review panels (e.g., the NSF and NIMH) involved reviewing up to 100 long proposals each year. In at least three years of the late 1960s I probably wrote detailed reviews of over 500 manuscripts and proposals per year.

There is one reviewer category, book reviewing, where I have barely held up my end. I am frequently invited to review books, and during the early career phase discussed here I sometimes accepted (McGuire, 1962b, 1962c, 1963a, 1964a). Subsequently, however, I have agreed to review books only under unusual circumstances (McGuire, 1993d, 1998). The early book-reviewing experience brought home to me how much a book is a final, unalterable product and how much work and emotion the author invests in writing one. Reluctance to criticize another's unalterable, major labor of love has led me to beg off book reviewing.

Is this onerous reviewing of manuscripts and proposals worthwhile to the extent that I would recommend it to young scientists? There are both pros and cons to which each researcher should assign his or her own egosyntonic weights. Taking on such gate-keeping functions – deciding which manuscripts are published and which proposals funded – would seem to give one clout to shape where the field will go, but actually the influence conferred is slight and reactive. One can choose only among options presented by the papers that arrive on one's desk but has little opportunity to encourage new, neglected lines of work. Such reviewing does allow one to keep up with the field by reading work that may not appear in print for several years; but one loses time for reading that is more focused on one's own area of work. Taking on such tasks does add to one's visibility: Few jobs are filled without the search committee's contacting the editor of the field's prime journal for names of up-and-coming candidates. Also one feels virtuous as a good citizen, doing one's share of the onerous evaluation tasks and offering suggestions to other researchers about their work. My biggest gratification from my heavy reviewing chores was pedagogic. I consider my main teaching contribution during 40 years in academia to be this Stakhanovite commenting on specific manuscripts from across the nation and the world rather than the teaching I did in the classroom. After the 1970s I reduced this manuscript reviewing work to a level below that in my heroic 1965–75 decade, but it remains heavy.

Rising stars may want to consider subtle reputational effects when deciding on whether or not to accept invitations to take on these gatekeeper reviewing roles. It might be thought that doing such review work is a mark of recognition that can only add to one's reputation, but there are cynical entrepreneurs who regard the reviewing of others' research as a foolish distraction from cultivating one's own garden. My own observations on peer-review panels and as a journal editor leave me feeling that the best researchers tend to be the best reviewers also, but others perceive the two activities as compensatory.

After one has established a track record by doing good research and exhibiting familiarity with an area for a half-dozen years, one is likely to be asked to write integrative reviews. My first major review of attitude research was for the 1966 *Annual Review of Psychology* (McGuire, 1966b). Next came invitations to do the chapters on attitude change in the main handbooks of social psychology, personality, and communication (McGuire, 1968b, 1969a, 1973a, 1985a). As I grew to "world's greatest authority" status I wrote the attitudes and persuasion chapters for the *Encyclopedia Britannica* and other encyclopedias (McGuire, 1974b, 1974c, 1977a, 1977b, 1983b,1989c). My narrower reviews were on subtopics of attitude change (McGuire, 1966c, 1968f, 1970c, 1972a, 1973b, 1975, 1982d, 1993c), whereas others were on topics as broad as social psychology (McGuire, 1972b, 1974a, 1976e, 1980d, 1985b, 1986a). This chapter samples various types of my attitude-change reviews.

THE ORIGINS OF ATTITUDES

[Adapted with permission from W. J. McGuire, 1985a, Attitudes and attitude change, in G. Lindzey and E. Aronson (Eds.), *Handbook of social psychology,* 3rd ed., Vol. 2, pp. 233–346. New York: Random House. Copyright © The McGraw-Hill Companies). Many citations, omitted here, can be found along with the full references in the original publications.]

Attitude-change research in psychology (such as that discussed in chapters 2–5 of this volume) is concerned almost exclusively with persuasive communication as its determinant. As a correction to this narrowness I shall here briefly review four other relatively neglected classes of variables that affect attitudes: genetic endowment, transient physiological states, direct experience with the attitude topic, and institutional structures.

Genetic Determinants of Attitudes

It is uncomfortable for most psychologists to conjecture about genetic influence, but the very repugnance of the heredity hypothesis merits disciplined attention to compensate for pusillanimous neglect. Genetic factors are likely to affect the dynamic aspects of attitudes and may also affect their directive aspects. Animal research shows that genetic factors affect dynamic levels of both aggressive (J. P. Scott & Fuller, 1965) and altruistic proclivities (Allee, 1938; E. O. Wilson, 1975). Some theorists (Schacter, 1982; Buss, 1994) go further and postulate genetic influence also on the directive aspects of attitudes, channeling destructive or constructive proclivities into specific behaviors or toward particular targets. It is not necessary to postulate Platonic idealism, transmigration of souls, Kantian synthetic a priori, Lamarckian transmission, or divine infusion. Natural variation and adaptive selection suffice to account for genetic determination of the directive aspects of attitudes, such as liking neotenic people with large pupillary dilation (Hess, 1975), or feeling nurturant toward those with large head-to-body ratios (Alley, 1981), or disliking those ethnically different from oneself (Campbell, 1965; Holldobler & Lumsden, 1980). Even attitudes detrimental to personal survival or reproduction, such as altruistic self-sacrifice and homosexuality, might be selectively bred into the species if their disadvantages to their possessors were sufficiently compensated for by their inclusive fitness in enhancing the survival of their own kind within a common gene pool (Campbell, 1975, 1979; E. O. Wilson, 1978; Boorman & Levitt, 1980; A. M. McGuire, 1993). Quantitative models for the genetic determination of beliefs have been presented tentatively by Cavalli-Sforza and Feldman (1981) and vigorously by Lumsden and Wilson (1981).

Transient Physiological Determinants

Aging and attitudes. Transitory physiological fluctuations associated with aging, illness, or body chemistry may also affect attitudes.

Critical-period theorists have proposed that the self-identity (E. H. Erikson, 1950/1964) and lifelong political ideology of a generational cohort (Kertzer, 1983) are determined by the socioeconomic conditions in one's cohort's adolescence (Mannheim, 1923/1952; Bengtson & Laufer, 1974; Graubard, 1980), but empirical results are mixed on this elusive "generational" issue (Himmelweit et al., 1981). Some life span researchers report that men tend to undergo dramatic shifts in attitudes during midlife crises (Levinson, 1978), but there is considerable ideological continuity over the life span (Brim & Kagan, 1980; Kahle, Klingel, & Kulka, 1981; D. O. Sears, 1983b) and such age-linked changes as do occur may reflect social rather than physiological changes with age (P. E. Murphy & Staples, 1979).

Attitudinal correlates of illness.   Novelists have associated certain illnesses with specific attitudes – euphoric optimism (*spes phthistica*) with tuberculosis, or irritable stubbornness with epilepsy. Sontag (1978) describes a peculiar contrast in the metaphoric use of tuberculosis versus cancer in society and in literature. The attitudinal malaise widespread among nineteenth-century French writers such as Baudelaire, Rimbaud, and de Maupassant, paradoxical in that it occurred at a time of more than typical social and economic progress in France, has been attributed by R. L. Williams (1980) to jaundiced outlooks produced by the diseases prevalent among the era's authors. As life imitates art, these literary manifestations deserve attention.

Body chemistry and neural states affecting attitudes.   Attitudes can be altered by various physiological manipulations, including hormones (androgen, epinephrine), drugs (barbiturates, hallucinogens, caffeine), deprivations (of sleep, food, stimulation, etc.), hyperventilation, rhythmic stimulation, lobotomy and other psychosurgery, and electroshock "therapies." Other physiological treatments may lower persuadability by disrupting cognitive processing of persuasive arguments or raise persuadability by weakening the tendency to counterargue. Central depressant drugs such as thiopental sodium and norepinephrine's MHPG metabolite (Maas, 1978) can reduce the impact of complex messages while enhancing susceptibility to simpler suggestions. Sensory deprivation may enhance persuadability more by destabilizing initial attitudes than by producing a stimulus hunger for the attacking information (Suedfeld & Borrie, 1978).

Direct Experience with the Object

Single significant experiences. Psychologists' preoccupation with attitudes' indirect determination by persuasive communications from third parties about an object neglects attitude determination by direct experience with this object. It is the stuff of legends but may nevertheless be true (Knapp, Stohl, & Reardon, 1981) that a streak of lightning can turn the village atheist into God's devotee, or that a traumatic childhood incident can lead to a lifelong aversion (Loewenberg, 1971), or that love may strike at first sight. Studies of war neuroses, childhood traumas, political zealotry, critical-period imprinting, religious conversion (Rejai & Phillips, 1979; Paloutzian, 1981; Ullman, 1982) and product use (Olson & Dover, 1979) all suggest that a single significant experience can be critical (Read, 1983). Psychobiographical analyses report that critical incidents in their childhoods account for the ideological appeal of Hitler's National Socialism (Merkl, 1980), at least to Protestant youth in 1932 Germany (Loewenberg, 1971), but leave unclear why the Hitler movement did not have a comparative appeal for Catholic youth (Broszat, 1968/1981; Schellenberger, 1975; R. F. Hamilton, 1982). Mass shifts in attitude have been attributed to the Martin Luther King, Jr., assassination (Riley & Pettigrew, 1976) and to media events, real and fictitious (E. Katz, 1980).

Evidence for such one-trial attitude acquisition comes mainly from anecdotal research marred by postfactum rationalizations, selective recall, and lack of control groups. However, the possibility of sudden ideological reversals (Weiss, 1963) deserves sympathetic consideration to counterbalance the strong gradualist bias of twentieth-century science. Signs that this gradualist bias may be abating are recent conjectures of evolutionary discontinuities in the rate of species' emergence (Stanley, 1981) and disappearance (Kerr, 1980; but see Archibald & Clemens, 1982). "Cataclysmic" explanations may increasingly corrode science's gradualist bias if suitable mathematical analyses (perhaps chaos theory) are developed (A. L. Robinson, 1982) to handle discontinuities better than has catastrophe theory (Kolata, 1977; Saunders, 1980; I. N. Stewart & Peregoy, 1983), and if scientists such as the cladists revive the metatheoretical Marxist-Leninist predilection for revolutionary rather than gradual change, despite the collapse of the Soviet Union.

Effects of mere exposure on liking. Conventional wisdom has it that social movements, fads, and fashions exhibit a nonmonotonic inverted-U life cycle, such that a fad at first gains popularity as exposure increases, until overexposure eventually dissipates its appeal. However, Vanbeselaere (1983) reports the opposite "decrease followed by increase" relation, and a large body of mere-exposure research (Zajonc, 1965; Schaffner, Wandersman, & Stang, 1981) indicates that, with some rare exceptions (G. N. Cantor, 1968; Zajonc et al.,1972), increasing exposure results in monotonically increasing liking for the object, even when exposures are carried to very high levels, occur in negative contexts, under low-recognition conditions, with stimuli only partially similar (Gordon & Holyoak, 1983), and at a variety of presentation intervals (A. A. Harrison, 1977). The mere-exposure phenomenon poses challenging questions to the theories of semantic satiation, arousal, and opponent-process motivation.

Interpersonal contact effects on liking. Contact among strangers in natural living situations is reported (Newcomb, 1961, 1981) to increase familiarity with one another's attitudes, liking for each other, and attitudinal similarity, although for so bidirectionally plausible a relation the effect size is modest (Klineberg, 1981). Such contact-acquired attitudes may be stronger (Zohar, Cohen, & Azar, 1980) and be better predictors of behavior (Fazio, Zanna, & Cooper, 1978) than are attitudes based on third-party communication, although at some levels of cognition the third-party messages can have more impact than direct contact (P. Katz & Zalk, 1978; Olson & Dover, 1979; Tyler, 1980).

Results are less clear when the contact is forced and involves hostile groups, a situation relevant to both theory and social policy in the important area of integrating groups previously segregated on bases such as religion, class, ethnicity, and sex (D. L. Hamilton, 1981; Bochner, 1982; N. Miller & Brewer, 1984). It is usually hoped that enforced racial integration will enhance intergroup liking and harmony, but a likely alternative is that it will lead to intensifying preexisting attitudes, making those initially positive more favorable and those initially ill-disposed more hostile (Amir, 1976). Research suggests (Mumpower & Cook, 1978; Tajfel, 1981, Patchen, 1982) that to enhance intergroup liking the integration should be long sustained, be experienced as voluntary, disclose ideological similarity, involve an intimate level of contact, provide mutual goal facilitation, include intrinsically attractive others, and occur on an equal-status basis and within a broader cultural context that is supportive of intergroup mixing. Even where such formidable conditions have been approximated by heroic efforts (S. W. Cook, 1978, 1979; D. L. Hamilton, Carpenter, & Bishop,1984), the amount of increase in liking tends to be modest.

Social Institutions as Attitude Determinants

Institutions may affect attitudes, not only by their explicit persuasive communications, but also by their structures' determining the stimulus situations to which the person is exposed, the response options made available, the level and type of motivation aroused, and the schedules of reinforcements administered. The influence of a half-dozen varied types of institutions illustrates such effects.

Parental introjection.   The importance of the person's early cultural experience (Zern, 1983), especially the childhood home, in establishing her or his lifelong conformity level and orientations is suggested by the abiding similarity of children's political attitudes to those of their parents and siblings (D. O. Sears, 1975; Berger, 1980; Himmelweit et al., 1981; Jessop, 1982; but see Jennings & Niemi, 1974, 1981; Abramson, 1983). Such across-generation ideological similarity could be due to the direct influence of the childhood home or to social continuity such that parents and child are usually exposed to similar conditions. Even parent–child dissimilarity could be evidence of parental influence (Kraut & Lewis, 1975), as when the 1960s peaceniks carried out their parents' moral injunctions more than did the parents themselves, the children following parental preaching rather than practice.

Peer-group norms.   Nonkin institutions such as peer groups, schools, the "helping" professions (Lasch, 1977), and the mass media are probably diminishing the family's influence on ideology, as modernization reduces parental control, presence, and prescriptiveness (Andrews & Kandel, 1979; Cherlin, 1981, 1983; but see Seward, 1978). Urbanization, population growth, and mass media, which bring large numbers of homogeneously aged children into contact and expose them to common experiences have produced a distinctive centripetal youth culture as regards art forms, values, and life-styles (Reisman, 1980; Conger, 1981; Veroff, Douvan, & Kulka, 1981; Yankelovich, 1981; Caplow et al., 1982).

Ideological schooling.   School curricula include, besides knowledge and skills training, attitudinal indoctrination under such rubrics as citizenship training, global outlook, multiculturalism, and civics (Barrows, 1981). School exposure has surprisingly little effect on knowledge and attitudes on specific issues (Feather, 1973; Barrows, 1981), but may affect general orientations (Rutter et al., 1979; Olmsted & Smith, 1980). Amount of education, even with other demographic variables controlled, is associated with increase in some "liberal" values such as ethnic tolerance (Schönbach, 1981) and respect for civil liberties, but fails to enhance other "liberal" values such as attitudes on the death penalty, abortion, and gun control (Hyman & Wright 1979). Type of school also makes a difference: Himmelweit and Swift (1969) report that the British streaming of youths into different school systems has a long-term effect on their attitudes and behavior. Greeley (1977) reports that the relatively low racism of Catholics declines even further with the number of years of education in Catholic schools, even when other factors are held constant (Greeley, McCready, & McCourt, 1976).

Legislating morality.   Doubt that society's laws affect the masses' behaviors and attitudes is epitomized in Sumner's (1906) claim that stateways cannot change folkways and in Dwight D. Eisenhower's contention that one cannot legislate morality. A contrary view of internalization and "identification with the aggressor" is expressed in Lyndon B. Johnson's contention that if one grabs the enemy by his arm (or whatever) and pulls, his heart and mind will follow. Empirical data are equivocal regarding how legalization of homosexual behavior affected its judged morality (N. Walker & Argyle, 1964; Berkowitz & Walker, 1967); how civil rights legislation affected southerners' attitudes on integration (Wirt, 1970; Rodgers & Bullock, 1972); and how the Schempp ruling outlawing prayer in the public schools affected the public's attitudes regarding school prayer (Muir, 1967; Birkby, 1969). Further research is needed on this important issue.

Mass media indoctrination. In the past half-century television (and other mass media) may be replacing home and school as society's primary institutions for inculcating or eradicating social values (Conway et al., 1981), although chapter 5 in this volume describes the surprising weakness of evidence that the media have massive effects on public attitudes.

Social control by art and rituals. The efficacy of ritual (Frischer, 1982; Winner, 1982) and ceremonial rites (Elliott, 1982; V. Turner, 1982) to influence public attitudes and behaviors, as in Hitler's use of pageantry to seize the public imagination (Riefenstahl, 1934), is implied by ethological, role, and rule theories (Goffman, 1959, 1976; Biddle, 1979; Harré, 1981). Ideological uses of ceremonies on the national scale have been described by Geertz (1980) in his theater-state analysis of Balinese society; by Weissman (1981), Goldthwaite (1981), and Trexler (1980) on how power was communicated through architecture and pageantry in Medici Florence; by A. Guttmann (1981) on the political use of sports spectacles; by Luttwak (1977) on how the Roman Empire positioned its army to dominate by ceremonial display of power rather than by actual application of military force; and by Rosen's (1982) description of the post-1964 use of the U.S. armed forces in Vietnam in accord with the limited-war doctrine of sending a signal to the enemy rather than destroying enemy forces. Elliott (1982) describes press conferences as political ritual; C. Lane (1981) describes the Soviet Union's use of May Day and other domestic rites to proselytize for Marxism-Leninism; Guilbaut (1981) argues that abstract expressionist art was a Cold War weapon; E. Katz (1980) argues that media events manipulate public opinion; and Vélez-Ibañez (1983) describes rituals of marginality used to control impoverished barrio populations. Bassiouni (1982), Schmidt and deGraaf (1982), and Weimann (1983) describe terrorists' use of violence as ritual communication; Ankerl (1981), the use of architecture to influence social relations; and Paige and Paige (1981), the use of reproductive rituals (puberty ceremonies, birth practices, etc.) in the war between the sexes.

Total institutions. It is widely believed that dramatic attitudinal changes can be produced in total institutions such as the preschool home, hospitals, prisons, military camps, residential college campuses, religious communities, and "cult" or political communes. Such changes tend to be transient for most members. Where they are effective, such thought reform procedures probably involve qualitatively different processes from those involved in ordinary persuasive communications.

INTERPRETATIONS
OF PERSUASION RESEARCH

The preceding section describes how forces other than persuasive communications affect attitudes; the remaining sections of this chapter describe how communication variables affect attitudes, ranging from my earliest (McGuire, 1966b) to my latest (McGuire, 1994b) reviews. The first, the 1966 *Annual Review of Psychology* selection, covers the then overly popular topic of dissonance theory and the neglected topic of attitude formation in natural communities. Festinger's dissonance theory dominated the field during the three years covered in this 1966 *Annual Review* chapter, so it was inevitable that my review discussed it at length. It was a controversial area full of nonreplications, but I tried to sketch the reported results in an evenhanded way. I had been Festinger's first postdoctoral fellow in 1955–6 at the University of Minnesota when his basic dissonance volume (Festinger, 1957) was being written, and many dissonance researchers and opponents of the theory were my close friends and colleagues, although my direct involvement in it was limited (McGuire, 1960b).

Dissonance Theory Research on Forced-
Compliance and Disconfirmed Expectations

[Adapted with permission from W. J. McGuire, 1966b, Attitudes and opinions, *Annual Review of Psychology*, vol. 17, pp. 475–514 (Palo Alto, CA: Annual Reviews, Inc., copyright © 1966).]

Dissonance theory in general. During the 1963–6 period reviewed here, dissonance theory (Festinger, 1957, 1964) generated more research and more hostility than any other approach. Brehm and Cohen (1962) reviewed the initial dissonance conceptualizations and added the variables of volition and commitment to Festinger's discrepancy and importance variables. Festinger (1964) grants that commitment is an important condition while contending that cognitive reorganization occurs postdecisionally, rather than predecisionally as implied by conflict theory, and that behaviors influence attitudes as well as the more obvious effect of attitudes on behavior. The heart of the controversy regarding forced compliance and disconfirmation of expectancy phenomena pits theories predicting commonsense reinforcement-maximizing behavior against dissonance theory's predictions of nonobvious postfactum cognitive justifications for one's own behavior and for things as they are.

Discussion of how and when forced overt compliance results in internalized attitude change goes back at least to Anna Freud and Bruno Bettelheim, and perhaps even to the Comte-Spencer disagreement, which is epitomized in Sumner's contention that stateways cannot change folkways. The issue has implications for social policy as regards the persuasive impact of "legislating morality," discussed above. Festinger (1957) used dissonance concepts to argue that the results of Kelman's (1953) "response restriction" study indicate that the less the external inducement used to justify overt compliance in defending a disliked position, the greater will be the complier's internalized opinion change toward the compliant position in order to justify having behaved counterattitudinally for so little inducement.

The twenty-dollar misunderstanding. The controversy gained new vigor when Festinger and Carlsmith (1969) induced students to lie to other students that a boring study was quite interesting in order to help the experimenter entice the others into participating in it. Participants who were given $20 for telling the lie ended up believing their own lie less than participants given only $1 (supposedly because so paltry a payment would not have justified telling the lie, so one convinced oneself that what one said was true). Chapanis and Chapanis (1964) argued that the large reward may have backfired by arousing the participants' suspicions, $20 seeming (in the words of Emilia) to be a great price for a small vice. Some participants in the $20 condition did indeed refuse to lie or became suspicious and had to be eliminated, but this happened in the $1 condition as well; also, the payment was given, not just for lying to one potential participant, but for being on call in the future for similar services as needed by the experimenter. The incredulity interpretation is further questioned by Brehm's and Cohen's (1962, pp. 74–8) study, in which participants were given financial inducements in small steps ($0.50, $1.00, $5.00, or $10.00) for writing a counterattitudinal essay, and it was found that the lower the pay, the greater the internalized opinion change, even at quite modest and credible reward levels (Lependorf, 1964). M. J. Rosenberg (1965) attributed the greater effect of the lower awards to negative affect and evaluation apprehension, to control for which he separated the two parts of the study; however, Festinger and Carlsmith (1959) and Nuttin (1964) had also separated them and still found the paradoxical negative relation between reward size and internalization.

The commonsensical self-indoctrination outcome is illustrated by the Janis and King (1954) role-playing finding that when a writer gets more money for writing a counterattitudinal essay he or she is motivated to write a more convincing essay and so talks himself or herself into the position advocated. Dissonance theorists predict the opposite, that the better-paid persons may write better essays but the extrinsic money reward will justify the effort without the writers' having to internalize the defended position. Bostrom, Vlandis, and Rosen (1961) assigned different grades randomly to students for essays involving counterattitudinal advocacy, and those awarded the highest grades showed more internalization of the overtly defended position, a finding in accord with the commonsense incentive-theory prediction (Janis & Gilmore, 1965) and against the counterintuitive dissonance prediction.

A reconciliation?   The seemingly opposite incentive theory self-indoctrination prediction versus dissonance theory insufficient-justification prediction in the forced compliance studies can be reconciled as an interaction effect. The dissonance inverse relation between reward and internalization will be more pronounced when participants simply commit themselves to the counterattitudinal advocacy but have not yet carried out the advocacy. Once the agreed-to advocacy is actually carried out, the positive relation between reward size and internalization predicted by incentive theory will be more pronounced. Janis and Gilmore (1965) support this interactional reconciliation, as do Brock and Backwood (1962), but Elms and Janis (1965) do not. Brehm (1965) argues that their experimental conditions were not appropriate for testing dissonance theory. Also in keeping with the reconciliation is that Carlsmith, Collins, and Helmreich (1965) find the dissonance inverse relation after public counterattitudinal advocacy and the incentive-theory positive relation after private, essay-writing advocacy. A subsequent study by Collins and Helmreich (1965) sounds a discordant note on which to end this dissonant symphony:

Their $0.50 versus $2.00 reward manipulation produced no main or interaction effect on attitude change, but, oddly, more attitude change occurred in the impersonal, anonymous condition than in the signed, persuasive condition, despite the fact that better essays were written under the latter condition. A series of unpublished studies by Collins raises as many questions as they answer. Five years of effort by numerous researchers have not fully answered the $20 question. Dissonance theory's counterintuitive insufficient-justification prediction fares better, as would be expected, when the task does not involve counterattitudinal advocacy. Related dissonance derivations receiving some support were (1) that students liked eating grasshoppers more if they had tasted them at the behest of unpleasant rather than pleasant leaders (Zimbardo et al., 1965); and (2) children forbidden to play with a preferred toy showed more internalized attitudinal derogation of the forbidden toy if forbidden by a mild than by a severe threat.

Effort and attitude changes.   A related paradoxical dissonance prediction is that overt compliance entailing large effort produces, because it has to be justified, more internalized attitude change toward the discrepant position advocated than does low-effort advocacy (Cohen, 1959; Aronson, 1961; Jansen & Stolurow, 1962). For example, Lawrence and Festinger (1962) report that habits acquired by rats under high-effort conditions are more resistant to extinction than those learned under low effort, but this outcome need not be embarrassing to incentive theorists who already swallowed the finding of the greater resistance to extinction with intermittent than with 100% reinforcement. Hess (1959, 1962, 1964) reported similar effort "paradoxes" as regards imprinting, but see Moltz (1960, 1963). Zimbardo (1965) manipulated the difficulty of giving a counterattitudinal speech by using delayed auditory feedback and confirmed the dissonance prediction of more attitude change with the more confusing feedback, but this could have been due to the feedback being a distraction that reduced counterarguing.

Surprised by joy.   Aronson and Carlsmith (1962) pitted a dissonance hypothesis based on confirmation-of-expectancy motivation against a more commonsensical one based on achievement motivation, predicting that an expected failure is preferred over an unexpected success. They reported that students who did better on a test than their previous failures would have led them to expect tended to change more answers when allowed to retake the test than did participants who expected to do poorly and actually did get a low score, the changed answers being a deliberate effort to lower their scores to the expected poor level. Two confirmations were reported by Brock and Edelman (1964) and a partial replication by Cottrell (1965), but Brock, Edwards, and Schuck (1964), Ward and Sandvold (1963), Lowin and Epstein (1965), and Conlon (1965) failed to confirm the paradoxical dissonance prediction.

Recommended Research on Attitude Formation in Natural Communities

My social psychological review written in the 1960s naturally had to cover these popular dissonance topics. More idiosyncratic was my covering of a neglected topic, community controversy, which I hoped (unavailingly) to popularize by giving it *Annual Review* coverage.

Resolution of community controversy.   Discrepancy models, like Anderson-Hovland's linear operator, underlie much of the theorizing about opinion formation in the natural environment, for example, during political campaigns or fluoridation referenda. Such models generally specify (*a*) the probability of a persuasive contact between any two community members and (*b*) the attitude change that results (e.g., that the contacters adjust opinions toward one another). Such a discrepancy-resolution model leads to the peaceable but implausible prediction that community controversies tend to universal agreement in the form of unanimous convergence on a moderate position. Abelson and Bernstein (1963), in their computer simulation of community voting on the fluoridation issue, save the model by assuming, like Hovland and Sherif's (1961) assimilation-contrast model, possible boomerang effects such that, when (rarely) very discrepant people interact, their interaction drives them still further apart. It is worthwhile to distinguish among process simulations, outcome simulations, and mathematical models. A mathematical model applicable to the same fluoridation problem was described by Abelson (1964). One might have to do a computer simulation even though a mathematical model is available, because one's computer cannot handle the mathematical model (e.g., the IBM 7090 can handle only communities of up to 900 people with Abelson's simulation program, and this despite its being written economically in FAP). The other computer approach to community controversy is represented by various "outcome simulations" of political contests such as those of the Coleman group (1964), of McPhee (1961), and of the Simulmatics group (Pool & Abelson, 1961; Pool, Abelson, & Popkin, 1964). The latter simulation, with its 480 different demographic types of U.S. voters, has been viewed with alarm by nonscientists such as Lasky in his John F. Kennedy biography and Eugene Burdick in his "480" novel.

Kreweras (1963) has suggested that another reason community controversies are not always resolved by monolithic agreement regarding all outstanding issues, as predicted by simple discrepancy models, is because communities (e.g., a parliament) have two classes of members, changers and nonchangers. In this case the whole community will ultimately divide in the same ratio as that in which the nonchangers were initially split, even when the nonchangers form a small minority and are quite atypical of the whole community as regards initial split. Converse (1966) has been led, by analysis of the U.S. elections, to a similar suggestion that the electorate is made up of party loyalists versus constant changers. This approach will be made more plausible and elegant when the changer–nonchanger dichotomy is developed into a continuum. A broad approach to the problem of attitude stabilization in communities is provided by Coleman (1964).

Opportunistic research in natural communities. Two additional lines of research on opinion formation in naturalistic settings deserve more attention, one dealing with President John F. Kennedy's mode of entering office and the other, of his leaving it. The Nixon–Kennedy presidential debates produced crash research on such topics as the effects of attitudes on perceptions of the debaters, and the effects of the debates on attitudes and voting (Kraus, 1962; Stephenson, 1964). The Kennedy assassination evoked even more precipitous attitude and communication studies (Sheatsley & Bradburn, 1964; Sheatsley & Feldman, 1964; Parker & Greenberg, 1965). Such salient natural events offer unusual opportunity for research, but their research potential might better be exploited by setting up a permanent panel of investigators who are familiar with the tactical problems of opportunistic research and are ready to move quickly when such events arise. The successes and failures of earlier "disaster" panels should be studied before setting up such a quick-response research group. Meanwhile, more predictable social innovations offer research opportunities of a less frenzied nature: for example, the growing trend toward changing traditional laws dealing with such attitude-encrusted topics as narcotics use, sexual behavior, school prayer, and the death penalty (Walker & Argyle, 1964).

Persistence of Induced Attitude Change

[This section is adapted with permission from McGuire, 1985a.]

Temporal decay of induced attitude change.   The persistence of induced attitude change is another topic deserving more research attention regarding both its temporal decay and, conversely, delayed-action attitude impacts. One should not expect a single decay curve to describe all attitude change, any more than one would expect a single forgetting curve for all material learned. Decay parameters vary wildly: Some studies report that most of the initially induced attitude change persists for months (Watts, 1967; Nuttin, 1975; Rokeach, 1975; P. B. Smith, 1976); others report intermediate decay rates suggesting a half-life of one or two weeks for induced attitude change (McGuire, 1957; Watts & McGuire, 1964c); and still others report precipitous and complete decay in short periods (Ronis et al., 1977) as if persuasive communications produce only superficial "elastic" changes (McGuire & Millman, 1965c, and chapter 3 of this volume; Cialdini et al., 1976; Hass & Mann, 1976). The shape, and even the direction, of the attitude-change decay curve varies with many factors (T. D. Cook & Flay, 1978).

Delayed-action effects of persuasive communications.   The vicissitudes of the discounting-cue sleeper effect hypothesis have been used (Greenwald et al., 1986) to vindicate keeping faith in a plausible theory even in the face of contrary evidence. Inspired by the reminiscence phenomenon in learning, Hovland, Lumsdaine, and Sheffield (1949) analyzed tenaciously for any slight delayed-action effects in their World War II army data. They conjectured that, when a discounting cue (e.g., attribution to an untrustworthy source) accompanies a persuasive message and muffles its immediate impact, then this incidental discounting cue may be gradually dissociated from the retained persuasive arguments, resulting in an initial phase of delayed-action impact, or at least slower decay (relative delayed action) than without a discounting cue (Watts & McGuire, 1964; T. D. Cook et al., 1979). Early statements of the theory assumed that the discounting cue had to be forgotten more rapidly than the convincing arguments, but McGuire (1961b, 1968b) showed that the nonmonotonic inverted-U relation can be derived algebraically without this ad hoc assumption (see chapters 1 and 3 of this volume). After several early replications (Hovland & Weiss, 1951; Kelman & Hovland, 1953; W. Weiss, 1953; S. J. Weber, 1972), the sleeper effect nodded off and was given premature burial in the 1970s after several failures to find empirical signs of life (Capon & Hulbert, 1973; Gillig & Greenwald, 1974). Heroic resuscitation efforts in the 1980s breathed life back into the discounting-cue explanation (T. D. Cook et al., 1979); at least when the persuasive content is strong, the discounting cue is substantial enough to suppress initial impact, the ensuing delay period is of appropriate duration, and relative as well as absolute delayed-action trends are considered (T. D. Cook & Flay, 1978).

This excessive concentration on the discounting-cue explanation provoked me to propose a dozen alternative mechanisms for producing delayed-action attitude-change effects. Besides the discounting-cue explanation, a second and third involve interpersonal processes. (2) Those who are little influenced immediately may show delayed-action impact due to their being subsequently proselytized by the more immediately affected majority. (3) There may be a two-step impact such that only the attentive group leaders are immediately affected, and they subsequently convince the passive masses.

Nine other explanations assume that intrapersonal processes underlie delayed-action persuasive impact. (4) A sensitization or agenda-setting hypothesis suggests that initial communications on a topic may sensitize receivers, enhancing their attentiveness to subsequent arguments on the topic. (5) The initial converts may seek out further bolstering arguments to enhance their confidence (McGuire, 1964b). (6) Delayed-action effects could reflect a consistency reaction in before-after experimental designs such that a person who has just reported "before" attitudes on a questionnaire may feel inhibited about showing a change of attitude on the immediately-after measure but might reveal change on a measure taken later, when its departure from the premeasure would not be so salient. (7) Reactance might be involved in that the person resists while under immediate pressure to change and shifts later when the external pressure subsides (Brehm & Mann, 1975; T. D. Cook et al., 1979). (8) Another delayed-action explanation is that situational factors might impede the receiver's immediate acceptance of the position, with agreement emerging as that situation changes over time. (9) A temporal-inertia explanation (McGuire, 1960c, 1981a; see chapter 6 in this volume) predicts that a sinking-in interval is needed before a persuasive communication's implications seep to related issues, especially if the communication is at all subtle (D. Katz, Sarnoff, & McClintock, 1956), as in Riley and Pettigrew's (1976) finding of a delayed-action impact of the Martin Luther King assassination on European-Americans' attitudes toward African-Americans. (10) Incubation-of-anxiety spread sometimes shown in verbal conditioning studies (Mednick, 1957) may be a related mechanism, reflecting a gradual spread of affect. (11) A "Bartlett effect" explanation (Papageorgis, 1963) is that, when a persuasive message argues for its position with qualifications and reservations, then recall for the incidental qualifications may decay rapidly, allowing the impact of the central point to manifest itself more sharply over time. (12) In the cluttered communication context, an issue on which there is initial resistance to change may gradually be assimilated to the bulk of the issues on which there are immediate changes (Leippe, Greenwald, & Baumgardner, 1982). As compared with these dozen explanations lying in wait to account for delayed-action effects, empirical corroborations are rare and slight.

FUTURE DIRECTIONS: PROMISING OUTPUT VARIABLES REGARDING HOW PERSUASION WORKS

[The following section is adapted from W. J. McGuire, 1994b, Using mass media communication to enhance public health, in L. Sechrest et al. (Eds.), *Effective dissemination of clinical health information,* pp. 125–51 (Rockville, MD: Public Health Service).]

Invitation to a Forecasting

When one becomes a recognized expert in an area one is asked not only to review what has been done but also to identify topics with a promising future (McGuire, 1966a, 1976b, 1976d, 1994b). Prognosis is useful to public and private granting agencies such as the National Science Foundation and the Marketing Research Institute in identifying research topics especially deserving of encouragement and support. When asked in 1991 to identify promising lines of research relevant to persuading people to adopt more healthful life-styles, I conducted a tour of the horizon, identifying dozens of promising persuasive communication topics, organized in terms of the well-known input/output model of the communication-persuasion process (see Table 5.1). The output side of the persuasion process (depicted as the row titles in Table 5.1) is a series of successive mediating steps by which persuasion occurs, including the audience's successively being exposed to the persuasive material, attending to it, and so on, through agreeing with its position, and acting on this agreement, and so on, and on to postaction steps such as ideological consolidation and proselytizing others. The input side of the communication/persuasion matrix, shown as the column headings in Figure 5.1, are the categories and subcategories of communication variables out of which persuasive campaigns can be constructed, the five broad categories being source, message, channel, audience, and target (or, interrogatively, "Who says what, via which medium, to whom, regarding what"). First I shall identify several dozen promising output (row) topics, in five groups, which provide insights into how persuasion works, and then identify a second set of several dozen promising input topics, that is, with the classes of variables (source, message, channel, audience, and target) shown as the major column headings in Table 5.1, out of which one can construct the communication to enhance its persuasive impact.

Promising Research Issues Having to Do with How People Use the Media

Advertisers and other media people have long recognized the need to know more about how people behave while being exposed to the mass media, but it is expensive and intrusive to "watch people watching television." Advertisers' growing dissatisfaction with Nielsen ratings, which simply measure whether someone's television set is turned on and tuned to a given channel, or whether a panel member's diary logs an exposure, has led to the development of new procedures, but these tend to evoke resistance, at least initially. I shall single out three promising issues.

The divided-attention issue. When people's television sets are turned on they are also doing numerous things besides viewing (D. R. Anderson, 1985). Basic research indicates that high levels of such distraction can lower persuasive impact by interfering with the encoding of the persuasive material; on the other hand, moderate levels of distraction may enhance impact by allowing the basic message to get through but interfering with the audience's counterarguing against the persuasive material. Current work on mood suggests that persuasive impact will be influenced by the affective quality of the distraction. A pleasant concurrent activity such as eating and drinking adds to persuasive impact (Janis, Kaye, & Kirschner, 1965; O'Quin & Aronoff, 1981), and an unpleasant mood (such as recalling a troubling event or loss of self-esteem) can reduce message impact (Zellner, 1970). It pays to get one's message on the tube when the viewer is likely to be mellowed by quaffing a can of beer or watching a pleasant program.

Channel surfing and selection.   Viewers engage in a high level of channel switching: 30% of watchers change channels at the beginning of a commercial break, suggesting that public health messages, now usually presented in public service announcements shown during commercial breaks, should rather be incorporated into the program itself (Geller, 1989; McGuire, 1984b; Piotrow et al., 1990). We need to know more about who controls the remote when several viewers are present and how to rivet that person.

Social contexts of media exposure.   Data suggest that people are more persuaded (but, puzzlingly, like the source less) when exposed to a message when they are alone rather than watching with other people present (Keating & Latané, 1976), even when these others are noninteracting strangers, as if resistance-conferring solidarity develops automatically within a watching group. Research is needed on the mechanisms involved and on whether the immunizing effect of others' presence is magnified when the others are familiars, such as family members. Health ads may be more effective when aired during programs shown at hours when viewing is solitary (e.g., late-night movies). More complex than the passive presence of others is the effect of interacting others: Do comments of parents watching with the child enhance the prosocial and lessen the antisocial impacts of programs and commercials (J. L. Singer & D. Singer, 1981)?

Promising Issues Having to Do with Paths and Mediators of the Persuasive Impact

Multiple paths.   There are multiple pathways to persuasion, each involving a different subset of mediating processes among those listed in the rows of Table 5.1. Three pathway issues particularly deserve research attention. Multistep central routes to persuasion, involving the whole complex chain of behaviors shown in Table 5.1, would be used to the extent that the audience feels vitally concerned. Petty and Cacioppo (1986a) and Chaiken (1980) have shown that certain variables (e.g., argument strength) are more important in central multistep processing of highly involving topics, while other variables (e.g., source credibility) are more important with quick-and-dirty shortcut paths used in peripheral processing of less important issues. Considering the heterogeneity of the at-risk population, one's set of health communications should be designed to have persuasive impact via both central and peripheral routes.

Sequences of mediating processes.   Paths to persuasion differ in regard to not only which of the Table 5.1 steps are involved but also the order in which the steps are performed. In the perceptual distortion and selective exposure phenomena, Step 7 would precede Step 4 and Step 2, in that the person's attitude on the communication's conclusion determines what arguments the person learns from the message or whether the person attends to the message, rather than the commonsensical attention → learning → attitude order shown in Table 5.1. Dissonance theorists argue that Step 7 often precedes Step 11, in that people adjust their attitudes to justify their actions rather than adjusting their actions to accord with their attitudes. If, as Zajonc (1984) has argued against Lazarus (1984), the person reacts affectively to a message before he or she can report what the content says, then Steps 3 and 4 reverse, making health campaigns more difficult because high-risk people for whom the advice is unpleasant might be able to shut out the message before perceiving what it says.

Message recall and liking as mediators of persuasion.   The two mediating processes in terms of which practitioners usually measure advertising effectiveness are Steps 3 and 4, ad liking and ad comprehension (recognition). These steps are far from the payoff action Step 11 (e.g., buying, voting, etc.), which is expensive and time-consuming to measure directly. Using the early Steps 3 and 4 as criteria for selecting ads may be a false economy. Step 11 may depend less on Step 4 (learning the information explicitly contained in the message) than Step 5 (evoking information already possessed by the recipient that is not explicitly mentioned in the message [Petty, Ostrom, & Brock, 1981]). Step 3, ad liking, is used by practitioners almost as much as ad comprehension as an index of persuasive effectiveness. That ads are selected on the basis of Steps 3 and 4 (ad liking and recall) may explain why more than half of all commercial ads use humor to enhance interest in and liking for the ad, even though humor may reduce agreement with the message.

Promising Research Issues Regarding Decision Processes in Persuasion

Topics under this heading have to do with how the decision to comply is evoked by a persuasive communication. Three promising decision-making topics deserve research.

Shortcut heuristics in making decisions. During the past half-century there have been three great leaps forward in selective biases and simplified approximations that people use in reasoning. Such "heuristics" serve as quick-and-dirty shortcuts that under usual conditions yield an approximation of the decision that would have been arrived at laboriously by making full use of all the available information within an elegant and exhaustive cognitive algebra (e.g., the full Subjective Expected Utility model). The first surge of interest in identifying such shortcuts in reasoning was shown by Woodworth and his colleagues in the 1930s (Woodworth & Sells, 1935), the second by W. J. McGuire (1960c), and the most recent by Tversky and Kahneman (1974). Sherman and Corty (1984) and Caverni, Fabre, and Gonzalez (1990) provide reviews of recently proposed cognitive heuristics such as availability, simulation, and anchoring and adjusting. The affirmational bias, people's underuse of cognitively negational information (but less so of affectively negative information), has been described by McGuire and McGuire (1992c). The operation of shortcut heuristics is likely to be particularly pronounced in health decision-making, where high risk and high uncertainty produce thought-distorting anxiety (Covello, von Winterfeldt, & Slovic, 1990).

Remote ramifications of persuasive communications. The study of how persuasive communications affect the audience's attitudes, not only on the explicit issue, but also on unmentioned related issues, promises to throw light both on the persuasion process and on the structure and function of human thought systems (McGuire & McGuire, 1991c; see chapter 6 in this volume). These remote impacts spread across dimensions (e.g., from the likelihood to the desirability of an outcome) and especially across topics (from events to their consequences). This approach has led also to the internal method of persuasion which involves, not presenting the audience with new information from an outside source, but rather using Socratic questioning or directed-thinking tasks to enhance the salience of information already within the audience's cognitive field (McGuire & McGuire, 1991c; chapter 6 in this volume). These considerations show the importance of work on the public's implicit biology (i.e., people's delusional systems about how the body works, the nature of illness and recovery, etc.), which may, even in the educated public, be primitive in ways that have major implications for how health messages are processed by the public (Burbach & Peterson, 1986; Leventhal, Meyer, & Nerenz, 1980; Pennebaker, 1982).

Processes to supplement the basic decision model. The subjective expected utility (expectancy × value) model is often assumed to be the central subprogram within the decision process. To this core process different theorists add a variety of additional terms to depict a broader decision model. The theory of reasoned action (Fishbein & Ajzen, 1975) adds a "subjective norm" term; N. H. Anderson's (1981) cognitive algebra model adds an initial apperceptive mass term; Ajzen (1991) adds perceived behavioral control; Bentler and Speckart (1991) add past habits; Gorsuch and Ortberg (1983) add sense of moral obligation; Fazio (1990) adds definition of the situation; Bagozzi and Warshaw (1990) add attitude toward trying; Sheth (1974) suggests four kinds of additions, and Triandis (1980) seven. Many plausible add-on processes have not proved cost-effective in improving the predictive power of the model. Another elaboration of the model is tracing out alternative paths by which the attitudinal and decision processes relate to one another (e.g., attitudes may affect behavior via paths other than behavioral intention). The substantive work on multiple paths to persuasion (Chaiken, 1980; Petty & Cacioppo, 1986a) and methodological advances that use structural equation models to test among alternative paths (Bagozzi, 1982; Bentler & Speckart, 1979) promise to enrich the yield of this approach.

Promising Innovations in Measuring Output Processes

Progress in a field depends in part on improved measures of its dependent variables. Four types of currently promising advances in attitude-change measurement deserve mention.

Advances in physiological and nonverbal measures.   In the last 10 years there has been progress in the use of physiological indices (Wagner & Manstead, 1989) to measure attitudes and persuasive impact, for example, the Cacioppo and Petty (1983) work using computer analysis of facial musculature (EMG); the Janick, Goldberg, and Wellens (1983) work monitoring autonomic cardiovascular responses such as pulse rate and amplitude; and Alwitt's (1985) use of electroencephalographic (EEG) indices such as type and location of brain waves, including hemispheric lateralization (Olson & Ray, 1989; Reeves, Lang, Thorson, & Rothschild, 1989). Improved recording and theorizing and the availability of computer analyses that untangle complexly interrelated sets of indices (e.g., facial EMG, PET, and magnetic resonance imaging) have made research on physiological indices sufficiently promising to warrant a decade of funding.

Research has flourished recently on using nonverbal behavior both to induce and to measure attitude change, but only the latter is pertinent here. People are highly sensitive to others' nonverbal cues, both intended and unintended (Rosenthal, Hall, DiMatteo et al., 1979). Friedman, DiMatteo, and Mertz (1980) have shown that the facial expressions of TV news readers can reveal their attitudes about the persons and events on which they are reporting. Vocalic (prosodic) nonverbal cues, as well as visual ones, can be used to interpret the speaker's attitudes (Frick, 1985).

Because research on physiological and nonverbal indices is expensive, it would be cost-effective to establish a few accessible regional laboratories at major research universities near major airports, to be shared with outsiders. Each laboratory would have recording stations for simultaneously monitoring several dozen audience members in regard to physiological indices, along with lighting and cameras capable of videotaping speakers and audience members. The latter would be provided with sophisticated multichannel graduated response levers. The laboratory computers would be programmed to provide complex stimuli keyed to ongoing analyses of multiple streams of data.

Advances in questionnaire measures.   Despite all the high-tech developments on (or over) the horizon, attitude questionnaires are likely to continue to be the quotidian workhorse measure of attitudes. Three current lines of advance on opinionnaires have promise: (*a*) question wording, (*b*) question ordering, and (*c*) the kind of response options allowed.

(*a*) Slight variations in the wording of survey items can sizably affect responses; for example, although 40% of members of the American public would "not allow" public speeches against democracy, only 20% would "forbid" such speeches (Schuman & Presser, 1981), an asymmetry that may reflect affirmational bias (McGuire & McGuire, 1992c). More empirical and theoretical analyses are needed to account for some large effects of what seem like small changes of wording.

(*b*) Effects of prior questions on the responses to later questions were first studied in the theory-guided work on the Socratic effect (McGuire, 1960c), but even atheoretical, routine counterbalancing of the ordering of questions in surveys has shown that at least four factors affect how the attitudinal response to an item can vary sizably as a function of which questions preceded it (Tourangeau & Rasinski, 1988). Because this work on question-context effects has theoretical and practical relevance in both cognitive and social psychology, and can sometimes be done economically by secondary analysis of available data, the current research enthusiasm deserves to continue.

(*c*) Some progress has been made recently on improving questionnaire items by presenting better response options to the audience, for example, by using more pertinent labels with "thermometer" or probability-type scales (Wilcox, Sigelman, & Cook, 1989; Krosnick & Berent, 1993). It seems better to label the response levels fully rather than partially, and with numerical rather than verbal labels (Jaffe-Katz, Budescu, & Wallsten, 1989). The old question of which expressions serve best as labels for different levels of subjective probability has been investigated further by Reagan, Mosteller, and Youtz (1989) and by Hamm (1991).

Progress in reducing artifact distortions. Even survey researchers recognize that questionnaire measures are distorted by artifacts arising both from these instruments per se and from their administration. Identifying and reducing these artifacts is progressing on three fronts: (*a*) how to use "Don't know" responses; (*b*) how to adjust for refusals to participate; and (*c*) how to handle interviewer effects. Issue (*a*) arises because respondents report attitudes even on topics to which they have given no thought, which decreases validity and reliability

(Converse, 1970). Employing filter questions that invite "Don't know" responses does, as hoped, increase by 20% the use of that option (Bishop, Oldendick, & Tuchfarber, 1983) but may not yield more valid response measures (Poe, Seeman, McLaughlin, Mehl, & Dietz, 1988; Goldsmith, 1989). More work is needed on the comparative utility of using various in-between response options such as "No opinion," "Not sure," and "Neutral," or "Ambivalently conflicted" (Duncan & Stenbeck, 1988) and on whether there is something special about the neutral midpoint on a scale that inhibits crossovers (Fishbein & Lange, 1990).

(*b*) Advertising and marketing researchers are bothered by the overall refusal-to-participate rate of about 38% (National Steering Committee, 1986; Coleman, 1991a). It was biased response rate rather than biased sampling that caused the infamous *Literary Digest* error in the 1936 U.S. presidential forecast (Squire, 1988). Response rates to mail surveys can be raised by a variety of devices (Fox, Crask, & Kim, 1988) but basic researchers have neglected the topic because of its lack of theory relevance, although it may attract interest due to its relation to the fashionable research on "compliance-gaining" tactics (Cialdini, 1993).

(*c*) Survey researchers' perennial worry about interviewer bias currently focuses on minority ethnic groups, as when New Mexican Spanish versus English speakers make different use of the "Don't know" response option (Briggs, 1986). B. A. Anderson, Silver, and Abramson (1988) have shown that, in national election surveys, African-American respondents exaggerate their voting rate more and then actually vote more often when interviewed by African-Americans than by European-Americans. Training of interviewers can improve response validity (Billiet & Loosveldt, 1988). Research on interviewer effects promises marginal improvements and lacks glamour for basic researchers but is cost-effective when studied as methodological add-ons to ongoing research or by secondary analysis of archived survey data.

New technologies for measuring independent and dependent variables. Periodically small high-tech companies in science parks announce new gadgets under development (e.g., eyeglasses that record and transmit continuously what the person is watching, wristwatches that measure exposure to magazine advertisements by recording transmissions from microchips embedded in the pages). Step 11, purchasing behavior, is now measured by high-tech supermarket cash registers that provide scanner data identifying each purchase as regards product, brand, size, and price, along with the date, hour, and place of purchase. These data can be transmitted from a sample of checkout counters to a central computer, where they can be related to previous hours' product advertisements in the region. Even health campaigns can be so evaluated when their target behavior is use or nonuse of products carried in supermarkets (e.g., campaigns urging the purchase of low-salt variants, dental floss, or condoms; or urging nonpurchase of beer, cigarettes, or junk food).

Promising Statistical Advances

Two analysis topics deserve mention as particularly promising for the near future. Meta-analysis allows aggregating slight relations obscured by noise in individual studies (Eagly & Carli, 1981; Bornstein, 1989a), but it may be hypersensitive. I used to joke that however strong a relation really is, behavioral science methods can manage not to detect it; now meta-analysis has provoked the contrary worry: that no relation is so weak in the environment that meta-analysis will fail to report it as significant. Hence, effect-size estimates should be included routinely in meta-analysis. A second promising mode of analysis is using structural equation models to test alternative causal paths among multiple input and output variables in the persuasion process (Bagozzi, 1982; Breckler, 1984).

FUTURE DIRECTIONS: PROMISING INPUT VARIABLES REGARDING WHAT ENHANCES PERSUASIVE IMPACT

The vast amount of research done on input variables that make communications more persuasive is unmanageable unless it is organized in some conceptual framework such as source, message, channel, receiver (or audience), and destination (or target) variables, each of which can be further subdivided, as shown in the Table 5.1 column headings. I shall here single out from each of these five broad categories a few variables that are especially deserving of further research.

Source Variables That Affect Persuasive Impact

The conventional analysis of perceived source variables. Three main categories of source variables – credibility, attractiveness, and power – are usually presented as enhancing persuasive impact via three processes, internalization, identification, and compliance, respectively (Kelman, 1958). The source's credibility derives from her or his seeming expert and trustworthy, that is, knowing the facts on the topic and reporting them honestly. Perceived expertise derives from such variables as the source's general education level, familiarity with the subject matter, and speaking in an authoritative tone; whereas perceived trustworthiness derives from such variables as the source's general reputation for honesty, being in a trustworthy profession, not standing to profit personally from convincing the audience, and emitting honest-appearing nonverbal cues. The source's attractiveness derives from variables such as her or his pleasantness, beauty, familiarity, and similarity. The source's perceived power derives from her or his perceived control over the audience's rewards and punishments, apparent desire for the audience's compliance, and ability to scrutinize the extent of this compliance.

Most research on source (and other) variables in persuasion uses such obvious analyses (e.g., it is hypothesized that physical attractiveness enhances liking for the source and therefore persuasive impact). Similarly plausible and prosaic analyses guide persuasive research on communication variables in the other four input categories (message, channel, audience, and target), leading to fairly obvious hypotheses. Such codified common sense is not nothing. It is better than uncodified common sense or codified nonsense; still, in Hollywoodese, it is good but not great.

Elsewhere (McGuire, 1983a, 1989b, 1997b) I have described dozens of discovery techniques that empirical researchers can use to go beyond demonstrating such banalities. Eight such creative techniques will be used here to generate interesting hypotheses about source effects in persuasion. (1) One can partition an obvious independent variable such as source–audience similarity into subvariables, as in the controversy between Rokeach and Triandis on whether the source's ideological or demographic similarity enhances persuasive impact the more. (2) One can conjecture multiple conflicting mediators of the relation (e.g., source similarity increases perceived likability but decreases perceived expertise, as in Brock, 1965a). (3) One can subdivide the dependent variable, as when one analyzes how source power affects differently public versus private attitude change. (4) Alternative mediational theories can be used to derive distinctive interaction effects that intensify the banal relation (see chapter 12). (5) One can conjecture alternative and reciprocal causal connections (e.g., among liking, similarity, and familiarity of the source as they affect and are affected by attitude change and by one another). (6) The quantitative parameters of the relation can be provocative, as when one investigates whether source similarity works as a cue or a reinforcer by examining whether issue importance affects the intercept or slope of the relation between similarity and persuasive impact. (7) More dramatically, one can assert the contrary of a banality and conjecture circumstances in which this counterintuitive contrary would obtain. (8) One can redefine the independent variable in novel ways (e.g., defining source attractiveness in terms of overlooked nonverbal or physical beauty indices). Rather than extending this list of eight, I shall describe the last two discovery techniques in more detail.

Reversing commonsense source-persuasion relations. The seventh of the novelty-enhancing techniques just mentioned, asserting the contrary to an obvious relation and conjecturing contexts in which this contrary might obtain, can be used with each of the three usual banal source variables – trustworthiness, likability, and power. As regards source credibility, revealing the source's persuasive intent in advance is typically predicted to lower persuasion by reducing the source's perceived trustworthiness. However, the contrary hypothesis, that disclosing the source's persuasive intent will enhance persuasive impact, is also plausible. This counterintuitive prediction might obtain, for example, in anticipatory belief change situations where the audience, fearful of appearing gullible, will, when forewarned of a persuasive attack, shift their opinion to the source's position even before receiving the persuasive communication (McGuire & Millman, 1965c; McGuire, 1969c; see chapter 3 in this volume). Forewarning might also enhance persuasive impact by clarifying the point of an abstruse message and in situations where the audience are trying to ingratiate themselves with an attractive or powerful source (Mills & Aronson, 1965).

In regard to source attractiveness, the contrary of the usual banal relation calls for conjecturing contexts in which the less attractive source is the more persuasive, as in the "insufficient justification" grasshopper-eating experiments (Zimbardo et al., 1965). In regard to source power also, one can hypothesize many conditions where the paradoxical contrary obtains, in that the source's perceived power decreases persuasiveness, for example, in the minority influence phenomenon (Moscovici, 1985); or when having a large number of sources backfires when one's arguments are weak (Petty & Cacioppo, 1986a); or the "dominating through weakness" phenomenon, when the source has a stigmatizing handicap; or when the "my hands are tied" ploy can gain acceptance of one's position better than does being perceived as having more discretionary power. My perspectivist theory of knowledge (McGuire, 1983a, 1989b; chapter 12 in this volume) encourages these reversal-of-commonsense exercises by pointing out that all propositions, even contradictory ones, are false and therefore all are occasionally true under specifiable circumstances.

Sources' nonverbal cues that contribute to persuasiveness. The eighth of the above-listed ways of going beyond the obvious calls for using more novel manipulations of the independent variable, for example, using nonverbal cues to manipulate source credibility, likableness, or power. One might start with a tree-diagram dividing nonverbal cues into visual versus vocalic; then subdividing visual cues into facial cues, posture, movement (kinesics, including touching), closeness (or proxemics), and dress (adornment); and subdividing vocalic (prosodic) cues into speed of speech, tone, inflections, fluency, and nonsemantic components. Partial definitions of the source variables in terms of nonverbal cues can enhance the interestingness even of the old banal prediction that source likability increases persuasive impact, for instance, defining likability as percent of time the source maintains eye contact. More interesting advances come when one identifies contradictory meanings of the nonverbal cue (e.g., the audience perceiving the source's eye contact not only as indicating liking but also as threatening or distrusting) and so produces a net nonmonotonic relation with most persuasive impact occurring at intermediate levels of eye contact, the exact shape of the relation depending predictably on personal and situational interaction variables. The nonverbal cue areas are rich in reversals of the banal suppositions, as when the hackneyed hypothesis that the "fast-talking used car salesman" is perceived as untrustworthy is reversed by the empirical finding that faster speakers are perceived as more expert and even more trustworthy and produce more attitude change (Miller et al., 1976).

Sources' physical appearance and persuasiveness.   The eighth of the above-listed ways for going beyond banality, novel redefinition of the hackneyed independent variable, can be illustrated also by taking the trite hypothesis that the source's beauty enhances persuasive impact and defining beauty more provocatively in terms of averaging and neoteny. Surprisingly, faces appear beautiful to the extent that they approximate the average human face: When digitized individual faces are mathematically averaged, the resulting composite is judged as increasingly attractive the greater the number of individual faces that went into the composite, even aggregating across sex (Langlois, Roggman, & Musselman, 1994). Novelty may also hide in the details. The source can improve upon nature by personal embellishments of various sorts, as when perceived attractiveness goes up with formality of costume, perhaps more for female than for male observers (Townsend & Levy, 1990), and by females' use of cosmetics, although this may affect male viewers more than it does females (Cash, Dawson, Davis et al., 1989). Flashing a smile is a cheaper and surer way of enhancing perceived attractiveness (Reis et al., 1990).

The neoteny-maturity variable also has interesting effects on perceived source beauty and persuasibility. In humans, as in other mammals, the proportionate sizes and shapes of features differ between infant and adult faces; infantile features are particularly appealing to adults, presumably because they reflect the evolutionary survival value of having the dependent neonate elicit the parent's nurturant behavior. Mammalian infantile features differ from mature ones by having large eyes-to-face ratio, small rounded chin, nonprominent cheekbones, bulging forehead, and slight eyebrows. This configuration is closer to the adult female than to the adult male face; and adult female faces tend to be judged as more attractive and adult male faces as less attractive to the extent that they approximate the neonatal configuration. Because faces that stay closer to the neonatal shape are judged less dominant, female faces that are perceived as more dominant are also perceived as less attractive (Keating, 1985). Neotenous (and therefore female) faces are perceived as less expert but more trustworthy (Brownlow & Zebrowitz, 1990) and so will make a source more persuasive when delivering a message whose acceptance depends on perceived trustworthiness and less persuasive when it depends on perceived expertise.

Sources' group characteristics and persuasiveness. My distinctiveness theory of perception (McGuire, 1984a; McGuire & Singer, 1976a; see chapter 8 in this volume) predicts on purely cognitive grounds that, as one's society becomes more diverse (e.g., more ethnically integrated), the diversity characteristic will become more salient in one's sense of self. This "us-them" distinctiveness may become an "us-versus-them" divisiveness, characterized by ingroup favoring and solidarity and by outgroup distancing and homogenization (Campbell, 1965), positions adopted also by social identity theory (Tajfel, 1982) and self-categorization theory (Turner et al., 1987). Thus, as the society becomes more diverse (integrated) on ethnicity (or other demographic characteristics), source-audience similarity on the characteristic increasingly affects persuasiveness. Distinctiveness theory predicts (McGuire, McGuire, Child, & Fujioka, 1978a) that the source's ethnicity has less effect on majority audiences than on minority ethnics (Banks, Stitt, Curtis, & McQuater, 1977; Clore, Bray, Itkin, & Murphy, 1978; Ramirez, 1977).

I've considered this first "source" class of communication inputs to the persuasion campaign in some detail to demonstrate how the usual trite hypotheses (e.g., "source's likability increases persuasive impact") can be made more interesting by a variety of cognitive transformations. These same interest-enhancing transformations can be applied to the next four classes of inputs (message, channel, audience, target), but details will be left to the reader as an exercise.

Message Variables That Affect Persuasive Impact

Promising message variables come from such subcategories as the kind of arguments used, type of motivational appeals, style of presentation, what is included versus what is omitted, how the included material is ordered, amount of persuasive material, and how discrepant from the audience's initial position is the position urged. I shall single out currently promising variables in selected subcategories.

The structure of argument. Assuming that attitudes are organized into systems (see McGuire, 1960c, 1989a; and chapter 6 in this volume) a persuasive communication that deals explicitly with one topic is likely to have remote ramifications also on unmentioned related topics. It should be possible also to change attitudes, not only by presenting new information from an outside source, but also by increasing the salience of information already within the audience's own cognitive system by a directed thinking task or by Socratic questioning. Basic research and applied persuasion campaigns have neglected these persuasion-from-within possibilities and remote persuasive impacts on related but unmentioned issues.

The relative persuasiveness of different types of arguments fascinated the classical rhetoricians: Aristotle's *Rhetoric* lists 38 types of arguments in just one category, and Cicero and Quintilian list many additional ones; but modern empirical researchers have neglected their study. Both cognitive and social psychology would be advanced by going beyond simple compliance-gaining tactics (e.g., foot-in-the-door, door-in-the-face, low-balling, etc.), as reviewed by Cialdini (1993), to studying how argument structure affects message impacts.

Types of appeals. I have identified (McGuire, 1985a, 1991b; see chapter 5 in this volume) as many as 16 types of motives to which persuasion campaigns (e.g., against substance abuse) can appeal, but the current experimental work is confined almost entirely to threat appeals, which is high in both theoretical interest and relevance to public health campaigns (Covello, von Winterfeldt, & Slovic, 1990). Two advances have suggested new complexities in this issue. The "message-framing" approach that grew out of Kahneman and Tversky's (1982) prospect theory asserts that people are risk-aversive in choosing among positively framed alternatives and risk-seeking in choosing among negatively framed alternatives, but the empirical results have been mixed (Maheswaran & Meyers-Levy, 1990). The other innovation has come from work on positive-negative asymmetry (Peeters, Czapinski, & Lewicka, 1991), where McGuire and McGuire (1992c) have analyzed cognitive versus affective components of positive-negative asymmetries (see chapter 9 in this volume).

Message style variables: Figurative language. Stylistic variables (e.g., message clarity, forcefulness, literalness, humorousness, etc.) have been surprisingly neglected in empirical research, except for the "vividness" hodgepodge (Taylor & Thompson, 1982) variable of arguing by factual examples versus abstract principles (Reyes, Thompson, & Bower, 1980). Literal versus figurative language is a promising style variable. Classical rhetoricians reported that metaphorical language adds to persuasive impact, but differed on whether the mechanism was perceived source expertise, positive mood, depth of meaning, or enhanced attention. More research is needed on the mechanisms by which similes and metaphors enhance persuasiveness (Bowers & Osborn, 1966) and on the mechanisms by which the many alternative figures of speech (Lanham, 1991) affect impact (McGuire, NIMH proposal, 1992).

Message style variables: Persuasive effects of humor.   Among style variables, humor deserves special attention. Half of radio and television advertisements employ humor, and there are numerous theorized mechanisms for why humor should enhance persuasive impact by increasing source attractiveness, attention to the message, retention, and mood positivity. Humor thus deserves to have considerable impact, but empirical support is surprisingly weak in showing humor's hypothesized main, interactional, or mediational impacts on persuasion (Markiewicz, 1974; Brown & Bryant, 1983; Scott, Klein, & Bryant, 1990). Humor's surprisingly poor track record in past research is no laughing matter and demands more study.

Effects of repetition on persuasion.   Length and repetition of persuasive communications are of great practical importance because costs of producing and especially of broadcasting ads increase almost rectilinearly with their length and number of showings. Sometimes persuasive impact increases with up to a dozen exposures (Eaton, 1996), but repetition of an ad (even in varied form) more often yields diminishing returns, asymptoting after three to five receptions (Cacioppo & Petty, 1979; Calder & Sternthal, 1980), perhaps because continuing presentations of the ads tend to evoke more negative thoughts (relative to positive) about the product (McCullough & Ostrom, 1974). The elaboration-likelihood model (Petty & Cacioppo, 1986b) and the minority-influence work (Kruglanski & Mackie, 1990) raise the possibility that repetition can, under specifiable conditions such as weak arguments, actually reduce persuasive impact.

Drastic methods of persuasion.   Drastic methods of persuasion such as hypnosis (Gheorghiu et al., 1991), brainwashing (Barker, 1984), and subliminal messages (Belay & Shevrin, 1988; Bornstein, 1989b; Hardaway, 1990; Janiszewski, 1990; Greenwald, 1991; Brannon &

Brock, 1994) seem hothouse laboratory curiosities rather than practically worrisome modes of influence in the natural environment. To the degree that they could be persuasive in society, they raise ethical questions that go beyond those raised by social influence in general, as discussed in chapter 11 of this volume.

Channel Variables That Affect Persuasive Impact

Comparative media effects are of crucial interest to practitioners but are largely neglected by basic researchers because of low theoretical relevance. There is little evidence that any one medium has a generally greater persuasive impact, so comparative media effects are probably best sought in interactions rather than in main effects (Chaiken & Eagly, 1983). Full-court-press multimedia campaigns to induce whole communities to adopt more healthful life-styles, like the Stanford three-city and five-city studies (Flora, Maccoby, & Farquhar, 1989), may provide suggestive data on channel issues.

Sparse evidence for intended and unintended television effects.   Network executives and other friends of television, and its enemies, and relatively neutral academic researchers on the topic, all seem agreed, if on nothing else, on the proposition that television has major impacts on the viewing public. Yet my review of the findings (McGuire, 1986b, 1989d; see chapter 5 in this volume) yields surprisingly weak evidence that television has massive impact either on its intended targets (commercial ads' effects on buying, political ads' effects on voting, etc.) or on its unintended effects (program violence effects on viewer aggression, biased portrayals on viewer stereotypes, etc.). Chapter 5 also presents five classes of excuses that might salvage belief in ubiquitous massive media impacts.

Context effects.   The United States has entered an information age when the ten mass media transmit trillions of words each year, growing at an annual rate of 9%, whereas per capita communication consumption has grown at only 1% per year (Pool, 1983), a disparity suggesting that there are defenses against being inundated (Graber, 1984). Information overload raises a "more is less" specter, that the vast number of messages impinging upon the audience may produce a dazzle effect that diminishes, not just average, but total impact (Malhotra, 1984). Another context effect arises when health ads or political appeals are presented during breaks in entertainment or information programs whose contents may affect processing of the ad. For example, there is sometimes a contrast effect such that attractive sources used in the ads may appear less attractive when the ad is presented embedded within a program with even more attractive actors (Kenrick et al., 1994); and sometimes there is an opposite assimilation effect such that the ad source appears more attractive by being assimilated toward the even more attractive actors in the program (Geiselman, Haight, & Kimata, 1984). The program context may influence also the audience's moods or cognitions about people in ways that affect the persuasive impact of the inserted ad (Hornstein et al., 1975; Krugman, 1983). Advertisers should give more thought to the programs in which their ads are placed; indeed, health campaigners should consider presenting their message within the program itself rather than confining it to the commercial breaks (e.g., an appropriate character in the show might be depicted as incidentally going for a mammogram, rather than presenting a PSA during the program break urging the viewer to get a mammogram; McGuire, 1984b; Piotrow et al., 1990).

Another context consideration is the distracting situational clutter in which many persuasive messages are presented, which might either enhance or reduce the message's persuasive impact. If the viewer is engaged in some pleasant concurrent activity, such as eating and drinking, the persuasive impact of a communication tends to be enhanced (Janis, Kaye, & Kirschner, 1965), whereas being in a negative mood can decrease persuasive impact. Incidental factors in the persuasion situation, such as ambient temperature or background music, may affect impact by cognitive or by affective processes (Gorn, 1982; Kellaris & Cox, 1989). Such situational clutter acts also as distraction, either enhancing persuasive impact when at moderate levels by reducing audience ability to counterargue, or reducing persuasive impact when it is so severe that it interferes with message reception. Appropriate research designs can untangle such complexities (Bless, Bohner, Schwarz, & Strack, 1990).

Audience Variables That Affect Persuasive Impact

My general theory. Persuasion campaigns aimed at large and varied audiences, like many public health campaigns, may require several components to reach varied subgroups. My general personality-persuasibility theory (McGuire, 1968a, 1968b, 1989e), summarized in chapter 3 of this volume, describes a half-dozen principles that constitute an axiomatic theory to account for correlates of susceptibility to social influence. The theory predicts that under a wide range of conditions many personal characteristics (e.g., age, intelligence, self-esteem, anxiety, etc.) will be related to persuasibility by an inverted-U nonmonotonic function, with maximum persuasibility occurring in people who are at intermediate levels on the variable. My multipostulate theory is complicated but, as Oscar Wilde wrote, the truth is never pure and rarely simple.

Special target groups.   Public policy and theoretical considerations have made the influenceability of certain age, sex, and ethnic groups of special interest. As regards age, some television critics have asserted that young children are particularly influenceable, but my mediational theory (see chapter 3) and empirical findings imply a nonmonotonic inverted-U shaped relation with maximum suggestibility occurring around age 9 (Eron, Huesmann, Brice et al., 1983), conformity maximizing at about age 12 (Costanzo & Shaw, 1966), and susceptibility to argumentation (e.g., in political campaigns) peaking somewhat later in adolescence (Krosnick & Alwin, 1989; Tyler & Schuller, 1991). The nonmonotonicity reflects opposing mediators: As people mature, their improving ability to understand what they are being told makes them more vulnerable to influence, but their decreasing tendency to agree with what they are told protects them from persuasion. The movement of the inflection point of maximum persuasibility to older ages as we go from suggestibility to conformity to persuasion reflects that these three kinds of influence place progressively more demand on comprehension, at which the older children are more competent than the younger, and less demand on agreement, to which younger children are more prone. More empirical work is needed, pitting these elegant nonmonotonic predictions against the usual assumption of a monotonically decreasing influenceability with age, chronological or mental.

With regard to audience's sex as it affects susceptibility to social influence, there is a formidable literature and considerable controversy. The bottom line (McGuire, 1968b, 1985a; Eagly, 1983) is that there is a slight sex difference such that, across conditions studied, women are slightly more influenceable than men, but it is unclear which of the output steps in Table 5.1 account for this slight difference – for example, women's higher comprehension (Step 4) or their higher tendency to agree (Step 7). More deserving of conceptual and empirical confrontation are interactions between sex and other communication variables (e.g., eye contact, formality of dress): A number of such variables affect influenceability oppositely in males as compared with females (Comadena, 1982; Cash, Dawson, Davis, et al., 1989; Orpen, 1989). Audience ethnic differences in persuasibility have been less studied than sex differences; any obtained differences may be due to ethnicity per se or to ethnicity's being accidentally confounded with such variables as education, status, and numerical preponderance.

Target Variables That Affect Persuasive Impact

Beliefs versus attitudes versus behaviors.   Regarding the impacts of communication input variables on beliefs versus attitudes versus behaviors, there tend to be positive correlations among the three but they are of discouragingly low magnitude. Future researchers should take a more systemic approach and look for molar rather than molecular correspondences (McGuire, 1989a; chapter 10 in this volume) between attitude and action systems. Causal models promise to untangle multiple direct and indirect paths among these three components and other components in the system (Bagozzi, 1982; Breckler, 1984).

Persistence of persuasive impact.   Both practitioners and basic researchers assume that the attitude change induced by a persuasive communication is at a maximum immediately after the audience receives the communication, after which the induced change decays progressively as time passes, perhaps traversing a negatively accelerated curve. As pointed out earlier in this chapter, one can identify a dozen situations where there may be an opposite delayed-action effect rather than the usually assumed temporal decay of persuasive impact with time passage.

Inducing resistance to persuasion.   McGuire (1964b; chapter 2 of this volume) discussed numerous procedures for inducing resistance to subsequent persuasive attacks (e.g., prior commitment, anchoring, pretraining, inoculation, etc.), which deserve more research, for both their practical and their theoretical implications. I have in this last "inputs" section selected some especially promising independent variables from each of the five major communication components (source, message, channel, audience, and target), singling out variables that have been shown by recent research either to be ready for application to public health or to be promising enough to warrant research support. Fuller discussions of them are conveniently available elsewhere (McGuire, 1985a, 1994b; Eagly & Chaiken, 1993).

5

Developing Effective Persuasion Campaigns

Most attitude-change work done by myself (chapters 2 and 3) and by others (chapter 4) is basic research undertaken for relevance to theory, but much of it has practical relevance as well, providing guidance for constructing persuasion campaigns in fields as diverse as advertising, marketing, politics, law, religion, and public health. I have often been consulted about such campaigns, by the marketing and media sectors in the 1960s and 1970s and by the public health sector in the 1980s and 1990s. This consultation usually produced in-house reports but has resulted also in some practical-application publications, often on how the findings of basic attitude-change research can be applied to designing more effective public health persuasion campaigns. Some of these publications were tailored to a specific topic, such as prevention of harmful addictions (McGuire, 1970b, 1974d, 1991b, 1992d, 1995) or improved nutrition (McGuire, 1982c), while others were more general regarding explicit target (McGuire, 1966a, 1971, 1976b, 1977c, 1978b, 1980b, 1980f, 1981c,1982b, 1984b, 1986g, 1989f, 1994b). Others were on tangential issues, such as how to search the attitude-change literature more cost-effectively (McGuire, 1978c, 1978d), the modest evidence for mass media impact (1974e, 1976d, 1986b, 1988b, 1992a), or the design of warning labels on products (McGuire, 1980g). From these varied applied publications, 5 kinds of work will be discussed in this chapter: (1) institutional versus personal approaches to influencing the public; (2) my 7-step "RASMICE" procedure for developing a persuasion campaign; (3) the communication/persuasion matrix as a way of carrying out RASMICE Step 6, constructing the persuasive communication; (4) 16 partial views of the person, each suggesting appeals to be used in this Step 6 communication construction; and (5) evaluation of mass media impact size.

INSTITUTIONAL VERSUS PERSONAL
APPROACHES TO CHANGING ATTITUDES
AND BEHAVIOR

[Adapted with permission from W. J. McGuire, 1984b, Public communication as a strategy for inducing health-promoting behavioral change, in *Preventive Medicine, 13,* pp. 299–319. Copyright © 1984 by Academic Press.]

Biomedical and epidemiological research has identified numerous health problems and found promising solutions to some of them. Social and behavioral science research suggests two general strategies by which these medical solutions can be brought to bear on improving public health. The first strategy involves engineering the public's behaviors in a health-maintaining direction by making structural changes in society's institutional arrangements – for example, by banning products, prescribing their specifications, taxing their use, restricting their sales, and taxing their purchase. Policy studies can contribute to this institutional approach by identifying economic factors and regulatory processes that led to the banning of cigarette advertising on television, or by doing taxation studies on the price elasticity of cigarette purchases (Murphy, 1980). A second, more person-focused strategy (and the one with which this chapter is mainly concerned) involves persuading individuals to exercise personal responsibility for their health by adopting more healthful life-styles, as when schools or the mass media are used to inform the public about dangers, motivate them to reduce risks, or acquaint them with health-promoting options available to them.

Some health problems, such as reducing environmental noise or water pollution, call mainly for the institutional approach. Others, such as obesity and accident-risking carelessness, call more for the second approach of encouraging individuals to take responsibility for maintaining their own health. Still other health risks are amenable to both approaches, as when cigarette smoking and alcohol abuse may be reduced both by the government's imposition of high taxes, restrictions on sales, or other deterrents, and also by educational campaigns to increase schoolchildren's motivation and ability to refrain from cigarette smoking or alcohol abuse. The next section discusses briefly the first institutional class of strategies whose implementation entails manipulating the policies of governmental and private institutions. Subsequent sections discuss more fully the second strategy of persuading individuals to take personal responsibility for adopting more healthful life-styles.

Punitive Strategies for Promoting Healthful Life-styles

Governmental punitive strategies. One way in which governments can reduce health risks is by imposing design specifications on manufacturers, as when seat belts, head supports, and air bags are mandated for automobiles. Toy and lawn mower manufacturers may be forbidden to market items with certain dangerous features, and some clothing, furniture, and building materials must be made fire-resistant. Government sometimes imposes self-protective behavior on the individual members of the public, for example, by requiring motorcyclists to wear helmets or car occupants to fasten seat belts. The government can reduce health risks in dangerous environments by regulating practices such as toxic waste disposal. Occupational injuries can be reduced both by legislating work-site modifications and by requiring injury-reducing behavior by the individual worker such as wearing hard hats, ear plugs, or goggles.

An extreme governmental punitive option is outright banning of health-threatening behaviors and products, such as the 1920s "noble experiment" by the U.S. federal government in prohibiting alcohol and, currently used by many governments, banning the use, sales, or possession of some addicting drugs (heroin, cocaine, etc.). Short of prohibiting alcohol sale or use, the government can prohibit automobile driving by those who have recently consumed more than a specified amount of alcohol. Of course, legislation is one thing and compliance is something else: When Glendower boasts, in *Henry IV, Part 1,* "I can call spirits from the vasty deep," Hotspur ripostes, "But will they come when you do call for them?" Laws may prohibit driving while intoxicated but the annual occurrence of over 25,000 alcohol-related highway deaths in the United States raises the question of whether the proscriptive legislation provides adequately for detection and discouragement through fines, license suspension, jail terms, or car confiscation. Short of outright banning, the government can also reduce health risks by impeding access to health-threatening products. Most governments have attempted to reduce alcohol consumption by restricting the hours, places, or amounts in which alcohol can be sold and the ages at which bought. In recent years many European and American governments have prohibited the advertising of cigarettes on the electronic and billboard media.

Another type of punitive option available to the government is to require health-promoting behaviors as a condition for the receipt of services, for example, forbidding school entry to uninoculated children. The state may also mandate health examinations and the correction of detected health problems as a condition for immigration, obtaining working papers, entering governmental employment, and holding food-handling jobs. The government's power to tax can also be used as a tool to channel behavior in healthful directions. "Sin" taxes on legal addictive substances not only raise revenue but also make use of the demonstrated price elasticity of substances such as cigarettes (Murphy, 1980).

A rapidly growing form of government regulation is mandating that products be labeled as regards their risks and benefits (Morris, Mazis, & Barofsky, 1980), thus disclosing to the public nutritional or undesirable ingredients in foods and the possible side effects of medications, and then leaving it to the individual to decide whether the benefits are worth the risks. Such a laid-back approach is in tune with the current popular "marketing economy" philosophy that risk ought to be managed by the individual. This informed-consent, laissez-faire philosophy contrasts with the more authoritarian banning approach popular during the 1960s when Establishment consensus favored governmentally imposed solutions, as manifested in the Delaney clause prohibiting the sale of foods containing any trace of any substance found to cause cancer in any animal. Still another governmental coercive option is legal regulation of health services, as in licensing medical and paramedical personnel, inspecting hospitals, certifying medical schools, monitoring pharmaceutical manufacturing, and requiring evidence of effectiveness and safety before allowing the marketing of new drugs.

Punitive strategies by nongovernmental organizations.   Governments tend to monopolize coercion and the power to inflict punishment, but a variety of "activist" private organizations have recently been using economic and other punitive sanctions available in the private sector to reduce health risks. For example, organizations opposed to advertising "junk" food or depicting violence on Saturday morning "kidvid" have used public-pressure campaigns against network officials, boycotts against advertisers, and petitions for FTC and FCC regulation. Private coercion has also been exerted by bringing class-action suits against environmental polluters or manufacturers of dangerous items; fear of costly litigation and settlements may induce private industry to take anticipatory precautions in the design and manufacture of their products or services. Also, private insurance companies can increase premiums for smokers or accident-prone drivers.

Private agencies may protect public health also by professional or industry self-regulation and policing, as when physicians' associations require a certain level of continuing education to certify the competence of their members, or when hospitals routinely do pathology tests or autopsies, or otherwise check the performance of individual staff members, or when industry members (often to forestall outside imposition) join in adopting a product safety code and inspection procedures to enforce it.

Promotive Strategies by Governmental and Nongovernmental Organizations

Institutional approaches to promoting public health may use the carrot as well as the stick. Contributing funds to support biomedical research is a positive institutional contribution to health maintenance, whose level has increased greatly in North America and Europe during the past 20 years, although it still represents only 2% of all expenditures for health. Earlier in the twentieth century private agencies had contributed a substantial proportion of biomedical research support, but increases in governmental funding in recent decades have turned many private health organizations into money-absorbing rather than money-dispersing institutions. Studies are needed of the cost effectiveness of biomedical research (Lewis, 1982), of how the structure and conditions of biomedical research institutes enhance their productivity (Andrews, 1979), and of the cognitive and motivational factors that promote creativity in the individual scientist (Stein, 1974, 1975; Goodfield, 1981; Hare, 1982). Public and private institutions can also improve the supply of trained health personnel by funding medical schools and supporting students, by developing curricula for training medical and paramedical personnel, and by improving certification procedures for evaluating training institutions, the individuals they employ, and the students they turn out. Volunteers can be trained in risk-reducing skills such as CPR and lifeguarding, and in relevant occupational skills (e.g., training restaurant workers to recognize choking symptoms and execute the Heimlich maneuver). Cost/benefit analyses of these various activities are needed, along with an overall program that organizes these many types of institutional approaches into coordinated, full-court, press public health campaigns.

Government and private agencies can enhance public health by supporting programs to provide nutritious school lunches and free clinics, by dispatching hypertension detection units to communities deficient in ordinary medical facilities, or by establishing blood and organ donation programs. Treatment facilities can be made more available by organizational lobbying to provide Medicare, Medicaid, private health insurance programs, or corporation self-insurance. Also useful are demonstration programs, such as regional arthritis centers sponsored by the National Institutes of Health, the MRFIT program, or private corporations' programs for detecting hypertension, reducing occupational health hazards, or treating alcoholism among their employees. Rather than expanding this list of punitive and supportive strategies available to governmental and private institutions for promoting public health, I shall discuss more fully the alternative strategy for promoting health and reducing risk – namely, education and persuasion campaigns aimed directly at the general public (or at high-risk subpopulations) to induce individuals to adopt more healthful life-styles.

THE "RASMICE" PROCEDURE FOR DEVELOPING INFLUENCE CAMPAIGNS

Public communication campaigns to induce individuals to adopt more healthful life-styles have had only modest success. Many campaigns have not been adequately evaluated, and studies with appropriate evaluations often reveal no appreciable health gains or, at best, gains that are statistically significant but have an effect size of doubtful cost-effectiveness. Encouraging preliminary results have been indicated by a few careful studies such as the Stanford Three-Cities Project (Maccoby & Alexander, 1980) and the Northern Karelia program in Finland (Puska et al., 1979), although their benefits need fuller evaluation relative to true costs.

Elsewhere (McGuire, 1980b) I have analyzed why public communication campaigns are likely to have limited effectiveness. For example, their impact on the desired health behavior depends on their eliciting a whole chain of a dozen responses (see Table 5.1), such as exposure to the health communication, attending to it, becoming involved in it, comprehending its contents, agreeing with what it says, retaining the agreement, and acting on the basis of it. Each of these responses has a modest probability of being elicited, so that the ultimate payoff in behavior compliance will be the very small product of multiplying a series of modest probabilities. Developing cost-effective communication campaigns thus requires heroic efforts, such as the seven-step procedure described here, given the acronym RASMICE: 1. Reviewing the realities; 2. Axiological analysis; 3. Surveying the sociocultural situation; 4. Mapping the mental matrix; 5. Isolating the issues; 6. Constructing the communication; and 7. Evaluating the effectiveness.

Step 1: Reviewing the Realities

The first step in developing a public health campaign is reviewing the biomedical and epidemiological research on health problems and solutions in order to assign priorities to proposed targets for a health-promoting communication campaign on the basis of three considerations: How serious is the health problem, how efficacious is the proposed solution likely to be, and to what extent can persuasive communications achieve this solution? Mounting a mass media campaign to urge people in the United States to add vitamins to their diet might not satisfy the first criterion because vitamin deficiency is not a widespread problem in the general public. A proposed campaign to teach Type-A personalities how better to handle stress may fail the second criterion because effective training programs for improving stress management may not be available. A television campaign counseling heroin addicts how to quit may fail the third criterion because quitting requires motivation, skill acquisition, and social support systems, not easily provided by mass media. Alternatively, an antiheroin campaign might better be aimed at prevention than cure, or might simply give a telephone number that could put the addict in touch with a treatment center.

The first criterion, assigning priorities on the basis of the seriousness of the health problems, calls for weighing the suggested problem by the number of people it affects and the extent to which it impairs functioning and causes suffering and other costs to the afflicted person and to the broader society. The biomedical and public health

Establishments have carried out such target evaluations (U.S. De partment of Health and Human Services, 1991). Hit lists of priority targets for public health campaigns need three reemphases: more consideration of (1) morbidity relative to mortality costs, (2) life-loss relative to lives-lost, and (3) initial causes rather than end outcomes in the causal chain leading to illness and death.

(1) The current overemphasis on mortality relative to morbidity is unwise, considering that prolonged serious morbidity may impose more human cost than does mortality. When a dreadful automobile accident kills one young person and permanently incapacitates another, both losses are catastrophic; however, although the death tends to evoke more dismay than the injury, the total social costs are likely to be greater for the injury. More attention should be paid to predisposing conditions like cigarette smoking and alcoholism that contribute diffusely to both mortality and morbidity. Alcoholics may be a long time dying from cirrhosis of the liver, but they live diminished lives, diminish the lives of others, and when they go may take others with them, as is indicated by the annual involvement of alcohol in 25,000 highway deaths and thousands of homicides and fire deaths each year. Chronic diseases like asthma and arthritis that cause much misery should be given more attention even though they lack the macabre glamour of appearing among the top ten "Leading Causes of Death."

(2) A second needed corrective is to give more weight to life-loss relative to lives-lost in determining priorities among competing health problems; that is, account should be taken of the average age at which various problems inflict mortality or morbidity costs on their victims. Cardiovascular disease and cancer cause many deaths but tend to strike victims at advanced ages when their life expectancies and likely further contributions to society are relatively small. Fewer lives are lost to accidents, suicides, homicides, and AIDS, but these deaths usually occur early in the victim's productive life, resulting in the loss of considerable life expectancy to the victim and of likely long service to society. Among people in their twenties, accidents cause ten times as many deaths as cancer and a hundred times more deaths than cardiovascular diseases. Suicides and homicides also vastly outweigh cardiovascular and cancer deaths among young people. Considering life-lost rather than lives-lost would alter priorities among public health campaign targets.

(3) A third needed corrective is to give more weight to earlier links in the chain of events terminating in illness and death. While treating

terminal diseases is useful, it would be more efficient to induce people to adopt healthful practices in childhood, such as increasing dietary calcium or not starting to smoke. Cohen and Lee (1979), in calculating how much life loss could be prevented by the achievement of various health goals, report that if all heart diseases were prevented life expectancy at birth would increase by six years, which is slightly less than would be gained by stopping males from smoking cigarettes. Eliminating all cancer would lengthen life expectancy by three years, appreciably less than could be added by weight reduction among those who are 30% overweight. The really formidable statistical health threat is being unmarried, single males living ten years less and single women four years less than those unwed (and this before AIDS). Hence, to increase life expectancy substantially one has only to eliminate heart disease or cancer; to increase life expectancy even more, one should eliminate cigarette smoking or obesity; but to really be a lifesaver one should go after the big one and open a marriage bureau. Of course, epidemiological statistics should not be interpreted so naively: The relation between marital status and life expectancy is probably bidirectional and due in part to their being coeffects of pre-existing physical conditions. Still, the life-style associated with being unmarried probably contributes to the ten-year shorter life span of single relative to married males. Death and the single man may deserve more attention than sex and the single man.

Social scientists can contribute to this initial step of reviewing the realities, especially in respect to the third criterion of judging whether the problem and the solution involve life-style changes that can be effectively produced by persuasive communications. Applying this criterion involves analyzing life-styles associated with the health threat, identifying changes that could reduce the risk, devising ways in which desired life-style changes could be effected, and judging the feasibility of mass media and other communication channels (e.g., school-based programs) for economically achieving the needed changes in life-style with a minimum of undesirable side effects. One takes into consideration several principles regarding the feasibility of behavioral change. Can the change be induced simply by providing information or must motivation also be supplied? The former is more achievable by mass communication than the latter. To what extent does compliance require skill acquisition and social support, thus lessening the suitability of a mass communication solution? Does the "psychographic profile" of the at-risk subpopulation include a focused pattern of media exposure, making it cost-effective to reach the high-risk population by a specifiable media mix?

Step 2: Axiological Analysis

Once a hit list of health problems has been assembled and given priorities on the basis of the three reality criteria just discussed in Step 1, the chosen targets should be subjected to an ethical appraisal that may modify some of the targets or alter the priority ordering. Such value analyses should consider the campaign's costs as well as benefits, its indirect unintended effects as well as its direct intended effects, its general psychological as well as specific physiological effects, and its effects on the broader society as well as on the target individuals. For example, before urging people to alter their life-styles by engaging in a jogging or other exercise program, one should weigh the health benefits to the physically underconditioned (e.g., weight loss, improved coronary blood supply, muscle tone, etc.) against possible health costs in knee injuries, muggings, dog bites, and automobile accidents. One should also consider the subtle, indirect benefits of the exercise (e.g., improving the person's general feeling of well-being, providing opportunities for pleasant social interactions, etc.) and indirect costs (e.g., guilt feelings when jogging leaves less time for one's family and work). Effects on the broader society must also be considered; for example, before trying to slow down Type-A executives, one should consider the cost to society of lessening the contributions of these highly productive workers. One has also to consider that the effects of communication campaigns can seldom be fine-tuned or monitored, so that a campaign to induce more physically active life-styles could become all too successful if jogging is taken up by people who should not engage in such heavy exercise or if it is adopted too suddenly, too vigorously. A campaign to reduce obesity must take care not to increase the incidence of bulimia in the already underweight, or to lower self-esteem or decrease social and economic opportunities for heavier people. Carrying out a value analysis calls for imagination, perspicacity, and objectivity.

In the ordering of RASMICE steps ethical examination has been placed early because it is important to consider ethical aspects before one gets so involved in the campaign that it becomes awkward to raise such issues, and when slight early modifications may correct the problem with little conflict or lost time. When moral qualms arise later it may leave one with such painful choices as insisting on laborious and disruptive campaign alterations, or an embarrassing withdrawal from it, or halfhearted and stressful continuation in an enterprise about which one feels ambivalent. Hence, an early value analysis of the campaign's goals is desirable. However, one should not, after this initial appraisal, lay one's ethical concerns to rest but rather should return to the ethical evaluation of both the means and the ends that are subsequently adopted as the campaign develops.

Step 3: Surveying the Sociocultural Situation

The purpose of this third step in designing a health-maintenance campaign is to study the at-risk people in their natural environment in order to identify situational circumstances that instigate and impede health-threatening life-styles, so identifying cost-effective points at which social influence can effectively redirect behavior into risk-reducing channels. Step 1 calls for wearing biomedical and epidemiological hats and Step 2 requires playing the philosopher, clergyman, or ethician; now, this third step calls for adopting anthropological and ecological techniques such as situational inventories, participant observation, use of informants, and market segmentation. In developing a smoking prevention campaign, the high school culture in which smoking begins might be studied by interviewing informants such as schoolteachers, principals, coaches, and the adolescents themselves, perhaps using peer leaders and "focus group" techniques, while recognizing that much of the obtained reports will be false (e.g., students report that most teachers smoke although actually most do not). If one is endeavoring to promote seat-belt use or hypertension checkups, one might interview those who have and those who have not adopted the risk-reducing practice in order to discover variables that have induced or discouraged taking the desired step. One could also serve as a participant observer at a highway tollbooth, recording seat-belt usage as a function of theory-relevant variables, such as the demographics of driver and passengers, the type of car, time of day, and weather conditions. Also usable in this third step are psychographic profiles employed in consumer research that segment the population into subgroups varying in risk and compliance, identifying the characteristics, life-style, and media-consumption habits of high-risk segments in order to ascertain the most cost-effective media mix to reach subpopulations most in need. Step 3 calls for identifying the demographics of the risk groups and the situational circumstances that increase the risk and identifying critical choice points at which social pressure exerted through a communication campaign can promote healthful behaviors with minimal disturbance of the target group's preferred life-style.

Step 4: Mapping the Mental Matrix

The previous Step 3 of surveying the sociocultural situation called for interpersonal analysis; Step 4 calls for intrapersonal analysis, getting inside the person's head to see how he or she conceptualizes and feels about the health-maintaining behavior that the campaign is designed to produce. Hence, whereas Step 3 called for anthropological and sociological techniques, Step 4 calls for cognitive and clinical psychology techniques in order to map the directive and dynamic mental structures that determine how the persons at risk selectively perceive the situation and the motives that direct their behavior into health-threatening or health-maintaining channels. In this fourth step one ascertains the kinds of (mis)information that people in the target at-risk group have about the relevant health dangers, their knowledge of risk-reducing alternatives, and their grasp of connections between their own life-style and the relevant health problems and solutions. Besides mapping these informational structures that direct perception and behavior, one also ascertains the relevant dynamic motivations and values that propel the person's behavior into health-threatening channels and those that could divert her or his behavior into risk-reducing paths.

A variety of psychological techniques, including reactive survey questionnaires and less structured clinical projective techniques, can be used for mapping these directive and dynamic psychological orientations relevant to the health-risk behavior. Leventhal, Meyer, and Nerenz (1980) and Pennebaker (1982) demonstrate techniques for identifying a person's implicit theories of biology, of health, and of medical and surgical treatments, revealing that even well-educated persons have distorted views of human anatomy and physiology, of the meaning of symptoms, and of how treatments work. One can use critical-incident analysis or TAT-type projective techniques to ascertain the thoughts and motives that precipitate at-risk individuals to obtain hypertension or cancer diagnoses or to stop smoking or to donate blood. One may find that cosmetic needs are more powerful than health needs for improving dental hygiene; or that in getting people to stop smoking or use seat belts altruistic appeals (e.g., to their responsibility as parents not to be health-threatening role models to their children) may be more effective than appeals to people's self-interest to preserve their own life and health. Use of the subjective expected utility technique with a standard set of values (Murray's, Rokeach's, or McGuire's, discussed later in this chapter) might reveal, for example, that sunbathers can be more effectively deterred by warnings about the cosmetic damage of tanning (skin aging) than by warning of its carcinogenic dangers. Even humanistic techniques can be useful, as illustrated by Sontag's (1978) revealing analysis of the depiction of tuberculosis and cancer in literature as indicative of the very different ways in which these two diseases are perceived by their potential victims.

Step 5: Teasing out the Target Themes

The first four steps involved divergent, information-accumulating operations that tend to inundate campaign developers with a wealth of options. In Step 5 one narrows down this *embarras de richesses* by teasing out a subset of high-priority campaign themes. The selection can be guided by a number of social and behavioral science principles. Most drastically, the Step 5 analysis may indicate that the problems are not sufficiently amenable to persuasion but call for one of the institutional-change strategies considered earlier. For example, Steps 3 and 4 may reveal so many situational and dispositional difficulties in further raising the proportion of automobile passengers who voluntarily use seat belts that it will be more cost-effective to add the institutional approach of passing legislation that will require automobile manufacturers to install side protective air bags or will induce governmental gatekeepers to enforce the seat belt law.

It will be usually found possible to design a communication campaign that promises to reduce the target health risk cost-effectively. One can then set priorities among possible themes by using psychological principles, such as that it is easier for mass-media communication to provide needed information than needed motivation (e.g., nutrition messages to reduce sodium intake can more effectively provide information on making food tasty by using herbs instead of salt rather than persuading people to like low-salt foods). Again, mass media can more effectively communicate "what" than "how," so that nutrition messages might more effectively urge the family shopper to read the salt content on food labels than retrain the family cook to prepare gourmet meals without salt. In general, the message should devote time less to pointing out the seriousness of the danger and more to describing the efficacy and availability of ways to cope with it. The public is all too well aware of the undesirability of cancer and tetanus; what they need to know are effective and available ways of avoiding these conditions (Leventhal, Singer, & Jones, 1965).

If it does become necessary for a health campaign to induce motivation as well as communicate information, a useful principle is that it is easier to manipulate perceived instrumentality than to change subjective value. For example, people at noisy work sites can be induced to wear protective ear coverings more effectively by giving periodic hearing tests that demonstrate to noncomplying workers their progressive hearing loss than by trying to make hearing loss seem more terrible or the wearing of ear protectors less unpleasant (Zahor, Cohen, & Azar, 1980). Motivational appeals should also concentrate on the values that are important to the people at risk rather than on the ones the campaign designers think should be important. For example, health professionals may feel that using sunscreen at the beach is important because it reduces the incidence of melanoma, but if the people at risk are more influenced by its averting premature skin aging, then, for effectiveness, the cosmetic appeal should be used, even if professionals regard the public's value hierarchy as distorted.

This fifth step entails not only teasing out the most cost-effective target themes but also defining subpopulations particularly at risk and identifying their media consumption habits in order to develop an optimal media mix for reaching those most in need. Toward this end, marketing and advertising techniques like psychographics and market segmentation are useful. Step 5 involves choosing a few particularly promising themes for emphasis and identifying particularly high-risk subpopulations and efficient channels for getting the campaign to them. For example, if one's objective is to decrease reckless and drunken driving in teenage males, one should be aware that the riskiness theme might backfire for the high-risk "macho" youth. One might make this problem part of the solution by appealing to youthful drivers to take manly responsibility for the well-being of their passengers. Also, with this target group one might try to get one's public service announcements not transmitted in the breaks in popular prime-time television shows with large but age-scattered Nielsen ratings, but rather embedded in lyrics of songs played on late-night rock music AM radio stations whose low general Arbitron ratings are cost-effectively concentrated on the high-risk young target group.

Step 6: Constructing the Communications

Having identified the themes to be stressed and the target subpopulations to be reached, health campaign designers can turn to the sixth step, constructing the communication, the task preeminently within the expertise of two complementary types of communication specialists, the artistic and the scientific. The artistic includes writers, directors, and production people from the media who know many rules of thumb (some of which deserve to be true but are not), such as that one can enhance the impact of communicators by photographing them full-face, at eye level, and while they are receiving audience approval (Noelle-Neumann, 1980). The second group of communication specialists are the social and behavioral scientists, who use empirically tested, theoretically derived principles to identify which communication variables should be used to enhance impact. Because my T-shirt proudly proclaims "Social Psychologist" I shall discuss primarily the scientists' contributions to Step 6.

A vast body of scientific research has been done on how communication variables can be manipulated to maximize informational, attitudinal, or behavioral impact. Over 1,000 published studies on this topic are summarized annually in the *Psychological Abstracts*. Lipstein and McGuire (1978c) compiled a bibliography with abstracts of 7,000 persuasion studies, indexed according to their input and output communication variables. I shall return to Step 6 in the next two sections of this chapter, after completing this overview of the RASMICE procedure by describing Step 7.

Step 7: Evaluating the Effectiveness

Any undertaking as complicated and important as a health campaign should include an end-point appraisal of its overall effectiveness as well as diagnostic measures of the effectiveness of its separate inputs and its impact on each of the critical at-risk subgroups. In this way evaluation serves, not simply as a report card on the given campaign, but also as a diagnostic guide for future health-promoting campaigns. End evaluation should be done immediately after the campaign and also after a delay of three months to a year to ascertain persistence of impact.

Evaluation also should be done not only after but during the campaign development as one is faced with choosing among alternative options and with detecting and strengthening weak points. Such during-campaign checks may be as simple as getting judgments of options by a diverse set of experts or involve more complex procedures such as getting multiple measures of crucial variables. For example, the Step 3 analysis of the sociocultural situation leading to children's beginning to smoke cigarettes can be pursued by open-ended and by structured questionnaires and by observational methods, yielding supplementary information and providing mutual cross-validations. In the Step 6 communication constructing, one can use copy-testing procedures with rough or final forms of the ads in order to determine the best of several promising alternatives before investing heavily in producing and broadcasting a final set of health-promoting ads. These ongoing evaluations during a campaign serve to improve both it and later campaigns.

Obviously, a thorough implementation of each of the seven steps that I have outlined here constitutes a formidable task, calling for prodigious efforts and an intimidating range of skills. Few individuals feel comfortable serving as a biomedical scientist, epidemiologist, moralist, cultural anthropologist, cognitive psychologist, clinical psychologist, media expert, attitude-change maven, and program evaluator. Nonetheless, that the task is so difficult is not an excuse to despair or to do a sloppy job but rather an impetus to try harder. Resources are finite and compromises must be made, with the result that some of the steps will be neglected relative to others in any campaign, but recognition of the whole spectrum of steps allows the sacrifices to be made as informed and rational choices rather than by default. The wide range of needed expertise makes it desirable that a health promotion campaign be a team effort rather than a one-person show. Although the team approach can add a wide range of talent and special knowledge, each team member, besides taking the lead in steps particularly relevant to her or his expertise, also should contribute actively to numerous other steps by making suggestions, raising questions, and generating and choosing among alternatives rather than abandoning these steps to inside experts. Social psychological expertise is most relevant to Step 6, and the majority of questions brought to us social psychologists by campaign developers do deal with Step 6 issues.

However, the social psychological basic researcher, after concentrating on the Step 6 issues on which he or she has been consulted, should raise questions relevant to the other six RASMICE steps, lest issues bearing on the other steps be overlooked.

USING THE COMMUNICATION/PERSUASION MATRIX IN "RASMICE" STEP 6

I return here to RASMICE Step 6, constructing a persuasive communication by selecting out of the wide spectrum of communication input variables sketched in Table 5.1 a subset adequate to evoke the desired behavioral outputs. I emphasize this sixth step because it is the one that most calls for my own special training and skills as a social psychologist and communication researcher. My communication/persuasion matrix approach to Step 6 involves using checklists of communication input variables to construct an effective campaign, and then using checklists of desired output processes to evaluate and improve its effectiveness. These input and output variables can be organized into the matrix shown in Table 5.1, whose input column headings are the independent variables (communication components) out of which the persuasive communications can be constructed, and whose output row headings are the mediating and dependent variables, the successive responses that the communication must evoke in order to induce the desired changes in attitudes and behaviors. In each cell of this input/output matrix is entered the demonstrated or theorized relation between the cell's column communication-input variable and its row behavioral-output variable.

Input and Output Factors in Persuasive Communications

Lasswell's (1948) classical interrogative analysis of persuasion as a matter of who says what, via which medium, to whom, aimed at what target effect, indicates that communication input variables fall into five broad classes: source, message, channel (or medium), receiver (or audience), and destination (or target). Each of these five sets of variables can be further subdivided, as shown in Table 5.1 (e.g., message variables can be divided into style, type of appeal, argument structure, what is included or left out, how the included material is organized, the amount of material, extremity of claim, etc.); and further subsub-

Table 5.1

The communication/persuasion, input/output matrix as an aid in constructing persuasive communications

Persuasion outputs: Mediating and Dependent Variables[b]	Communication Component Inputs: Independent Variables[a]							
	SOURCE			MESSAGE	CHANNEL (medium)	RECEIVER (audience)	RESPONSE TARGET
	Credibility	Attractiveness	Power	Arguments	Modality	Demographics	Purchasing
	Expertise	Similarity	Control	Inclusions	Context	Personality	Voting
	Trust	Familiarity	Scrutiny	Orderings	Nonverbal	Ability	Violence
	. . .	Neotony	Concern	Discrepancy	. . .	. . .	. . .
		. . .	. . .	Style			
				. . .			

1. Exposure
2. Attention
3. Liking
4. Comprehension
5. Cognitive elaboration
6. Skill acquisition
7. Agreement
8. Memory storage
9. Retrieval
10. Decision making
11. Acting on decision
12. Cognitive consolidation
13. Proselytizing

[a] The column headings are the categories and subcategories of inputs (independent variables) out of which the persuasive communication can be constructed.
[b] The row headings are the output steps (mediating and dependent variables) the evocation of which enhances persuasive impact.

divided (e.g., message style can be divided into vividness, literalness, humorousness, etc.). Lists of inputs expanded from those in the Table 5.1 column headings serve as checklists to suggest variables out of which effective communications can be constructed. As regards the output side of the persuasion process, the row headings in Table 5.1 list mediating and dependent variables that may have to be promoted by the communication if it is to have persuasive impact. Alternative output analyses, some fuller and most shorter, are available elsewhere (McGuire, 1978d; Petty & Cacioppo, 1986).

Uses of the Communication/Persuasion Matrix

Such a communication/persuasion matrix serves multiple purposes. First, in constructing a new campaign one can judge the net effect of adding a proposed input factor by doing a thought experiment or a prestudy to estimate that factor's likely impact on each of the output processes. For example, if one is considering adding humor to the communication in order to elicit attention or increase liking (output Steps 2 and 3) one must weigh any such benefits against humor's possible detrimental effects in being distracting or in seeming facetious and so interfering with Step 4 or Step 7. Another illustration is that if one is considering beefing up the elicitation of the agreement step by vividly portraying dreadful physiological damage done by smoking, one should weigh any such Step 7 agreement elicitation against the possibility that the anxiety aroused by the vivid portrayal of dangers will interfere with Step 2, 3, or 9, attention, liking, or retention (Lazarus, 1980; Leventhal, 1980).

A second use of the communication/persuasion matrix is that, once a tentative overall campaign has been put together, the list of output steps can serve as a diagnostic checklist for evaluating the extent to which the input components already in the campaign will suffice to evoke each of the needed output steps. When the combined inputs seem deficient in eliciting one of the needed output steps, the checklists of possible inputs provided by the column headings of the Table 5.1 matrix can be used to suggest additional communicating variables whose manipulation promises to evoke the neglected output step without interfering disproportionately with other output steps. A third use of the matrix is that, when one is mastering or keeping up with the literature, the matrix provides a conceptual framework for assimilating new findings about relations making up the attitude-change process so that this new material is available for creative retrieval. A fourth use of the matrix is to reveal gaps in the existing knowledge by the comparative fullness of the relation entries in its various cells. A cell with many entries as regards relations between its column input and its row output raises the question of whether this heavily studied topic has a lower priority for research funding than a neglected relation indicated by a relatively empty cell. The final section of chapter 4 used the matrix for this purpose of identifying currently promising lines of attitude change research (McGuire, 1994b).

A fifth use of the communication/persuasion matrix is that it protects the designers of a public health or other applied persuasion campaign from a half-dozen fallacies commonly made by persuasion practitioners. (*a*) The great-expectation fallacy of thinking any campaign will produce large changes is avoided by realizing that payoff Step 11, the audience's taking action, is the joint probability of all ten preceding steps; multiplications of 10 probabilities, most substantially less than the 1.00 maximum, yield small products. (*b*) The distal-measure fallacy is also reduced: Practitioners tend to evaluate persuasive communications in terms of Steps 3 and 4 (ad liking and ad recall), which are only distantly related to payoff Step 11, so that a better-liked ad (Step 3) may be inferior in inducing action (Step 11) due to its poor performance on intervening steps. (*c*) The matrix also helps preserve the practitioner from the neglected-mediator fallacy, as when vivid animation is introduced to enhance Step 3 (interest) while overlooking that animation may distract from Steps 4 and 5 (comprehension and cognitive responding). (*d*) The matrix calls attention also to the compensatory principle that any communication input factor in a given campaign tends to enhance impact via some mediators and reduce impact via others (e.g., fear appeals may facilitate Step 7, agreement, but interfere with Step 3, liking for the message). This compensatory calculus yields a "golden mean" corollary, such that an intermediate level on any input variable tends to have more persuasive impact than very high or very low levels of that variable. (*e*) The matrix also helps prevent the "if some is good, more is better" fallacy (e.g., if moderate source expertise is more effective than low expertise, then very high credibility is better still); on the contrary, the characteristic inverted-U relation indicates that intermediate levels of the input have maximum persuasive impact. (*f*) Also prevented is the extrapolational fallacy when the matrix reminds the practitioner that a set of communication inputs that worked well in one campaign will have to be modified in specifiable ways in other situations to the extent that the situations differ in the variance contributed to the payoff Step 11 by the various intervening steps. Further discussion of these and other uses of the communication/persuasion matrix can be found in McGuire (1969a, 1985a, 1978d, and chapter 3 of this volume).

PERSUASION APPEALS THAT CAN BE USED
IN STEP 6 CAMPAIGN CONSTRUCTION

[Adapted with permission from William J. McGuire, 1991b, Using guiding-idea theories of the person to develop educational campaigns against drug abuse and other health-threatening behavior, *Health Education Research: Theory and Practice, 6,* 173–184. Copyright © 1991 by the Oxford University Press. A fuller description can be found in McGuire, 1985a, pp. 294–304.]

The preceding section zooms in on Step 6 of the seven-step RASMICE procedure, describing how the communication/persuasion matrix can be used to construct persuasive communications. Now I zoom in more narrowly still, focusing within Step 6 on just one category of message input variables, namely, motivational appeals that can be used in the persuasive communications. McGuire (1985a, 1991b) identifies 16 popular guiding-idea theories of what moves people, each theory suggesting a family of motivational appeals that can be used in a persuasion campaign. Each is a partial view of human nature that focuses attention on one limited aspect of the person (e.g., the person as a learning machine, as a consistency maximizer, as a tension reducer, a meaning seeker, an ego defender, etc.) and thus provides creative insights into appeals and arguments that can be used to make a message persuasive. These partial views of the person will be illustrated here by the appeals they suggest for use in a campaign to deter people from getting involved in drug abuse.

Creative Provocativeness of Guiding-Idea,
Partial-View-of-the-Person Theories

The approach proposed here to developing appeals for use in a persuasion campaign against drug abuse is theory guided, gratification oriented, and eclectic, in contrast to most antidrug persuasion campaigns, which are atheoretical, negatively oriented, and narrow (which may explain their disappointing outcomes). Firstly, developing more imaginative campaigns against drug abuse calls for using general theories of human needs, not just needs peculiar to substance abuse. Secondly, whereas campaigns against drug abuse are usually negatively oriented in focusing on drug abuse's bad effects (which tend to be well known to addicts without deterring their drug abuse), the theories used here focus on the positive appeals of drugs, the better to argue against them. Thirdly, rather than the usual doctrinaire insistence on one preferred theory, here 16 complementary theories are used eclectically to identify diverse human needs that may sustain drug abuse.

One workshop on drug abuse in which I participated was shrewdly designed so that half the participants were applied researchers specializing in reducing drug abuse and the other half were basic researchers doing theory-guided studies on social influence. It soon became obvious that the applied people were in possession of a treasure house of specific facts about drug abuse, while the basic researchers (including me) had a cornucopia of theories purporting to account for why in general people do what they do – two supplementary bodies of knowledge that badly needing bridging. Whenever a question arose about the incidence of drug abuse in a certain demographic subgroup, the applied people would flip through their printouts and give impressive statistics on amount and type of drug usage, broken down by time of day, cities, sex, age, and other variables. Whenever a question arose about the motivational basis of drug abuse, we basic researchers would ride off in all directions, each on his or her own hobbyhorse theory that emphasized a human need such as accommodation, achievement, affiliation, assimilation, attribution, or autonomy, just to mention theories at the top of the alphabetical list. To avoid monolithic theorizing, the present discussion will be promiscuously eclectic in laying out a broad spectrum of guiding-idea theories of the person and in examining the implications of each specifically for appeals usable in campaigns against drug abuse, although the approach is equally relevant to other targets.

A first creative reversal: Accentuating the positive.   Antidrug campaigns tend unwisely to focus on the drug's harmful effects. Considering how damaging drugs can be, it is not surprising that the appeals used are typically negative, stressing detrimental effects even though these are already familiar to abusers without having deterred them. An alternative, know-your-enemy approach would mention and rebut the neglected benefits that have enticed so many people into drug abuse. Drugs' gratifications extend far beyond physiological pleasures (the mood highs, the reduction of anxiety and depression, the narcosis, the intensifying of experience, etc.), as is shown by the high recidivism rates of treated drug abusers even after they are physiologically detox-ified. Identifying the wide range of gratifications provided both by the drugs per se and by drug-related life-styles gives insights into reasons for drug abuse's persistence and prevalence despite its generally rec-ognized detrimental effects. By confronting these benefits one can at-tack the drug from within the abuser's own perspective.

A second creative reversal: Shifting from dependent to independent variable.   Circumventing a first creative block by switching one's thinking from the evils of drug abuse to its gratifications leads to a second block, one's inhibition against thinking productively of the benefits of a behavior that one regards as heinous. One can come up with a few plausible benefits, but this goes so against the grain that one's creativity is quickly stifled. A tactic useful in circumventing this second type of creative block is to switch one's attention to the other variable in the relation under study. Instead of generating heroin ad-diction's many gratifications one can undertake the less repulsive task of taking a diverse list of human needs and then reactively generating ways in which heroin addiction may satisfy each need. One can start out with a ready-made needs list such as Murray's (1938), Maslow's (1970), or Rokeach's (1973). I suggest here an organized set of 2^4 hu-man gratifications (McGuire, 1991b), each a partial view of the per-son that has been used creatively in personality and social psycholog-ical research and that taken together can diversify one's insights into the appeals of drug abuse.

Generating 16 Guiding-Idea Theories
of the Person

The 2^4 array of basic human needs shown in Table 5.2 was assembled by listing some well-known partial views of human nature (e.g., the person as a consistency maximizer, an information seeker, a tension reducer, an ego defender, etc.), each of which some researchers have

Table 5.2

Psychology's guiding-idea theories about motivational bases of human behavior usable in developing persuasion campaigns

Action-Terminating Dimensions		Action-Instigation Dimensions			
		STABILITY		GROWTH	
		Active	Reactive	Active	Reactive
Cognitive States	Internal Relations	1. Consistency	2. Categorization	5. Stimulation	6. Coping
	External Relations	4. Hermeneutic	3. Rationalization	8. Autonomy	7. Template-Matching
Affective States	Internal Relations	13. Tension-reduction	14. Ego-defense	9. Affiliation	10. Identity
gion	External Relations	16. Expression	15. Repetition	12. Assertion	11. Conta-

found provocative of insights into human behavior. I then abstracted from this initial accumulation of needs some basic differentiating dimensions and dichotomized each dimension into polar-opposite views. These dichotomized dimensions were then organized orthogonally into an economical matrix structure into whose cells were sorted the guiding-idea theories on our initial list. Each cell that remained empty was filled by generating an additional type of partial view of human nature whose characteristics could be identified by the empty cell's column and row descriptors. This augmented list of needs suggested additional dimensions, producing new cells that could be filled in with new partial views generated to fit the descriptors of the new cells. By this recursive procedure I ended up with a 2^4 matrix, the entry in each of whose 16 cells identifies a set of the human needs that motivate people's behavior. This set of 16 needs can then be used, for example, to explain what makes drug-abuse behavior attractive to abusers and to suggest appeals that can be used in antidrug persuasion campaigns.

The 16-cell $2^2 \times 2^2$ matrix shown in Table 5.2 is organized in terms of what instigates versus what terminates human actions. The four column headings are 2×2 dichotomous dimensions that distinguish motivational theories on the basis of what instigates people to action. The first, "being versus becoming" behavior-instigating column dichotomization, reflects whether the person is theorized as acting to maintain the current stability (homeostasis, equilibrium) or to attain a higher level of complexity (transcendence, growth). The second instigation dimension dichotomizes whether the person is depicted as incited to action by internal stresses or in reaction to external presses. The four row headings are 2×2 dichotomous dimensions that distinguish motivational theories on the basis of what terminates action, whether action is terminated with the attainment of a cognitive state or an affective state, and whether action is terminated with the attainment of some internal relation among components of the person or with the attainment of some favorable external relation between the person and his or her environment. Each of the 16 cells in the Table 5.2 matrix contains the name of a distinctive family of theories of the person, each a partial view of human motivations. There is room here to discuss adequately only the four families of theories shown in the upper left quadrant of Table 5.2. The other 12 are described more fully in McGuire (1985a, 1991b).

Cognitive Stability Theories of the Person

All four families of theories in the upper-left quadrant of Table 5.2 agree that action is instigated by the person's need to maintain a present equilibrium (rather than to grow transcendentally to some higher level of complexity) and is terminated with the attainment of some cognitive (rather than affective) end state. What differentiates theories in the four cells of this quadrant are their assumptions on the other two dimensions. I shall discuss the four, starting with consistency theories in the upper left cell and proceeding clockwise around the other three cells of the quadrant.

(1) Consistency theories.   The Cell 1 theories in this cognitive stability quadrant depict the person as a consistency maximizer instigated to action by the need to reduce internal imbalances arising among

thoughts, feelings, and actions; and they depict action as terminating with the restoration of a balance among the components within the individual's personality (rather than between the person and the outside environment). Such theories were popular during the 1960s, as reviewed by Abelson et al. (1968) and McGuire (1966c). Examples include Osgood and Tannenbaum's congruity theory, Heider's P-O-X balance theory, Festinger's dissonance theory, Newcomb's ABX theory, and McGuire's probabilogical theory (see chapter 6 in this volume).

As regards drug-abuse gratifications, consistency theories suggest that the drugs' narcotic effects or the distracting demands of the drug life-style may serve to protect the person from painful recognition of the discrepancy between his or her real self and his or her ideal or moral self (Higgins, 1987). Such self-discrepancies seem especially prevalent in situations where drug abuse is also common – for example, in adolescence, with its impossible dreams, and in cosmopolitan cities, where relative deprivation is salient. The obsessing demands of the drug life provide a connected and coherent integration of thought, feeling, and action that eminently satisfies the need for consistency. Drug prevention campaigns have the challenging task of providing high-risk groups, before they get hooked, with an attractive and coherent life-style and mentality in which drug abuse would be a discordant element.

(2) Categorization theories. These Cell 2 theories in the cognitive stability quadrant depict the person as filing clerk, constantly struggling to cope with an overload of incoming information (Poole, 1983) by sorting arriving stimuli into his or her stereotypic categories, which trigger customary responses to cope with that class of stimuli. Complex observations are simplified by assimilation to partially fitting preexisting categories, with such distortions as are necessary, and with occasional readjustments of categories to accommodate compelling novelties. This view of the person was particularly popular during the 1930s perceptual era and has been used creatively by such researchers as Bartlett, Sherif, Luchins, Gordon Allport, Piaget, Asch, Lévi-Strauss, Tajfel, and Moscovici and other social representationalists.

Application of categorization theories to drug-abuse behavior is epitomized in the formula that social influence involves, not so much changing the person's attitudes or actions toward a given situation but rather changing his or her perception of what is the situation to which he or she is reacting. Drug addicts tend to be responding to a different phenomenal reality from that assumed by antidrug campaign designers. The ineffectiveness of most antidrug campaigns may reflect this perceptual gap. What needs to be changed is not so much addicts' attitudes to drug abuse as their perceptions of the drug situation. A difficulty is that the rich street culture and rituals of the drug life may have provided the addict with a richer set of relevant categories than the antidrug campaigner can easily offer. However, campaigns aimed at prevention rather than cure may be able to develop and work effectively within the available categories of the not-yet-addicted, even those in high-risk groups.

(3) Rationalizing theories.   Cell 3 theories depict the person as unreflective, behaving without much thought or self-examination; only when outside pressure requires an explanation does the person generate a rationalization of his or her current behavior. Often this response involves self-labeling that channels the person's behavior in future situations. These theories stress that one's self-concept derives in part from interpreting one's own overt behavior, just as one conceptualizes other people on the basis of their overt behavior. This behavioral-derivation notion is adumbrated by Marx's materialistic epistemology that ideology is shaped by social and ultimately material conditions, by Freud's notion of rationalization, by William James's theory of emotion, by symbolic interactionists' "looking-glass self" notion, and by the existentialist notion that being precedes essence. More empirically oriented versions of this partial view of the person are Festinger's social comparison theory, Bem's (1972) radical behaviorism, and Freedman's foot-in-the-door and other self-labeling approaches.

Drug abusers tend to live in a segregated subculture where their behavior, although aberrant in the larger culture, is not uncommon and where sustaining rationalizations are rarely challenged, suggesting that the effectiveness of an antidrug campaign is enhanced by putting the (potential) drug abuser into an environment where, when self-definition is called for, attractive drug-free self-characterizations are saliently available. Because considerable resources are needed to create such environments, their use in prevention campaigns seems more hopeful than in campaigns aimed at the already addicted.

(4) Hermeneutic theories. These partial views stress the person's need for meaning, for interpretations and explanations of the nature of the world, of what happens in life, and especially of one's own experiences and behaviors. This guiding idea of the person was especially popular in 1970s conceptualizations such as attribution theory, just-world assumptions, blaming the victim, and the person as an implicit psychologist, economist, biologist, or whatever. The working idea is that the person, including the addict, acts in accord with his or her own schema, implicit theories to account for common domains of experience (health, ethics, etc.), which schema may be very different from those which guide antidrug professionals.

Drug abuse may be consonant with various tacit views of the world. For example, the person may, from experience or indoctrination, view society as oppressive and resent authority figures such as parents, teachers, or police, so that drug abuse is seen as a mode of resistance. Because illegal drug abuse elicits further oppression from society this meaning attribution has a self-confirming quality. For a person of low self-esteem, becoming hooked on drugs may provide a chemical or life-style explanation for failure that is less painful than blaming his or her inherent inadequacy. Campaigns to lessen drug abuse may have the formidable task of providing high-risk youth with acceptable and satisfying theories of society and of themselves within which their becoming addicted to drugs would be a highly discordant cognition. Again, this might be achievable primarily in prevention campaigns that abandon hope for the already addicted.

Cognitive Growth Theories of the Person

The next four families of theories, those in the upper-right quadrant of Table 5.2, all depict the person as terminating action with the attainment of some cognitive state, as did the four in the upper-left quadrant just discussed; but they differ from those four in postulating that behavior is instigated by the need to achieve some form of cognitive growth rather than to maintain one's current cognitive homeostasis. This second tetrad of theories, like the first, differ among themselves in their assumptions regarding the other two dimensions that differentiate theories about the driving forces in human nature.

(5) Need-for-stimulation, or "stimulus hunger" theories. These theories stress people's need for exploration and varied experience, the

driving power of curiosity, the human zest for novelty. They flourished in psychology during the 1960s as a reaction against the passive drive-reduction concept of the organism popular during the preceding stimulus-response behaviorist ascendancy. Researchers who made creative use of this novelty-seeking concept of the person include Harlow, Howard Kendler, Dember, Berlyne, Maddi, Bieri, and Zuckerman (1983). Earlier theorists viewed such stimulus hunger as healthy, but more recently it has been perceived as dysfunctional hyperactivity calling for the pharmaceutical subduing of large numbers of children. Current media critics worry that the animated style of television programming for children has aggravated this need, producing a hyperactive generation with short attention span, avidity for change, and intolerance for boredom, which disturbs the peace and renders the Television Age cohort unsuitable for many educational and work environments.

Stimulus hunger may predispose youth to exciting life-styles, including the hectic music, recreation, socializing, and adornment associated with drug abuse. Drugs with contrasting effects (e.g., heroin vs. cocaine) may appeal to this need in different ways. However, even drugs whose actual pharmaceutical effects dull the senses may be regarded by users as expanding consciousness, sharpening sensation, or reducing inhibitions. That former addicts typically return to drug use, even after physiological detoxification, may reflect attraction to the exciting hustle of street life in contrast to the dullness of available post-addictive life-styles. To antidrug campaigners the street drug scene may seem terrifying and exhausting, but this may appeal to the stimulus hunger of subcategories of addicts. The addict life-style may fill every moment with the purpose and excitement of getting the next fix. To offer an alternative, preventive and therapeutic environments may have to provide demanding, obsessive boot camp regimens. Space is not available here to describe this cognitive growth quadrant's other three cells – (6) coping theories; (7) template-matching theories, and (8) autonomy theories – but further details can be found in McGuire (1985a, 1991b).

Affective Growth and Stability Theories
of the Person

The eight partial views of the person shown in the just described top half of Table 5.2 all depict the person as striving toward some cognitive end state; the eight in the lower half all depict the person as striving toward some affective end state, either for affective growth (as in the case of the [9] to [12] families of guiding-idea theories in the lower-right quadrant) or for maintaining their current affective equilibrium (as in the case of the [13] to [16] theories in the lower-left quadrant). These eight affective theories are described in McGuire (1985a, 1991b) as regards their core concepts, variant proponents, and implication for appeals to be used in antidrug campaigns.

Concluding Considerations Regarding These
Partial Theories of the Person

The mutual supplementation of these partial views of the person. Each of these 16 guiding-idea theories singles out a type of want that propels the person to action and a type of gratification that terminates action. They are mutually supplementary rather than exclusive, but in the heat of controversy proponents of one view sometimes talk themselves into denying the validity of others. Each human in any situation has some mix of these 16 aspects and others. Effort devoted to arguing that one partial view is more useful than another might better be spent on exploiting the creative potential of each.

Either/or controversies among these 16 partial views of the person tend to be wasteful, but integrative confrontations of pairs can be stimulating. For example, Cell 8 autonomy theorists versus Cell 9 affiliation theorists constitute thesis versus antithesis, as do Cell 5, stressing the need for excitement, versus Cell 13, tension reduction, the need to escape excitement. Although it seems superficially contradictory, humans do seek both excitement and relief from it. Such apparently contradictory needs can serve as Hegelian or Saussurean oppositions for generating a higher synthesis, as when Berlyne (1960) and Apter (1992) deduce that an intermediate level of arousal is optimal. Analyzing how the parameters of this inverted-U-shaped relation are affected by diverse dispositional and situational variables can yield a rich set of interaction predictions, as described in chapters 1 and 3. Alternatively, these seemingly opposite Cell 5 sensation-seeking and Cell 13 tension-reduction theories can be reconciled by arguing that the person seeks excitement in order to have the high level of stimulation that allows gratifying drive-reduction to occur; Cell 13 tension-reduction theories can then be subdivided into those postulating that having an absolutely low tension level is gratifying versus those defining gratification rather in first-derivative terms, as reducing tension from any initial level to a lower level.

Some general correctives offered by this approach. Regarding drugs' pharmaceutical effects, users' expectations (derived from peer culture, parents, teachers, the media, etc.) may be as influential as any actual physiological effects. Schoolchildren perceive that the proportion of teachers who smoke is vastly higher than is actually the case. Exaggerations of a drug's pharmaceutical effects voiced by parents or other authority figures may paradoxically make drugs more attractive and enhance their placebo effects.

Beyond the pharmaceutical attractions, real or imagined, the distinctive life-styles associated with drug abuse may provide a wide range of satisfactions. Most of the negative aspects of drug abuse stressed in antidrug campaigns can actually attract members of the high-risk groups, as when stressing the riskiness of drugs to macho male teenagers can actually increase their appeal. The obsessive street-life pressure on the addict desperate to obtain multiple daily fixes may seem horrendous to the antidrug professional but may attract people stifled by boredom. For lives so liturgically and socially impoverished, the little rituals involved in the use of drugs, ranging from cigarettes to heroin, may provide ceremonial gratifications that explain the partial persistence of needle sharing despite its known danger for spreading hepatitis and AIDS.

In sum, a campaign to discourage drug abuse should take into account its many appeals rather than just insisting on its dangers and should be multifaceted to wrestle with drugs' diverse gratifications. No one magic bullet will shoot down drug abuse. Rather, it will require a full-court-press strategy and a recognition that taking addicts off drugs will leave them with many unfulfilled needs likely to result in recidivism if alternative gratifications are not available. Campaigns should not only present negative arguments about the dangers of drug abuse but also substitute new gratifications for the needs that the drugs have been satisfying.

WHO'S AFRAID OF THE BIG BAD MEDIA

[Adapted with permission from the chapter of the same name by W. J. McGuire, 1991e, in A. A. Berger (Ed.), *Mass media USA: Process and effect,* 2nd ed., pp. 272–280 (New York: Longmans. Copyright © 1991 by Addison Wesley Educational Publications). My fuller discussion of the topic can be found in W. J. McGuire (1986b).]

Advertising executives usually equate research with the critical (that is, copy-testing or evaluation) aspect and overlook its relevance to the creative, hypothesis-generating aspect of the process; hence the "research" departments of ad agencies are often limited to the task of testing the copy already developed by "creative" departments. In my consultation work in the advertising-marketing community I have urged that research has much to offer to the creative, option-generating process as well as to the critical, option-choosing process to which it is often relegated. Hence, the preceding sections of this applied chapter 5 are devoted to showing how the RASMICE procedure, the communication/persuasion matrix, and the 16 partial views of the person's wants can put basic attitude-change research to use in creating applied persuasion campaigns.

My corrective insistence that research can be useful in creating persuasion campaigns does not deny that it can also serve critical, evaluative purposes. The final section of this chapter will discuss a central evaluation topic in basic and applied persuasion research – namely, how big are the effects of mass media. On this topic I take a skeptical position, arguing that the evidence for massive television effects is surprisingly weak: The null hypothesis of no television effects has not, of course, been proven, but neither have widespread massive television effects. At some time in the future, evidence for massive media effects may have accumulated, but one goes beyond current evidence if one claims that a pervasive pattern of massive media effects has already been demonstrated. In the first section below I argue against the claim that massive effects have been established, and in the second section I keep alive (in intensive care) the belief in such effects by mentioning five classes of excuses for frequent failure to find the anticipated massive effects. More detailed evidence is presented in McGuire (1986b).

Television has been credited with – and blamed for – having major impacts on the public. The high-consumption life-styles often portrayed in media programs and encouraged by interspersed advertisements are accused of creating insatiable desires and materialistic value systems in the public; and ads for specific products and brands are assumed to determine purchases and use. The violence pervading television shows has been blamed for high levels of crime. The media's biased depiction (or nondepiction) of nonfashionable groups like the elderly purportedly contributes to their stereotyping (or invisibility) in the public mind. The superficial political ads presented during election campaigns are said to trivialize political campaigning and voters' decision making. The media's preemption of most of the public's leisure time is blamed for the decline of family life, of social interaction, and of the pursuit of higher culture. Agitated animation in cartoon programs is accused of lowering the child viewers' attention span and educability. That there is widespread agreement that the mass media, and especially television, have enormous impacts on the public does not establish that this is true. Indeed, any judgment receiving universal acceptance should evoke the suspicion that it may have escaped critical scrutiny because its acceptance serves diverse constituencies.

Origins of the Belief in Large Mass-Media Effects

It is in the interest of each of the contending factions to maintain that the mass media have large effects. Self-interest compels the managers and owners of television stations and other media to insist that their messages have sizable impact, because their economic well-being depends on advertisers' being convinced that ads sell. These advertisers who buy the time and space have, in turn, their own reasons for being true believers in massive media impacts (e.g., it would take heroic virtue for marketing executives to admit that the billions of their companies' dollars they spend each year on advertising are ineffectual). Enemies of the media are equally motivated to insist on massive impacts because their criticisms and urgings that the media be regulated are based, not on the media's ineffectualness, but on their massive malevolent impact. Even supposedly neutral academic basic researchers have much to gain by reporting that the media are highly effective and therefore an important topic to study. It is in the self-interest of all the contending factions to insist that the media have massive impacts.

To deny that vast media effects have been pervasively demonstrated also violates a number of commonsense informal observations suggesting that the media, especially television, must be having vast influence on the public. For example, there is so much exposure to the media that it *must* be producing considerable effect. The average American spends three hours a day, 20% of his or her waking life, watching television; the average child sees over 20,000 ads and 7,000 acts of violence each year on television and reaches age 18 having spent more time in front of the home television set than in front of the schoolteacher and has seen 13,000 violent deaths on television. Surely all this exposure must be having a formidable effect? The buying of time for commercial advertising is another commonsense argument: Hard-headed business executives, who, it is assumed, must know the value of a dollar even if nothing else, spend 50 billion of them each year on mass-media advertising. They must know what they are doing, and if marketing departments were not able to document the effectiveness of such a vast investment would they not have been fired by their companies or eliminated by market forces? Another commonsense argument is that television violence must be inciting viewers to antisocial aggression, considering that there is so much violence on television and that television's advent in the 1950s was quickly followed by a frightening rise in crime and violence.

Considering its self-interest and the a priori plausibility of the claim, the evidence that the media have massive impacts on the American public is surprisingly weak. This paucity of evidence does not result from lack of research, of which there has been plenty. Nor is it due to inadequacies in the research: Much of the evaluation research leaves room for improvement, but often the better the methods the less impact found. Reported effects do sometimes reach the conventionally accepted .05 level of statistical significance, but the effect sizes tend to be slight in magnitude, accounting for only a few percent of the variance in the dependent-variable target behavior of buying, aggression, or whatever. These customarily modest results do not disprove the existence of massive pervasive impacts, but they should inhibit us from claiming that the research has clearly demonstrated such effects.

Weakness of the Evidence for Massive Impacts of Media Advertisements

Evidence in support of the claim that the media have sizable direct impacts on the general public is weak as regards each of the dozen most often mentioned intended and unintended effects of the media. My judgment is that the 6 most commonly studied intended effects (in declining order of study level) are: (1) the influence of commercial advertising on buying behavior; (2) the impact of political campaigns on voting; (3) public service announcements' efficacy in promoting social or personal benefits; (4) prolonged multimedia campaigns' effects on life-styles; (5) monolithic indoctrination effects on ideology; and (6) the role of ritual displays in mobilizing social energies and maintaining social control. The six most commonly studied unintended effects of the mass media (in declining order of study) include: (1) program violence effects on viewers' antisocial aggression; (2) manner of media representation as it affects the public's stereotypes of groups; (3) effects of amount of media representation on social visibility; (4) erotic materials' arousal of sexual behavior; (5) how media presentation style affects viewers' cognitive processes; and (6) effects on thought processes produced by the introduction of new media. Space limitations have confined my discussion here to evidence regarding the most studied topic in each category: the intended effect of commercial advertising on buying behavior and the unintended effect of program violence on viewer aggression. A fuller discussion of all 12 effects can be found elsewhere (McGuire, 1986b, 1988b).

Effects of television ads on buying behavior: Econometric (macro) evaluations. The ultimate payoff measure for whether American advertisers are getting their dollars' worth for the 50 billion spent each year is how much goods and services the ads sell relative to their costs. Usually ad impact is evaluated, not in terms of the payoff response of buying (Step 11 in Table 5.1) but in terms of the more convenient but less valid measures such as brand liking or salience (Steps 3 and 2). Four popular research strategies include two macro (econometric) approaches, brand share and product class; and two micro (behavioral) approaches, laboratory and field. Brand-share studies involve tracking competing brands of a product (e.g., brands of beer or makes of cars) and measuring the percentages of the industry's total ad budget and total sales racked up by each brand in each month for a several-year period, then analyzing whether rises and falls in a brand's advertising share lead to rises and falls in its share of the product's total sales at any time lag between the two measures. Such brand-share studies typically find surprisingly little effect, often not statistically significant or with an effect size that may not justify the cost of the advertising. Even reviews sponsored by the advertising agencies themselves (Albion & Farris, 1981) report modest impact size.

The other macro approach, product-class studies, indicates only similarly modest impacts. This type of evaluation tracks a whole product class over time for all brands combined (e.g., total cigarette ad spending and total cigarette sales each month for a several-year period) and analyzes whether fluctuations in the tobacco industry's total advertising lead to fluctuations in total cigarette sales at any time lag. Typical of the results is the Federal Trade Commission study (Murphy, 1980) on cigarette smoking, which found that annual fluctuations in cigarette advertising (or indeed, in anticigarette advertising) bore little relation to annual cigarette sales, even though the same research was sensitive enough to pick up sizable "price elasticity" effects on smoking in that raising the price of cigarettes does sizably diminish cigarette sales (Murphy, 1980).

Effects of television ads on buying behavior: Behavioral (micro) evaluations. Micro-level or "behavioral" studies evaluate advertising effects on the level of the individual person, in either field or laboratory situations. A dozen respectable field studies (e.g., Milavsky et al., 1975) lead me to estimate that exposure to televised over-the-counter drug ads accounts for less than 5% of the variance in legal drug use, and an even lesser proportion of illegal use. Typical studies involve monitoring the TV viewing of large groups of adolescents to measure how many drug ads they have been exposed to during successive time periods and monitoring the concurrent drug use of these adolescents. Results show little relation between number of ads seen and subsequent levels of legal (or illegal) drug use. In an illustrative laboratory study, children may be divided randomly into two equivalent groups and one group exposed to fruit ads and the other to candy ads. The children are then allowed to pick their prizes out of a basket of mixed fruit and candy to determine if the ads affect the choices. These laboratory studies often show significant ad effects, but are inconclusive because of weak methodology, artificiality, and modest effect sizes.

In summary, these four approaches to commercial advertising evaluation have yielded surprisingly weak support for the contention that advertisements have large direct impacts on the consumers' buying behavior (or even on their liking for or awareness of the product). Evidence is even weaker for large impacts of the other five classes of intended media effects listed above (McGuire, 1986b).

Unintended effects: Television violence and viewer aggression: Theory. As regards the half-dozen unintended effects purportedly produced by the mass media mentioned above, the best-studied has been how watching violent television programs affects the viewer's subsequent antisocial aggressive behavior. By the 1960s television had spread to most U.S. households and the average American was spending several hours a day watching programs that became increasingly violent. Contemporaneously, the U.S. crime rate rose dramatically, naturally leading to the charge that TV violence was to blame for the rise in crime, riots, and assassinations, just as violent comic books had been so accused in the 1950s (Wertham, 1955) and violent films in the 1930s (Peterson & Thurstone, 1933). Television programs are indeed saturated with violence: Prime-time shows average a half-dozen acts of violence per hour, and Saturday morning children's programs average three times that level. Such violence counts can be criticized in regard to what is scored as violent and how units are defined, but in any case the daily body count on television is appalling. To put television's avid taste for blood into perspective, however, it must be admitted that the violence levels may be even greater in popular novels and films, and that throughout history people have always enjoyed violent spectacles (Goldstein, 1983). The other premise of the argument is that viewers emulate what they see on the TV screen and so are provoked to aggressive behavior by watching violence. It is this second premise of the argument that is theoretically and empirically suspect.

Most theories predict that viewer aggression will increase with amount of violent television watching, but a few theories predict a negative relation (see Table 5.3). I shall first mention six theories that explain the relation by assuming the obvious causal direction: that TV violence affects viewer aggression. A positive effect of television violence on viewer aggressiveness is predicted by four theories (social learning, disinhibition, arousal, and mood theories), and a negative relation by two theories (catharsis and time-monopoly theories). Social learning theory, the most popular of these views, asserts that people model their own behavior on behavior they witness in others, especially when they see that behavior being rewarded. Disinhibition the-

Table 5.3

Classification of some theories to account for relations between exposure to televised violence and viewer aggressiveness, showing, underlined, the name of each theory (and, in parentheses, a leading proponent; and a predicted interaction variable)

Direction of the relation	Direction of causality	
	Exposure to TV Violence Affects Viewers' Aggressiveness	**Viewers' Aggressiveness Affects Exposure to TV Violence**
Positive relation	1. Modeling, social learning (A. Bandura; violence rewarded)	7. Ostracism (L. R. Huesmann; unattractiveness of perpetrator)
	2. Disinhibition, legitimizing (L. Berkowitz; attractive perpetrator)	8. Predilection (A. Fenigstein; violence available in other media)
	3. Arousal (P. H. Tannenbaum; pre-angering)	
	4. Mood (J. P. Leyens; presence of guns)	
Negative relation	5. Catharsis, Vicarious Expression (S. Feshbach; imaginativeness)	9. Conventionality (R. Jessor; attractive home)
	6. Time preemption (J. P. Robinson; joblessness	

ory asserts that, because violence is shown pervasively, it comes to be perceived as banal and even as socially condoned, thus lowering viewers' inhibitions against hurting other people. Arousal theory posits that violent depictions are exciting and so intensify the vigor of viewers' responses, making them more destructive. Mood theories say that exposure to violence induces anger and other negative feelings that provoke antisocial behaviors. As for the two theories predicting a negative relation, catharsis theory asserts that watching violent programs enables a person to release aggressive tensions in fantasy so that he or she will be less aggressive in overt behavior; and time-monopoly theory asserts that watching a lot of television preempts the viewer's time, leaving little opportunity for going out on the street and perpetrating mayhem.

Three other theories predict the reverse direction of causal flow: that it is the person's level of aggression that affects the amount of televised violence to which he or she gets exposed. Ostracism and predilection theories predict a positive relation, and conventionality theory a negative relation. Ostracism theory implies that antisocial, aggressive people are shunned by others and so stay home and watch television's predominantly violent shows. Predilection theory hypothesizes that predilections toward aggressiveness lead both to more violent behavior and to preferring violent TV shows for entertainment. Conventionality theory predicts a negative effect of personal aggressiveness on exposure to televised violence on the grounds that conventional, unaggressive adolescent boys stay home passively watching television (and inevitably its ubiquitous violent shows) while more aggressive types are out clobbering people, which leaves relatively little time for passively watching television. These nine theories and their distinctive interaction predictions are more fully described in McGuire (1986b).

Television violence and viewer aggression: Empirical evidence. With all these theories and with all the research carried out in both the laboratory and the natural world, the frequency and size of demonstrated impacts of televised violence on viewer aggression remain surprisingly modest. Laboratory studies have typically used two readily available populations: young children and college students. Two groups of matched preschoolers might be shown a moderately violent cartoon in contrast to a similarly exciting but less violent cartoon, and then, as the aggression measure, put in play situations where they are invited to emulate an adult model by kicking an inflated clown doll. Alternatively, two matched groups of college students might be shown a violent prizefighting film compared with a nonviolent but equally exciting noncontact sports film, and the students' subsequent aggression measured in terms of how much electric shock they then administer in training a fellow student. In these laboratory studies the group exposed to the more violent material often scores significantly higher on aggression, especially if they are persons predisposed to violence or are pre-angered when they enter the study; but the modest effect size and the artificiality of the aggression measures and other conditions make it hazardous to generalize from these laboratory findings.

Violence-evaluation research carried out in natural-world situations includes concurrent and retrospective subtypes. A concurrent correlational study might investigate a junior high school population repeatedly over several years, measuring monthly both their reported television program watching (to calculate the amount of television violence to which each child has been exposed) and their aggressiveness as indicated by peer or teacher ratings, by delinquency records, and so on (Milavsky et al., 1982b). The extent to which later aggression levels can be predicted from the level of prior violence exposure is then calculated. An alternative, manipulational subtype of concurrent study is to divide an institutionalized population (e.g., incarcerated juvenile delinquents) into matched or random subgroups and to manipulate the amount of violent television shown to the captive subgroups and then measure the amount of aggression in each subgroup to analyze if being exposed to more violent television increases subsequent aggressive behavior.

The retrospective (or "archival") type of natural-world research involves analyzing recorded levels of violent crimes for the time periods around highly publicized violent spectacles (e.g., heavyweight championship prizefights) to determine if national crime statistics increased from before to after the prizefights as compared to matched control periods (Phillips, 1986). Findings in some natural-world studies, both concurrent and retrospective (Milavsky, Kessler, Stipp, & Rubens, 1982; Huesmann, Lagerspetz, & Eron, 1984; Phillips, 1986), find a significant positive relation, but the effect size is modest relative to the massive media impacts usually expected. The bottom-line impacts for the other five unintended media effects are comparably modest (McGuire, 1986b), occasionally attaining the .05 statistical significance level, but are of too small an effect size to support the common belief that the media have massive impacts.

Excuses for Keeping the Faith in Massive Media Impacts

So far I have argued that the results of empirical research do not provide strong support for the common belief that mass media have large direct impacts on the people exposed to them, but here I switch sides to argue for caution in rejecting belief in pervasive massive impacts. I shall mention briefly five well-filled classes of excuses that argue for keeping the faith regarding massive media impacts even though they have seldom been found in past research. McGuire (1986b) discusses these excuses more fully.

Methodological weaknesses may obscure effects.   A first type of excuse is that massive effects usually do occur but are missed because the evaluation research is so methodologically flawed. Media evaluations do, of course, have serious flaws, including: (1) crude measures of the independent variables (e.g., the amount of exposure to specific types of ads or to violent shows); (2) crude measures of the dependent variables (such as the levels of viewers' purchases or of antisocial aggression); (3) poor descriptive statistics for estimating the relations between the two; (4) poor controls of extraneous variables; (5) poor manipulations of the independent variables; (6) possible experimenter biases; and (7) restricted range on the independent variable (see McGuire, 1986b, for details). However, these inadequacies provide only weak excuses for the failure to obtain evidence for massive media impacts because improvements in method often reduce rather than increase the impact size reported. Although meta-analyses tend to yield significant effects, the effect sizes are modest (and meta-analyses tend to be wonderfully and worrisomely powerful in detecting effects).

Communication conditions may obscure media impact.   A second class of excuses is that mass media impacts are potentially vast but are masked by obscuring conditions. For example, (1) it may be that people selectively avoid messages with which they do not already agree and so are seldom exposed to the disagreeing media material that would have converted them had they received it. (2) The media often transmit opposed sets of messages (e.g., from rival politicians or from competing brands of a product) that mutually cancel one another's effects. Also, media messages often come in obscuring environments clouded by (3) advertisement clutter, or by (4) being embedded in more interesting entertainment programs, or by (5) distracting conditions in the viewer's environment. (6) Societal forces may develop to dampen the impact of the plethora of messages (e.g., media credibility may decline with familiarity). Granting that such conditions exist and could have an obscuring effect, then the media might have large impacts in some hypothetical world where these conditions were absent; but in the world as we find it such conditions may well reduce media impacts even more substantially than they do in controlled research situations.

Circumscribed effects may be missed in the search for general effects. Another set of excuses is that even if the media do not generally have large effects, in special subdomains of behavior they may have sizable effects that are lost in evaluations that are looking only for broad spectrum effects. For example, (1) even if media campaigns do little for familiar products or known candidates, they may help new ones get an initial visibility and hearing; or (2) media may not convert the opposition but may keep the faith of those already convinced (the "law of minimal effect"); or (3) media may have sizable effects only on highly involving issues (or only on unimportant issues); or (4) media may have little impact by themselves but may synergistically multiply the impacts of other factors like personal experience; or (5) media may speed up the performing of responses like buying or aggression, even if they do not affect the amount of the response in the long run; or (6) media may affect the form if not the level of the activity; or (7) although ordinary media material may not affect viewers, sensational "media events" (e.g., news reports showing Sadat visiting Jerusalem or the *Roots* miniseries) may have sizable impacts. Such circumscribed effects are plausible, although they are a considerable retreat from general massive impacts and none has been firmly established by research (except possibly the greater media impact on a new product or an unfamiliar candidate).

Effects may focus on especially susceptible subpopulations. An alternative fallback strategy is the excuse that, even if the media do not have large effects on everyone, they do sizably affect certain highly susceptible subpopulations who get lost in evaluations typically designed to detect universal effects. Among the subpopulations suggested as being especially susceptible are (1) children, (2) certain personality types, (3) elites who monitor the media carefully and serve as opinion leaders or, conversely, (4) apathetic viewers with no initial stands of their own, or (5) new viewers who have not yet become jaded with the medium. Also, (6) although program violence does not raise the aggressiveness of most viewers, it may trigger violence in acutely angered individuals or those possessing high chronic aggressiveness. However, where the evidence indicates that some special subgroup is more susceptible than is the general population, the effect size tends to be modest even among these susceptibles. (See McGuire, 1986b, for a fuller discussion.)

Indirect effects may be missed in the search for direct impacts. A fifth category of excuses to defend the hypothesis of massive media impact despite weak empirical corroboration is to argue that sizable effects occur, but only indirectly and over time, and so are lost in evaluations designed to pick up only immediate direct affects. A number of interesting theories use such salvaging excuses. (1) Two-step flow theory asserts that the media may not directly effect the general public but do affect media-monitoring opinion leaders, who later convince the general public to adopt positions that the leaders derived from the media. (2) Agenda-setting theory argues that the media do not change the public's stands on issues but do determine which issues are salient to the public when they make their decisions. (3) Spiral-of-silence theory asserts that the media do not convert the public directly, but that, by endorsing the "politically correct" stand on an issue, the media silence the opposition by giving them the impression that they stand alone, this silence resulting in the eventual dominance of the media view. (4) The continuous presentation of a behavior in the media may gradually establish a consensus that such behavior is normative (e.g., it may legitimize violence). (5) The media may not have great direct impact but the belief that they do determines institutional practices (e.g., even though the television charisma of candidates has not been proven to win elections, belief that it does win affects what kind of candidates get nominated and how they behave during the campaign and in office). Evidence is available that supports some of these conjectured indirect effects (e.g., see Iyengar & Kinder, 1987, on agenda setting) but the effect size continues to be unimpressive.

Conclusion Regarding Media Effects

Although the general public and diverse interest groups who are closely involved with the media may be convinced that the mass media have vast direct persuasive impacts on the public for evil or good, considerable empirical research on the topic has demonstrated only modest effects. Media effects are sometimes confirmed at the .05 level of statistical significance but are usually quite small in magnitude. The null hypothesis is hard to prove, and many types of excuses such as the dozens mentioned above could explain away these failures to confirm large media effects. However, even if failures to confirm do not rule out the possibility of massive media effects, they make it improper to claim that the available empirical results already support this general belief. For the present, a Scotch verdict of "Not proven" seems indicated on the proposition that the mass media have vast direct impacts on the public exposed to them.

6

Thought Systems: Their Content, Structure, and Functioning

Some persisting cognitive issues underlie much of my seemingly heterogeneous work. One abiding interest has been selective perception, or what variables determine which aspects of a complex stimulus get selectively noticed (McGuire, 1984a; McGuire & McGuire, 1988a; chapter 8 in this volume). Another abiding interest, described in this chapter, is the structure and functioning of thought systems: how a person's thoughts are linked to one another, so that when a change is induced in one thought, there tend to be remote ramifications on unmentioned but related thoughts in the system. The first quarter of this chapter describes my initial work on thought systems (McGuire, 1960a, 1960b, 1960c, 1968c, 1968d, 1968e), which was done in the mid-1950s during my last graduate student year at Yale University and the following postdoctoral year at the University of Minnesota. The remainder of the chapter describes the yield of my return to the topic, with some shifts in theory and method, around 1990 (McGuire, 1989a, 1990, 1991d; McGuire & McGuire, 1991c).

MY 1955 CONCEPTUALIZATION OF THOUGHT SYSTEMS

Origins of My Approach

One of the seven basic themes in science fiction involves means becoming ends. Archetypically, a cosmic disaster threatens Earth as we know it, astronomical observations and theory having revealed that the sun will explode into a supernova within a few decades. A disillusioned, reclusive master scientist has a general cosmogonical theory that indicates how such stellar cataclysms can be reversed, but implementing this reversal requires approaching to within a few thousand miles of the sun's chromosphere, where the heat is so intense that all known materials would vaporize. The master scientist and his two young assistants (his daughter and his postdoctoral student, but theirs is another story, developed more fully in the film version) work feverishly in materials science until they come up with an alloy of rare earth metals that can be made into a heat shield that operates by converting heat energy into matter, thus making possible a sufficiently close approach to the sun. A space laboratory is constructed of the alloy, and the master scientist and his two assistants are rocketed into position near the solar chromosphere. There they labor for several years, applying the master's theory and successfully averting the solar cataclysm. During their years of solar labor they have been out of contact with Earth because the solar wind interferes with radio transmission. Thus, when they return to Earth they find to their amazement that Terrestrials have almost forgotten the purpose of the trio's solar mission, having been diverted by living a vastly more affluent lifestyle because the alloy heat-to-matter converter, invented by the master scientist only as a means to allow a sufficiently close approach to the sun to implement his theory and defuse the solar cataclysm, has itself solved the Earth's economic problems by creating a limitless abundance of energy and materials. The reclusive master scientist returns to his isolated laboratory shaking his head, appalled but not surprised at Earthlings' preoccupation with what to him was merely a means to the end. His daughter and the postdoc buy a condo an hour north of Salt Lake City, where they produce software from a home office.

When the human comedy moves offstage, the dramatic irony tends to be more poignant. In real life it is not just others who let our means become their ends; it is we ourselves whose growing preoccupation with our means causes us to forget the ends they were intended to serve. My own attitude-change research (described in chapters 2–5 of this volume) began as a tool to be used to study the structure and functioning of thought systems. I entered psychology graduate study with an interest in how thought systems are structured and operate. A physiological course in my first year at Yale described the technique of tracing the histological structure of the nervous system by administering a lesion or electrical impulse to a specific nerve fiber in the vertebrate's spinal cord and tracking this excitation's remote ramifications to study organization in the central nervous system. The analogy occurred to me that one might introduce a change of attitude on a specific issue in a thought system and map the organization of mind by tracing the phenomenological ramifications of this experimentally induced local alteration in belief as it spread to adjacent thoughts. I recognized that I would have to produce a whopping attitude change on the explicit target issue because of likely attenuation of such a spread of effect. Hence, I became interested in developing powerful persuasive communications as a tool for studying the operation of thought systems. Before long the tool itself became so interesting, and Carl Hovland's "attitude-change" project at Yale (McGuire, 1996a) so inviting, that I was diverted into a decade of studying the tool – attitude change (see chapters 2 and 3 and other topics such as selective perception) – before getting back to this thought-systems work.

[Adapted with permission from W. J. McGuire, 1981a, The probabilogical model of cognitive structure and attitude change, in R. E. Petty, T. M. Ostrom, & T. Brock (Eds), *Cognitive responses in persuasion*, pp. 291–307. (Hillsdale, NJ: Lawrence Erlbaum Associates, copyright © 1981.]

Terminological Clarification

Some conceptual clarifications help reduce confusion. It is useful to distinguish between a thought per se and the various ways of expressing that thought. Also, I use *thought* atypically broadly as an inclusive label for many types of predispositions or representations to which other students of the topic give separate labels (e.g., attitude, belief, opinion, cognition, judgment, etc.). One should not adopt a distinction until it has been shown to make a difference; it is better to lump together similar concepts until there is reason for distinguishing them (e.g., when they are found to relate differently to a third variable), because overlumping tends to be self-correcting whereas oversplitting is not.

Furthermore, if and when it is found that a distinction ought to be made, care must be taken in labeling the components to be distinguished. For example, when it appears that evaluative and expectancy thoughts (judgments) relate differently to important third variables, some students of the topic use *attitudes* to label evaluative thoughts (desirability or "goodness" judgments) and *beliefs* to label expectancy thoughts (likelihood or "truth" judgments). I advocate instead the use of labels that are less confusing and more informative, usually a noun (e.g., *judgment*) that conveys the common genus of the two types of thoughts to be distinguished, and add pertinent adjectives that convey their distinctive features (e.g., *evaluative judgments* vs. *expectancy judgments*). Precedents can be found for employing *attitudes* versus *opinions* to convey this evaluative-versus-expectancy distinction, but precedents can be found also for using these two terms to label other distinctions (McGuire, 1969a, 1985a). Hence, labels such as *attitudes* versus *opinions,* or *beliefs* are doubly faulted.

Content of Mind

An inclusive theory of thought systems ought to explain their contents, static structure, and dynamic functioning – three topics discussed successively in the next three sections. Regarding the content of thoughts, I prefer a topics-on-dimensions analysis that defines an elemental thought as the thinker's response that indicates where he or she perceives a topic of meaning to fall on a dimension of judgment. "Topics of meaning" and "dimensions of judgment" as primitive terms are not strictly definable, but I shall clarify them by listing examples and subtypes. A half-dozen alternative definitions of individual thoughts are discussed in McGuire (1989a) and in chapter 10 of this volume.

Topics of meaning.   The topical components of thoughts include anything about which a judgment can be made, or can be distinguished from at least one other topic, or to which at least one property can be predicated – three equivalent criteria. Some topics of meaning are simple, or at least simply labeled (e.g., George Washington, London, my breakfast today, the American flag, etc.). Other topics are more complex in being collective (e.g., the human race, violent crime in America, etc.) or more abstract (e.g., justice, betrayal). Still more complex are topics that are syntactical combinations of more simple elements; for example, the "NASA budget," an "astronaut," or "Mars" is each a topic of meaning, as is the composite, "increasing the NASA budget for a program to put an astronaut on Mars," because each of the components and the composite is a topic about which one can make judgments, discriminate reliably from other topics of meaning, and predicate properties.

Dimensions of judgment.   The other component of individual thoughts, dimensions of judgment, are the axes of the conceptual space in which topics of meaning fall. Any aspect with respect to which two or more topics of meaning can be perceived to differ constitutes a dimension of judgment. Some dimensions are transcendental in that all topics of meaning may be projected on them. Classical transcendental attributes are truth and goodness. Truth includes any veridicality judgment about topics of meaning (e.g., expectancy, likelihood, existence, occurrence, etc.); goodness includes any evaluative judgment (e.g., desirability, liking, attractiveness, choosing, preferring, etc.). Still other transcendental dimensions of judgment on which all topics of thought can be projected are meaningfulness (familiarity, categorizability, etc.); importance (involvement, relevance, centrality, etc.); complexity; activity; potency; and so on. My own empirical work has focused on philosophy's and psychology's two favorite dimensions, truth and goodness, here called "expectancy" and "evaluation" judgments.

Besides these transcendental dimensions on which all topics of meaning can be projected, there are also circumscribed dimensions of judgment on which only a specifiable subset of topics of meaning can be literally projected. For example, only physical topics can properly be projected on the size and weight dimensions; only people (and perhaps a few other "higher" animal species) can be projected on the guilt and loyalty dimensions. A broader range of topics can be projected figuratively on some circumscribed dimension, as when one speaks of "a weighty decision" or "a cruel winter."

Propositions.   My theory applies to thought systems insofar as their contents can be inventoried as lists of propositions that assign topics of thought to positions on dimensions of judgment. For example, a proposition such as "There is no chance that astronauts will visit Mars in the twentieth century" assigns the object of thought, "astronauts visiting Mars in the twentieth century," to a position on the expectancy dimension of judgment. Another proposition, "I hope that astronauts will visit Mars in the twentieth century" assigns this same object of thought to a position on the evaluation dimension. There probably are additional nonverbalized contents of thought systems, but my model has so far been developed primarily to handle such verbal propositional thoughts.

Structure of Mind

When the contents of mind are defined as propositions that locate topics of meaning on dimensions of judgment, then the structure of mind (the organization among these propositions) reduces to the interrelations among the topics or the dimensions of these propositions. I postulate a connectedness and coherence among thoughts such that people tend to interrelate thoughts and the propositions that express them and to prefer congruent patterns (to be described) of interrelations. A simple within-dimension type of thought microsystem involves the organization among a set of propositions all of which assign their topics of meaning to the same dimension of judgment (e.g., "I'll reduce my intake of any food ingredient that aggravates high blood pressure," "Sodium in one's diet aggravates high blood pressure," "I'll reduce sodium levels in my diet," each of these three syllogistically related propositions assigning its topic of thought to the expectancy dimension of judgment). Among such sets of within-dimension thoughts, like the syllogistic triad just listed, I postulate a congruence describable by the axioms of logic and probability theory.

An across-dimension type of simple thought system assigns a single topic of meaning to positions on multiple dimensions of judgment (e.g., the propositions "It would be a good thing to reduce my intake of any food ingredient that aggravates high blood pressure" and "I am going to reduce my intake of any food ingredient that aggravates high blood pressure," which project the reduced-intake topic on the evaluation and expectancy dimensions, respectively). Between evaluation and expectancy thoughts I postulate a hedonic consistency (in either the wishful thinking or the rationalization causal direction), just as for material topics I postulate a consistency between the perceived size and weight dimensions (resulting in the "size-weight illusion"). Still more complex thought systems ("ideologies" – see chapter 10) arise when many topics are projected on multiple dimensions, as discussed in McGuire 1989a. The thought systems studied here tend to be mesosystems, bigger than the microsystems just mentioned but smaller than ideologies.

Mental Functioning

The line between structure and functioning being blurry, my dynamic functioning postulates are natural outgrowths of the model's structural postulates. The 1955 model focused on two types of tendencies guiding thought-system functioning: (1) rational "probabilogical" consistency tendencies which posit that people's patterns of thoughts follow the axioms of logic and probability theory; and (2) add-on arational motivational tendencies including hedonic consistency processes such as rationalization and wishful thinking, plus economizing "cognitive miser" processes such as loose-linkage and temporal and spatial inertia.

The probabilogical model. The model's basic postulate is that thought processes follow the axioms of logic, as illustrated by syllogistic reasoning and probability theory. Suppose the person is presented with the following triad of syllogistically related propositions: (*a*) Swimming at the city beaches is a recreation that is becoming a serious threat to the health of the participants; (*b*) the city health authorities will prohibit any recreation that becomes a serious threat to the health of the participants; (*c*) the city health authorities will prohibit swimming at the city beaches. The person is then asked to judge the probability that each proposition is true and perhaps responds that $p(a) = .55$, $p(b) = .60$, and $p(c) = .40$. I postulate that relations among these subjective probabilities will approximate the principles of logic and probability theory. In general, to the extent that the person judges the two premises, *a* and *b*, to be highly probable, she or he should judge the conclusion *c* also to be highly probable. More exactly, the probabilogical model postulates that there will be logical consistency in this syllogistic minisystem that will take the form of:

$$p(c) = [p(c/(a \ \& \ b)) \times p(a \ \& \ b)] + [p(c/{\sim}(a \ \& \ b)) \times p{\sim}(a \ \& \ b)],$$
(Equation $p(c)$)

where the slash mark can be interpreted as "follows on the basis of" or "given that"; "&" can be operationalized as "and"; and "~" as "not." As a simpler inequality, $p(c) \geq p(a) \times p(b)$, a formula to which our above-stated obtained values conform, namely, $.40 \geq .55 \times .60$. (Note that, although this respondent would be logical in terms of our probability-scaled logic, he or she might be illogical in terms of a two-valued (true, false) Aristotelian logic. If the respondent judged "true" any proposition with a subjective probability of .50 or higher and judged "false" any with .49 or less, then the resultant TTF obtained response pattern in the case above would be illogical by Aristotelian logic.)

Turning from the static structure to dynamic functioning, if a person's belief is changed on one of the premises (e.g., if the subjective probability of premise *a*, $p(a)$, is raised by a communication that experts agree that the city's beaches are polluted to a degree that is becoming a serious health menace), then the probabilogical model's required resultant change on the conclusion, $\triangle p(c)$ (the increase in the subjective probability judgment that swimming will be prohibited), is as follows:

$$\triangle p(c) = \triangle p(a \ \& \ b) \times [p(c/(a \ \& \ b)) - p(c/\sim(a \ \& \ b))].$$

(Equation $\triangle p(c)$)

We have focused on a syllogistically related set of beliefs because the syllogism is a well-known logical structure, widely used (at least implicitly) in thinking. However, the probabilogical model can be generalized beyond the syllogism to any other sets of beliefs in well-formed relations (McGuire, 1960c).

Alogical auxiliary functioning postulates.   The probabilogical model in isolation depicts people as acting like logic machines, but theoretical analyses and everyday observation make it unlikely that people have evolved to be purely logical. My model postulates that additional, alogical rules operate within thought systems. Besides a realistic logical consistency, people's thought systems show a need for autistic hedonic consistency such that the person's perceptions of a topic's position on the expectancy dimension and on the evaluative dimension tend to be assimilated toward one another. That is, the person's expectancy belief on a conclusion (that swimming will be prohibited), $p(c)$, will be assimilated, not only to his or her subjective probabilities of the premises, $p(a)$ and $p(b)$, but also to his or her judgment of the desirability of c, Des(c). The person thinks in an honest-broker manner, such that his or her expectancy on the conclusion $p(c)$ is a "least-squared deviation" compromise between these realistic and autistic consistency needs, with the exact point of compromise shifting with dispositional and situational interaction variables that affect the relative salience of realistic or autistic needs. Experimental manipulation of the salience of one or the other need can affect its contribution to the compromise.

The salience postulate is an important part of the probabilogical model. Some prescriptive "laws of thought" cognitive simulations treat all mental contents as being equally available (as they are for the computer metaphor), ignoring the obvious constriction of foveal awareness and the limitations of recall. Salience is a matter of degree, and even low-salient related premises will have some impact on conclusions, but my functioning model predicts that the impact of any one belief on another is directly proportional to its momentary salience, which can be manipulated by operations such as Socratic questioning and directed-thinking tasks. Hence, attitude change can be induced by manipulating the salience of material already within the person's cognitive system, even without presenting any new information from an outside source.

Our own full model (McGuire, 1960c; McGuire & McGuire, 1991c) adds postulates about various adaptive "fallacies" in thinking, including ones described in antiquity such as undistributed middle and amphibology; those described earlier in the first half of this century such as the atmosphere and the wariness effects (Wilkins, 1928; Woodworth & Sells, 1935); those described in the second half, which inaugurated the social cognition era, such as spatial and temporal inertia, wishful thinking, and rationalization, discussed by McGuire 1960c and below; and those later introduced, such as retrievability and anchoring (Wason & Johnson-Laird, 1972; Tversky & Kahneman, 1974).

EMPIRICAL RESULTS ON THE 1950s PROBABILOGICAL MODEL

My 1950s probabilogical model yields predictions about four aspects of thought systems' content, structure, and functioning: (1) it illustrates the initial steady-state static structure of the thought system; (2) it demonstrates the efficacy of the "Socratic method" of changing attitudes simply by asking questions that increase the salience of biased subsets of the person's thoughts on related issues without communicating any new information from an outside source; (3) it indicates how a belief's resistance to a persuasive communication from an outside source is affected by the cognitive embeddedness of the belief; and (4) it shows the remote ramifications of persuasive communications on thoughts that are not mentioned in the communication but are related to the explicit target thought. For each of these four areas of empirical work, I shall first describe the basic main-effect predictions and then mediational or interactional predictions that clarify the underlying processes or suggest limitations to their operation.

Static Structure of Thought Systems: The Relations among Initial Attitudes

The person's thought system surrounding any core judgment is postulated to be determined by a variety of forces, of which logical consistency and hedonic consistency are central to this research program. Logical consistency in the initial state of a thought system is measured by the extent to which a person's probability judgment of the truth of a given proposition, p(c), relates, as specified in Equation p(c), to his or her probability judgment of the truth of antecedent premises *a* & *b,* from which conclusion *c* logically follows. Hedonic consistency in the initial thought system is measured by the extent to which the conclusion's (or any other proposition's) judged likelihood correlates with its judged desirability.

Initial logical consistency among contemporaneous beliefs.   The basic prediction here is that the expectation judgment regarding a logical conclusion (its subjective probability of occurrence) will be related to the subjective probabilities of its logical antecedent premises as specified by Equation p(c). In the first wave of my thought-systems research (McGuire, 1960c) highly significant correlations of about +.50 to +.70 were typically found between the obtained subjective probability of the conclusion and that predicted from the premises by Equation p(c). With Wyer and Goldberg's (1970) improved operationalizations, the correlations between observed and predicted values have been as high as r = +.94 and remain high even when the sets of propositions are in relations more complex than syllogistic triads. These correlations are admittedly somewhat inflated by being based on grouped data, but are still impressive considering the limited reliability of the individual belief measures and the complex combinatory rules, and the low experimental demand for consistency (e.g., logically related propositions were typically scattered over a long questionnaire), and that these high correlations are obtained without taking into account the additional variables in my model.

Several lines of evidence suggest that adherence of actual thought systems to the probabilogical model is automatic rather than thought out. If it were intellectually reasoned one might expect it to be correlated with intelligence, but both Dillehay, Insko, and Smith (1966) and Holt and Watts (1970) report that low- and high-intelligence students showed equal consistency (though admittedly college student participants do not reflect the full range of intelligence). Automaticity is suggested also because manipulating the salience of the interrelations among the antecedents and consequents (e.g., by grouping vs. scattering triads of syllogistically related propositions over a long questionnaire) did not affect initial logical consistency (Holt & Watts, 1969). Rosen and Wyer (1972) did find an increase in consistency when it was explicitly mentioned to the participants that some of the items in the scattered questionnaire were interrelated; but their participants were about equally consistent regardless of whether or not mention was made of the desirability of being consistent. The probabilogical model predicts equally well relations among high as low importance issues, and for evaluations as for expectancies, without pronounced interactions (Wyer, 1974b). Hence, the probabilogical model proves impressively robust in predicting interrelations among initial sets of judgment under a wide range of conditions, and even when consistency and interrelatedness are deemphasized. Some provocative interactions have been found and deserve more study; for example, the union relation between propositions does not fit the probabilogical model quite as well as do implication and intersection relations (Wyer, 1974b).

Initial hedonic consistency.   A positive correlation is predicted between the expectation and evaluation judgments on any set of topics of meaning. Such "hedonic consistency" can be a rational way of thinking (McGuire, 1960c) rather than a blatantly illogical distortion, as proposed by some researchers (Lund, 1925; Cantril, 1938; McGregor, 1938). I postulate that causality flows in both directions, reflecting both a "wishful thinking" tendency such that people bring their expectations in line with their desires, and a "rationalization" tendency such that they bring desires in line with expectations.

Results inspired by this model show a substantial level of hedonic consistency over a variety of measurement tactics. The overall correlation between the expectations and the evaluations of topics of thought tends to exceed r = +.40, substantial if somewhat less than the correlation obtained for logical consistency. The correlation goes up to r = .85 when both logical and hedonic consistencies are taken into account simultaneously (McGuire, 1960c). The use of college student respondents may contribute to the finding of stronger logical consistency than hedonic consistency, although the higher level of logical than hedonic consistency was found even with the high school and community college students deliberately employed in the original studies (McGuire, 1960a, 1960b). The stronger logical than hedonic consistency might also reflect the concentration in these studies on the more objective expectation dimension of judgment, but the probabilogical model has been applied also to the evaluation dimension (Wyer, 1975, pp. 234–5), with the logical consistency tendency seeming as powerful in accounting for initial structures among evaluation as among expectation beliefs. There is an interaction effect such that hedonic consistency is greater with low- than high-intelligence participants (Dillehay, Insko, & Smith, 1966; Watts & Holt, 1970. Intelligence may reduce hedonic consistency rather than raise logical consistency.

The Persuasion-from-Within Approach: Socratic Questioning

Theory. A second innovative line of work emerging from my thought-systems approach is its implication that a person's attitudes can be changed simply by manipulating the salience of information already in her or his cognitive repertory, without presenting new information from an outside source. Salience of a biased subset of related beliefs can be manipulated either by the reactive Socratic-questioning task or by the more active "directed-thinking" task. Socratic questioning involves asking the person questions the answering of which enhances the salience of a subset of beliefs that the person already accepts; then to be consistent with that subset of beliefs made more salient, the person must change his or her initial belief. In the eponymous example, Socrates, simply by asking questions, persuaded Meno's slave to change his preconceptions regarding the Pythagorean theorem. The alternative, more active "directed-thinking" self-persuasion technique involves changing the person's judgment by giving him or her a biased scanning task (e.g., raising the person's evaluation judgment about an event by asking him or her to list desirable consequences that the event promotes). My theory assumes that a person's momentary expectancy on any topic is the result of multiple forces, including a pressure to both logical and hedonic consistency as well as pressures to inconsistency due to a variety of factors (e.g., conflicting partial information, disagreements among one's valued reference groups, the person's response biases, spatial and temporal inertia, and attention limitations that leave much of one's sample of information nonsalient).

Empirical studies. The empirical track record of the Socratic-questioning predictions is good across a variety of manipulations and measures. In the original study (McGuire, 1960a) the Socratic effect was tested in terms of the prediction that if people are asked their probability judgments on the likelihood of syllogistically related premises and conclusions in a first session it will sensitize them to inconsistencies among these judgments. Hence, when they are asked to judge these propositions a week later, this second set of judgments will better approximate the Equation $p(c)$ relations than did the initial set of judgments. This was found even controlling for regression and even when the logically related beliefs are scattered through the questionnaire and no mention is made in either session of their interrelatedness or of the importance of being consistent. A dozen studies by Watts and Holt (1970) and by Wyer and his students (Rosen and Wyer, 1972; Wyer, 1974b; Henninger and Wyer, 1976), using the criterion that judgments on related premises and conclusions will be closer to Equation $p(c)$ in a second than in the first session, have found significant evidence of the Socratic effect. Only isolated studies by Holt and Watts (1969) and Dillehay, Insko, and Smith (1966) fail to confirm. The Socratic effect is robust over time intervals between sessions, ranging from immediately, ten minutes, two days, to seven days.

I began the Socratic effect research expecting that it would be a laboratory curiosity requiring delicate teasing out, but it has proven to be surprisingly robust, respectable in effect size and reliability. The Socratic effect has sufficient power to resolve theoretical niceties, such as showing (Wyer, 1974b) that the McGuire (1960c) probabilogical model simulates actual cognitive consistency better than does the Osgood-Tannenbaum (1955) congruity theory, the Heider (1958) balance theory, or the Abelson and Rosenberg (1958) psycho-logic theory. Far from its being an elusive laboratory novelty, survey researchers have come to realize that the Socratic effect is a constant intruder that introduces order-of-questions "artifacts" into real-life surveys (Schwarz & Strack, 1991).

Although the Socratic effect dependably shows up as a greater consistency (by the Equation $p(c)$ criterion) in the second than in the first session, the further prediction that it will show up even within the first session (in the form of greater logical consistency in the later than earlier elicited beliefs within a syllogistic system of beliefs) receives confirmation only occasionally and within limited circumstances (McGuire, 1960a; Holt, 1970; Henninger & Wyer, 1976). This weakness of the Socratic effect within as compared to across sessions separated by an interval may be due to the temporal-inertia process (discussed further below), such that information needs time before it percolates through the thought system.

Variables accentuating the Socratic effect.   The theory underlying the Socratic effect implies that there will be a number of multiplying interaction effects, but their empirical confirmation has been spotty. Grouping the related propositions closely together, or explicitly mentioning the desirability of being consistent, or pointing out that some of the propositions are interrelated, usually fails to yield stronger Socratic effects. The failures to confirm such salience interaction predictions suggest that the Socratic effect is automatic rather than based on explicit recognition and correction of inconsistencies. McGuire (1960a) found that the Socratic effect adjustment is made on the major premise and the conclusion more than on the minor premise, perhaps because the predicate variable (which is in the major premise and conclusion but not in the minor premise) tends to be the most affect-loaded term in syllogisms of the type used in these studies.

As for dispositional interactions, predicting how the respondent's intelligence will affect the magnitude of the Socratic effect is hazardous because alternative plausible mediators imply opposite interactions: More intelligent respondents would tend to show less Socratic effect because they would have greater consistency among their beliefs from the outset; or, conversely, the more intelligent persons may be more perceptive of and bothered by any initial inconsistencies that do arise and so show greater corrective Socratic adjustments. A suitable test thus calls for a design where the relation between intelligence and the Socratic effect could be adjusted for the magnitude of the initial inconsistency. Three studies have failed to show an interaction between intelligence and magnitude of Socratic effect, but without employing the full design suggested here.

Cognitive Linkage and Resistance to Persuasion

The previous two sections have reviewed empirical work testing my theory's predictions regarding the effects of thoughts already in the person's cognitive system. The next two sections will discuss the theory's predictions regarding the processing of new information communicated to the thinker by an outside source. This section reports how resistance to a persuasive attack on a target judgment is affected by that judgment's embeddedness in broader cognitive structures that are not explicitly mentioned in the attacking message; and the subsequent section reports the remote cognitive ramifications of a persuasive message on judgments not themselves explicitly mentioned in the message but related to the explicit target judgments that are argued.

This probabilogical thought-system approach has implications regarding resistance to persuasive attacks. Firstly, the more the person is sensitized to a given belief's embeddedness in a thought system, the more inhibited he or she will become about changing the belief because that will require onerously changing beliefs on the related issues as well (and then on issues related to the related issues), or else aggravating the inconsistencies in his or her thought systems. A number of studies support such implications. Resistance to the persuasive information is increased by use of a "before" measure (Watts and Holt, 1970); by grouping together the syllogistically related propositions (Holt & Watts, 1969); by having the believer participate actively in linking the belief to cherished values (Nelson, 1968); and even by passive linkage (Holt, 1970). Also as implied, persons cognitively tuned (Zajonc, 1960) to be receivers rather than senders of further messages are more resistant (Watts & Holt, 1970).

A second resistance-to-persuasion implication of this thought-system theory is that if the persuasive message is arguing in a direction that aggravates any initial inconsistency then the person will be more resistant to attack. McGuire (1960b) confirmed the implication that a person will be more resistant to a communication arguing for the likelihood of a relatively desirable judgment than of an undesirable one, controlling for regression and ceiling effects. The further prediction that the induced changes on the explicit premises will be more persistent when the change is in the direction that increases logical consistency as defined by the probabilogical Equation $p(c)$ was not confirmed. Failure to confirm several persistence predictions has led to alterations in my theorizing. I now postulate that at any given moment the person's thought system manifests a balance between hedonic and logical consistency that reflects the person's momentary internal and environmental demands. Experimental manipulations can induce changes in a thought system by shifting this balance momentarily, but after the person leaves the experimental situation the balance tends to revert to its initial chronic state.

Remote Ramifications on Unmentioned Related Judgments

The probabilogical model's richest set of implications concerns a fourth area, the remote cognitive ramifications of persuasive communications. The study of how persuasive communications affect not only their explicit target judgment but also unmentioned related judgments has been relatively neglected in other programs of attitude research. Tracing the cognitive ramifications of the communication-induced change as it spreads from the explicit target judgment to unmentioned parts of the thought system is interesting, not just for its attitude-change implications, but especially because it provides a powerful method of investigating the content, structure, and functioning of thought systems.

Evidence for remote impacts on unmentioned judgments. The probabilogical model implies that a persuasive communication that affects the judgment about which it explicitly argues will affect also, as specified in Equation $\triangle p(c)$, unmentioned judgments that are logically or hedonically related to that judgment. The point can be illustrated by the syllogistic example used earlier: A communication arguing persuasively that the city beaches are becoming dangerously polluted should affect the audience's likelihood judgments, not only on this explicit premise a, that the beaches are growing dangerously polluted, but also on the unmentioned implied conclusion c, that swimming will be forbidden at these beaches, and on the copremise b, that dangerous recreations will be forbidden by the city. The hedonic consistency postulate further predicts that this likelihood persuasive message will affect also the desirability judgments on propositions a, b, and c. There are now numerous studies confirming that a persuasive communication affects not only the premise with which it explicitly deals but also the unmentioned consequences that follow from that premise. Such remote ramifications occur robustly over a wide range of situational and dispositional conditions. Some survey researchers (Converse, 1964) have questioned the connectedness and coherence of people's belief systems, but these remote ramifications findings provide evidence that people do connect their beliefs and tend to maintain coherence among them.

Variables that multiply remote ramifications. The magnitude of these remote impacts has been predicted to depend on a number of interacting variables. As predicted, remote impacts increase when the communication argues in a direction that would increase initial inconsistency as defined by Equation $p(c)$ (McGuire, 1960b); when the person is cognitively tuned (Zajonc, 1960) as receiver rather than as sender (Watts & Holt, 1970); and when the person is less committed to his or her judgment on the remote issue (Holt, 1970). Some predicted interactions (e.g., that a "before" measure would affect size of remote impacts) were not confirmed (Watts & Holt, 1970). Remote ramifications were predicted to increase with intelligence, but, curiously, Dillehay, Insko, and Smith (1966) found significantly more remote ramifications for those below median intelligence than for those above; conceivably, more intelligent believers are able to spread the remote changes over a broader spectrum of implications so that each individual remote change is small.

The spatial inertia postulate.   Another postulate in my theory applies a loose-link metaphor to thought chains such that when one link in the belief chain is pulled (e.g., by a persuasive communication giving experts' discrepant norms on the explicit issue) some slack has to be taken up before this exerts a pull on the next premise in the chain, implying that the remote impact on the unmentioned conclusion will fall short of the directly induced change on the explicit premise for two reasons: (1) the probabilogical model Equation $\Delta p(c)$ predicts that the change on the unmentioned consequence will be attenuated due to the direct change on the explicit premise, $p(a)$, being multiplied by the lower-than-1.00 probability of the copremise, $p(b)$; and (2) there is an additional "spatial inertia" that results in the actual change on the conclusion being even less than this attenuated $\Delta p(a)$ change logically required, due to the slack in the loosely linked system of related beliefs.

The empirical evidence is mixed. Spatial inertia was found in both of McGuire's (1960a, 1960b) studies and two of the three studies by Watts and Holt (1969, 1970), in one of the three McFarland and Thistlethwaite (1970) studies, in one of the two by Dillehay, Insko, and Smith (1966), and in Spellman, Ullman, and Holyoak (1993). It should be noted that where the spatial inertia postulate was not confirmed, it was not because of a lack of remote ramification but, on the contrary, because the remote ramification on the unmentioned conclusion was large, the full amount required by the probabilogical model's Equation $\Delta p(c)$. The person shows not only a significant tendency to behave like a probabilistic logic machine but to behave precisely like a logic machine, making superfluous alogical "lazy organism" postulates like spatial and temporal inertia that I added to account for expected shortfalls from the probabilogical model.

The temporal inertia postulate. Another postulate in the theory is that when a persuasive communication produces an immediate change on its explicit target premise this change percolates through the system only gradually, producing delayed-action changes of judgments on related but unmentioned consequences (although the net remote impact should be reduced over time by concurrent decay of the immediate impact on the explicit premise). This delayed-action prediction has had only moderate empirical confirmation (Hovland, Lumsdaine, & Sheffield, 1949; Stotland, Katz, & Patchen, 1959). Several studies using a one-week delay interval found modest delayed-action effects (e.g., in one of two tests by McGuire [1960a, 1960b] and in one of two studies by Dillehay, Insko, and Smith [1966]). Holt and Watts (1970), using a briefer delay interval of ten minutes, found sizable short-term delayed-action effects on the unmentioned logical conclusion, suggesting that the spread of effect occurs mainly in the first few minutes after the initial change. The overall decay curve is predicted to be an inverted-U whose time parameters need further exploration.

Ramifications across dimensions of judgment. Another alogical postulate of our theory is that consistency is maintained, not only across topics of meaning on a single dimension, as just described, but also across dimensions of judgment (e.g., in the form of hedonic consistency tendencies, in both wishful thinking and rationalization directions, to bring into alignment one's expectation and one's evaluation regarding any topic of meaning) as well as within-dimension consistency (e.g., probabilogical consistency, discussed above). My own earlier work (McGuire, 1960c) demonstrates such cross-dimensional hedonic consistency and my later 1980s work gives it more attention, as described in the next section of this chapter. Most of the empirical work on the probabilogical theory has concentrated on within-dimensional consistency (and especially within the expectancy dimension); but Wyer (1974a), measuring evaluations on a probabilistic scale, found that the Socratic effect holds up as well for evaluations as for expectancies (Wyer, 1974b). As regards causal direction of these across-dimension hedonic consistency ramifications, McGuire (1960a) showed its occurrence in a rationalization direction and Holt (1970) in the wishful-thinking direction. Our newer research (McGuire & McGuire, 1991c), described in the next part of this chapter, found stronger evidence in the rationalization than in the wishful-thinking direction.

NEW DIRECTIONS IN OUR 1980s THOUGHT-SYSTEMS RESEARCH

[Adapted with permission from W. J. McGuire and C. V. McGuire, 1991c, The content, structure, and operation of thought systems, in R. S. Wyer, Jr., & T. K. Srull (Eds.), *Advances in social cognition, Vol. 4*, pp. 1–78 (Hillsdale, NJ: Erlbaum, copyright © 1991).]

Changes from the 1950s Research Program

Our return to research on thought systems in the 1980s had considerable continuity with the 1950s research described so far as regards both the general assumption that thought systems are systemically organized and many of the specific postulates. However, four changes should be noted, two substantive and two pertaining to method. Regarding substance, a first change is that my 1950s theorizing had depicted thinking as being basically logical with some alogical add-ons (e.g., hedonic consistency and cognitive miserliness tendencies); in contrast, our 1980s theorizing depicts realistic and autistic thought processes as equally basic. Secondly, the 1950s work concentrated more narrowly on antecedents as the topics of meaning and on likelihood as the dimensions of judgment; in contrast, our 1980s program of research gives equal attention to antecedent and consequence topics and to likelihood and desirability dimensions.

As regards methods, one change is that the new work presents a lower profile to the participants, allowing their free associations to define what thoughts are related to a given core event, instead of our 1950s practice of a priori designating thoughts as obviously related. A second methods change is that we have backed down tactically from the attempt in the 1950s probabilogical work (McGuire, 1960c) to be highly quantitative from the outset. This new research settles for counting rather than scaling or weighing (e.g., settling for qualitative contrasts between number of desirable versus undesirable consequences without quantifying how desirable; and settling for dichotomous promotive versus preventive relations between events without weighing them for the subjective conditional probabilities linking the events). The remaining sections of this chapter describe our second round of thought systems research, first as regards its general theoretical postulates and then as regards the obtained empirical results.

Theoretical Assumptions

Coping postulates, realistic and hedonic. We assume that people have both realistic coping needs to adjust to the actualities of the external environment and autistic coping needs to maintain hedonically comfortable phenomenal states. Specifically, we postulate three realistic and two autistic tactics for coping with possible events. A more masterful, destiny-controlling realistic tactic is a "principle of sufficient reason" process of deciding on the core event's likelihood by identifying antecedents whose manipulation would promote or prevent the core event's occurrences. A more conservative, destiny-resigned realistic tactic is the "utility maximizing" process of focusing on the core event's desirability, letting happen what will but identifying and preparing for the event's pleasant and unpleasant consequences, for example, by damage-control tactics. A third, good-brings-forth-good, coping tactic is for the person to estimate the core event's desirability by the net desirability of its antecedents, a "congruent origins" process.

Also postulated are two autistic tactics for coping with possible events by keeping a hedonically gratifying congruence among one's thoughts: One such tactic, wishful thinking, calls for the person's assimilating his or her judgment of an event's likelihood to its judged desirability (and so the pleasantness of its perceived consequents). The other autistic coping tactic, rationalization, calls for the person to assimilate his or her judgment of an event's desirability to its judged likelihood (and so to the likelihood of its perceived antecedents). Three of these five coping tendencies (utility-maximizing, congruent origins, and rationalization) are postulated to govern the structure and operation of desirability subsystems, and the other two coping tendencies (sufficient reason and wishful thinking) are postulated to govern the likelihood subsystems. These five coping postulates and their specific implications are discussed further below, when empirical studies relevant to each are described.

Auxiliary postulates. Besides these five coping postulates, our theory also contains a series of auxiliary postulates, most of which deal with the person's "cognitive miserliness" tendency to reduce much cognitive effort at only slight loss of coping optimization. These auxiliary postulates were already proposed in the 1950s probabilogical research (e.g., salience effects, temporal inertia, and spatial inertia, etc.) and so were discussed earlier in this chapter. Additional economizing processes, such as the postulate that desirability thought systems are more tightly linked than likelihood thought systems, will be discussed further below. Predictions stemming from the coping postulates and the auxiliary postulates were tested in a series of experiments reported in the next three sections, which deal successively with thought systems' content, their static structure, and their dynamic functioning.

STUDIES OF THOUGHT SYSTEMS' CONTENT

Content of Thought Systems: Theory

Our basic theoretical postulate is that thought systems develop around the person's perceptions of possible events and help the person to cope, realistically or autistically, with these events. The content of thought systems is operationally defined as the thoughts that the person generates when asked to free-associate about a designated core event, and predicted to consist primarily of the core event's antecedents and consequences projected primarily on the desirability and likelihood dimensions of judgment. Our five specific coping postulates make further predictions about how the relative prevalence of various types of antecedents and consequences will be affected by dispositional variables like the thinker's sex and by situational variables like the controllability of the events.

Realistically, a person's judgment about an event's desirability should be related to the pattern of the salient consequences that it evokes (e.g., the prevalence of favorable over unfavorable salient consequences). The person's judgment about the event's likelihood should be realistically related to the pattern of its salient antecedents (e.g., the prevalence of promotive over preventive antecedents). Thinking about either its antecedents or its consequences can help the person to cope realistically with the core event, but focusing on its antecedents is the more masterful mode of coping in that it offers some possibility of controlling one's destiny by acting on these antecedents to manipulate whether or not the event will occur. Thinking about the event's consequences, on the other hand, allows only the more limited coping tactic of letting happen what will but taking preparatory actions like damage control. Thus, thinking about the event's antecedents reflects a willingness to take effective control, whereas thinking about its consequences reflects being resigned to one's fate and attempting to make the best of it. An implication is that the more the person feels a sense of control in a given conceptual domain, the greater will be the ratio of antecedents to consequences among the thoughts evoked by mention of a core event from that domain, which implies situational and dispositional interaction effects. An auxiliary positivity-bias postulate implies that when a person is asked to free-associate on a core event there will be a preponderance of promotively over preventively related antecedents and consequences. We theorize further that slight ability differences tend to develop into large proclivity (preference) differences (McGuire & McGuire, 1992c).

Content of Thought Systems: Methods

Procedures. Yale College students were paced through an experimental booklet whose early pages manipulated the independent variables and whose later pages measured the dependent variables. On the top of each of four early pages was printed the statement of a core eventuality (e.g., "Drug abuse is being largely eliminated in the United States"), and the participant was given three minutes to write down on that page all of the thoughts evoked by the mentioned event (or, in some conditions, all thoughts of a designated type, e.g., all the desirable consequences that the core event would tend to promote). The numbers from 1 to 12 were spaced down the lefthand margin of each of these pages and participants were asked to start each new thought next to a new number. After three minutes the signal was given to proceed to the next page, on the top of which was presented still another core event and a new thought-generating task.

Content analysis of the evoked thoughts. The evoked thoughts written down by the participant beneath the core-event heading on each page were then content-analyzed by trained coders into 15 broad categories (see Table 6.1), including the eight types of antecedents and consequences (in a $2 \times 2 \times 2$ design), with which our predictions mainly deal. The 8 include: (Desirable vs. Undesirable) $\times$ (More vs.

Less likely) × (Antecedents vs. Consequences of the core event), yielding the 8 types, DMA, UMA, . . . , ULC, where DMA refers to *D*esirable *A*ntecedents that make the core event *M*ore likely; and ULC refers to *U*ndesirable *C*onsequences that the core event makes *L*ess likely. Intercoder agreement on classifying the evoked thoughts on the eight categories averaged 94%.

Core-event stimuli used to evoke the related thoughts. Our half-dozen content studies were systematically varied regarding the types of core events used to evoke related thoughts. The first content study cast a wide net by including 36 diverse topics, selected by prestudies from long lists of events in each of 6 diverse topic areas: economics, health, international affairs, life-style, politics, and sports. Prestudy participants rated each event on desirability, likelihood, and importance. On the basis of these judgments 36 core events, 6 from each of the 6 topic areas, were selected for diversity as regards perceived desirability and likelihood. In the first study a subset of 96 Yale students free-associated for 3 minutes on each of these 36 events.

A second content study used 8 of these 36 core events, all near the neutral .50 point on our .00 to 1.00 desirability and likelihood scales, Des(CE) and Lik (CE), to allow counterbalanced designs in which judgmental changes can be manipulated either upward or downward without introducing scaling asymmetries. In this second content study, 128 Yale students were first given experts' purported norms on the core events' desirabilities or on their likelihoods and then were asked to free-associate on the core events. The core events used in these first two content studies were all general societal events (e.g., a vaccine against AIDS being developed; the United States having a severe economic depression). A third study used instead personal events of matched desirabilities (e.g., "Your having a highly satisfying social life at Yale next term"; "Your becoming very disappointed in future years in your chosen field of work"). Each of 64 students free-associated on a subset of these personal core events.

In the first three content studies just described participants were asked to free-associate on the core events. In contrast, a fourth content study used a biased-scanning, directed-thinking task: Participants were asked to generate for each designated core event a specified one of the eight types of antecedents and consequences (e.g., participants in the DMA-generating task condition on the drug-abuse-eliminating core event were instructed to "Generate all the desirable antecedents that you can think of that would help eliminate drug abuse in the

United States"). The free-association task used in the first three studies gets at the thinker's proclivity, that is, at the types of antecedents and consequences of the core event that participants prefer spontaneously to think of when given no specification of what kinds of thoughts are to be generated. This fourth content study, by using a directed-thinking task, gets at ability rather than proclivity; that is, at how able the participant is to generate on demand one versus another designated type of antecedent or consequence.

Contents of Thought Systems: Empirical Results

Number of thoughts generated. Yale students were sufficiently fluent at generating thoughts evoked by the core events during the three-minute free-association period. In the first content study, Yale undergraduates free-associating on 36 very diverse core events of an impersonal societal nature generated an average of 5.34 thoughts in three minutes. The number generated was unrelated to the rated desirability, likelihood, and importance judgments of the 36 core events but did vary among the six topical areas, with the most thoughts ($p < .05$) being evoked by sports and life-style events and the least by economic and political events. The 2 most thought-evocative of the 36 core events were "Most shopping will be done from home computer terminals rather than in stores" and "Admission prices will increase substantially for major sports events," which evoked means of 6.50 and 6.42 thoughts, respectively; the two least evocative were "A sizable amount of poverty will continue to exist in the United States" and "Political campaigns will focus on issues rather than on personalities," which evoked means of 3.91 and 3.90 thoughts. Further evidence of Yale students' parochialism (which may be even more pronounced in the general population) is that, in our third study (Columns d and e in Table 6.1), in which participants free-associated either on 8 societal events of polarized desirabilities (e.g., a vaccine against AIDS being developed) or on 8 personal events of matched desirabilities (e.g., oneself having good health in one's later life), the mean number of thoughts evoked were 5.59 versus 7.45, respectively, a parochialism bias in thought fluency significant at the .001 level.

Sex differences in thought fluency. Because a sex difference indicating that females show greater verbal fluency has been often reported, at least until recently (Feingold, 1988), we tested whether the core events evoke more thoughts in women than in men. The picture that emerges across three content studies suggests a sex × thought-domain interaction effect, in addition to (or instead of) a main effect of sex on number of thoughts evoked. In the first content study, where the task was to free-associate on 36 diverse societal events, there was only a trivial gender difference in number of thoughts generated. In the second content study, which used eight neutral societal events, women did generate somewhat ($p < .05$) more thoughts than men; and on the eight highly polarized personal events used in the third content study women generated far more (19% more, $p < .001$) thoughts than did men, whereas for eight general societal events of matched polarized desirabilities the men generated (trivially) more thoughts than the women. Overall, women had slightly richer thought systems, especially thought systems around core events of high personal relevance.

The prevalence of antecedents and consequences. Turning from general fluency effects to types of thoughts evoked as specifically implied by our coping theory of thought systems, the basic hypothesis that most of the thought topics evoked by mention of a core event will be the event's antecedents and consequences receives support in all three free-association studies. In the first content study, using 36 varied core events of a general societal nature, 78% of all evoked thoughts were antecedents or consequences (see Column a in Table 6.1). In the second content study, using 8 societal core events neutral in desirability and likelihood, antecedents and consequences composed 82% of all thoughts listed (Columns b and c in Table 6.1); in the third content study, using eight societal and eight personal core events highly polarized in desirabilities, antecedents and consequences composed 76% and 77%, respectively, of all generated thoughts (Columns d and e in Table 6.1). Particularly prevalent are UMC free associations, that is, *U*ndesirable *C*onsequences that would be made *M*ore likely by occurrence of the core event, which perhaps reflects a "minimax" damage-control coping strategy of getting ready to mitigate the harm done by undesirable consequences.

Association of antecedents with likelihood and of consequences with desirability. Our coping theory about the thought systems that develop around events that might befall the person identifies two general modes of realistic coping, either sufficient-reason thinking of the event's likelihood-determining antecedents or utility-maximizing thinking of the event's desirability-determining consequences. These two modes of thinking, predicting that likelihoods would be linked with antecedents and that desirabilities would be linked with consequences, were tested in the second content study, using eight core events of a general societal nature that were neutral in judged desirability and likelihood. Participants' thoughts were first directed toward either the desirability or the likelihood dimension by giving experts' purported ratings of core events' desirabilities to half the students and giving experts' purported likelihood norms to the other half of the students. Most of those reported experts' ratings were near .50 (as were the judgments of prestudy students) to lend plausibility, but a few were discrepantly high or discrepantly low to evoke attention. Then the participants were asked to free-associate on four of the eight core events and their generated thoughts were content-analyzed.

The linkage predictions are confirmed by the results shown in Table 6.1, Columns b and c. Participants whom experts' norms had presensitized to the core event's desirabilities generated more ($p < .001$) consequences than antecedents, 55% versus 31% of all listed thoughts (see Column b in Table 6.1). Participants presensitized to the likelihood norms generated fewer ($p < .001$) consequences than antecedents, 22% versus 56% of all evoked thoughts (see Column c in Table 6.1). The presensitizations to the desirability (vs. likelihood) of events increase the salience of all four types of consequences (or antecedents), including those that would account for and those that would go against the specific expert norms that had been presented. As Petty and Cacioppo (1986) predicted, presensitization to one versus another dimension evokes both congruent and counterargument consequences or antecedents.

Antecedent focus as more masterful: Event-domain interactions. It was postulated that both the antecedents/likelihood and the consequences/desirability modes of coping serve adaptive functions, but that the former is more masterful in that it gives one a chance to take control of one's destiny by manipulating the antecedents and so affect whether or not the core event will occur. Focusing on the consequences/desirability, on the other hand, limits one to the more reactive coping mode of accepting one's destiny and making the best of it by the damage control allowed by anticipating and preparing for the event's consequences. This postulate was tested in terms of its

Table 6.1

Results of four studies of thought systems' contents: How the proportion of thoughts evoked by mention of possible events is distributed among the 15 content analysis categories

	Content study 1: Free assoc. on 36 varied societal events	Content study 2: (8 neutral societal events)		Content study 3: Polarized core events		Content study 4: 12 neutral societal events	
		After Norms on Desir.	on Likeli.	Societal events	8 Personal events	8 associa- tion	Free Directed generating
Categories	(a)	(b)	(c)	(d)	(e)	(f)	(g)
DMA	.10	.14	.23	.08	.16	.14	.13
UMA	.14	.09	.15	.17	.12	.14	.13
DLA	.03	.05	.10	.04	.07	.04	.12
ULA	.03	.04	.07	.03	.03	.02	.11
(Σ ANTEC)	(.30)	(.31)	(.56)	(.32)	(.39)	(.33)	(.49)
DMC	.19	.25	.11	.15	.20	.20	.17
UMC	.25	.28	.11	.24	.15	.27	.16
DLC	.03	.00	.00	.04	.02	.04	.09
ULC	.02	.01	.01	.01	.01	.03	.08
(Σ CONSEQ)	(.48)	(.55)	(.22)	(.44)	(.38)	(.54)	(.50)
HI-DES	.01	.01	.00	.01	.03	.00	
LO-DES	.02	.01	.00	.01	.02	.02	
HI-LIK	.01	.00	.02	.01	.02	.00	
LO-LIK	.03	.03	.04	.03	.03	.04	
METH	.04	.03	.03	.06	.05	.04	
PERS	.03	.03	.04	.03	.07	.02	
OTHER	.08	.04	.10	.09	.01	.02	—
(Σ misc)	(.22)	(.15)	(.22)	(.24)	(.23)	(.14)	
Total Proportion	1.00	1.00	1.00	1.00	1.00	1.00	1.00
Mean Total Number of Evoked Thoughts	5.34	5.29	5.63	5.59	7.45	5.52	3.34

implied situational and personal interaction predictions. One situational interaction implication of the auxiliary assumption that people feel they have more control over the events in their personal lives than over events in broader societal domains is that free-associating on personal core events will evoke a higher ratio of antecedents to consequences than will free-associating on societal core events. Table 6.1 results are weakly (p ≈ .10) in the predicted direction: Personal events (Column e) evoke trivially more antecedents than consequences, whereas matched societal events (Column d) evoke substantially more consequences than antecedents.

A further topical interaction is implied within the eight personal events. Assuming that a person feels more control over his or her friendships than over his or her abilities, there should be a higher antecedents-to-consequences ratio evoked by the four social events (e.g., "Your social life at Yale will improve next term") than by the four achievement events (e.g., "Your grades at Yale will improve next term"). The results support this interaction prediction. Free-associating on the four affiliative interpersonal-relations events evoked more (p < .001) antecedents than consequences, 3.57 versus 2.02; free-associating on the four achievement events showed a difference in the opposite direction, evoking more (p < .001) consequences than antecedents, 3.60 versus 2.21.

Antecedent focus as more masterful: Time-perspective interactions. If a personal core event is impending in the students' immediate future (the next few months), he or she will tend to feel less power to control it than if it is in the distant future (midlife or beyond), when there is still time to intervene effectively. Results support this interaction prediction (p < .05) in that when free-associating on distant future events students generate more antecedents than consequences, 3.02 versus 2.33 (41% vs. 31% of the total generated), but when free-associating on impending events students generate more consequences than antecedents, 3.29 versus 2.77 (44% vs. 37% of the total).

Antecedent focus as more masterful: Sex interactions. The hypothesis that focusing on antecedents/likelihoods of core events is a more masterful mode of coping than is focusing on their consequences/ desirabilities implies sex interactions. On the auxiliary assumption that men feel more empowered than women in contemporary society, the prediction follows that there will be a higher ratio of antecedents to consequences in men's than in women's free associations evoked by societal core events. In the first content study, in which participants free-associated on 36 varied societal core events, this interaction prediction was supported in that the ratio of evoked antecedents to consequences was slightly higher (p < .05) for men than for women. However, this sex difference in the antecedents/consequences ratio did not replicate in the second content study that used 8 societal core events neutral in desirabilities and likelihoods.

The third content study investigated a higher-order sex difference interaction, assuming that men feel more empowered in the public (societal) domain and women in the private (personal) domain. The results support this triple interaction effect (men vs. women) × (societal vs. personal event domain) × (evoked antecedents vs. consequences). For societal (public economic and political) events, there was a higher ratio of antecedents to consequences in men's than in women's free associations; but for personal events (involving one's own interpersonal and academic outcomes), the antecedents-over-consequences ratio was higher in women than in men.

Prevalence of promotive over preventive thoughts.   Our positivity-bias postulate (McGuire & McGuire, 1992c) predicts that when free-associating on core events participants will generate more antecedents and consequences in a promotive than in a preventive relation to the core event. Using the symbolism of Table 6.1, it is predicted that in free-associating, promotive _M_ thoughts (DMA, UMA, DMC, UMC) will be more prevalent than preventive _L_ thoughts (DLA, ULA, DLC, ULC). Table 6.1 shows that the three content studies strongly support this prediction. In each of the three free-association content studies (Columns a through f in Table 6.1) participants generated more (p < .001) promotive (_M_) antecedents and consequences than preventive (_L_), 68% versus 11%, 68% versus 14%, and 64% versus 12% in the three studies. This cognitive positivity bias evoked by the free-association tasks in the first three studies can reflect both proclivity and ability. A fourth content study reduced the proclivity component by prescribing a constrained association task (e.g., a core event was presented and the person was asked to generate one specified type of the eight types of antecedents and consequences). When performance was thus determined by ability more than proclivity, excess of the promotive over preventive antecedents and consequences still emerged (Column g in Table 6.1), 59% versus 40%, p < .01, but much smaller in magnitude than in the first three, proclivity, studies.

Summary of the content findings. These thought-fluency results indicate a pronounced parochialism, even among Yale undergraduates, in that they generated many more thoughts about core events in the shopping and sports domains that affected their everyday personal lives than about more cosmic events, such as an AIDS cure and an economic depression in the United States, even though they reactively rated the latter as much more important. Having richer thought systems around personal core events than societal ones is especially pronounced in women. People distribute their thoughts over topics in proportion to the topics' personal relevance to them rather than how important they judge the topics to be.

As predicted, antecedents and consequences were common in these thought systems, accounting for over three-quarters of all thought topics evoked in three minutes of free-associating on a wide variety of possible core events. A rational linkage of topics and dimensions was found, in that when the desirability dimension was made more salient the person thought predominantly of core events' consequences, whereas when likelihood was made more salient the person thought primarily of events' antecedents.

Our postulate that the antecedent/likelihood mode of thinking reflects a greater sense of empowerment in the thinker than does the consequences/desirability mode is given some support by several situational and dispositional interactions. (a) The ratio of antecedents to consequences is slightly higher ($p \approx .10$) in thought systems surrounding personal than the less controllable societal core events; (b) this antecedents-over-consequences ratio is higher around affiliative than around less controllable achievement personal events; (c) this ratio is higher around future events for which there is still time to influence their occurrence than around imminently impending events; and (d) the ratio is higher in women than in men around personal as compared with societal core events. Also supported is the affirmational-bias auxiliary postulate that people tend to generate more antecedents and consequences that are in a promotive than in a preventive relation to the core events, particularly in free-association (proclivity) tasks, as compared to directed-thinking (ability) tasks.

STUDIES ON THE STATIC STRUCTURE OF THOUGHT SYSTEMS

The preceding studies dealt with thought-systems' contents (i.e., the meaning topics that are salient to people and the dimensions of judgment on which people project these topics) as defined by what thoughts people generate when asked to do free or directed thinking regarding a wide range of core events that might befall themselves or their society. I here turn to the structural organization of thought systems, which raises issues regarding the interrelations among the thought systems' contents at a given moment in time. The following sections describe in turn the theorizing, methods, and results regarding such structural issues.

Theory Regarding the Static Structure of Thought Systems

Our coping and auxiliary postulates yield predictions about the static organization of thought systems' contents at a given moment in time, particularly about how the person's judgments of the desirability and likelihood of a core event, Des(CE) and Lik(CE), will be related to the relative salience (the number evoked) of the eight types of antecedents and consequences, #DMA, #UMA, . . . , #ULC, which constitute about 80% of the contents of the thought system elicited by the core event.

The five coping postulates (utility maximizing, congruent origins, rationalization, sufficient reason, and wishful thinking) and auxiliary postulates (salience effects, positivity bias, loose linkage, etc.) make predictions regarding the type of antecedent and consequence topics that will be evoked by core events. The eight types of antecedents and consequences are studied in a $2 \times 2 \times 2$ design: *Desirable An*tecedents that make the core event *M*ore likely (DMA) versus *L*ess likely (DLA); and *U*ndesirable *A*ntecedents that make the core event *M*ore likely (UMA) versus *L*ess likely (ULA); and *D*esirable *C*onsequences that are made *M*ore likely (DMC) versus *L*ess likely (DLC) by the core events; and *U*ndesirable *C*onsequences that are made more likely (UMC) versus *L*ess likely (ULC) by the core events. The thoughts evoked in participants when they free-associated on the core events were content-analyzed into these eight categories with a high degree (94%) of intercoder agreement. The five coping postulates and the auxiliary postulates predict how these eight types of salient antecedents and consequences will be related to the core event's judged desirability and likelihood, Des(CE) and Lik(CE). These structural predictions were tested in two studies. One study used the thought system surrounding each of 36 diverse societal events; the other study used thoughts surrounding eight personal events. Here only the first study will be reported. The second structure study (McGuire & McGuire, 1991c) yields similar implications.

Methods for Studying Structures around Societal Core Events

The first structural study used the 36 varied impersonal societal core events (6 from each of 6 varied domains, as described above). The Yale introductory psychology students worked through a booklet at a carefully timed pace. On each of four early pages participants were asked to take three minutes to list all the thoughts evoked by one of the 36 possible events stated in a box on the top of the page. These free associations were later content-analyzed into the 15 Table 6.1 categories, of which the number evoked of each of the 8 types of antecedents and consequences (#DMA, #UMA, . . . , #ULC) were of primary theoretical interest. After these four free-association pages, later pages of the booklet asked the participants to use a .00 to 1.00 scale to rate all 36 core events for desirability and likelihood, Des(CE) and Lik(CE).

Results Regarding Coping Structures around Desirability Judgments, Des(CE)

By including in our experimental design 36 thought systems (each consisting of a different core event and the antecedents and consequences commonly evoked by free-associating on it) we were able to use correlation coefficients across the 36 events as our descriptive statistics to test the five coping postulates' structural predictions as specified in Formulae 1a through 5a shown in Table 6.2. Across the 36 belief systems we correlated whether the numbers of evoked antecedents and consequences (#DMA, . . . #ULC) on the right side

Table 6.2
Static-structure study on how the judged desirabilities and likelihoods of possible events, Des(CE) and Lik(CE), correlate with types of antecedents and consequences evoked by those events.

Predictions	Correlations
Formulae 1a, utility maximizing:	
1a+ Des(CE) $\propto$#DMC + ULC	+.46 (p < .01)
1a− Des(CE) ∞# UMC + DLC	−.43 (p = .01)
Formula 2a, congruent origins:	
2a+ Des(CE) $\propto$#DMA + #ULA	+.71 (p < .01)
2a− Des(CE) ∞#UMA + #DLA	−.67 (p < .01)
Formula 3a, rationalization:	
3a+ Des(CE) $\propto$#DMA + #UMA	trivial
3a− Des(CE) ∞#DLA + #ULA	trivial
Formula 4a, sufficient reason:	
4a+ Lik(CE) $\propto$#DMA + #UMA	+.21 (not sig.)
4a− Lik(CE) ∞#DLA + #ULA	−.34 (p = .05)
Formula 5a, wishful thinking:	
5a+ Lik(CE) $\propto$#DMC + #ULC	trivial
5a− Lik(CE) ∞#UMC + #DLC	trivial

$\propto$ indicates direct proportionality
∞ indicates inverse proportionality

of the proportionality sign were related to the core event's judged desirabilities, Des(CE), on the left side, as predicted in Formulae 1a, 2a, and 3a; and were related to the core's judged likelihoods, Lik(CE), as predicted in Formulae 4a and 5a. The obtained correlations are shown in Table 6.2.

These data confirm the Formula 1a utility-maximizing, "by their fruits you will know them" (Matt 7:17–20), prediction that the judged desirability of the core event, Des(CE), will be related to the net favorableness of the pattern of consequences that the core event evokes when the person free-associates on it. As predicted in Formula 1a+ the mean judged desirabilities of the 36 core events, Des(CE), correlate positively (r = + .46, p < .01) with #DMC + #ULC (i.e., the number of desirable consequences that the core events are perceived as making more likely plus the number of undesirable consequences that the core events are perceived as making less likely). Also, as predicted in Formula 1a−, the 36 mean Des(CE) scores correlate negatively ($r = -.43$, $p = .01$) with the number of unfavorable consequences, #UMC + #DLC, evoked (i.e., the number of undesirable consequences it is perceived as making more likely and the number of desirable consequences it is perceived as making less likely).

Even more strongly confirmed were the congruent-origins postulate's Formula 2a+ and 2a−predictions that the relations between the core event's judged desirability, Des(CE), and its pattern of evoked antecedents will follow a like-begets-like, "by their seed you will know them" rationale (James, 1902; Katona, 1975). Across the 36 core events, mean judged desirabilities, Des(CE), correlated positively ($r = +.71$, $p < .01$) with the salience of favorable antecedents (#DMA + #ULA), as predicted in Formula 2a+, and correlated negatively ($r = -7$, $p < .01$) with the salience of unfavorable antecedents (#UMA + #DLA), as predicted in Formula 2a−.

No support was obtained for the third, rationalization, postulate of an autistically gratifying hedonic consistency such that Des(CE) will be brought autistically into hedonic congruence with Lik(CE) and therefore with the preponderance of promotive over preventive antecedents. The data confirmed neither the "sweet lemon" rationalization prediction (that Des(CE) would correlate positively with promotive antecedents, #DMA plus #UMA, as specified in Formula 3a+) nor the "sour grapes" rationalization prediction (that Des(CE) would correlate negatively with preventive antecedents, #DLA plus #ULA, as specified in Formula 3a−).

Results Regarding Coping Structures
around Likelihood Judgments, Lik(CE)

Two other coping postulates predicted relations between the core event's judged likelihood, Lik(CE), and its pattern of salient antecedents and consequences. The Table 6.2 data show only weak support for the Formula 4a sufficient-reason structural predictions, and no support for the Formula 5a wishful-thinking predictions. The realistic principle of sufficient reason predicts, as specified in Formula 4a+ of Table 6.2, that the judged likelihood of the core event, Lik(CE), will be positively correlated to the salience of promotive antecedents (#DMA + #UMA); the results show only a nonsignificant trend in this direction (r = +.21, p > .05). This sufficient-reason postulate also predicts, as specified in Formula 4a−, that Lik(CE) will be negatively correlated to preventive antecedents (#DLA plus #ULA), a prediction that was confirmed just at the .05 level of significance (r = −.34, p = .05). The final coping postulate of an autistic wishful-thinking hedonic congruence tendency, as defined by Formulae 5a+ and 5a−, received no support from the obtained data.

Table 6.2 shows some weak support for the loose-linkage auxiliary postulate that desirability subsystems are more tightly organized than likelihood subsystems. The six predicted relations (Formulae 1a+, 1a−, 2a+, 2a−, 3a+, and 3a−) specifying correlations between Des(CE) and its patterns of salient antecedents and consequences are sizable in magnitude and significant at the .01 level. In contrast, of the four Formulae 4a+, 4a−, 5a+, and 5a− predictions of correlations with Lik(CE), only one is of a magnitude sufficient to attain a borderline .05 level of significance. A second static structure study of thought systems surrounding highly polarized personal events (McGuire & McGuire, 1991c) yields results similar to this first study.

STUDIES ON THE DYNAMIC FUNCTIONING OF THOUGHT SYSTEMS

We theorize that the forces specified in our coping and auxiliary postulates govern thought systems as regards, not only their content and static structure, but also their dynamic adjustments over time in response to localized changes introduced in the system. The same forces that have shaped the thought system's static structure at a given moment will also, whenever this initial balance is disturbed by a localized change induced at one point in a thought system, produce remote ramifications at other points, in directions and amounts specified by the same five coping and auxiliary postulates. These dynamic readjustments are predicted to move in both causal directions, from attitude change to salience change and from salience change to attitude change. If changes in attitudes, $\triangle$Des(CE) or $\triangle$Lik(CE), are directly introduced on desirability or likelihood judgments on the core event (e.g., by presenting the person with discrepant expert judgments about the core event), then there should be remote changes in the salience of the antecedents and consequences of that core event,

△#DMA, △#UMA, . . . , △#ULC, as specified by the five coping and the auxiliary hypotheses. Dynamic Study 1 used experts' discrepant norms to test the predicted adjustments in this attitudes-to-salience direction. Dynamic Study 2 tested the predicted adjustments in the opposite, salience-to-attitudes, direction by using Socratic questioning that manipulated the relative salience of the eight types of antecedents and consequences (△#DMA, . . . , △#ULC), and then tested for the changes in attitudes on the core issues, △Des(CE) and △Lik(CE), predicted by the coping and auxiliary postulates. These two dynamic operations studies will be described in turn.

Dynamic-Operation Study 1: Manipulating Des(CE) or Lik(CE) Attitudes to Affect Salience of Antecedents and Consequences

Predictions. Directly inducing △Des(CE) or △Lik(CE) changes in judgments of the core event by presenting experts' discrepant norms is predicted to result in justifying remote changes in the salience of the eight types of the core event's evoked antecedents and consequences (△#DMA, △#UMA, . . . , △#ULC), as measured by a content analysis of the free associations evoked by the core event after being presented with experts' discrepant norms. The specific remote changes on antecedent and consequence salience are predicted on the basis of the five coping and the auxiliary postulates as specified in Table 6.3.

Methods in attitudes-to-salience dynamic operation study. Participation in this study involved working through three successive sections of an experimental booklet, paced by the experimenter. The first section presented experts' discrepantly high (or low) norms to manipulate the independent variable, namely, to move the participants' judgments of the core events' desirabilities upward or downward, △Des(CE) or ▽Des(CE); or to move their likelihoods upward or downward, △Lik(CE) or ▽Lik(CE). The second section of the booklet measured the resulting remote impact on the dependent variables, the salience of the eight types of antecedents and consequences, #DMA, . . . , #ULC, as measured by having the participants free-associate on the core event after receipt of the experts' discrepant judgments, and then content-analyzing the generated associations. The third section of the booklet measured the participants' judgments of the desirabilities and likelihoods of the core events, Des(CE) and Lik(CE), to provide a check on the effectiveness of the independent variable manipulations, the experts' discrepant norms. Eight core events were used in the experimental design, all of which were impersonal societal events shown in a prestudy to be near the midpoint on both the desirability and likelihood scale (which facilitated use of a counterbalanced design with upward and downward attitude manipulations).

Attitudes-to-salience Dynamic Study 1 results: Effects on attitudes. The check on the manipulations shows that presentation of discrepant expert norms on the desirabilities or likelihoods of the core events was moderately successful in directly manipulating the independent variables, participants' judgments of the core events' desirabilities and likelihoods. The mean Des(CE) judgment was .42 for participants in control conditions (who received no expert norms) and went up to .51 after discrepantly high desirability experts' norms and down to .37 after discrepantly low desirability norms; the .51 and .37 levels are significantly different ($p < .01$) from one another and from the .42 control level. Lik(CE) was .47 in the control conditions, .54 after discrepantly high likelihood norms, and .38 after discrepantly low likelihood norms, the .54 versus .38 means being again significantly ($p < .01$) different from one another and from the .47 control level.

The direct within-dimensional attitudinal effects (i.e., how presenting experts' discrepant desirability [or likelihood] norms affected participants' judgments of the core event's desirability [or likelihood] judgments of the core events) were trivially greater for likelihood than for desirability norms, .16 versus .14 for Lik(CE) versus Des(CE). However, the between-dimensional effects went, as predicted, in the opposite direction. The .14 direct within-dimensional Des(CE) changes produced by experts' discrepant desirability norms spread 71% across dimensions to Lik(CE), but the .16 direct intradimensional Lik(CE) change spread only 25% across dimensions to Des(CE).

Attitudes-to-salience Dynamic Study 1 results: Tests of the three coping postulates predicting how Des(CE) manipulations affect thought-topic availability. The data in Table 6.3 confirm the main predic-

Table 6.3

Dynamic-operation Study 1: From attitude change to salience change. How using experts' discrepant norms to induce increases or decreases in the judged desirabilities or likelihoods of core events, Des(CE) or Lik(CE), affects the number of the eight types of associated antecedents or consequences (#DMA, #UMA, ... #ULC) that are evoked by free associating on the core events

Postulate	Direction of attitude manipulation	Antec. (or Consequences) Predicted to Increase Number Generated	Mean number of these antec./conseq. actually generated	Antec. (or consequences) predicted to decrease in number generated	Mean number of these antec. (or conseq.) actually generated	Diff. between numbers actually generated	Prob. of this diff.
A. EFFECTS OF PRESENTING EXPERTS' HIGH-VERSUS-LOW DESIRABILITY NORMS							
Formula 1: Utility maximizing	△Des(CE)		1.703		1.031	+0.672	
	▽Des(CE)		1.094		1.750	−0.656	
	Diff. △#minus#▽	△(#DMC & #ULC)	+0.609	▽(#UMC & #DLC)	−0.719	+1.328	(p < .01)
Formula 2: Congruent origins	△Des(CE)		1.188		0.625	+0.563	
	▽Des(CE)		0.750		0.813	−0.062	
	Diff. △#minus#▽	△(#DMA & #ULA)	+0.438	▽(#UMA & #DLA)	−0.188	+0.625	(p < .05)
Formulae 3: Rationalization	△Des(CE)		1.516		0.297	+1.219	
	▽Des(CE)		0.844		0.719	+0.125	
	Diff. △#minus#▽	△(#DMA & #UMA)	+0.672	▽(#DLA & #ULA)	−0.422	+1.094	(p < .01)
B. EFFECTS OF PRESENTING EXPERTS' HIGH-VERSUS-LOW LIKELIHOOD NORMS							
Formula 4: Sufficient reason	△Lik(CE)		2.672		0.594	+2.078	
	▽Lik(CE)		1.469		1.594	−0.125	
	Diff. △#minus#▽	△(#DMA & #UMA)	+1.203	▽(#DLA & #ULA)	−1.000	+2.203	(p < .01)
Formula 5: Wishful thinking	△Lik(CE)		0.734		0.547	+0.188	
	▽Lik(CE)		0.547		0.547	+0.000	
	Diff. △#minus#▽	△(#DMC & #ULC)	+0.187	▽(#UMC & #DLC)	−0.000	+0.188	(trivial)

tions derived from each of the three coping postulates regarding the remote effects on the pattern of salience among the eight types of antecedents and consequences (#DMA, #UMA . . ., #ULC) produced by directly changing $\triangle$Des(CE) attitudes by presenting experts' discrepant desirability norms. The utility-maximizing postulate (Formula 1) predicts that manipulating $\triangle$Des(CE) upward by presenting experts' discrepantly high norms will have the remote effect of increasing the net favorableness pattern among the salient consequences (increasing the salience of favorable consequences, $\triangle$#DMC & $\triangle$#ULC, and decreasing the salience of unfavorable consequences, ∇#UMC & ∇#DLC). Conversely, manipulating ∇Des(CE) downward by presenting experts' low norms on the core event is predicted to have the opposite remote effect of lowering the net favorableness of evoked consequences (decreasing the salience of ∇#DMC and ∇#ULC and increasing $\triangle$#UMC & $\triangle$#DLC). The results are in accord with each of these eight utility-maximizing predictions, as can be seen in the top triad of Formula 1 rows of Table 6.3. After the $\triangle$Des(CE) manipulation, compared to after the ∇Des(CE) manipulation, there is an increase of +0.609 in the evoked number of favorable (#DMC plus #ULC) consequences; and there is a -0.719 decrease in number of evoked unfavorable (#UMC plus #DLC) consequences. All eight components of the utility-maximizing postulate are in the predicted direction, and the bottom-line difference-between-differences of +1.328 is significant at the $p < .01$ level.

As shown in the second triad of rows in Table 6.3, the results also confirm the congruent-origins postulate's predictions, Formula 2. Raising the judged desirability of the core event, $\triangle$Des(CE), increases the salience of the core event's favorable antecedents (#DMA and #ULA) and decreases salience of unfavorable antecedents (#UMA and #DLA); and lowering the judged desirability of the core event (∇Des(CE)) has the reverse effects on antecedent salience. All eight component predictions are in the predicted direction; the bottom-line net +0.625 obtained congruent-origins predicted difference-between-differences is significant at the .05 level.

The third triad of rows in Table 6.3 shows that all four remote effects predicted by the rationalization postulate, Formula 3, are also confirmed. Directly raising (vs. lowering) the perceived desirability of the core event affects the excess of promotive over preventive antecedents (i.e., the excess of #DMA & #UMA over #DLA & #ULA) as shown in Table 6.3. The net rationalization difference-between-differences effect of +1.094 is sizable and significant ($p < .01$), even though it is across-dimensions as well as across-topics and therefore is two steps removed from the direct manipulation of Des(CE).

Tests of the two coping postulates that predict how Lik(CE) manipulations affect thought-topic availability. Here we turn from remote effects of the $\triangle$Des(CE) manipulation to remote effects of the $\triangle$Lik(CE) manipulation. The results relevant to these fourth and fifth dynamic-operation predictions, Formulae 4 and 5, are shown in the last two triads of rows in Table 6.3. The fourth, sufficient-reason, postulate predicts that presenting experts' discrepantly high (vs. low) likelihood norms on the core event (thus manipulating upward [vs. downward] the participant's Lik(CE) judgment) will result in appropriate remote readjustments of the salience of the four types of antecedents, increasing (decreasing) the number of promotive antecedents (#DMA and #UMA) and decreasing (increasing) the salience of preventive antecedents (#DLA and #ULA). These eight sufficient-reason predictions of remote changes in antecedents' salience were highly significant (p < .01) separately, as was the obtained +2.203 bottom-line difference-between-differences effect. Alone of the five coping postulates, rationalization (Formula 5) predictions received little support from Dynamic Study 1 results, as can be seen in the last triad of rows of Table 6.3. Directly manipulating the participant's Lik(CE) judgment by presenting experts' discrepant norms did not have the predicted rationalization effect on the net favorability pattern of salient consequences.

Support was found also for the auxiliary affirmational-bias postulate that the remote impacts predicted in Formulae 1 through 5 will operate more strongly through promotive than preventive links, that is, more via the _M_ than the _L_ antecedent and consequences in these formulae. Each of the five coping postulates allows two such promotive-versus-preventive comparisons. Nine of these 10 (p < .05 by the sign test) independent comparisons are in the affirmational-bias direction.

Dynamic-Operation Study 2: How a Socratic-Questioning Manipulation of Antecedent or Consequence Salience Affects Des(CE) and Lik(CE) Attitudes

Further dynamic-operation studies were designed to test the same coping and auxiliary postulates as they operate in the opposite causal direction. This calls for reversing the independent and dependent variables of Dynamic Study 1 by directly manipulating the salience of one or another of the eight types of antecedents and consequences ($\triangle$#DMA, . . . $\triangle$#ULC) and then testing for the coping postulate's predicted remote changes on the judged desirabilities and likelihoods of the core events (on $\triangle$Des(CE) and $\triangle$Lik(CE)). Our several reverse-direction studies differed from one another in how they manipulated the independent variables, $\triangle$#DMA, . . ., $\triangle$#ULC: One study used a reactive Socratic-questioning task and the other used a more active biased-scanning task. Both involved "persuasion from within" (producing attitude change by manipulating the salience of information already in the person's own thought system, without presenting new information in a persuasive communication from an external source). I shall describe here only the study that used the Socratic-questioning manipulation. The other study yielded similar results and is described in McGuire & McGuire (1991c).

Predictions in the salience-to-attitudes dynamic-operation study. The five coping-postulate predictions about the effect of such Socratic questioning are expressed in the five pairs of formulae, 1e to 5e, shown in Table 6.4 and discussed in the Results section below. The first three pairs of formulae state predictions of the three desirability coping postulates (utility maximizing, congruent origins, and rationalization) regarding how prior questioning that sensitizes the person to designated types of antecedents and consequences will affect the core events' judged desirabilities, Des(CE). The final two pairs of Formulae, 4e and 5e in Table 6.4, state predictions of the two likelihood coping postulates (sufficient reason and wishful thinking) regarding how Socratic questioning about designated antecedents and consequences of the core events will affect Lik(CE).

Methods in the salience-to-attitudes dynamic-operation study. The salience of one of the eight types of the core event's antecedents and consequences (DMA, . . . , ULC) was manipulated by Socratic questioning (McGuire, 1960c; Rosen & Wyer, 1972) that directed the participant's attention to that type of antecedent or consequence. By a prestudy using free association we identified, for each core event, the four most commonly generated examples of each of the eight types of antecedents or consequences, DMA, UMA, . . . ULC. Questions were then made up asking the person to judge the desirability or likelihood of these eight salient antecedents or consequences of the given type for a specific core event. For example, for the core event that an increasing proportion of meals would be eaten in restaurants rather than at home, a commonly generated UMC (i.e., an *U*ndesirable *C*onsequence that this core event would make *M*ore likely) is that it would reduce family togetherness. Half the participants were asked categorical questions on each such item (e.g., "How likely (desirable) is it that there is going to be a reduction in family togetherness," which constitutes a $QLik(UMC_{ij})$ (or $QDes(UMC_{ij})$) for this UMC_i consequent of core event j. The other half of the participants were asked conditional questions, $QLik(UMC_{ij}/CE_j)$, such as "How likely is it that if an increasing proportion of meals are eaten in restaurants rather than at home that it would reduce family togetherness?"

To manipulate the independent variable (salience of the given type of antecedent or consequent), the participant was first asked a series of such categorical or conditional questions on a subset of antecedents or consequences of the core events. Of the 64 introductory psychology participants, half were asked questions about the core events' commonly mentioned antecedents, and the other half were asked about commonly mentioned consequences. After this questioning the participants were measured on the dependent variables (judged desirability and likelihood of the core event, Des(CE) and Lik(CE)). This allowed us to determine if manipulating the pattern of salience among the eight types of antecedents and consequences by asking the various types of questions had the effects predicted by the coping postulates on judgments of the core events desirability and likelihood.

Results in the salience-to-attitudes dynamic-operation study. The results of the Socratic-effect manipulations are shown in Table 6.4 regarding each of the five coping postulates. The results for each coping postulate are shown in three rows of data. The top row of the triad gives the mean Des(CE) or Lik(CE) dependent variable judgments after each of the four types of Socratic questioning predicted by that coping postulate to raise these judgments; the second row of each triad gives the mean Des(CE) or Lik(CE) judgments after each of the four types of Socratic questioning predicted to lower these judgments; finally, the bottom row of the triad gives the algebraic difference in Des(CE) or in Lik(CE) for the first minus the second row of that triad, that is, for $\triangle$ minus $\triangledown$. The critical prediction for each of the five coping postulates is that means in this bottom row of each triad of rows (equal to row 1 minus row 2) will be significantly positive. As can be seen in Table 6.4, the overall difference is positive, as predicted, with 17 of the 20 relevant differences being positive. The mean of the four differences for each of the five postulates is positive, with the size of this mean difference reaching the .05 level of significance for three of the five postulates.

The results in the top, $1e$ triad of rows in Table 6.4 confirm the utility-maximizing predictions of remote Des(CE) attitude effects produced by Socratic questioning on designated types of consequences. After Socratic questioning on any of the four beneficial types of consequences (DMC, DMC/CE, ULC, or ULC/CE) that were predicted to raise the judged desirability of the core event, the resulting $\triangle$Des(CE) was substantially higher (p < .01) than after Socratic questioning on any of the four corresponding types of detrimental consequences (UMC, UMC/CE, DLC, DLC/CE) predicted to lower the judged desirability of the core event, $\triangledown$Des(CE). Overall, the mean Des(CE) after answering questions about any of the four beneficial types of consequences (Formula $1e_1$) was .48; and after questions on any of the four detrimental types of consequence (Formula $1e_2$) the mean was .40, p < .01 for this .08 overall difference.

The congruent-origins predictions (Formula $2e_1$ minus $2e_2$) about Des(CE) were also confirmed, the overall .08 difference between the .46 minus .38 means shown in the $2e_1$ minus $2e_2$ rows of Table 6.4 being significant at the .01 level. The Table 6.4 results relative to the third, rationalization, postulate's predictions regarding Des(CE), as expressed by Formula $3e_1$ minus $3e_2$, is in the right direction but of trivial statistical magnitude. The fourth and fifth coping postulates' predictions deal with remote effects of Socratic questioning on Lik(CE) rather than on Des(CE). Of these fourth and fifth postulates, the fourth (sufficient reason) postulate (Equation $4e_1$, minus $4e_2$) shows an effect in the predicted direction that reaches the .05 level of significance. The wishful-thinking predictions given by Formula $5e_1$ minus $5e_2$ in the final three rows of Table 6.4 are in the predicted direction but of trivial statistical significance.

A surprising finding apparent in Table 6.4 is that Socratic questioning on eight types of the categorical antecedents or consequences (DMA, UMA, . . . ULC) was as effective in producing the predicted remote $\triangle$Des(CE) or $\triangle$Lik(CE) attitude effects as was Socratic questioning on the eight types of conditional antecedents and consequences propositions (CE/DMA, CE/UMA, . . . ULC/CE). A priori it seemed likely that presensitizing the person to antecedents and consequences by categorical questions would have fewer remote effects on core events' attitudes than would questions on the corresponding conditional propositions in producing remote effects on the core-event judgments, Des(CE) and Lik(CE). Categorical questions mention only the antecedent or consequences, whereas conditional propositions explicitly mention not only the antecedent or consequence but also the core event itself and its logical relation to the antecedent or consequence. That cryptic categorical questioning had as much remote attitudinal effect as fuller conditional questioning for all three confirmed postulates (utility-maximizing, congruent origins, and sufficient reason) suggesting again that the cognitive processing that channels remote effects is automatic rather than explicitly reasoned.

CURRENT STATUS OF THE THEORY
AND FUTURE DIRECTIONS

Evaluation of the Coping Postulates

The coping postulates' confirmation ratio in our two static and three dynamic studies (including those described above) ranges from perfect (for the utility-maximizing and congruent-origins postulates) to nil (for the wishful-thinking postulate, which was not confirmed in any of the five studies); the rationalization and sufficient-reason postulates had an intermediate, mixed pattern of confirmations. The uniformly confirmed utility-maximizing postulate predicts that the judged desirability of the core event, Des(CE), will be directly proportional to how beneficial is its pattern of salient consequences, going up with the number of favorable DMC and ULC consequences that the core event evokes and down with the number of unfavorable UMC and DLC consequences that it evokes. The congruent-origins postulate, also invariably confirmed, predicts that Des(CE) will be directly proportional to the net pleasantness of its pattern of salient antecedents, going up with the number of pleasant DMA and ULA antecedents that it evokes and down with the number of unpleasant UMA and DLA antecedents evoked. That both postulates were confirmed above the .05 level in all five studies indicates that the desir-

Table 6.4

Dynamic operation Study 2: how an induced change in salience of antecedents and consequences affects attitudes. Tests of the five coping postulates of how Socratic questioning that enhances the salience of the various types of antecedents and consequences of a core event affects the judged desirability or judged likelihood of that core event, Des(CE) and Lik(CE).

---

1. Utility-Maximizing Postulate: Remote effects on Des(CE)

$1e_1$ $\triangle$Des(CE) after questioning regarding beneficial consequences:
DMC & DMC/CE & ULC & ULC/CE = .52 & .51 & .44 & .47, mean = .48

$1e_2$ ∇Des(CE) after questioning regarding detrimental consequences:
UMC & UMC/CE & DLC & DLC/CE = .38 & .44 & .41 & .38, mean = .40
$\triangle$ minus ∇ Differences = .14 & .07 & .03 & .09, mean = .08 ($p < .01$)

2. Congruent-Origins Postulate: Remote effects on Des(CE)

$2e_1$ $\triangle$Des(CE) after questioning regarding beneficial antecedents:
DMA & CE/DMA & ULA & CE/ULA = .44 & .52 & .40 & .46, mean = .46

$2e_2$ ∇Des(CE) after questioning regarding detrimental antecedents:
UMA & CE/UMA & DLA & CE/DLA = .32 & .43 & .37 & .38, mean = .38
$\triangle$ minus ∇ Differences = .12 & .09 & .03 & .08, mean = .08 ($p < .01$)

3. Rationalization Postulate: Remote effects on Des(CE)

$3e_1$ $\triangle$Des(CE) after questioning regarding promotive antecedents:
DMA & CE/DMA & UMA & CE/UMA = .44 & .52 & .32 & .43, mean = .43

$3e_2$ ∇Des(CE) after questioning regarding preventive antecedents:
DLA & CE/DLA & ULA & CE/ULA = .37 & .38 & .40 & .46, mean = .40
$\triangle$ minus ∇ Differences = .07 & .14 & –.08 & –.03, mean = .03 (not sig.)

4. Sufficient-Reason Postulate: Remote effects on Lik(CE)

$4e_1$ $\triangle$Lik(CE) after questioning regarding promotive antecedents:
DMA & CE/DMA & UMA & CE/UMA = .49 & .49 & .48 & .53, mean = .50

$4e_2$ ∇Lik(CE) after questioning regarding preventive antecedents:
DLA & CE/DLA & ULA & CE/ULA = .42 & .45 & .44 & .45, mean = .44
$\triangle$ minus ∇ Differences = .07 & .04 & .04 & .08, mean = .06 ($p < .05$)

5. Wishful-Thinking Postulate: Remote effects on Lik(CE)

$5e_1$ $\triangle$Lik(CE) after questioning regarding beneficial consequences:
DMC & DMC/CE & ULC & ULC/CE = .54 & .50 & .50 & .52, mean = .52

$5e_2$ ∇Lik(CE) after questioning regarding detrimental consequences:
UMC & UMC/CE & DLC & DLC/CE = .45 & .51 & .48 & .50, mean = .49
$\triangle$ minus ∇ Differences = .09 & –.01 & .02 & .02, mean = .03 (not sig.)

---

ability of a core event, Des(CE), is tied in tightly with the net pleasantness of its salient consequences and (more surprisingly) of its antecedents, whether we look at the thought system statically at a given point in time or as dynamically readjusting after a localized change is introduced at one point in the system. It is reassuring regarding human rationality that Des(CE) reflects the commonsensical utility-maximizing postulate, the Matthew (7:17–20) biblical prescription that "by their fruits, you shall know them." It is more bothersome that Des(CE) equally reflects the congruent-origins postulate's more sentimental, atmospheric "by their seeds [roots] you shall know them" principle that William James (1902) warned us against and whose prevalence worried Katona (1975).

Results were more mixed on a third, rationalization, postulate that the judged desirability of the core event, Des(CE), will show an across-dimensional effect, such that the event's judged desirability will be adjusted to its judged likelihood and so reflect the preponderance of promotive over preventive antecedents. As regards static structure, this rationalization postulate was confirmed for thought systems surrounding highly polarized personal core events but not for the less personally relevant societal events; as regards dynamic operation, it was confirmed for how a directly induced $\triangle$Des(CE) change in judgment affected the salience of antecedents but not for how a manipulation of antecedents' salience affected judgments. It appears that this rationalization tendency is detectable only when the within-system articulation is particularly tight.

The other two postulates, sufficient reason and wishful thinking, have to do with likelihood instead of desirability subsystems, that is, with thought systems consisting of antecedents and consequences surrounding Lik(CE) thoughts rather than Des(CE) thoughts. Results were mixed on the realistic sufficient-reason postulate that the judged likelihood of the core event will be a positive function of the excess of salient promotive (_M_) over preventive (_L_) antecedents. Despite its being an axiom of logic, this sufficient-reason postulate received only borderline confirmation in one of the two static structure tests and in two of the three dynamic-operation studies. The final, wishful-thinking postulate, that Lik(CE) will be related to the preponderance of salient favorable consequences (DMC and ULC) over unfavorable consequences (UMC and DLC), was clearly the weakest among our five coping postulates, receiving no support in any of the five studies, perhaps because wishful thinking calls for a response in the less tightly articulated likelihood subsystem rather than the desirability subsystem and because it involves an across-dimensional as well as a within-dimensional effect, both of which would tend to loosen the structural links within a thought system.

General Implications

This pattern of confirmations and nonconfirmations of the five cop-ing postulates across the two static-structure and the three dynamic-operations studies has several broad implications regarding the organization and functioning of one's thought systems surrounding events that might befall oneself. In general, it supports the auxiliary postulate's prediction that the more involving desirability subsystems surrounding Des(CE) are more tightly organized than the likelihood subsystems surrounding Lik(CE). The three Des(CE) postulates (utility-maximizing, congruent origins, and rationalization) each made two general predictions in each of the 5 relevant static and dynamic studies, and 24 of these 30 Des(CE) predictions were significantly confirmed. (All six nonconfirmations occurred with the across-dimensional rationalization predictions.) Much less support is obtained for the two Lik(CE) postulates (sufficient reason and wishful thinking), in that only 5 of the 16 Lik(CE) predictions were significantly confirmed (all 5 being confirmations of sufficient-reason predictions and none confirming wishful-thinking predictions). One might well have predicted the opposite, that likelihood subsystems would be more tightly organized, on the assumption that people would try to be logically consistent in the more objective likelihood domain while tolerating personal idiosyncrasies and arbitrariness in the domain of taste, as in *de gustibus non est disputandum*. However, the results suggest that the person's greater emotional involvement in his or her desirability judgments outweighs any permissiveness of caprice in this domain of taste.

A second general implication of the obtained pattern of results across studies is that the two most rational-coping postulates (utility maximizing and sufficient reason) are confirmed more often and more strongly than the two autistic-coping postulates (wishful thinking and rationalization). Across the five studies these two rational-coping postulates were significantly confirmed in 15 of the 18 relevant tests, whereas the autistic-coping postulates were significantly confirmed in only 4 of the 18 tests. It appears that both the judged desirability and the judged likelihood of the core event are brought into relation to the patterns of salient antecedents and consequences more in order to adjust to the perceived realities of the external environment than to serve the autistic need for inner hedonic concordance.

A third general across-study implication is that thought systems are more tightly organized within than across dimensions of judgment.

The three postulates (utility maximizing, congruent origins, and sufficient reason) that deal with the organization of thought within a single dimension were significantly confirmed in 25 of the 28 relevant tests. The other two postulates (wishful thinking and rationalization) that deal with the organization of thought systems across dimensions were significantly confirmed in only 4 of the 18 relevant comparisons. Thought systems seem to be organized mainly within single dimensions of judgment (as would be realistic), with only weak connectedness across dimensions, even across dimensions as closely related psychologically as are evaluation and expectancy (desirability and likelihood).

Needed Future Elaborations of the Theory

Quantification needs. The experiments reported here tested our theory in a semiquantified "counting" form, in that relations between the judged desirability or likelihood of the core event, Des(CE) or Lik(CE), and the numbers of salient antecedents and consequences of the eight qualitatively contrasting types, #DMA, . . . , #ULC, were predicted without taking into account quantitative weightings of the components. The desirability (or likelihood) of antecedents and consequences was manipulated and scored only on a dichotomous desirable-versus-undesirable scale, without being weighed as to degree of desirability; also, the implications between propositions were scored only on a dichotomous promotive versus preventive scale, without weighing the links for their subjective conditional probabilities. What is needed is quantification that takes degree of desirability, and especially of likelihood, into account. These and other quantification refinements are needed in the model, not only to make the old predictions more precise, but also to allow testing additional predictions.

Needed work on the loose-link spatial attenuation postulate. Another variable in the theory that needs greater quantification and investigation is the amount of "give" in the thought systems, as assumed by our postulate that the chain of thought is loosely linked, resulting in a spatial attenuation such that obtained remote effects will fall short of the amounts required by my logic/probability theory, and that this shortfall will aggregate over successive links. At each link some slack must be taken up before any pull is exerted on the next thought. Our informal explorations of this loose-linkage "give" in the system suggest that when Des(CE) or Lik(CE) thoughts are measured on a .00 to 1.00 quasi-probability scale a change of about .07 to .10 is necessary to take up the slack before any remote change occurs on the connected thoughts. We predict that the amount of give is greater in likelihood subsystems than in desirability subsystems, with negative than with positive links, and for conditional than for categorical judgments.

Needed work on the temporal-inertia, delayed-action postulate. The spatial-attenuation postulate just discussed and the temporal-delay postulate are analogous inertias in space and time, respectively. The temporal-delay postulate predicts that the system responds lethargically, and so there will be delays before the appearance of remote systemic effects caused by a locally induced change. Both inertias help to maintain the stability of thought systems, allowing them the flexibility of being responsive to sizable and persistent internal or external pressures while maintaining stability by dampening hyperactivity to slight, transient, and mutually canceling perturbations.

Empirical work is needed to determine the parameters of the temporal lag with which the induced change seeps through the system from the point of direct application through the successively more remote links in the chain of implications. Systematic work on the topic has been sparse, but delayed-action seepage has been detected over intervals varying from a few minutes to two days and a week (McGuire, 1960b; Dillehay, Insko, & Smith, 1966; Watts & Holt, 1970; Higgins & Rholes, 1978). Quantification of the decay rate is complicated by the fact that, as time passes after the locally induced change, not only is that change gradually seeping to more remote points in the system, but also the direct change itself is gradually decaying at its initial point of induction. Hence, because it is the resultant of two opposed mediators, the net remote-effect time trend will be a nonmonotonic inverted-U (see chapters 1, 2, and 3 in this volume). Differential delayed-action effects are also predicted: The delay will be greater in likelihood than in desirability subsystems, via negative than positive links, on categorical than in conditional thoughts, and in low- than high-salient antecedents and consequences. Again, in this respect the spatial-attenuation and temporal-delay postulates are yoked, with high-inertial links showing both more spatial attenuation and greater delay.

Study of five-level thought systems. To test the implications of these and other postulates, a new round of prestudies is needed to expand the three-level thought systems so far used (antecedents → core events → consequences) to five-level systems that include antecedents of antecedents → antecedents → core events → consequences → consequences of consequences. To this end, a new round of prestudy participants will free-associate on the commonly evoked antecedents and consequences of the core events, so that further content-analyses can identify salient antecedents of the antecedents and consequences of the consequences. These five-level belief systems will allow better tests of directional predictions, such as that induced local changes spread vertically more than horizontally, and spread via unidirectional paths more than via paths that involve changes in direction. Also, future experiments should use two sessions to test predictions about differences in patterns of remote effect immediately-after versus delayed-after the directly induced change. Immediate remote impacts are predicted to involve large changes on a few thoughts, especially on conditional propositions; as time passes, the remote impacts spread out more flatly, affecting many remote thoughts, but each slightly (below the loose-linkage .10 slack) and focused more on the subtler conditional propositions.

7

A Topography of the Phenomenal Self

The research program reported in this chapter maps the contours of the self as phenomenally experienced, a terrain little explored in the vast empirical literature on the self. Traditional studies of the self have a narrow, impoverished quality because they examine a hypothetical as-if self by asking people where they would place themselves on some dimension that conventionally interests researchers without getting information on how often, if ever, people do in fact think of themselves on that dimension. In place of this hypothetical as-if self, I study the actual as-is self, identifying characteristics in terms of which persons actually do think of themselves. Participants are presented with open-ended probes (e.g., "Tell us about yourself," "Tell us what you are not," in McGuire & McGuire, 1991a) that allow them to describe themselves on dimensions of their own choosing. Then, by content-analyzing these free self-descriptions it can be ascertained which characteristics are spontaneously salient in people's sense of self and what determines the salience of one versus another dimension.

Our studies investigate both the contents and the processes of the phenomenal self: the contents as revealed by the nouns used in people's flowing self-description in response to probes such as "Tell us about yourself," and the processes as revealed by the verbs used in these self-descriptions. Our noun/content studies investigate the salience and correlates in the phenomenal self of such dimensions as physical features (height, weight, etc.), demographic characteristics (ethnicity, sex, etc.), the representation of the child's school experiences in the self, and the social self (the significant others who occupy self-space). The verb/process studies deal with topics such as how children's thought processes about themselves change as they grow older, how their multiple self-concepts differ in home versus school contexts, and how their thought processes differ when conceptualizing the self compared to other people. I shall discuss these topics in the order mentioned.

GENERAL PURPOSE OF THESE PHENOMENAL SELF STUDIES

[Adapted with permission from W. J. McGuire & C. V. McGuire, 1988a, Content and process in the experience of self, in L. Berkowitz (Ed.), *Advances in Experimental Social Psychology, 21,* pp. 97–144. Copyright © 1988 by Academic Press.]

Research on the self, everyone's favorite topic and arguably psychology's most interesting one, has been distinguished more by quantity than by quality. The modesty of its yield stems less from failure to answer the questions posed than from avoidance of questions that make the self so fascinating a topic. Avoidance of gripping issues occasionally derives from an explicit ideological stance, as when a radical behaviorist in approaching the self assumes that people have little interior life to be studied, or when a positivist assumes that the person's subjective sense of self is not a proper topic for scientific study. More often, gripping issues are inadvertently screened out by use of reactive methods. Psychological research often has a Sadim (reverse-Midas) touch in turning to dross such golden topics as self, love, creativity, or anxiety by cutting the topic to fit a Procrustean bed of conventional methods, rendering it dead on arrival at the laboratory. The research program described here chooses methods to get at issues that make the experienced self an interesting topic.

Two Common Shortcomings in Past Studies of the Self

Loss of information in reactive measures of the self. Since William James (1890/1981) identified self as psychology's central concern, there has been a steady stream of research on the topic, summarized by Wylie (1974; 1979), Rosenberg (1979), Gecas (1982), Greenwald and Pratkanis (1984), Markus and Wurf (1987), and Banaji and Prentice (1994). Most of this research uses a "reactive" approach, in that the investigator presents a dimension (typically evaluation) to respondents and asks them to characterize themselves by indicating where they fall on this dimension. The respondent is limited to placing her-

or himself on this researcher-chosen dimension, so that only as-if information about a hypothetical self is obtained – indicating where the person would perceive her- or himself as falling on the researcher's dimension if she or he ever thought of it, but with no indication of how often she or he does in fact think of this characteristic, which is the more interesting information about content salience and process modes in the experience of self.

Confinement to the evaluative dimension.   An aggravating narrowness of the usual reactive approach is that, not only is the person limited to describing the self on a researcher-chosen dimension, but further, almost all researchers choose the same dimension, self-evaluation. A sampling of the thousand self-concept studies cited by Wylie (1974, 1979) shows that over 90% are focused on the evaluation dimension, so that her volumes could accurately have been retitled more narrowly as "Self-Esteem" rather than "Self-Concept." The two terms have come to be used interchangeably, so excessively has self-research been confined to the evaluative dimension, as if people think about themselves and others solely in terms of how good or bad they are.

Evaluation may well be the most important single dimension and so deserving of intensive study, but is hardly so exclusively important that it should interdict research on other dimensions. When children and adolescents are allowed to describe themselves in whatever terms they wish (McGuire & Padawer-Singer, 1976a; McGuire, McGuire, & Winton, 1979a), fewer than 10% of all their self-descriptive thought segments are explicitly evaluative, including physical self-evaluations ("I have terrible hair"), intellectual ("I'm pretty good at math"), conduct ("I'm not a troublemaker like most of the kids around here"), and emotional ("I cry too easy"). The other 90% of self-descriptive thoughts are not explicitly evaluative (e.g., "I like to go off by myself on long bicycle rides," "I have brown hair," "My best friend lives next door but we go to different schools," "I work part-time at McDonald's"). Any self-descriptive statement can be reduced to an evaluative component by obtaining a rating of its social desirability, but treating diverse descriptions of the self as equivalent just because their social desirabilities are equal loses much information. This usually lost, other-than-evaluative, information is a main focus of the research program reported in this chapter.

Measuring the Phenomenal Self-Concept

Permissively presenting a lower profile to participants allows them leeway to describe themselves in their own ways on dimensions of their own choosing. We present open-ended probes such as "Tell us about yourself," "Tell us what you are not," "Tell us what you look like," "Tell us about your family," and ask participants to respond for three or five minutes with whatever comes to mind. The evoked self-descriptions are content-analyzed to determine what topics are salient in the person's sense of self and the way the person thinks about these topics. Admittedly, content analyses are labor-intensive. Open-ended responses are a *camino real* in the sense that they lead to interesting realms of information but not that they provide easy passage. Open-ended methods were used by a few mid-twentieth-century self-concept researchers (Bugental & Zelen, 1950; Kuhn & McPartland, 1954; Kelly, 1955) but then fell into neglect, as the potentially rich information elicited was often reduced to the evaluative self-esteem component (Spitzer, Couch, & Stratton, 1971). Such usage makes the open-ended methods the worst of both worlds, requiring laborious data collection and analysis but yielding only an evaluation score that could have been obtained more simply and reliably by reactive measures. The present research program exploits content analyses of open-ended responses for the rich content and process information they yield, justifying the formidable effort involved. We shall report first our research on the noun content of the perceived self, and then that on the verb processes.

NOUN CONTENTS IN THE PHENOMENAL SELF

The data base for our research program to map the topography of the phenomenal self is largely the noun content of the free self-descriptions given by a wide range of schoolchildren, ages 6 through 18, in oral and written self-descriptive free associations in response to "Tell us about yourself" and other probes. Our findings on the noun content of self are described in the next four sections in terms of salience in the phenomenal self of four types of personal characteristics, including: (1) salience of one's physical characteristics such as weight and hair color; (2) salience of one's demographic characteristics such as ethnicity and sex; (3) salience of the school domain in children's sense of self; and (4) salience of significant others in self-space, the "social self." Then the second half of this chapter will turn from these noun contents to the verb processes of the phenomenal self.

Salience of Physical Appearance in Children's Self-Concepts

[Adapted from W. J. McGuire & C. V. McGuire, 1981b, The spontaneous self-concept as affected by personal distinctiveness, in M. D. Lynch, A. A. Norem-Hebeisen, & K. Gergen (Eds.), *Self concept: Advances in theory and research,* pp. 147–171 (Cambridge, MA: Ballinger, copyright © 1981). See also related work in W. J. McGuire & A. Padawer-Singer, 1976a.]

Method.   Schoolchildren in their normal classroom settings were asked to respond to "Tell us about yourself" probes. They were told that their responses would be anonymous and that there were no right or wrong answers so they should just write down whatever came to mind. The children were then asked, "Tell us about yourself," and given five minutes to write down next to a column of numbers all the thoughts that occurred to them. A later page in the booklet explicitly asked the children to report their hair color, eye color, age, birthplace, whether they wore eyeglasses, and their height and weight, absolutely and compared with the other children in their class.

To score the dependent variable (salience of the physical characteristics in the spontaneous self-concept), judges read each child's responses to the "Tell us about yourself" probe and scored any mention of seven physical or demographic characteristics: height, weight, hair color, eye color, eyeglass wearing, birth date (or age) and birthplace. The 1,000 participants included 100 boys and 100 girls each from the fifth, seventh, ninth, eleventh, and twelfth grades (aged 11 to 18 years) in the schools of a medium-sized industrial New England city.

Results.   The students' responses were divided into subject/verb/complement thought units. Over all five grade levels the mean number of thought units reported in five minutes was 16.1 per student. The girls' response protocols were 22 percent longer ($p < .01$) than the boys', and eleventh graders' were 27 percent longer ($p < .01$) than fifth graders'. The age $\times$ sex interaction effect on length was negligible.

Height was mentioned as part of their spontaneous self-concept by 19 percent of the children, higher (p < .01) than the 11 percent who mentioned their weight, explainable (see chapter 8 on distinctiveness theory) by height's being varied and changing more than weight in this age range. There was no gender difference in the mention of height or weight and no age difference in mention of height, but weight was mentioned by twice as many eleventh and twelfth graders as by fifth and seventh graders, indicating a growing concern about weight during adolescence. Hair color was mentioned by 14 percent of the respondents and eye color by 11 percent. Self-description in terms of these two characteristics was twice as high (p < .01) for girls as for boys; and both were mentioned more often (p < .05) by younger than by older children. Birthplace is a less salient characteristic, being mentioned by only 6 percent of the children, without significant gender or grade differences, but age is highly salient, being mentioned by 31 percent of the respondents, twice as often (p < .01) by the younger than by the older children, perhaps reflecting a "Weber-Fechner" effect, in that a year's aging represents a larger proportionate change for younger children. Eyeglasses were mentioned by only 2% of the respondents (significantly more often by younger and by female students). In general, physical appearance looms somewhat larger in girls' than in boys' sense of self, with four of these seven varied physical characteristics being mentioned significantly more often by girls than by boys, and none of the seven significantly more often by boys. How distinctiveness of one's position on these physical characteristics affects their salience in the self-concept is discussed in chapter 8.

Salience of Ethnicity in One's Sense of Self

[Adapted with permission from W. J. McGuire, C. V. McGuire, P. Child, & T. Fujioka, 1978a, Salience of ethnicity in the spontaneous self concept as a function of one's ethnic distinctiveness in the social environment, *Journal of Personality and Social Psychology, 36,* pp. 511–520. Copyright © 1978 by the American Psychological Association.]

Method.   We orally interviewed individually 560 students drawn from six schools in a medium-sized industrial New England city. There were 70 boys and 70 girls at each of four grade levels, the first, third, seventh, and eleventh (mean ages 7 to 17 years). Alone with the interviewer in a small room at school, each child was asked the general affirmational self-concept question "Tell us about yourself" and given five minutes for a tape-recorded reply without further prompts. Then he or she was asked the negational self-concept question "Tell us what you are not" and given three minutes to respond. Prestudies had suggested that appreciable numbers of children tended to run out of ideas and feel awkward when allowed more than five minutes. The responses were then transcribed and judges scored each protocol for "mention" versus "no-mention" of ethnicity as the dependent variable measure. The interviewer recorded a judgment of the child's actual ethnicity, based on appearance, accent, and name, as the independent variable measure.

Determinants of ethnicity salience in the phenomenal self. Of the 560 respondents, the interviewers judged 82% (n = 460) to be European-American, 9% (n = 48) African-American, 8% (n = 44) Latino-Americans; and 1% (n = 8) uncertain or other, a distribution that approximated that in the city at large. In keeping with the distinctiveness postulate, members of the ethnic minorities described themselves in terms of their ethnicity more often (p < .01) than members of the majority group: 17% of the African-Americans and 14% of the Latino-Americans mentioned their ethnicity versus only 1% of the majority European-American children. (These distinctiveness-theory predictions are discussed more fully in chapter 8.) Ethnicity was mentioned trivially more often by boys than girls, and there was no sex × race interaction effect. Several past studies suggest that girls have more ethnic self-consciousness than boys (Goodman, 1964; Schofield & Sagar, 1977), or that there is an interaction effect such that African-American girls and European-American boys are more ethnically self-conscious (or racially hostile) than European-American girls and African-American boys (St. John, 1975; Singer, 1967), but such tendencies did not show up in our data. There was a sizable age trend (p < .01) for ethnicity to increase in salience as the child became older, in agreement with Brand, Ruiz, and Padilla (1974).

Ethnicity was mentioned in 3% of the affirmational ("Tell us about yourself") self-concept, lower (p < .05) than the 6% mention in the negational ("Tell us what you are not") self-concept. That people are twice as likely to think of other ethnicities as something they are *not* than of their own ethnicity as something that they *are* is especially striking, considering that the participants had five minutes to give affirmational and only three minutes to give negational self-concepts, and considering that they generated twice as many affirmational as negational self-descriptive thoughts.

Salience of Sex in One's Sense of Self

Chapter 8 reports results confirming the distinctiveness-theory prediction that the child's sex becomes more salient in her or his self-concept increasingly as the other sex becomes more numerically preponderant in her or his classroom (McGuire & Padawer-Singer, 1976a) or household (McGuire, McGuire, & Winton, 1979a). Here we report findings on factors other than distinctiveness that affect the salience of sex in the self-concept.

Sex salience in the general versus physical self-concept. McGuire & Padawer-Singer (1976a) asked 252 sixth-grade students (age 13) in 10 schools in an East Coast U.S. metropolis to free-associate for seven minutes in response to a general "Tell us about yourself" probe and for five minutes to a physical-self "Describe what you look like" probe. Each child's responses to each probe were then scored for whether or not the child spontaneously specified her or his sex in describing the self. Sex was mentioned equally often (by about 20% of the children) as part of the general self-concept and of the physical self-concept. On the general self-concept, girls were slightly more likely than boys to mention their sex, whereas on the physical self-concept boys were much more likely (p < .01) than girls to mention their sex. Thus girls are more likely to mention their sex as part of their being rather than their appearance, 23% versus 10%; conversely, boys are more likely to mention their sex as part of what they look like rather than what they are, 26% versus 18%. This interaction might reflect biology's or society's impressing upon females that their sex is part of their being while on males that it is only a part of their physical appearance; or perhaps boys regard their sex as a more circumscribed physical attribute and girls regard it as a more pervasive characteristic; or it may be that, among 12-year-olds, girls are more shy than boys about thinking of their sex as part of their physical appearance.

[Adapted with permission from W. J. McGuire, C. V. McGuire, & W. Winton, 1979a.]

Age and affirmational effects on sex salience in the self. A follow-up study of the salience of sex in the phenomenal self used oral self-descriptions evoked by affirmational versus negational probes (by "Tell us about yourself" versus "Tell us what you are not"). The 560 schoolchildren respondents included 70 boys and 70 girls at each of four grade levels, the first, third, seventh, and eleventh, participating individually and given five minutes to respond orally to the affirmational and three minutes to the negational self-probes. The child's responses were recorded and transcribed, and judges scored each protocol for mention versus nonmention of sex.

Sex proved to be a moderately salient characteristic in the spontaneous self-concept, mentioned by 9% of the 560 children. For comparison, 11% described themselves in terms of height, 6% weight, and 3% ethnicity. Sex became progressively more salient with age: From first to third to seventh to eleventh graders spontaneous mention of one's sex rose ($p < .01$) from 3% to 6% to 10% to 19%, respectively, rising even when adjusted for response length. This increasing salience with age during the pubertal and adolescent years is not surprising, considering fluctuations in society's demands for sex-differentiated behavior and the changing biological realities of sexuality in this age period. Trivially more girls than boys described themselves in terms of sex (11% versus 8%), and there was no appreciable sex × age interaction effect on sex salience.

The negational versus affirmational self-concept probes had a large effect ($p < .01$) on the salience of sex. Only 9% of the children mentioned their own sex as something that they are, but 25% responded to the negational "Tell us what you are not" probe by listing the other sex as something that they are not. (As described in the previous section, an analogous effect was found for ethnicity, which was also more salient in the negational than in the affirmational self.) That not being the other sex is so much more salient than one's being one's own sex is even more impressive considering that the affirmational self-concept evoked twice as many descriptors as the negational. Also of interest is the finding that there is a significant ($p < .05$) sex × probe interaction effect: In the affirmational self-concept sex was equally salient in boys' and girls' self-concepts; but in the negational self-concept, 30% of the girls mentioned that they were not boys while only 21% of the boys mentioned that they were not girls. That for both girls and boys (but especially girls) not being a member of the other sex is much more salient than being a member of one's own are main and interaction effects that deserve further study.

The Place of School in the
Child's Phenomenal Self

[Adapted from W. J. McGuire, T. Fujioka, & C. V. McGuire, 1979b. The place of school in the child's self-concept. *Impact on Instructional Improvement, 15*, pp. 3–10.]

The three worlds of childhood – family, school, and friendship group – can be expected to loom large in the child's phenomenal sense of self. For example, McGuire and Padawer-Singer (1976a) found that 17% of all self-descriptive thoughts of sixth-graders pertained to their school experiences. We report here a follow-up study using the 560 schoolchildren in a New England industrial town, including 70 boys and 70 girls at each of five grade levels, the first, third, seventh, and eleventh, which mapped in more detail the place of school in children's self-descriptions evoked by the "Tell us about yourself" probe.

Extent of the school domain in self-space. School topics occupy 11% of the child's thoughts about the self, trailing four other categories. Family mentions were most common, exceeding school mentions 17% to 11%, even though the responses were elicited in the school setting. After family came recreational activities (primarily hobbies, games, sports, and cars) at 14%, followed by daily life and demographic topics (for example, meals, clothes, age, gender), which occupy 13% of the child's self-thoughts, and friends and social relations, which constitute 11%. School mentions, at 11%, come fifth and exceeded mention of five further topics, including 10% mention of objects, 9% mention of formal activities (e.g., domestic chores, music and art, and work and career expectations), 6% mention of the natural environment (e.g., pets and other animals, plants, climate, etc.), 5% mention of broader societal concerns (e.g., economics, religion, politics, etc.), and 4% mention of health and appearance.

These figures, summed across the various grade levels, indicate that a respectable though not overwhelming proportion of the child's thoughts of self focused on school matters, but the prominence of school in the sense of self grows steeply from age 7 to 17 years. Going from first to eleventh grades, school mentions grew progressively from less than 5% to more than 15%. Indeed, by the eleventh grade the school experience became the most preoccupying topic in the child's self-space, while thoughts of one's family relations declined to less than 5%. These age trends, and the overall salience of school top-ics in defining the self, show up about equally in boys and girls.

Self-definition in terms of academic performance.   These scholastic mentions in children's self-descriptions are distributed over various aspects of the school experience. Across all age and sex groups about one-third of school mentions deal with academic concerns, such as the workload, grades, or future academic aspirations; another third in-volve social aspects of the school such as extracurricular activities or relations with other students or with teachers; 12% of the school men-tions concern institutional aspects such as school regulations or the physical condition of the school; and 26% are superficial mentions of school in general or reports on the child's own present grade level. Most of the one-third of school mentions dealing with academic con-cerns focus on one's own academic performance, split about equally between worries about and satisfactions with this performance. The remaining, impersonal academic concerns focus on the quality of the education being received (e.g., the adequacy of the teaching, the availability of courses in the curriculum, adequacy of educational ma-terials), plans for continuing education in high school or college, and comments on specific current courses. Breaking down these overall age trends for affect, as the child moves to higher grade levels com-plaints tend progressively to predominate (e.g., from first to eleventh grade there are increasing net expressions of dissatisfaction with own performance, of academic difficulties, and of dissatisfaction with the education being received).

Social aspects of school.   One-third of the scholastic self-definitions deal with the school's social aspects, mostly other students. First- and third-graders tended to mention specific students in their own class-room, whereas seventh- and eleventh-graders defined themselves more globally in comparison to students in general or broad types of students. Teachers are slightly less prominent in the child's self-concept than are students, and administrators do not loom large in the child's self-concept, only 8 of the 560 students mentioning principals or other administrative personnel and only 2 students mentioning service personnel such as school guards or janitors. Guidance and counseling people were mentioned by only 24 students, primarily those in the higher grades; remarkably, all 24 such mentions were made by boys, perhaps because boys see more guidance and remedial personnel or because such experiences have a bigger impact on the self-definition of boys. Sports and other extracurricular activities were mentioned in defining the self by only 2% of the students, almost all eleventh-grade boys, the group most likely to occupy important positions on varsity teams. School athletics seem to contribute almost nothing to the sense of self for the vast majority of students who are not on varsity teams.

The school's institutional setting. Institutional aspects supplied 12% of the school mentions, divided about equally among the school schedule, regulations, and the physical plant. Mentions of the physical plant dealt mainly with complaints about the conditions of the academic space, especially the student's current classroom: More than 60 of the students mentioned paint, ventilation, and so on of the current classroom; whereas only 12 of the 560 students mentioned the cafeteria or meals; and practically no children mentioned the gymnasium, lavatory, halls, or staircases as entering their self-consciousness. The students might prefer spending the school's refurbishment budget on the classrooms rather than on the other sites that visitors often complain about. The 3% of the scholastic mentions that focused on restrictions and regulations were mostly complaints and dealt with truancy, regulations against causing disturbances in class, and restrictions on smoking and other student activities. We had expected consciousness of the rules and discipline to increase with age, but it proves to be as high in the first as in the eleventh grade.

By the eleventh grade the child is more preoccupied with school experience than with any other part of the environment (it occupies far more self-space than family, friends, or recreational activities), suggesting that the school has considerable opportunity and responsibility for the broader development of the child, extending far beyond the acquisition of skills. The school experience impinges on the child's self-consciousness via a wide variety of scholastic aspects, each constituting a handle by which the school can affect the child's development. In apportioning their limited resources, teachers and educational administrators might give greater attention to those aspects of the school experience which loom large in the child's self-consciousness. School sports do not loom large in the sense of self, except for the few boys who are on varsity teams. It is disturbing that over the 12 years of primary and secondary education, as school preoccupation grows increasingly to fill the child's self-consciousness, there is a parallel monotonic age-shift toward increasing dissatisfaction with school and with one's own scholastic performance.

The Social Self: Significant Others in Self-Space

[Adapted with permission from W. J. McGuire & C. V. McGuire, 1982a, Significant others in self-space: Sex difference and developmental trends in the social self, in J. Suls (Ed.), *Psychological Perspectives on the Self, 1,* pp. 71–96 (Hillsdale, NJ: L. Erlbaum Associates, copyright © 1982).]

The content of self-space is operationally defined as the noun material that the person reports when asked in a nonspecific context to "Tell us about yourself." Our social-self study deals with the significant others who occupy self-space: who they are, how much space they occupy, and how this self-space varies with sex and age. We assume the person is highly dependent on and oriented toward other people and to a sizable extent defines him- or herself in relation to other people. Freud (1921) asserted that even in one's most autistic mental acts someone else is invariably involved (as a model, object, observer, helper, opponent, etc.). Because younger children are particularly dependent on others, we expect that the prevalence of other people in the phenomenal self-concept will be especially high in the young.

Method.   Our data come from five-minute oral responses to the "Tell us about yourself" probe given by 560 schoolchildren (70 girls and 70 boys in each of four grades, the first, third, seventh, and eleventh). The recorded responses were transcribed and content-analyzed by being divided into thought segments, each of which was reformulated into a three-unit "subject/verb/complement" format, and the contents of each of its units were translated into a 1,000-term dictionary that includes all of the significant other terms identified by prestudies or by a priori conjecture as likely to be salient to school-aged children.

Results: Prevalence of significant others in the sense of self.   Children's self-concepts are highly social in that, of the 30,603 noun concepts (i.e., all the contents of the first and third units of all thought segments produced by the 560 schoolchildren in response to a "Tell us about yourself" probe), no fewer than 7,170 (or 23% of the total) were mentions of significant others. Almost half (47%) of these references to significant others involved mentions of relatives; an additional quarter (24%) were mentions of friends. The remaining quarter included mentions of teachers and students (8%), broad categories of people (adults, boys, people in general, etc., 11%), and animals (11%).

Girls as more people-oriented than boys in their self-definitions. Our predictions about sex differences in the salience of significant others in the children's self-concepts derive from three postulates: (A) that in defining themselves girls are more people-oriented than boys; (B) that girls, being more restricted, protected, and domestically directed than boys, are more parochial than boys in the choice of the significant others in terms of whom they define themselves; and (C) that as regards salient nuclear-family significant others, children focus on other-sex siblings and same-sex parent. The results bearing on sex-difference predictions drawn from these three postulates are summarized in Table 7.1.

Postulate A, that girls are more preoccupied with people than are boys and therefore will define themselves in terms of relationships with other people more than do boys, is confirmed by all tests. Most basically, mentions of other people constitute a greater proportion of all the noun content in the self-concepts of girls than of boys. As can be seen in row A1.1 of Table 7.1, of all their self-concept nouns, for girls 24% are mentions of other people, higher ($p < .001$) than boys' 17%. A more subtle implication of Postulate A is that girls, being more person-oriented than boys, will differentiate people as specific individuals rather than making a deindividuating lumping of people into categories. This implication yields Table 7.1 predictions A2.1, A2.2, and A2.3, all three of which are confirmed at the $p < .001$ level. Girls' self-concepts more than boys' differentiate people into males versus females and into children versus adults and into specified family relationships (rather than referring to "my family" in general). A third implication of Postulate A, that fewer negatively valenced significant others will enter girls' than boys' self-concepts, is confirmed ($p < .001$) by the data in row A3.1 of Table 7.1.

Girls' social selves as more parochial than boys'. The predictions from Postulate B, that girls, being more confined than boys, are more domestic than boys in the significant others in terms of whom they define themselves, are largely confirmed, as can be seen in five of the seven B rows of Table 7.1. For girls a higher ($p < .001$) proportion of people mentioned are family members and a higher ($p < .05$) propor-

Table 7.1

Sex differences in defining the self in terms of significant others. The hypotheses are derived from postulates A (girls are more people-oriented), B (girls are more parochial), and C (orientation to own-sex parent and other-sex sibling). Numbers of cases are 280 boys and 280 girls.

Prediction		Sex of participants		Significance level
Number	*Comparison*	*Boys*	*Girls*	
A1.1	Sig.-others nouns ÷ all nouns	.17	.24	< .001
A2.1	"adults," "child"÷ all categ. others	.05	.35	< .001
A2.2	"males," "females," ÷ all categ. others	.06	.24	< .001
A2.3	specific family members ÷ all "family"	.78	.84	< .001
A3.1	friends ÷ friends and enemies	.87	.94	< .001
B1.1	kin mentions ÷ all human references	.49	.55	< .001
B1.2	nuclear family ÷ all family	.90	.90	not sig.
B1.3	romantic friends ÷ all friends	.11	.14	< .05
B1.4	pets ÷ all animals	.68	.88	< .001
B2.1	sib-age peers ÷ all household	.52	.62	< .001
B2-2	student-age peers ÷ students & teachers	.48	.66	< .001
B3.1	own-sex kin ÷ all kin	.53	.53	not sig.
C1.1	mother ÷ mother & father	.40	.67	<.001
C1.2	brother ÷ brother & sister	.49	.56	<.05

tion of friend mentions are romantic friends; and of animal mentions a higher (p < .001) proportion are pets rather than wild animals. That girls more than boys would mention their own age group rather than adults was confirmed (p < .001) for mentions of both family and school others (see rows B2.1 and B2.2 in Table 7.1).

Sex-difference Postulate C, that when children define themselves in terms of nuclear family members they will focus on their own-sex parent and other-sex sibling, is derived from the assumption that children, in learning their prescribed adult roles, must define themselves in terms of their same-sex parent (e.g., boys must focus on their fathers rather than their mothers); whereas in learning their prescribed procreative role with age peers, children must define themselves in relation to other-sex age peers (e.g., boys focus on their sisters rather than their brothers). Rows C1.1 and C1.2 in Table 7.1 show that both predictions are confirmed, girls tending to define themselves in relation to mothers and brothers, boys in relation to fathers and sisters.

Results regarding shrinkage of the social self with maturity. The most basic age postulate, D, is that as the person matures during childhood and adolescence, becoming less dependent on nurturing adults, the social realm becomes less significant in self-definition. This postulate's clearest implication is confirmed ($p < .001$) by the data in row D1.1 of Table 7.2, which shows that the proportion of all first- and third-unit self-thoughts that mention significant others declines progressively ($p < .001$) from .29 for 7-year-olds to .16 for 17-year-olds. A second D2 "deindividuating" implication, that as children mature they define themselves in relation to generic categories of people rather than specific individuals, yields four predictions. Rows D2.1 through D2.4 of Table 7.2 significantly ($p < .001$) confirm all four of these predictions. As the child grows older, he or she tends increasingly to describe the self in relation to people in general and decreasingly to differentiate these significant others in terms of their sex, age, or status. A final implication of postulate D, that as the child grows older there will be increasing self-definition in terms of negatively evaluated others, is supported ($p < .01$) by the row D3.1 data in Table 7.2. Mentions of friends, as might be expected from the person-positivity postulate, far outnumber mentions of enemies at all age levels, but enemies constitute a steadily growing minority of mentions as the child grows older.

Developmental postulate E, that the significant others in terms of whom one defines oneself progressively shift from adults to age peers through the childhood and adolescent years, is not confirmed as regards any of its three predictions, as shown in rows E1, E2, and E3. The third postulated age trend, F, is that during childhood and adolescent development, as children's autonomy and mobility grow, then social self-definitions become progressively more cosmopolitan in that nonkin persons constitute an increasing proportion of all significant others in terms of whom children define themselves. The three derived cosmopolitan developmental predictions are all confirmed

Table 7.2

Age trends in the salience of significant others in self-space. The predictions are derived from Postulates D (decreasing importance of significant others with age), E (increasing peer orientation), and F (increasing negativity). Each age group includes 70 boys and 70 girls.

Number	Predictions	Age group (in years)				Significance level
		7	9	13	17	
D1.1	Sig.-others ÷ all items	.29	.27	.24	.16	< .001
D2.1	"humans, etc." ÷ all sig. others	.06	.05	.10	.27	< .001
D2.2	"relatives, family" ÷ all kin	.11	.18	.22	.29	< .001
D2.3	"students in gen'l." ÷ all students	.03	.04	.40	.69	< .001
D2.4	"teacher in gen'l." ÷ all teacher	.09	.04	.13	.36	< .001
D3.1	"enemies" ÷ friends + enemies	.04	.08	.09	.13	< .01
E1.1	sibling ÷ sibling + parents	.56	.60	.69	.58	nonmonotonic
E1.2	cousins ÷ all extended family	.40	.38	.54	.32	nonmonotonic
E1.3	students ÷ students + teachers	.66	.65	.26	.58	nonmonotonic
F1.1	parents ÷ parents + teachers	.95	.78	.67	.58	< .001
F1.2	sibs ÷ (friends + students + sibs)	.63	.42	.51	.30	< .001
F1.3	extended family ÷all nonkin	.19	.11	.07	.02	< .001
G1.1	animals ÷ all sig. others	.09	.19	.10	.03	nonmonotonic

(p < .001) by data in the three F rows of Table 7.2. As the child grows older, the significant others in terms of whom children define themselves shift away from the family – from parents to teachers, from brothers and sisters to friends and fellow students, from extended-family members to nonkin others.

Self-definitions in terms of nonhuman animals.   Our prestudies indicated a prevalence of nonhuman animals in children's self-definitions, in keeping with reports that childhood fantasies (e.g., as manifested in dreams) reflect an identification with small animals. Perhaps for young children, so dependent and powerless relative to other humans, animals may provide one of the few outlets for nurturance and power needs. In this social-self study children defined themselves to a striking extent in terms of nonhuman animals. Across the age span from 7 to 17 years nonhuman animal mentions provided 11% of all significant others mentions, a proportion exceeded only by the inclusive human categories of friends (24%), siblings (20%), and parents (14%). Even though all the children had mothers and not all had pets, mentions of pets (8% of all significant others) exceeded mentions of mothers (7%). And among the particularly animal-oriented 9-year-olds, mention of nonhuman animals constituted an amazing 19% of all self-definitions in terms of references to significant others, a proportion exceeding even that contributed by core generic groups such as all friends or all siblings or both parents.

What are all these animals? Children (especially boys) tend slightly to be "dog" people, with 30% of all animal mentions referring to that species of pet, as compared with 23% dealing with cats, 8% with other small mammals (gerbils, etc.), 6% with birds, 5% with horses, and lesser incidence of fish and other pets. All in all, 78% of all animal mentions referred to pets and 22% to wild animals (usually fish, birds, and insects).

On the assumption that self-definition in terms of nonhuman animals represents rather "primitive" thought content, we predicted that the proportion of the social self occupied by nonhuman animals would decline progressively as the child develops through childhood and adolescence. However, the results in row G1.1 of Table 7.2 show a nonmonotonic developmental trend: It is not the youngest, 7-year-old group whose self-concepts are most concerned with nonhuman animals, but rather the 9-year-olds. For the 7-year-olds, animals furnish .09 of all self-definitions in terms of significant others, whereas for 9-year-olds this proportion more than doubles to .19; thereafter, the proportion falls precipitously to .10 among 13-year olds and .03 among 17-year olds. This inverted-U developmental trend, peaking at age 9, is quite stable across species, appearing similarly for each of the four equipotential subclasses of animals (dogs, cats, other pets, and wild animals). This nonmonotonic age trend may be due to the salience of animals deriving from two mediating factors with opposite developmental trends. A mediator increasing with age might be maturing needs for power and nurturing; a mediator declining with age might be the scarcity of other human beings toward whom one can exercise these nurturing needs. McGuire (1961b, 1968b, and chapters 1 and 3 of this volume) presents a quantitative model demonstrating that, under a wide range of parametric assumptions, such two-factor models yield a nonmonotonic, inverted-U function such that the dependent variable (here, salience of animals in the phenomenal self) peaks at an intermediate level of the independent variable (here, age).

Conclusions regarding the social self. As expected, the social self occupies a substantial proportion of total self-space (23% of all noun content). The social self is larger for girls than boys, and girls are more parochial in selecting the significant others in terms of whom they define themselves. Both boys and girls are oriented toward their own-sex parent and other-sex sibling in forming their self-concepts, a pattern that facilitates socialization into their prescribed adult sex roles. As children mature from ages 7 to 17, they define themselves decreasingly in terms of other people and these other people are more cosmopolitanly chosen. No confirmation was found for increasingly peer-oriented self-definition as the child matures. Nonhuman animals provide a substantial proportion of all significant others in self-space, with a nonmonotonic inverted-U developmental trend peaking around age 9 years.

VERB PROCESSES IN THE PHENOMENAL SELF

The studies so far reported in this topographical chapter have mapped the phenomenal sense of self as regards the noun content of children's free associations in response to probes such as "Tell us about yourself." The rest of the chapter moves from content to process, describing studies of the verb processes by which one thinks about this noun content, as revealed by the types of verbs used in the children's self-descriptions. The theoretical issues addressed in the three successive verb/process studies include: (1) age trends in how thought processes about the self change during childhood; (2) multiple-self manifestations of how thought processes about the self differ depending on which contextual self is involved; and (3) self–other distinctions regarding how processes in thinking about the self differ from those in thinking about other people. In these three verb/process studies we continue to let the person think in her or his own terms by presenting a general probe and then content-analyzing her or his free associations to it; but we change somewhat the nature of the probe, making it more situationally and less personally specific (e.g., "Tell us about school," "Tell us about your family") and we abstract self-descriptive (or other-descriptive) thoughts that arise in these contrasting contexts.

[Adapted with permission from W. J. McGuire & C. V. McGuire, 1988a. Additional details can be found in McGuire & McGuire, 1986f; McGuire, McGuire, & Cheever, 1986d.]

Methods Used in the Verb/Process Studies

Participants and data-collection procedures.   The three verb/process studies described here were replicated in oral and written response modalities. In the oral response replication 70 boys and 70 girls participated at each of four grade levels, the first, third, seventh, and eleventh (their mean ages being 7, 9, 13, and 17 years, respectively). In the written response condition, 100 boys and 100 girls participated at each of five grade levels, the fifth, seventh, ninth, eleventh, and twelfth (with mean ages of 11, 13, 15, 17, and 18 years, respectively). Participants in both oral and written conditions were given five minutes to free-associate to the "Tell us about yourself" probe, furnishing data for the first verb study on the ontogeny of self-conceptualizing processes, and were then given three minutes to free-associate to two other probes, "Tell us about school" and "Tell us about your family," order being counterbalanced, furnishing data for the second and third verb studies on how self-conceptualizing is affected by situational context and on how self-conceptualizing differs from conceptualizing other people.

The subject/verb/complement content analysis.   The oral and written responses which the participant gave to each of the three probes were transcribed and content-analyzed by a three-step procedure, including segmenting, formatting, and translating. Segmentation, dividing the responses into individual units of thought, was usually routine, the basic rules being that each predicate supplied a new thought segment and that compound subjects yielded multiple thought segments; for example, the child's response "Me and my sister work at Burger King. She's already finished school" was divided into three thought segments: "self/works at/ restaurant," "sister/works at/ restaurant," "sister/graduated/high school."

The second step of transforming each of these thought segments into a standard subject/verb/complement format was straightforward for most thought segments, except that details often had to be eliminated; for example, the child's expression, "I work four hours Friday and Saturday nights at McDonalds" was reduced to "self/works part-time at/restaurant." Occasionally the child's grammar had to be more drastically transformed, as when the rare passive expressions such as "The most baskets were gotten by me" was transformed into "self/performed well at/ basketball," or when the rare metaphor such as "I'd give my right arm for a Harley-Davidson" was translated into its literal expression, "self/wants/motorcycle." Depicting the flow of thought as a succession of subject/verb/complement segments has enjoyed popularity in social cognition research at least since its mid-twentieth-century use for meaning measurement by Osgood, Suci, and Tannenbaum (1957). It has proved useful in a wide range of social cognition research (Abelson & Rosenberg, 1958; Kreitler & Kreitler, 1976) and has received elegant formal development by Gollob (1974b). Aspects of its use continue to be debated (Anderson, 1977, 1979; Gollob, 1979; Wyer & Carlston, 1979, pp. 314–33), but the controversial aspects are not central to its usage in the present study. Its continuing popularity and use here derive from its being a simple form that closely fits the way people actually express most of their thoughts, except for loss of detail and connectives and for occasional transformations of the child's idiom. The third step in our content-analysis procedure was to translate the content of the three units in each thought segment into the thousand terms of our basic concept dictionary, which included 108 verb concepts used to encode the middle (verb) unit of each thought segment.

The focus on verbs.   We concentrated on verbs in these process studies because several lines of evidence indicate that verbs are particularly strong carriers of meaning. Verbs are the parts of speech most resistant to slips of the tongue (Meringer, 1908; Hotopf, 1980), to systematic distortions (Semin & Greenslade, 1985), and to alteration by speakers' purposes (Sandell, 1977, pp. 110–27). Verbs also make the largest contribution to judged similarity of thoughts (Healy & Miller, 1970), to perceived completeness of thoughts (Healy & Miller, 1971), to inducing general principles (Abelson & Kanouse, 1966), and to evoking agreement with propositions (Kanouse & Abelson, 1967).

A dictionary of 108 basic verb concepts was compiled to encode the contents of the middle (verb) unit of each subject/verb/complement thought segment. Both a priori and a posteriori methods were used to assemble this verb dictionary. Starting with published word-frequency counts and thesauri and with conjectures about verbs likely to be used in person descriptions, we assembled an extensive initial list of promising verbs. Prestudies boiled the list down to the final set of 108 verbs, usually by combining lesser-used verbs with others of similar meaning. Our current list of 108 could be shortened considerably with little loss of information.

Table 7.3
Verb classification system used to generate the six verb ratios

---

All verbs
 I. State verbs
    A. States of being (e.g., characterized by, situated at)
    B. Stages of becoming (e.g., attempt, improve)
 II. Action verbs
    A. Overt actions
       1. Physical acting on (e.g., move, eat)
       2. Social interacting with (e.g., talk, help)
    B. Covert reactions
       1. Cognitive (e.g., believe, interested in)
       2. Affective (e.g., like, feel)
All verbs
    Affirmative (e.g., being, doing)
    Negative (e.g., not being, not doing)

The verb classification. The 108 verbs in our basic concept dictionary were organized into the tree structure shown in Table 7.3, composed of a succession of branching dichotomies that reflect traditional grammatical and semantic distinctions among verbs and are relevant to hypotheses about person perception. The basic dichotomy is the traditional division of all verbs into verbs of state versus verbs of action. Using state verbs to describe oneself and other people reflects seeing them abstractly in terms of what they are, whereas using action verbs reflects seeing them concretely in terms of what they do. Verbs of state are then subdivided into being states versus becoming states, reflecting a view of persons as static versus as dynamically changing, as Apollonian versus Dionysian. Verbs of action, in turn, are dichotomized into overt action verbs versus covert reaction verbs, that is, thinking about persons in terms of their objective behavior versus their subjective experience. Overt action verbs are further partitioned into physical actions versus social interactions; and covert reactions are further partitioned into affective versus cognitive reactions. A sixth verb dichotomy cuts across these first five partitions, dividing the total set of verbs into affirmations (describing people in terms of what they are) versus negations (describing people in terms of what they are not). These six verb dichotomies provide the dependent variable dimensions in the hypotheses in the three process studies described below.

Verb/Processes Study 1: Developmental Trends in Self-Thought

Hypotheses and methods in the developmental studies.   The general postulate underlying our age-trend predictions (McGuire & McGuire, 1987) is that, as the person matures through childhood and adolescence, his or her modes of thinking about the self become more sophisticated in various ways, each manifested in an age shift in one of our six verb dichotomies toward increasing use of the more sophisticated branch of that verb dichotomy.

Because our hypotheses deal specifically with self-conceptualizing, we selected out of all thought segments elicited by the "Tell us about yourself" probe only the subset with "self" as subject. For example, when a child replies, "I get along well with my brother. He works at Livingston Tools," this material is coded as two thought segments, "self/friendly with/brother," and "brother/works at/factory." Only the first of these two segments is strictly a self-descriptive statement in having self as its subject, and so only it enters in the verb analyses for the six developmental hypotheses discussed below. The proportion of self-segments was substantially higher in the written than the oral condition: When responding to the "Tell us about yourself" probe in writing, 83% of all thought segments had "self" as subject versus only 61% in the oral condition. Perhaps the greater onerousness of written responding inhibits going off on tangents, or perhaps the slower pace imposed by writing allows better monitoring for self-relevance.

Age changes in the six verb ratios.   Significant monotonic age trends in the predicted directions were found for all of the six verb ratios in the written response modality, and for four of the six in the oral condition. The first prediction is that as one matures one perceives the self increasingly in more sophisticated abstract terms of what one is rather than what one does; hence, the ratio of state verbs relative to action verbs in describing oneself will increase with age. Both oral and written responses show the predicted monotonically increasing ($p < .01$)

use of state relative to action verbs in self-descriptions as the child grows older.

The second prediction is that, because as one matures one has had increasing opportunities to appreciate that the self changes, therefore the proportion of all self-descriptive verbs of state that are becoming verbs will increase with age relative to verbs of being. The results show such an increasing trend with age for becoming verbs to predominate over being verbs in both modalities, monotonic in the written condition but with a slight dip at age 13 in the oral responding.

The third prediction is of an age trend toward interiorization of self-thought (because as one matures one inhibits overt action in favor of covert analysis). This prediction was confirmed by a steady age shift from overt actions to covert reactions among those self-descriptive statements that used verbs of action, a shift steep ($p < .01$) in the oral-response condition but only borderline ($p = .08$) in the written.

The fourth prediction is that, when overt action verbs are used in self-descriptions, an age shift toward socialization of overt activity will be exhibited in the form of an increasing ratio of social interacting verbs relative to physical acting verbs. This prediction was confirmed by steady age shifts ($p < .01$ in both oral and written response modalities) from physical actions to social interactions in self-descriptions that used overt-action verbs. The fifth prediction, of an intellectualization of the covert self with age, was confirmed ($p < .01$) in the written-response condition by a steady age shift from affect verbs to cognition verbs among self-descriptions that used covert reaction verbs. However, in the oral condition (which taps earlier ages) this prediction was not supported in that the proportion of cognition verbs dropped from age 7 to age 9 before showing, from age 9 to 17, the predicted increase in cognitive relative to affective verbs.

The sixth prediction of a negational age trend from seeing oneself in simple affirmational terms of what one is to seeing oneself in more complex negational terms of what one is not was confirmed in both oral and written conditions by monotonic increases ($p < .01$) with age in the proportion of self-descriptions that are negational rather than affirmational. That negational thinking is more sophisticated is illustrated by the late appearance of negatives in children's speech (Bellugi-Klima, 1968; Maratsos et al., 1976; Kim, 1985; Akiyama, 1986) and by the difficulty even highly educated adults have in retrieving negational information (McGuire & McGuire, 1992c) and in using negative information in concept formation (Hovland, 1952) and in decision making (Wason, 1961; Slobin, 1966). Hence, all six developmental verb-trend predictions were confirmed significantly (one only borderline) in the written response modality; and four of the six in the oral modality. The predicted verb trends were robust across sex, appearing about equally in boys and girls, without any significant age × sex interactions.

Verb/Processes Study 2: Multiple Selves, Effects of Social Context on the Self-Concepts

[Adapted with permission from W. J. McGuire, C. V. McGuire, and J. Cheever, 1986d, The self in society: Effects of social context on the sense of self, *British Journal of Social Psychology, 25,* pp. 259–275. Copyright © 1986 by The British Psychological Society.]

The relation between self and society is intimate and intricate in the domain of thought as in the arena of actuality. From some perspectives the two appear as opposed thesis and antithesis, the self striving for distinctive identity and society imposing deindividuating collectivity; but from other viewpoints the two appear symbiotic, the sense of self developing out of social interaction and the society's institutions being formed on the template of self-identities. Interrelations between self and society are investigated in the present study by examining the ways in which even so personal an experience as one's phenomenal sense of self is colored by the social context in which the self-thoughts arise.

Theorists have long debated the extent to which the self-concept is social rather than individual. A strong social position has been taken by Marx in his notion of the person as a species being, as well as in his historical materialism; by looking-glass self theorists (Cooley, 1902; Sullivan, 1953); and by symbolic interactionists in the George Herbert Mead tradition (e.g., Strauss, 1964; Berger, 1966; Hewitt, 1983; Felson, 1985; Schafer & Keith, 1985), who stress that a person's sense of identity is always formed in the context of some specific social world. On the other hand, behavioristic (Kagan, 1981) and psychoanalytic (Wrong, 1962) theorists argue that social scientists have oversocialized the concept of self, though the founding father himself (Freud, 1921) asserted that self-perception always involves the self in relation to another person, even in one's most autistic thoughts. When the phenomenal sense of self is investigated empirically by having people report whatever comes to mind when asked "Tell me about yourself" the thoughts elicited are highly social: As reported earlier in this chapter, no fewer than 23% of all the noun content appearing in these free self-descriptions by children and adolescents are mentions of significant others (McGuire & McGuire, 1982a).

Theorists in the Durkheimian (1898) and Marxist traditions of collective consciousness and others who emphasize the social determination of self argue that a similar sense of self arises in all members of a community out of their common culture and shared social institutions and material conditions. In this study we make an opposite use of the social determinism position by assuming that modern society enmeshes the individual in multiple critical social contexts, each imposing a distinctive self-creating role, so that researchers should adopt William James's (1890) practice of speaking of the person's "selves" rather than self. Our research strategy here is to ask children and adolescents to give open-ended descriptions of two of their three main social contexts – their family world and their school world, leaving their peer/friend world for later study. We then examine the self-descriptive statements arising in each of these two social contexts to determine if the family-self and the school-self differ predictably in processes used in thinking about the self, as manifested in the six contrasting types of verbs used in the self-descriptive thought segments that arise in the two contexts, family and school. Our general contention is that the nurturing family is a more supportive, less challenging context, likely to engender a relatively passive sense of self; whereas the more demanding school context, designed to inculcate achievement, is likely to engender a more dynamic sense of self. Implications regarding the six verb-ratios are discussed below when the results are reported.

Methods in these multiple-selves studies. The participants were the same as in the previous study, the 560 schoolchildren who gave their responses orally and the 1,000 children who responded in writing. Each child free-associated for three minutes to each of two probes, "Tell us about school" and "Tell us about your family." The responses were transcribed and content-analyzed by the three-step procedure already described: (1) the free-flowing responses were divided into individual thought segments; (2) each thought segment was put into a subject/verb/complement format; and (3) the contents of the three units in each thought segment were translated into the vocabulary of our 1,000-term basic concept dictionary. Our hypotheses concern the middle (verb) unit translated into the 108 verb terms in the dictionary, which terms were sorted into the verb types in our tree-diagram classification shown in Table 7.3. Because our hypotheses apply specifically to self-thoughts, we selected for analysis only those evoked thoughts with "self" as their first-unit (subject) content. Thus, among the thoughts evoked by the school probe, the thought segment "I'm having trouble with arithmetic" would enter these analyses but not the segment "Some students in this school are bad news."

Fluency and self-salience in family versus school descriptions.   The children were similarly fluent in responding to family and school probes. In the oral condition, the mean number of segments spoken during the three minutes of response to "Tell us about your family" was 27.76, and in response to "Tell us about school" the mean was an almost identical 27.88 segments. This oral fluency in response to each probe increased steadily (p < .001) with age, as would be expected, from a mean of 18 segments for 7-year-olds to 39 segments for 17-year-olds. The girls were slightly (p = .08) more fluent than the boys; the sex × age interactions were trivial. Fluency was of course decidedly lower in the written condition: At a given grade level three times as many thought segments were evoked in the oral as in the written condition. In the written replication the number of segments elicited by the family and school probes were again approximately equal; fluency again increased steadily (p < .001) with age; again girls were more fluent than boys (p < .001) and the age × sex interaction effects on fluency were again negligible.

Although responses to family and school probes were almost identical in length, they differed sizably in the proportion of all generated thought segments that focused on the self (as defined by their having "myself" as the subject of the subject/verb/complement segments). In the oral condition only 25% of all the thought segments elicited by the family probe were self-segments, much lower (p < .001) than the 38% of those elicited by the school probe. An even more sizable (p < .001) context effect on self-salience appeared in the written condition, where only 27% of all segments evoked by the family probe were self-thoughts versus 49% by the school probe. This lesser proportion of self-references when describing family than school in both oral and written response conditions supports our general assumption that the sense of self is more subdued in the family than in the school context.

The proportion of self-segments did not vary with age or sex in either modality.

Effects of school versus family contexts on the six verb ratios. The six hypotheses about differences between the school-self and the family-self in the verb types used in self-descriptive thoughts elicited by "school" versus "family" probes were again tested in terms of the subset of evoked thought segments that had "myself" as their subject term. The first hypothesis is that the family context engenders a more passive self, one's seeing oneself in terms of ascribed rather than attained status, of abstract states and relations rather than of concrete acts, of what one is rather than what one does. The verb implication is that among all verbs, the proportion of state to action verbs will be higher in the family-self than in the school-self. This prediction is borne out ($p < .01$) in both response modalities. In the oral condition the proportion of all self-segments that uses state rather than action verbs is .22 in the family context versus only .14 in the school context. In the written condition the context effect is similar: The proportion of state verbs is .22 in the family-self versus only .11 in the school-self.

The second hypothesis is that the more changing, demanding, achievement-oriented school environment will result in a more dynamic, mutable sense of self; in the relatively constant, conservative family context the self will be more static. The verb implication is that when verbs of state are used in describing the self there will be a higher ratio of static verbs of being relative to dynamic verbs of becoming in family than in school contexts. The results confirm ($p < .01$) this prediction in both the oral condition (where, of all state verbs, 40% were "becoming" rather than "being" verbs in the school-self, versus only 21% in the family-self); and in the written condition (where the corresponding ratios were 53% versus 14%). The third hypothesis predicts that when verbs of action are used there will be a higher ratio of primitive overt-action verbs relative to mature covert-reaction verbs when the self-thoughts occur in the family than in the school context, because the school restrains physical acting out and promotes subjective reactions more than does the home. This prediction is strongly supported ($p < .01$) in both modality replications. In the oral-response condition, among all action verbs, 73% are covert reactions in the school-self versus only 27% in the family-self; in the written response condition the corresponding ratios are 89% versus 38%. The fourth hypothesis was also confirmed ($p < .01$) in both modalities (p < .01), in that when overt action verbs were used there was a larger proportion of simple physical actions (traveling, eating, etc.), relative to more demanding social interactions in self-descriptions in the family context than in the more challenging school context. The fifth prediction is that in the more engulfing family situations it is safer for the child simply to register a situation cognitively without affectively appraising it, whereas the more challenging school situation encourages the child to go beyond simple cognitive registration to affective judgment. The verb implication is confirmed (p < .01) in both modalities: When covert reaction verbs are used in self-descriptions, the ratio of affective appraisal verbs over cognitive registration verbs is significantly higher in the school-self than in the family-self.

A final prediction derived from the postulate of a less sophisticated self in the family context is that across all verbs the proportion of affirmations over negations will be greater in the family than in the school context. As cited above, past research shows that reflexive negational thinking, including conceptualizing oneself in terms of what one is not, is a more sophisticated mode of thinking than conceptualizing oneself affirmatively in terms of what one is. The prediction of more negations in the school- than family-self is confirmed (p < .01) in both written and oral modalities.

Overall, the six predicted context effects on modes of self-thought show up sizably and significantly on all six verb ratios in both oral and written response replications. Furthermore, the age trends for the six verb ratios, reported in the previous study for the "Yourself" probe, were replicated here with the "School" and "Family" probes. Rom Harré and Klaus Fiedler provide critiques of this study, to which the authors reply (McGuire, 1986e).

Verb/Processes Study 3: Self- Versus Other-Perception

[Adapted with permission from W. J. McGuire and C. V. McGuire, 1986f, Differences in conceptualizing self versus conceptualizing other people as manifested in contrasting verb types used in natural speech, *Journal of Personality and Social Psychology, 51,* pp. 1135–1143. Copyright © 1986 by The American Psychological Association.]

Occasional comparative studies have included self- and other-person conceptualizations within a single design to test theorized differences between the two (e.g., Farr & Moscovici, 1984; Figurski, 1986; Higgins, Klein, & Strauman, 1986; Kreitler & Kreitler, 1986; Prentice, 1990), but the only sustained comparative work is that pursuing the narrow Jones and Nisbett (1972) attributional hypothesis that people emphasize situational determinants in explaining their own behavior and dispositional determinants in explaining other people's behavior. Here we go further by carrying out a whole program of work, testing six postulates of how the thought processes differ between self- and other-conceptualizations, each of the six being tested in terms of the types of verbs used in free descriptions.

That differences between how one conceptualizes oneself versus other people might derive from the privileged knowledge one has about the self might be questioned by positivistic theorists. Radical behaviorists (Bem, 1972) contend that self-perceptions derive largely from one's observations of one's own overt behavior, just as one's perception of others is based mainly on observations of their overt behavior. Looking-glass self, symbolic interactionist theorists (Cooley, 1902/1964; Mead, 1934; Blumer, 1969) also downplay differences in conceptualizing self-versus-others because of their contention that one's self-concept is based largely on reflections back from how one is perceived by others. It is a challenging tour de force to see how far one can get by taking such a positivistic stance that minimizes differences between self-knowledge and knowledge of others; but it is also provocative to take the opposite stance, as we do here, of focusing on how differently one thinks about oneself versus others because of the contrasting sample of information one has regarding the two.

Method. We used the same data source as in the preceding Verb /Processes Study 2, collected from the 560 schoolchildren in the oral response modality and 1,000 children in the written modality. The children responded for three minutes to each of two probes, "Tell us about school" and "Tell us about your family." The responses were then content-analyzed by the three-step procedure described above. Two types of thought segments were partitioned out as our independent variable: (*a*) self-descriptive thought segments, that is, those with "self" as the first (subject) unit; and (*b*) thought segments describing other people, that is, those with other persons (e.g., "my mother") or groups of other persons (e.g., "people," "boys") as their first (subject) units. The verbs in the middle units in these two, self-versus-other, sets of thoughts were translated into the 108 verbs in our basic concept dictionary, which were organized into the Table 7.3 tree diagram to serve as our dependent-variable measures.

Results regarding the prevalence of persons in the child's self-concept. In the oral responses to "Family" and "School" probes combined, 32% of all thought segments described the self in that their first (subject) unit's content was "myself," and another 54% described other people in that their subject was a person or a group of people other than the self. The remaining 14% of the thought segments were not about people, but rather had animals, inanimate objects, or abstract concepts as their subjects. Thus, an impressively large proportion (86%) of all the spoken thoughts evoked by general Family and School probes were about people. In the written modality, 38% of all thought segments were self-descriptions and 46% described other people, a total person preoccupation (84%) similar to that in the oral responses. However, there were more self-thoughts relative to thoughts about other people in the written than in the oral response modality. Responding in the more private written condition may incline the person to be more introspectively self-focused than in the public oral responding where the child was in a one-to-one situation with the interviewer. In both modalities there were only negligible age and sex differences in proportion of self- versus other-person thoughts.

Self-versus-other differences in the six verb-ratio hypotheses. Our first verb-type prediction is that one's frequent opportunities to observe the self acting in a variety of contexts allows one to conceptualize the self more concretely in terms of specific actions; whereas other people, having been experienced in fewer specific situations, have to be conceptualized more abstractly in terms of general dispositions. The implication regarding our verb types is that the proportion of action verbs to state verbs will be higher in self-descriptions than in other-descriptions. This implication is strongly confirmed (p < .01) in both response modalities. In the oral modality, 82% of self-descriptions versus only 51% of other-descriptions used verbs of action; this self-versus-other difference is even more pronounced in the written replication, 84% versus 33%. The "fundamental attribution error," attributing others' more than one's own behavior to dispositional rather than situational factors, may be a special case of this first thought process, manifested in an excess of verbs of action over verbs of state (what one does vs. what one is) when expressing thoughts of self as compared to other people.

A second hypothesis focuses more narrowly on state verbs, predicting that the ratio of becoming to being state verbs will be higher in self-conceptualizations than in conceptualizations of other people (because one has the opportunity to observe the self more than other people as growing and changing over time). This second prediction was confirmed ($p < .01$) in each modality. The third hypothesis, focusing on action verbs, predicts that because one has privileged access to one's own interior experience, one will conceptualize the self more than other people in terms of covert reactions relative to overt behavior. This fairly obvious prediction also was strongly confirmed ($p < .01$) in both oral and written conditions. Hypothesis four concerns the physical versus social branches of overt action verbs and is based on the assumption that the self is often experienced in solitary as well as in social circumstances, whereas other people are usually experienced as socially interacting with the self or others, and so are thought of more as social beings than is the self. Hence, when overt-action verbs are used a higher proportion will refer to physical actions relative to social interactions in self-descriptions than in descriptions of other people, a prediction strongly confirmed ($p < .01$) in both modalities.

The fifth hypothesis is based on the assumption that people are more willing and able to discuss their thoughts than their feelings, and therefore an observer exaggerates the cognitive relative to the affective components of other people's interior lives. The verb implication is that when covert reaction verbs are used to describe a person, the proportion of affective relative to cognitive verbs will be higher in self-descriptions than in descriptions of other people. This implication was supported ($p < .01$) in both oral and written conditions. The assumption that, due to greater familiarity, one can think in more sophisticated terms about the self than about others yields a sixth verb-ratio prediction, that a higher ratio of more difficult negational thoughts (about what the individual is not) relative to easier affirmational thoughts (about what the individual is) will occur in describing the self than others. The obtained self-negational effect is modest

(p < .05) in the oral condition and more substantial (p < .01) in the written condition.

Overall, the verb/process studies reported in the last half of this chapter strongly support the predictions. All six predicted self-versus-others differences in verb ratios were confirmed in both oral and written response conditions, and were robust across sex and age of the students. Similarly, in the multiple selves study all six verb predictions about differences between the child's home and school self-concepts were confirmed in both oral and written replication. In the developmental study, all six verb predictions about age trends were confirmed in the written replication, and four of the six in the oral condition. Just as these three verb studies were revealing of the processes of thinking about the self, so also the noun studies reported in the first half of the chapter were revealing about the content of thinking about the self, identifying important determinants of how salient in the experienced sense of self are one's physical and demographic characteristics, as well as showing the ways in which the child and the adolescent define the self in terms of school experience and of significant others.

8

Distinctiveness Theory and the
Salience of Self-characteristics

The program of research reported in this chapter considers the person as an overloaded information processor who selectively notices the peculiarities in complex stimuli and ignores the more predictable. Bombarded by more information than she or he can effectively encode, the person copes with this overload by a number of techniques reviewed in McGuire (1984a) (e.g., parallel processing, temporary storage for subsequent processing, selective perception, etc.). The research reported here focuses on selective perception as a mode of coping, noticing only the more information-rich (unpredictable, peculiar, distinctive) aspects of a complex stimulus. For example, when one observes a person one is more likely to notice her unusual height than her average weight. When observing a crowd, one is more likely to notice a member's ethnicity the more ethnically heterogeneous the crowd is, as defined by (*a*) the number of ethnic groups represented and (*b*) the equipotentiality of the members' distribution over these ethnic groups (e.g., if 95% of people are right-handed, it is efficient not to notice handedness but to assume that everyone is right-handed, and almost always be correct). These predictions are made on a strictly cognitive basis, without recourse to motivational factors like perceived powerlessness of minorities or rareness value. This theorizing applies equally to noticing the color versus the size of people and of geometrical figures. In general, the relative likelihood of noticing one versus another characteristic of a stimulus is given by the information-theory general formula for uncertainty, $U(X) = -\Sigma p(x_i) \ln_2 p(x_i)$, where x_i is the proportion of stimuli having characteristic i on a dimension (e.g., x_1 might be the proportion of stimulus persons who have "brown" as their characteristic on the hair-color dimension).

As the stimulus studied we have typically used the self, a wonderfully complex stimulus whose complexities are well known to the person, so that he or she must be highly selective when responding to an open-ended request to "Tell us about yourself." Our strictly cognitive distinctiveness postulate yields predictions that people tend to perceive themselves (and other stimuli) in terms of their peculiarities. Thus, regarding the physical characteristics out of which people forge their self-identities, left-handers' sinistrality is likely to be more salient in their self-concepts than is right-handers' dexterity in theirs; hair color will be more salient for people with unusual colors than for those with common colors; weight will receive more spontaneous mentions in the self-concepts of children who are substantially heavier or lighter than their classmates than of those in the average weight range. Sex or ethnicity is likely to loom large in the person's self-concept to the extent to which people of the other sex or ethnicities predominate in her or his social contexts. There are many other determinants of a characteristic's salience in the self-concept (e.g., social desirability, situational relevance, past reinforcement, etc., as reviewed in McGuire, 1984a). We focus here on the distinctiveness determinant, without denying the predictive power of many additional cognitive and affective determinants.

My basic theoretical and exploratory empirical work was done in the late 1950s and presented in numerous public talks in the United States and United Kingdom (e.g., my keynote address at the 1970 London meeting of the British Psychological Society), in research proposals (e.g., my January 1966 proposal to the National Science Foundation), and in my classes. I did not go into print with the earlier studies (e.g., McGuire & Padawer-Singer, 1976a) until they had been replicated and extended by later studies in the research program. Most of the studies were published around 1980 (e.g., McGuire, McGuire, Child, & Fujioka, 1978a; McGuire, McGuire & Winton, 1979a; McGuire & McGuire, 1980a; McGuire & McGuire, 1981b). Summaries can be found in McGuire (1984a) and McGuire and McGuire (1988a). This chapter describes the theoretical background (McGuire, 1984a) and then excerpts the results from many of our empirical studies on distinctiveness theory.

[Adapted with permission from W. J. McGuire, 1984a, Search for the self: Going beyond self-esteem and the reactive self, in R. A. Zucker, J. Arnoff, & A. I. Rabin (Eds.), *Personality and the prediction of behavior,* pp. 73–120. (New York: Academic Press, copyright © 1984).]

The core of the person is the phenomenal self as experienced and as expressed in one's free-flowing self-perceptions. One's sense of self is easily accessible; indeed, is often too much with us, as on those dark nights of the soul of which Gerard Manley Hopkins (1933) wrote, "the lost are like this, and their scourge to be / As I am mine, their sweating selves; but worse." To be surprised by joy may require a release from this albatross of self, "Soul, self; come, poor jackself, I do advise/ You, jaded, let be; call off thought awhile/ Elsewhere; leave comfort root room." Thinkers wise and unwise from Socrates to Wagner have asserted as the human imperative "Know thyself," but most people live lives of quiet desperation in which they wrestle through the night, like Jacob, with this too-well-known stranger.

In chapter 7 I attributed the disappointing yield of thousands of psychological studies of the self to two restrictions: (1) their use of reactive methods, limiting the person to describing the self on researcher-chosen dimensions, which provides no information about how often, if ever, he or she thinks of him- or herself on that dimension; and (2) the use by over 90% of researchers of evaluation as the dimension to be studied. As a corrective, the research program reported in this chapter presents a lower profile to participants, permitting them to describe themselves more fully and meaningfully on dimensions of their own choosing, in response to generalized probes such as "Tell us about yourself" or "Tell us what you are not," and then analyzing the elicited material so as to retain much of its informational content. Our basic postulate is that what is spontaneously salient in the phenomenal self-concept (operationally defined as the self-descriptive thoughts evoked by such probes) is the person's distinctive (information-rich, unpredictable) characteristics.

Theoretical Bases of the Distinctiveness Postulate

Empirical work in psychology, even when carried out by philosophically concerned researchers, seldom makes contact with the researcher's fundamental philosophical musings. Hence it is unusual that my empirical work reported here flows directly from my basic epistemological and even ontological speculations, some of which depart from commonsense assumptions regarding the nature of knowledge and of existence. Because I wear a different school tie from most of my psychological colleagues, I am usually cautious about telling such tales outside of class, but here I shall let some of my philosophical slips show, blinding some with a light too bright for their eyes and raising the eyebrows and suspicions of others that the *numerus clausus* for my peculiar group may be too high. It might be wise for those who do not yet have tenure to play it safe by not revealing their own philosophical musings, even musings more orthodox than mine. Although the philosophical speculations here may seem extravagant, it will be seen that they do lead to rigorous empirical research.

A nonexistential philosophy: Much ado about nothing. I label the philosophy pursued here "distinctiveness theory," or more generally, "nonexistentialism," not to contrast it with some Heidegger-Jaspers-Sartre dictum about the precedence of existence over essence, but because my ontological and epistemological position stands on its head, like Marx did Hegel, the commonsense notion of what it is that exists. These nonexistential epistemological musings began when, as a philosophy major in college, I wrestled with the ontological problem of individuation within an Aristotelian-Thomistic approach. I could accept without logical strain the assertions either that nothing exists or that everything exists, because neither produces an intrinsic contradiction; but what gave me intellectual unease was to assert that two or more different things exist. Positing that being is multiple threatens to impale one on a dilemma, in that what distinguishes (individuates) different beings must itself either exist or not exist. If it does not exist, how can it distinguish other things? If it does exist, then it violates my intuition that being can never be heterogeneous to itself and furthermore raises the question of what distinguishes this discriminator from the first two beings, and so on in an infinite regress, salvaged at best by a "turtles all the way down" solution with which I am not comfortable.

The ontological problem regarding distinctive individuated existence seemed to underlie several bothersome cosmological issues. Cosmogony speculations on the origins and limits of the universe (whether one takes a theological, big-bang, or bubble stance; and even Hoyle's continuous-creation position does not completely escape this problem) make it difficult to imagine the existential status of the space within which the universe came into being or into which it is expanding. Related cosmological enigmas are how gravity and other forces can operate at a distance, how a probabilistic physical particle can disappear and seem to reemerge further on in a trajectory, how physical objects can be mostly empty space with a few isolated particles, how electrons jump discontinuously between the orbits, and how electromagnetic waves propagate through mediumless space (Cantor & Hodge, 1981; Grant, 1981).

My solution to this cluster of cosmological conundrums involves a figure-ground reversal that stands the usual conception of being on its head by asserting that what exists is that which is conventionally regarded as the absence of being, and what are commonly regarded as the existing entities are interruptions in reality. Thus homogeneous "empty" space is existent being, whereas the physical particles (electrons, muons, quarks, or whatever is one's preferred particle of the month) are holes in reality. This reversing of the conventional concepts of being and nonbeing makes more graspable the just mentioned cosmological conundrums. That particles disappear and reappear at a distance becomes more imaginable when they are represented as gaps in being rather than as entities; and the propagation of electromagnetic waves through space becomes more comprehensible when space is seen as the existent continuous medium in which particles and galaxies are gaps rather than a void containing a scattering of hydrogen nuclei. As regards cosmogony, the origin of the universe is revisualized as annihilation rather than creation, a localized big bang rending the seamless web of infinite homogeneous existence, introducing a gap of nonexistence that is metastasizing through space, producing the multiplicity of entities through negation.

Individuation is thus accomplished, not by what the individual thing is (because being is one and cannot be heterogeneous to itself) but rather by what it is not. On the cosmological actual level, electrons are holes in reality; on the personal perceptual level, what makes me be "me" to myself, and others to be their individual selves, is not what we are but what we are not, the consciousness of absences that distinguishes us from one another. On the cognitive level we are conscious of ourselves in terms of absences, by awareness of distinctive features that individuate us from one another by being absent in one of us. I exist to myself and others in terms of my differences. If a feature is always present it goes unnoticed, as with the fish being the last to discover the ocean. It is absences that make us present to ourselves and to one another.

Precursors of nonexistentialism. The few psychologists who return my secret handshake may suspect that my nonexistential position derives from Duns Scotus's relentless struggles with the problem of individuality and its intelligibility. I grant that the subtle doctor was slouching toward something profound in his haecceity solution (despite its obscurity having made his name contribute "dunce" to the language, dunce being one of the casual pejoratives like "hocus pocus" that persists due to insensitivity stemming from academic underrepresentation). I judge his solution and mine to be far apart, but I admit that Scotus's tortuous prose may have kept his secret intact from me, especially as it resonates so joyously with the cadences of Gerard Manley Hopkins's (1933) magnificent Scotist sonnet, "As Kingfishers Catch Fire, Dragonflies Draw Flame," which I believe to be the finest philosophical poem in English, among other reasons because it catches so magnificently Duns Scotus's passion for individuation and the self:

> Each mortal thing does one thing and the same:
> Deals out that being indoors each one dwells;
> Selves – goes itself; myself it speaks and spells,
> Crying what I do is me: for that I came.

If my nonexistential formulation did derive from Catholic philosophical speculations it may have come from Nicholas of Cusa's analysis of God as non-other (J. Hopkins, 1979). It is significant that God, even when being conceptualized as pure being, is often defined in terms of negation in theories as disparate as the Hindu Upanishad's depiction of Brahman as the not-this, not-that, not-other, to Simone Weil's (1952) conception of God's being in creation in the form of absences (an ethical solution of the problem of evil as well as a theological solution of the nature of God). The notion was encouraged in literature by Nietzsche and Valéry (1934) that "the only proper object of thought is that which does not exist" to current textual critics like Foucault and Derrida (1967), who hold that "God" or other constructs can be understood only by admitting the absence of a reference, only in the erasure of the "transcendental signified." Parallel structuralist traditions, precariously bridged by Heidegger, derive from de Saussure's (1916) relativistic epistemology that the meaning of a word can be grasped only in conjunction with its opposite. Related are Bloom's (1974) misreadings that there are no texts but only relationships among texts and Baltaxe's (1978) distinctive feature theory. In the Wienerkreis philosophy of science tradition, Popper (1959) suggests that the information content of a theory is a set of statements that are incompatible with the theory. Obviously, the classes and the masses have had no trouble thinking about and writing about nothing, even though philosophers from Parmenides to Wittgenstein have asserted that it cannot be done (Heath, 1967).

My own nonexistential position is probably intellectually closer to Isaac Luria's cabalism, as developed by Vital and Nathan of Gaza, in its doctrine of individuation, and particularly in its depiction of the origin of things being better understood as involving annihilation rather than creation, the world beginning with a *tsimtsum,* or contraction of God, this recoil leaving room in which the universe of discrete beings could emerge (Scholem, 1954, 1973). The interweaving of these strands that we have mentioned is illustrated by the fact that Martin Buber, well before he became a preeminent interpreter of Hasidic cabalism, wrote his doctoral dissertation on the problem of individuation in Nicholas of Cusa.

These abstract ontological and cosmological speculations lead to cognitive psychological theorizing through the "to be is to be perceived" principle. If the individuating essence of a being that makes it be itself is the distinctive absences that make it not be other things, then a cognitive parallel is that we perceive a thing not in terms of what is there but what is absent. Perceiving the self (or any other stimulus) involves recognizing the peculiar individuating ways in which this stimulus is not absolute being but differs from other individual things by absences. The person has evolved as an efficient recognizer of absences, information being defined as perceived distinctions, and distinctions being made possible only by absences. This information-theory linkage brings my philosophical metatheorizing to bear on a more familiar level of psychological theorizing, the distinctiveness postulate regarding what is salient in person perception.

Selectively Noticing the Distinctive as a Way of Coping with Information Overload

Given the vast number of entities in the world, each differing from others by multiple absences that constitute information on the basis of which individual objects can be discriminated and enter awareness, it follows that the perceiving person is often confronted by an astronomical amount of information. To some extent humans are spared from being drowned in information by having evolved with quite limited sensory capacities (e.g., we are able to sense directly only the tiny visible-light band within the vast range of the electromagnetic spectrum). Presumably species evolve adaptively so that their senses put them in contact with a subset of information that is cost-effective in terms of the organism's needs and capacities and the environment's possibilities, alerting people to differences among objects that are important for perpetuating relevant genes and that can be picked up by a sensory apparatus economical to develop and operate. Although receptor insensitivity to vast ranges of energy differentials protects humans from being completely swamped, even within this limited sensory capacity we are in a constant state of information overload (Blumenthal, 1977). Having a sensory capacity for taking in much more information than they can process centrally is characteristic, not only of humans, but also of laboratory albino rats, as Krechevsky (1932) demonstrated during the "continuity" controversy of the 1930s. Apparently there is a survival value in having sensory access at any given moment to vastly more information than one can centrally process, allowing one the flexibility of sampling a wide universe of environmental information constituted by the numerous sensible differences among things.

Varied modes of coping with information overload. Confronted chronically with more information about the environment than they can effectively encode, humans have evolved to handle this embarrassment of riches in a variety of ways, of which eight will be mentioned here (see McGuire, 1984a, for fuller discussion). (1) People can "chunk," changing the grain size by perception's "zoom lens" capacity; when a plethora of trees becomes overwhelming, one can take a broader perspective and perceive the forest as a whole. (2) One can cope with information overload by concept utilization, categorizing information so that a highly complex experience is reductively encoded by assimilation to an available prototype label. (3) The person can divert cognitive capacity from one function to another; for example, as one lies abed fantasizing the destruction of one's enemies or other delights, if something suddenly goes bump in the night one can cease reverie and divert more of one's cognitive capacity from fantasy into focused attention to external sounds. (4) Temporary storage for later processing is a fourth mode of coping with information overload. In a particularly rich sensory environment one can, like the cow chewing its cud, stuff information temporarily into push-down lists for later deliberative processing when the opportunity allows (dream work being one illustration of this reprocessing during quiet time). (5) One can shift attention from one aspect of the stimulus to another, as when one tours the horizon or breaks a complex problem into parts. (6) One can do parallel processing, for example, encoding some information in words and other information in images. (7) Diffusing attention to regions that are ordinarily peripheral so that they enter partial awareness, at some loss of attention to central concerns, is still another mode of coping with information overload. (8) Selective perception, attending to some categories of incoming information while disregarding others, is an eighth mode of coping that will be discussed more fully here because it is the mode investigated in the present distinctiveness-theory research.

Coping with information overload by perceptual selectivity. At any given moment the person tends to be oblivious to most of the information impinging on her or his senses, as can be illustrated by the armchair experiment of closing one's eyes and trying to recall the perceptible details of what has just been impinging on the retinal fovea. People shrewdly register some aspects of the retinal image while ignoring others. I shall mention here a dozen variables that affect what is selectively perceived versus ignored, discussing in more detail only the last of the 12, selection by distinctiveness, which bears directly on the empirical research reported in this chapter. The first 11 bases of selection are described more fully in McGuire (1984a).

One basis of selective perception is (1) chance, the person noticing a random subset of stimulus information; this austerely elegant selectional tactic, despite its conceptual vacuity, has been used creatively by stimulus-sampling theorists such as Estes. (2) Transient need state may determine selectivity: A person walking down the street with a letter to be mailed notices the mailboxes; and walking down the same mean street with an appetite, notices the restaurants. (3) During the midcentury "perceptual defense" era, the person's enduring values were stressed as a basis of selection, as when the person preferentially notices positive words from a valued domain and blocks out disturbing words. (4) Expectancy (set, familiarity) is another selectional basis, as demonstrated in tachistoscopic laboratory experiments where a person tends to notice aspects that fit his or her own chronic preconceptions or experimenter-established momentary sets; indeed, some hard-hatted theorists have argued that cognitive expectancy can account for the selective role attributed to affective constructs like momentary needs and enduring values. (5) An external determinant of selectivity is stimulus intensity, as when bright lights or loud noises attract more notice than faint ones. (6) A determinant emphasized in the 1950s era of "liberated" stimulus-response theory is acquired distinctiveness of cue: one selectively perceives aspects of a stimulus that one has been rewarded for noticing or punished for not noticing, as when the army recruit by the end of basic training attends closely to the various insignia of military rank that he or she disregarded in civilian days. (7) The "availability heuristic" is a currently fashionable determinant: One notices aspects of stimuli to the extent that their frequency, recency, and so on, make them readily retrievable. (8) Also currently fashionable is prototypicality, or encodability, as when a characteristic's regularity, meaningfulness, categorizability, or unusual departure from the prototype grabs one's attention. (9) Dimensional prepotency is another determinant in that some characteristics are more likely to be encoded than others, either in general or for some types of situations or observers, as when color-versus-form prepotency is used to diagnose chronic dispositions by the Vigotsky (1939) and Rorschach (1921) tests, or when children switch from color to form prepotency at 4 or 5 years of age. (10) Another selectivity determinant is vividness, in the sense that concreteness, imageability, or strikingness of an aspect attracts attention. (11) Selective attention may also be negatively affected by satiation (fatigue, reactive inhibition), as a central process analogous to peripheral sense organ adaptation or nerve-fiber refractory phase (Peeke & Herz, 1972). (12) Distinctiveness is another selectivity determinant, in that novel, peculiar, unexpected aspects of a situation tend to capture the person's attention. This distinctiveness basis of selectivity will be discussed in more detail here because the studies reported in this chapter derive from it. These dozen determinants of selective perception are discussed more fully in McGuire (1984a).

Vicissitudes of the distinctiveness postulate.   That a characteristic's distinctiveness (novelty, unexpectedness) enhances perceptual salience has been long postulated (see McGuire, 1984a) by diverse theorists, for example, from Pavlov's (1928) concept of the orienting reflex through G. A. Miller's (1953) information theory concept of communication. The distinctiveness notion flourished particularly in the 1960s (McGuire, 1966c), when a variety of theories stressed its motivating power in humans and other mammalian species under such terms as the curiosity drive, the need for varied experience, alternation behavior, exploratory drive, need for cognition, stimulus hunger, sensation seeking, cognitive complexity, and need for novelty. Surprisingly, the 1960s decade that saw this flurry of theories stressing the need for the novel and the unexpected also witnessed a flourishing of consistency theories, stressing the opposite need, a drive for congruence and the confirmation of the expected (congruity theory, balance theory, symmetry theory, dissonance theory, and probabilogical theory; see chapter 6). It is not unusual for such contrary views to flourish contemporaneously: Humans adapting to a complex environment can be expected to be guided by antagonistic tendencies (see chapters 3 and 12) whose relative ascendancies vary across persons and situations, so that a given tendency may be more powerful a predictor in one context, whereas a different, even contrary, tendency will predict better in a different context, a complexity that is used creatively in my perspectivist philosophy of science (McGuire, 1983a, 1986c, 1989b, chapter 12 in this volume). The paradoxical coexistence of contradictory postulates such as here – that expectedness and unexpectedness both enhance perceptual salience – is desirable because together they serve as thesis and antithesis whose internal contradiction can provide heuristic impetus to reach a powerful higher synthesis, as in the derivation that people seek out intermediate levels of unexpectedness, with the optimal level and other parameters shifting predictably as a function of dispositional and situational interaction variables (Piaget, 1936; Berlyne, 1960, 1970; Kagan, 1970; Veroff & Veroff, 1980; chapters 1, 3, and 5 in this volume).

Distinctiveness Theory's Implications
for Systematically Constructed, Artificial Stimuli

Our completed empirical studies, described later in this chapter, tested distinctiveness theory's predictions regarding a highly involving stimulus, the self, especially how one selectively perceives oneself in one's natural situations. However, in our 1966 NSF and 1978 NIMH research proposals we also described the theory's predictions regarding artificially constructed stimuli as they will be selectively perceived in simplified laboratory situations. These laboratory implications will be described briefly with regard to two types of artificial systematically constructed stimuli – geometric figures and political figures – because they allow the distinctiveness predictions to stand out more clearly, less confounded by other factors than when studying the self in its natural situations.

Selective perception of artificially constructed geometric figures. Suppose the participants' task is to learn to label, recall, and otherwise respond to a set of stimuli sufficiently complex so that each can be perceived only selectively. Specifically, we might use a dozen geometric stimuli, artificially constructed to differ systematically on four dimensions (e.g., color, shape, pattern, and border), two of which dimensions are two-valued and two of which are three-valued, and one of each pair is equally and the other is unequally distributed (e.g., if color is the two-valued, equally distributed dimension, then the dozen geometric stimuli might include six blue and six yellow figures; and if shape is the three-valued, unequally distributed dimension, then the 12 geometric stimuli might include six triangles, three circles, and three squares). Distinctiveness theory predicts that in this case participants will perceive, label, and otherwise respond to the 12 figures more in terms of the three- than the two-valued dimensions; more in terms of the equally distributed than the unequally distributed dimensions; and, among the unequally distributed dimensions, more in terms of the rarer characteristics.

Selective perception of artificially constructed political figures. Closely paralleling such a geometric-figure experiment would be an experiment where the task is to selectively perceive, label, and respond to 12 political figures. These 12 political candidates would, analogous to the geometric figures, be constructed to differ on four political issue dimensions (e.g., foreign-aid locus, urban-aid targets, tax sources, and welfare focus). If foreign-aid locus is the three-valued unequally distributed dimension, then the 12 political candidates might divide into 6 favoring aid to Latin America, 3 to Africa, and 3 to Eastern Europe.

Distinctiveness theory's predictions regarding how participants would label, recognize, and otherwise respond to these 12 political figures exactly parallel the three types of predictions just mentioned for the 12 geometric figures but with some additional variables entering, yielding additional predictions. A participant (voter) is likely to have his or her own preference on each political dimension (e.g., the participant him- or herself may prefer foreign aid to Africa rather than to Latin America or Eastern Europe) and is likely to perceive politicians in general as having preferences that distribute differently from those systematically reported for the set of 12 fabricated political candidates. Also, the participants will judge the importance of the four issues to vary sizably more than he or she will judge the shape-versus-color of the geometric figures to differ greatly in importance. These added independent variables arising with the political figures yield numerous additional predictions (e.g., that the participant will especially prefer candidates who agree with him or her on issues where he or she has a minority stand). These laboratory studies with artificially constructed stimuli deserve to be done; but in our own research program we gave priority to studies involving self-perception in the natural environment, to whose description we now turn.

Salience of Distinctive Characteristics in the Phenomenal Self-Concept

The diversity of distinctiveness formulations proposed during the past half-century provides encouraging evidence for the concept's utility but also requires clarification regarding which of the Protean distinctiveness notions we use in our self-concept studies. The postulate asserts that an individual exists insofar as he or she is different and that he or she is selectively perceived by self and others in terms of such differences. When one thinks of oneself generically as a group member, one thinks of characteristics by which one's in-group differs from out-groups; when one thinks of oneself as an individual member of one's in-group what is salient is ways in which one is different from other members of the in-group. Because one perceives oneself (and is perceived by others) in terms of characteristics that differentiate one from one's associates, one's phenomenal sense of self changes in predictable ways as one moves from one social setting to another. For example, an African-American woman while taking part in a committee meeting with 11 African-American men will be thinking of herself as a woman; when she then goes to a class with 11 European-American women, she will think of herself as an African-American. Richard Wright wrote that one of his gains in moving from Chicago to Paris was that in Chicago he was viewed by himself and others (typically white) as a black, a characteristic irrelevant to his vocation as writer; but in Paris he was perceived by himself and others (typically French-speaking) as an English-speaking person, an identity more central to his vocation.

Distinctiveness theory's application to the spontaneous self-concept can be illustrated by the salience of self-characteristics of the people in a group consisting of a black woman, a white woman, and three white men. In Table 8.1, the column headings are the five persons and the row headings are two personal characteristics, sex and

Table 8.1

Illustration of the distinctiveness postulate for the case of a mixed five-person group

Dimension (j)	Person (i)					
	Black woman	White woman	White man 1	White man 2	White man 3	Σ
Sex	3	3	2	2	2	12
Ethnicity	4	1	1	1	1	8
Σ	7	4	3	3	3	20

(salience of sex and ethnicity of each person in a group consisting of a black woman, a white woman, and three white men). Cell entries are the number of other group members who differ from the column person on the row dimension.

ethnicity, that distinguish these five group members. The numerical entry in each of the 10 cells indicates the number of others among the five people in the group from whom the column person differs on the row characteristic. For example, in the sex row, because there are two women and three men, each woman gets a discriminability score of 3 in her sex cell because her sex differs from that of the three men, and each man gets a score of 2 because he is distinctive from the two women in this regard. The row totals, column totals, and cell entries all yield salience predictions about what gets mentioned if we ask the five people in the Table 8.1 group to "Tell us about yourself." The row sums predict that sex is half again more likely than ethnicity to be mentioned by members of this group; the column sums indicate that the women are almost twice as likely as the men to describe themselves in terms of these two characteristics; and the cell entries show, for example, that the black woman is 33% more likely to mention her ethnicity than her sex, whereas the white woman is 300% more likely to mention her sex than her ethnicity. In general, the probability of noticing a given entity's, *i,* aspect on dimension *j,* (e.g., the probability of the black woman's femaleness in this group being noticed by herself or others) is given by the following formula:

$$p_{ij} \propto \frac{N - n_{ij}}{\displaystyle\sum_{j=1}^{x} \sum_{i=1}^{y} (N - n_{ij})}$$

where N is the number of entities (people or other stimuli) in the perceptual field and n_{ij} is the number of entities with i's aspect on the dimension j. This formulation constitutes our definition of a characteristic's distinctiveness, which determines its salience in the spontaneous self-concept. It can be seen that the characteristic's salience increases with the number of discriminable characteristics on the dimension with the equipotentiality of the stimuli (persons' or whatever) distribution among these categories, and whether the category is the majority or minority one on an asymmetrical characteristic.

The series of empirical studies reported below test distinctiveness-theory implications that, when children are asked to "Tell us about yourself," the probability of their mentioning their position on a given physical or demographic dimension (height, weight, age, sex, ethnicity, etc.) increases as their position on it is distant from the typical positions of their familiar others.

THE EFFECT OF DISTINCTIVENESS ON THE SALIENCE OF PHYSICAL CHARACTERISTICS

The Metropolis Study of Physical Characteristic Salience

[Adapted with permission from W. J. McGuire & A. Padawer-Singer, 1976a, Trait salience in the spontaneous self-concept, *Journal of Personality and Social Psychology, 33,* pp. 743–754. Copyright © 1976 by The American Psychological Association.]

Method.   In this early study testing the distinctiveness-postulate predictions that people think of themselves in terms of their unusual characteristics we asked sixth-graders (13-year-olds) in their normal classroom setting to respond in writing for seven minutes to a "Tell us about yourself" probe (the general self-concept) and to respond for four minutes to a "Describe what you look like" probe (the physical self-concept). Judges then scored each response protocol for mention versus nonmention of six characteristics (the respondent's age and birthplace, eye and hair color, height and weight), which served as the dependent-variable measure, namely, the salience in the self-concept of these six characteristics. Later each child in the classroom was explicitly asked to write down his or her height, weight, eye and hair color, age, and birthplace to allow scoring of the child's position on the independent variables, his or her distinctiveness on each of the six characteristics. Our sample, drawn from 10 sixth-grade classes in 5 elementary schools in a metropolitan city on the east coast of the United States, included 252 students, 127 girls and 125 boys.

Results. The distinctiveness-theory prediction regarding age was confirmed (p < .05), in that only 19% of children within six months of the modal age of the class spontaneously mentioned their age versus 30% of the younger and older children who deviated more than six months from the modal age. As regards birthplace, the distinctiveness hypothesis predicts that people born in places different from that of most of their associates are more likely to think of themselves in terms of their origin than those who share their birthplace with most of their associates. In confirmation, of the typical 70% of the sixth-graders who were born in the metropolis where the experiment was done, only 6% spontaneously mentioned their birthplace, whereas a much higher (p < .001) 22% of those born outside the city spontaneously mentioned their birthplaces. When we partition the respondents still more extremely on birthplace, 44% of the foreign-born versus only 7% of the U.S.-born children spontaneously mentioned their birthplaces (p < .001 for the difference). This birthplace confirmation is impressive considering that both social desirability and availability are pitted against it, and yet the net results go in the distinctiveness direction.

In regard to hair color, on the reactive questionnaire 88% of the respondents reported having brown or black hair, and the remaining atypical 12% reported blond or red. In response to the general self-concept probe, the typical brown- and black-haired participants described themselves in terms of hair color at only two-thirds the rate of the distinctive red- and blond-haired, a difference in the predicted direction but not attaining the .05 significance level. In response to the physical self-concept probe ("Describe what you look like"), 54% of those with brown or black hair and a much higher (p < .01) 79% of those with red or blond hair spontaneously reported their hair color. As regards eye color, on the general self-concept those with atypical blue or green eyes spontaneously mentioned their eye color half again more often than those with the usual brown eyes, but this difference does not reach the .05 level. On the physical self-concept, 56% of those with the typical brown eyes mentioned the fact versus a much higher (p < .01) 77% of those with the atypical blue or green eyes spontaneously mentioned eye color.

A similar picture emerges regarding weight. Children in the upper and lower quartiles in weight (above 46 kg or below 36 kg) spontaneously mentioned their weight half again more often than those in the middle half of the weight distribution, but the difference does not attain the .05 level. In responding to the physical self-concept probe, 37% of the middle half spontaneously mentioned their weight, versus a substantially higher (p < .05) 52% of those in the upper and lower quarters. The greater mention of weight by the atypicals was about equal for overweight and underweight children. Again with weight, the distinctiveness hypothesis is pitted against the social desirability hypothesis and still emerges as a powerful determinant of salience. The distinctiveness postulate received no support on the sixth dimension, height. Those in the upper quarter and the lower quarter of the height distribution spontaneously mentioned their height as part of both their general and physical self-concepts slightly more often than did those in the middle half of the height distribution, but both differences were of trivial statistical significance. Over all 12 comparisons (6 physical dimensions, each tested in the general and in the physical self-concept) all 12 were in the distinctiveness-theory direction; and the difference reached the .05 level of significance individually in 7 of the 10 meaningful comparisons (there being no age or birthplace predictions for the "Tell us what you look like" data).

The New England Study of Physical Characteristic Salience

[Adapted from W. J. McGuire & C. V. McGuire, 1981b.]

Methods. The just described metropolitan study of the spontaneous salience of physical and demographic characteristics in the self-concept was replicated in a middle-sized, inland New England city, using a larger sample more varied in age than were those in the metropolitan sample. We elicited the spontaneous self-concept from 100 boys and

100 girls at each of five grade levels – the fifth, seventh, ninth, eleventh, and twelfth grades, ages 11 to 18 years. The interviewer administered the test booklet in the students' usual classrooms, telling them that their responses were anonymous and that there were no right or wrong answers so that they should respond with whatever thoughts came to mind. The students turned to a sheet topped by the "Tell us about yourself" general self-concept probe and were allowed five minutes to write down all the thoughts it evoked. After these five minutes they were given three minutes to respond to the physical self-concept probe, "Tell us what you look like." Their free associations evoked by these two probes were scored for mention versus nonmention of seven dimensions (height, weight, hair and eye color, birthdate and birthplace, and eyeglass wearing) that served as the dependent variable measure, spontaneous salience of the dimensions in the general and in the physical self-concepts. The children were then given a reactive questionnaire explicitly asking them to write down their characteristics on the seven dimensions. On these responses the children were scored on the independent variables, namely, the distinctiveness of each child's characteristic on each of the seven dimensions, as compared with the other children of the child's own sex at his or her grade level.

Results.   The results show that atypicality of a child's height increases ($p < .05$) the salience of height in his or her spontaneous self-concept: only 17% of children of average height (within one inch above or below the grade-level mean for their sex) spontaneously described themselves in terms of their height, whereas 27% of the tall and short children (five inches below or above the mean height) spontaneously mentioned their height. Atypicality in either direction enhanced salience: 25% of those five inches above average and 31% of those five inches below average mentioned height, in contrast to the 17% mention by those within one inch of the mean height. Distinctiveness also enhanced ($p < .05$) the salience of weight, overcoming a social-desirability counterforce. Only 6% of the children of average weight (within six pounds above or below the class mean) spontaneously described themselves in terms of weight; whereas weight was mentioned as part of the spontaneous self-concept by 12% of the heavy and light children (those whose weight deviated by 14 pounds above or below the grade-level mean for their sex).

The distinctiveness factor operated less strongly in affecting the spontaneous salience of hair color and eye color. The effect of hair color just barely attained the .05 level of statistical significance: 13% of the black- and brown-haired majority spontaneously mentioned their hair color as part of their spontaneous self-concept, whereas 17% of those with the atypical blond and red hair colors spontaneously mentioned it. Distinctiveness had only a trivial effect on eye-color salience: 11% of the brown-eyed majority spontaneously mentioned their eye color as part of their spontaneous self concept, trivially fewer than the 13% mention by the blue-eyed minority.

The results on birthdate (age) did not significantly confirm the distinctiveness prediction, but the data on birthplace did. Of the modal-age children (those within seven months of their grade-level mean age) 30% spontaneously mentioned their age as part of their self-concept; and of the atypically young and old children (more than seven months above or below the mean for their grade level) 33% spontaneously mentioned their age, a difference in the predicted direction but of trivial statistical significance. The results for spontaneous mention of birthplace did support the distinctiveness hypothesis. Of the great majority born in the state in which the study was done, 3% spontaneously mentioned where they were born, much lower (p < .01) than the 15% self-description in terms of birthplace by those who were born outside of the state. Using a more extreme partition point, 5% of those born in the United States spontaneously mentioned their birthplace as compared with 18% of the foreign-born (p < .01), which is in accord with the distinctiveness postulate even though social desirability weighs against it.

The distinctiveness prediction is also confirmed (p < .01) as regards spontaneous mention of eyeglass wearing. Overall, 31% of these fifth- through twelfth-graders reported wearing eyeglasses when explicitly asked at the end of the session. To test the distinctiveness prediction, we partitioned the children into those from classes in which fewer than 30% of the children wore glasses versus those from classes in which 30% or more wore glasses. In those classes where wearing glasses was rarer, 8% of the wearers spontaneously described themselves as wearing glasses, whereas in classes where eyeglass wearing was more common (30% plus), fewer than 1% of the wearers spontaneously mentioned them. Thus, of the seven comparisons, all came out in the predicted direction, that salience was greater for distinctive self-characteristics, and 5 of the 7 individually reached the .05 level of significance.

Salience of Handedness in the Self-Concept

[Adapted with permission from W. J. McGuire & C. V. McGuire, 1980a, Salience of handedness in the spontaneous self-concept, *Perceptual and Motor Skills, 50*, pp. 3–7. Copyright © 1980.]

When I first proposed distinctiveness theory as having implications for what is salient in the sense of self and what one notices in other people, I used handedness as an illustration. Distinctiveness theory predicts that their dexterity will be less salient in their self-concepts to right-handers than is their sinistrality to the lefties; and that people notice left-handedness more than right-handedness in others. Left-handedness serves as a good illustration because, while hardly shameful, it has a slight negative evaluation (as illustrated by the terms "gauche," "sinister," etc.), and so suppression of socially undesirable traits has to be outweighed by the distinctiveness-theory cognitive effect that informative (uncommon, unpredictable) characteristics are more likely to be noticed. Simply by guessing that everyone is right-handed an observer can be correct over 90% of the time, so there is little gain in accuracy from the costly task of learning every individual's handedness.

In a first study with 291 college students the dependent variable, salience of handedness in the spontaneous self-concept, was measured by obtaining a 10-minute response to the general "Tell me about yourself" probe and scoring each respondent for mention versus non-mention of handedness. The independent variable, actual handedness, was measured by subsequent explicit handedness questions, responses to which indicated that 86% regarded themselves as exclusively right-handed and 14% as ambidextrous or left-handed. Handedness is very low in salience, with only 4 of the 285 students spontaneously mentioning it; but of the 4 who did, 3 were left-handed and only 1 right-handed. That is, only 0.4% of the right-handers spontaneously mentioned that they were right-handed, whereas a significantly higher 7.5% of the left-handers mentioned this characteristic spontaneously.

A similar study of the general self-concepts of 7- to 18-year-old children and adolescents also revealed that handedness has a negligible salience: Of the 1,560 children, only 1 mentioned handedness in response to the general "Tell us about yourself" question and only 9 in response to the physical self-concept (evoked by the "Tell us what you look like" question). In the physical self-concept, left-handers were more likely ($p < .05$) spontaneously to mention their handedness: 6 of the 1,288 right-handers versus 3 of the 159 left-handers (0.6% vs. 1.9%) spontaneously described themselves in terms of handedness.

SALIENCE OF ETHNICITY IN THE SELF-CONCEPT

Theory

[Adapted with permission from W. J. McGuire, C. V. McGuire, P. Child, & T. Fujioka, 1978a.]

Ethnicity is a demographic variable second only to sex in its political importance, human interest, and relevance to distinctiveness theorizing, which predicts in general that a person's ethnicity will be salient in his or her sense of self (and in others' perception of him or her) to the extent that ethnicity is informative (unpredictable, atypical) in that person's social milieu. This prediction is made as a strictly cognitive process over and above any affective process having to do with other variables such as power, disadvantage, eliteness, need for group solidarity, scarcity value, stigmatization, and false consciousness. From this general proposition can be derived a number of specific predictions. (1) As a society becomes more integrated, bringing people from multiple ethnic groups into contact, ethnicity will become more salient and be spontaneously mentioned more often by the society's members as part of their self-identities and perceptions of one another. (2) The greater the number of different ethnic groups over which a society's members are distributed, the more mentions of ethnicity in members' self-descriptions. (3) The more equally distributed the society's members are over its ethnic groups, the more salient ethnicity will be in self-descriptions. (4) When members are unequally distributed over the groups, ethnicity will be more salient in the self-descriptions of minority than of majority group members. (5) As an ethnic group grows in relative size, its members will become less likely to identify themselves in terms of their ethnicity but more likely to describe members of other ethnicities in terms of the others' ethnicity. (6) Ethnicity will be more salient for minority than majority group members in the affirmational self-concept (evoked by a "Tell us about yourself" probe), but (7) ethnicity will be more salient for the majority group than the minority group in the negational self ("Tell us what you are not").

Method

Students in the school system of a moderate-sized inland industrial city in New England were interviewed individually in a small room in their school. The 560 students included 70 boys and 70 girls at each of four grade levels (the first, third, seventh, and eleventh grades). The participant was told that the questions were quite general, with no right or wrong answers, and that he or she should say for tape recording whatever came to mind in answer to the questions. The general affirmational self-concept probe, "Tell us about yourself," was then presented and the student given five minutes to respond orally with whatever thoughts came to mind. Later in the booklet the negational self-concept probe "Tell us what you are not" was presented and three minutes allowed for the response. As the student responded, the interviewer checked a judgment of the child's ethnicity (based on physical appearance, name, and accent) as either European-American, African-American, Latino-American, or other (including mixed and uncertain). The tape-recorded self-descriptions were typed out and judges scored each protocol on the dependent variable, mention versus nonmention of ethnicity.

Results

Ethnic makeup of the sample.   Of the 560 respondents, interviewers scored 82% as European-American, 9% as African-American, 8% as Latino-American, and 1% as uncertain or other, a distribution representative of the region. The distinctiveness postulate predicts that ethnicity will be more salient in the self-concept of persons whose ethnicity is in the minority in the school (the African-Americans and the Latino-Americans) than in the European-American majority group. We found that 9% of the African-Americans, 8% of the Latino-Americans, and a significantly ($p < .01$) lower 1% of the students of

the numerically predominant European-American group spontaneously mentioned their ethnicity in responding to the "Tell us about
yourself" probe. Other studies have given at least suggestive support
to this basic prediction that ethnicity is more salient in the minority
children's self-concepts than in the majority's. H. Greenwald and Op-
penheim (1968) found that minority (African-American) 4-year-olds
were more accurate than the majority European-American preschoolers in indicating which dolls were black and which were white, and
that African-Americans were more likely to judge themselves to be
black than European-American children were to judge themselves as
white. Crooks (1970) also found that black preschool children were
more accurate than whites in indicating the ethnicity of dolls. Hoetker
and Siegel (1970) reported that minority black high school children in
interracial settings were more conscious of race than were the majority whites. Usually it is not feasible to counterbalance ethnic groups
as regards majority versus minority status, but Loomis (1943) did a
rare ethnically counterbalanced study in the high schools of two cities
in the Southwest, one with a Spanish-American and the other with an
Anglo-American majority. In keeping with the distinctiveness-theory
prediction, the minority ethnic group was more in-group oriented than
the majority, both when the Spanish-Americans and when the Anglo-
Americans were in the minority.

Within-ethnic effect of numerical preponderance.   Another distinctiveness-theory prediction is that, as a given ethnic group becomes numerically more preponderant in the social environment, ethnicity becomes progressively less salient in the phenomenal self-concept of
its members. The overall results for all three ethnic groups combined
support the prediction (although the relation is clearer in the European-Americans and Latino-Americans than in the African Americans). For those whose ethnicity was rare in their school (less than
30% at their grade level), 15% spontaneously mentioned their ethnicity; of those whose ethnic group constituted an intermediate 31% to
79% of the student body at grade level, 4% spontaneously mentioned ethnicity; and when fellow ethnics constituted a preponderant 80% plus at
grade level, 0% spontaneously mentioned their ethnicity. A number of
previous studies on school integration lend suggestive support to the distinctiveness-postulate prediction that when the student body is ethnically more heterogeneous the student's ethnicity becomes more
salient in his or her self-concept (Singer, 1967; Crooks, 1970;

Bochner & Ohsaka, 1977). Gerard and Miller's (1975) large-scale field study on school integration indicates that with growing ethnic integration schoolchildren increasingly identify and choose in terms of ethnicity.

Ethnic salience in the affirmational versus negational self-concept. A subtle prediction from distinctiveness theory contrasts the affirmational self-concept (elicited by asking, "Tell us about yourself," which directs one's attention toward characteristics that one has) versus the negational self-concept (elicited by asking, "Tell us what you are not," which directs one's attention toward characteristics found in others that one does not have oneself). Because the distinctiveness postulate predicts that in a stimulus complex one notices its peculiarities, the implication is that the majority European-American children will mention others' ethnicity as something that the self is not more often than they mention their own ethnicity as something that the self is; the African-American and Latino-American children, on the contrary, will mention the majority others' ethnicity as something that the self is not less often than they mention their own distinctive ethnicity as something that the self is. This interaction prediction is supported ($p <$ .01) by the data. Among the majority European-American children only 1% spontaneously mentioned their own ethnicity as part of their affirmational self-concept, whereas 5% spontaneously mentioned their not being of other (minority) ethnicities as part of their negational self-concept ($p < .01$). Among the minority African-American and Latino-American children, on the other hand, 15% mentioned their own ethnicity as part of their affirmational self-concept, whereas only 7% mentioned their not having the majority group's ethnicity as part of their negational self-concept.

Social and Political Implications

Confirmation of the distinctiveness postulate's predictions regarding ethnic salience has both theoretical and political relevance. On the theoretical side, the results suggest that people do act like efficient information-processing machines, noting aspects of their environment insofar as such aspects contain information (are distinctive, unpredictable). A policy implication is that people become more conscious of their ethnicity (or religion, sex, or whatever) to the extent that their social setting is ethnically integrated, especially if their own group is in the numerical minority. It has become U.S. public policy to reduce segregating people on such bases as ethnicity, sex, and religion. Advocates of integration often also aspire to make the society "color-blind," but distinctiveness-theory implications supported here indicate that integration heightens rather than erases consciousness of ethnicity (or sex, etc.), and so may heighten discrimination and hostility among members of different groups. This sensitization increases as the integrated groups approach equality in size. Recognizing this cognitive sensitizing effect of ethnic (and religious, sex, etc.) integration, regardless of the circumstances in which integration is achieved, raises the challenge of how society can enhance the beneficial effects of this sensitization and mitigate its detrimental effects.

SALIENCE OF SEX IN THE SELF-CONCEPT

Sex is another physical demographic characteristic whose spontaneous salience in the self-concept is of high theoretical and policy interest. The distinctiveness theory prediction is that one's sex becomes increasingly salient in one's identity to the extent that one lives in social milieux where the other sex is numerically preponderant. Of the three worlds of childhood – school, home, and friendship/peer group – we have studied this prediction in the first two. In the first of the studies reported below, the independent variable is whether the student's own sex is in the minority or majority of his or her sixth-grade classroom; in the second study, the independent variable is whether the child's sex is in the minority or majority of his or her familial household. In both studies the dependent variable is the salience of the child's sex in his or her phenomenal self-concept.

Effects of Classroom Sex Composition on Salience of the Student's Sex

[Adapted with permission from McGuire & Padawer-Singer, 1976a.]

Participants were 252 sixth-graders in 10 classes, 2 from each of 5 elementary schools in a heterogeneous district of an East Coast U.S. metropolis. The sixth-graders (13-year-olds), tested in their usual classrooms, were given 7 minutes to write down all the thoughts that occurred to them in response to the general affirmational probe "Tell us about yourself," and on a subsequent page were given 4 minutes to free-associate to a physical self-concept probe, "Tell us what you look like." Their free associations to each probe were scored for mention versus no-mention of their sex as part of these spontaneous self-concepts.

Across all 10 classes in the metropolitan study, there were almost exactly as many girls as boys among our 252 participants, 127 versus 125, but on a class-by-class basis, boys were in the majority in 5 classes and girls in the other 5. The discrepancy in each class was not great: the majority sex exceeded the minority by an average of 3 persons in these classes averaging over 25 students in attendance. The distinctiveness-theory prediction is that in each classroom members of the minority sex will more often spontaneously mention their sex than will the majority sex. There was an insignificant tendency in this direction with the general self-concept (in response to the "Tell us about yourself" probe). With the physical self-concept ("Tell us what you look like"), sex was more often mentioned and there was a more sizable and significant ($p < .01$) sex difference in the direction predicted: Across the 10 classes, 26% of members of the minority sex spontaneously described themselves in terms of their sex, whereas only 11% of those in the majority sex mentioned their sex. This sizable difference is especially impressive considering that the discrepancy in numbers between the two sexes in any classroom was not great.

Effects of Household Sex Composition on the Salience of the Child's Sex

[Adapted with permission from W. J. McGuire, C. V. McGuire, & W. Winton, 1979a, Effects of household sex composition on the salience of one's gender in the spontaneous self-concept, *Journal of Experimental Social Psychology, 15,* pp. 77–90. Copyright © 1979 by Academic Press.]

To test a further distinctiveness-theory prediction that children are more likely to think of themselves in terms of their sex increasingly to the extent that the other sex is numerically preponderant in their family households, we carried out individual oral interviews of schoolchildren, first measuring their affirmational self-concept as their five-minute tape-recorded oral response to a "Tell us about yourself" probe, then their three-minute response to the negational self-concept probe, "Tell us what you are not." Later each child was asked to report the sex composition of his or her household.

Method. The study, conducted in the schools of an intermediate-sized manufacturing city in New England, involved individual interviews of 560 children including 70 girls and 70 boys from each of four grade levels: first, third, seventh, and eleventh. In the first part of the interview the child was asked to free-associate to the affirmational self-concept probe, "Tell us about yourself," and then to the negational self-concept probe, "Tell us what you are not." Their responses were then scored for the dependent variable, mention versus no-mention of their sex. The independent variable of our hypothesis was the size of the numerical preponderance of the child's own sex over the other sex in her or his household. Data on this variable were obtained after the spontaneous self-concept responses by asking the child to list by initials all persons living in his or her household and to indicate the sex and relationship of each.

Effects of other sex's numerical preponderance in the household. Strong support was found for the basic prediction that sex will be more spontaneously salient in the self-concepts of children whose own sex is in the minority in their households. The households of the 554 respondents (omitting 3 boys and 3 girls among the total of 560 participants who were excluded because of ambiguities in their reports of the independent variable, household sex composition) were first partitioned on the independent variable into those with males in the majority (33%), those with equal numbers of males and females (29%), and those with females in the majority (38%). As predicted, boys are progressively more likely spontaneously to mention their being males as the proportion of females in the household increases ($p < .05$); and conversely, girls are progressively more likely to mention their being females as the proportion of females in the household decreases ($p < .05$). An incidental analysis suggests that the number of males may be more important than the number of females for this household sex-ratio effect.

Effect of father's absence on sex salience in boys. A further prediction, somewhat paradoxical and with social significance, is that their sense of themselves as males will be more salient in boys whose fathers are absent from the home than in those with fathers present. The effect of the father's absence on the boy's sex-typing has received considerable attention because of its prevalence and the association of father's absence with poverty, crime, family instability, substance abuse, and unemployment. Commentators, typically using social learning theory (if only implicitly), predict that boys from father-absent homes will be low in adoption of socially prescribed adult masculine behavior, due to a deficiency during childhood of role models and reinforcement for prescribed manly behavior. Distinctiveness theory makes the almost opposite prediction that absence of the father will enhance the boy's consciousness of being a male, because the boy's maleness will be more distinctive in a fatherless home. Although the flavor of their two predictions is opposite, social-learning and distinctiveness theories make predictions about somewhat different dependent variables rather than opposite predictions about a single dependent variable.

To test this prediction, we partitioned the 560 respondents into those from households with both mother and father present (the home situation for 446 of these children) versus those with mother but not father present (the home situation for 68 of the children, including 33 boys and 35 girls). (The remaining 46 respondents were excluded from this analysis as falling into more ambiguous household situations. Reanalyses done with other plausible assignments of these 46 ambiguous cases did not appreciably affect the conclusions reported here.) Our sample's having 13% mother-only households among the 514 classifiable cases is in good agreement with the national U.S. figure of 13% of family households that were at the time headed by women (U.S. Bureau of Census, 1976).

The results support the distinctiveness prediction that being male is more salient in boys from fatherless homes: Of the 33 boys who came from fatherless homes, 18% spontaneously mentioned that they were male, whereas only 7% of the 227 boys with both mothers and fathers present spontaneously mentioned their maleness, a difference in sex salience significant at the .05 level. Father's absence appears to make no difference in the extent to which girls are conscious of their femaleness: 11% of the 35 girls who came from fatherless homes and 12% of the 219 girls who came from homes with both mothers and fathers spontaneously mentioned that they were female. Other father-absence studies and studies of the sex of older siblings also find that the effect on girls is less than the effect on boys (Biller & Weiss, 1970;

Santrock, 1970). The prevalence of this sex asymmetry invites further research. We were unable to investigate the effect of mother-absence/father-presence on sex salience in boys and girls because so few of our participants' households fell into this category, reflecting its rarity in society in general. Distinctiveness theory's confirmed nonobvious predictions regarding the salience of sex in the phenomenal self, like those regarding ethnicity, have important implications for both theory and practice.

CONCLUSION: THICK TEXTURE
OF THE PHENOMENAL SELF

[Adapted with permission from W. J. McGuire, 1984a.]

This chapter and the preceding one (chapters 7 and 8) both focus on the phenomenal self; that is, both study which of the person's many characteristics are spontaneously salient in his or her sense of self as revealed when the person describes his or her self-concept in his or her own terms. This procedure corrects the usual narrowness of self-concept research due to the person's typically being restricted to defining the self on researcher-chosen dimensions, almost always just on the evaluative dimension. In these two chapters I have discussed the content and process of self-space analytically, as befits a nomothetic researcher who is interested in describing relations between abstract variables and so is willing to lose specific information about concrete individuals in order to abstract general principles that have wide, even if only partial and inexact, applicability to specific cases. To illustrate some of the information lost by our abstract level of discourse, I end these two chapters with some idiographic thick description (Geertz, 1973) in concrete protocols obtained in this spontaneous self-concept research. One participant whose self-descriptions are particularly evocative and provocative is a 14-year-old boy in the written-response condition, whose touching response to our "Tell us about yourself" probe was:

> I am a kid that has nothing and gets nothing. When I born I born trouble. My mother said to me that I was born just for trouble. I was born in New York. I used to think to myself that I should be dead. I never had a good time for long. When I come home I just get fust at. I was born just to be born. I am a kid that is hardly known to the

world. I am a human just like everybody you know and should be treated like one. Please be my friend.

His response to our "Tell us what you look like" probe was no less depressing:

> I have blue eyes, brown hair, black eyelashes. I am a kid that looks like a stupid donkey. I say deep down in my heart I am no good.

Nor was he much happier in his response to our "Tell us about your past life" probe:

> When I was growing up I had a hard life but I will tell you why. When I was born my parents said that I would grow with a hard life and I did. I had the hardest life. Thank you.

Yet in his response to our "Tell us about your family" request, this 14-year-old showed an appreciation of love and a ferocity for loving that few grasp even in their maturity:

> My family is the nicest parents in the world. Sometimes they can be mean and I think they no good. My mother said she hated me so I thought I shouldn't like her but I do. I love her very much and she loves me but she doesn't know it.

And his response to our "Tell us what you like best" probe shows that his heart could soar in the presence of beauty:

> I like Trudy Greenberg because when I went to school and saw her I said I like her. And I do like her because she pretty. I like her.

It was our request for his negational self-concept that elicited this boy's most self-affirming response. He replied to the "Tell us what you are not" probe as follows:

> I am not a hero or prince or king. But I can do some things well maybe better than anybody. Some people can do things better than me but I can top people in sports. I am not a prince or hero or king. But I am a kid that lives.

Few responses are as poignant as this boy's, but all children can be revealing when the researcher presents a low profile, allowing them to express themselves in their own terms rather than by restricting them to making check marks on semantic differential polar opposites of the researcher's (or C. E. Osgood's) choosing. Allowed to express themselves in their own words, these young people produce rich material, some of whose information is lost in aggregation across cases when one wants to abstract general principles; but the researcher can choose the level of abstraction. Before one rides off in one or more analytical directions one can confront the thick descriptions that disclose an individual person's realizing herself or himself at a certain moment in time, constituting one manifestation of the infinite variety of possible human epiphanies. The seventh-grader just reported shows himself to be a troubled boy, perhaps feeling too sorry for himself or perhaps entitled to every one of his sorrows. And yet from his valley of despondency he shows not only a capacity to be surprised by joy but an active avidity to "let joy size at God knows when to God knows what." His self-descriptions do not leave one sure that he will grow and prevail, or even to feel certain that he has survived until this reading, but they put us in the presence of a self at a moment fully lived, a self that can look at a face of truth and seek something finer, a self that makes selves worth studying.

9

Language and Thought Asymmetries

Two of our lines of research on asymmetries in thought and language will be reported here: first our work on positivity biases in thinking (McGuire & McGuire, 1992c), which grew out of our earlier research (McGuire & McGuire, 1991a) on the phenomenal self (chapter 7) and on thought systems (chapter 6); and then our more autonomous line of asymmetry research on seemingly arbitrary word-order asymmetries (McGuire & McGuire, 1992b).

COGNITIVE AND AFFECTIVE POSITIVITY ASYMMETRIES IN THOUGHT SYSTEMS

[Adapted with permission from W. J. McGuire & C. V. McGuire, 1992c, Cognitive-versus-affective positivity asymmetries in thought systems, *European Journal of Social Psychology, 22,* pp. 571–591. Copyright © 1992 by John Wiley & Sons Ltd. See also McGuire & McGuire, 1996b.]

Psychologists and people in general use the terms *positive* and *negative* ambiguously to refer to both cognitive and affective dimensions. One can study positive versus negative thinking about a person in the cognitive sense of what the person has versus what he or she lacks, what he or she is versus what he or she is not. The participant can be asked, "List all the characteristics that your best friend has (or that France has, or that democracy has)" versus "List all the characteristics that your best friend (or France, or democracy) does not have." Quite independently, one can study positive versus negative thinking in the affective, desirable versus undesirable, sense of thinking about good versus bad characteristics of the topic. The participant can be asked, "List all the desirable characteristics that your best friend (or France, or democracy) has" versus "List all the undesirable characteristics that your best friend (or France or democracy) has."

These cognitive versus affective positivity-negativity dimensions are distinct both logically and operationally. Cognitive × affective positivity can be studied in an orthogonal 2 × 2 experimental design by using four tasks: "List all the desirable (undesirable) characteristics that France has (does not have)." Despite their logical and operational distinctness, ambiguity of labeling confuses these cognitive and affective dimensions; hence, we shall clarify the distinction by describing several commonly studied subtypes of positivity asymmetries of each kind, cognitive versus affective.

Illustrative Positive–Negative Asymmetries

Cognitive asymmetries. Among the wide range of thinking tasks that exhibit a robust cognitive positivity bias such that people are better able to think affirmationally than negationally (i.e., are able to think more effectively about what a topic is than about what it is not) we shall mention six varied examples. (1) Woodworth and Sells (1935) found that people can judge the logical validity of a syllogism more accurately the fewer the negative propositions that it has. (2) Hovland (1952) showed that in concept-learning tasks people make fuller use of the information in positive than in negative instances. (3) Regarding memory, Fiedler, Fladung, and Hemmeter (1987) showed that people remember better characteristics that stimuli are reported to have rather than lack. (4) In psychophysical studies reaction times are faster in making "same" than "not-same" judgments (Farell, 1985), even though "not-same" judgments logically require less information. (5) People are more fluent in listing characteristics that a topic has than those it does not have, even though there are many more characteristics that the topics do not have than they do have. (6) Mentioning a characteristic to negate it may be distorted to an affirmation (e.g., if a product is explicitly labeled "Nontoxic," consumers may perceive it as more toxic than if the toxicity had been left unlabeled) (Rozin, Markwith, & Ross, 1990).

Affective asymmetries. Positive–negative thought asymmetries in the affective sense concern whether people think more effectively about the desirable or the undesirable characteristics possessed or lacked by a topic of thought. Five varied examples illustrate the range of affective asymmetries. (1) Retrospective voting studies (Kieweit and Rivers, 1984) show that incumbent leaders and parties tend to be re-elected if the economy has been prospering just prior to the election and tend to be voted out if the economy has been performing dismally, but with an affective negativity bias such that incumbents are hurt by deteriorating economic conditions more than they are helped by prosperous conditions, especially when the economic conditions are experienced by the voter personally (Ansolabehere, Iyengar, & Simon, 1990). (2) Some research on fear appeals indicates that people are more influenced to adopt a healthful behavior if the message stresses the undesirable effects of not complying rather than the desirable effects of complying (Meyerowitz & Chaiken, 1987), but results are mixed (Sutton, 1982) and affective and cognitive bias tends to be confounded in these studies. Perhaps negativity bias operates for effects on realistic health behavior and positivity bias operates for effects on autistic self-esteem (Robberson & Rogers, 1988), and people may be risk-aversive on gains and risk-seeking on losses (Tversky & Kahneman, 1981). (3) Studies on defensive pessimism (Norem & Cantor, 1986) suggest that, when asked to predict whether a situation's outcome will be desirable or undesirable, some people take a defensive pessimism stance as if to soften the blow, with expected failure being less disturbing than unexpected failure (Feather, 1969).

The three asymmetries just mentioned are affective biases in the negativity (undesirability) direction, but in other situations affective positivity biases are found. (4) When people are asked to evaluate an unknown stimulus person, they tend to have a positivity (desirability) bias, rating the unknown person on the positive side of the evaluation scale's neutral point (Anderson, 1981) and ascribing more desirable than undesirable traits to a stranger. This affective positivity bias may be especially pronounced for persons, as when positivity bias is greater for political leaders than for the political parties they lead (Sears, 1983); however, these U.S. findings may reverse for countries like Sweden, where in politics parties loom larger than personalities. (5) Another affective positivity bias shows up in triadic structures (Heider, 1958; Insko, Songer, & McGarvey, 1977): When people think about structures consisting of oneself, another person, and one or more other components, they prefer balance (defined as not having an uneven number of negations in the links between pairs of components) but also prefer positivity, that is, prefer a balance achieved with a minimum number of negations. Thus, although cognitive asymmetries are usually sizable and in the positive direction, affective asymmetries are slighter and vary between negativity and positivity biases among tasks, depending on dispositional and situational interacting variables.

Theorizing That Guides This Research Program on Positive–Negative Asymmetries

The ability–proclivity distinction. It is clarifying to distinguish also between ability (capacity) and proclivity (preference, style) when theorizing about positive versus negative thinking. Ability (capacity) is studied when the instructions specify whether positive or negative thinking should be done (e.g., "List all the desirable [undesirable] characteristics that Italy has [does not have]"), and then counting how many thoughts of each designated type the participants are able to generate. Proclivity (preference) is studied by giving participants an open-ended task where instructions do not specify whether positive or negative thinking should be done (e.g., "List all the thoughts that occur to you when you think about Italy") and then counting how many positive or negative thoughts the participant spontaneously generates. We predict relatively small differences in ability (capacity) to think positively versus negatively when necessary, on the assumption that varied environmental demands will have required the person to develop at least moderate proficiencies in both positive and negative thinking when needed. However, we assume that small differences in ability are magnified greatly in proclivity (preference); for example, if a person is able to think just slightly better affirmatively than negationally, then he or she will, when given the option, think preponderantly affirmatively to the virtual exclusion of the only slightly more difficult negational mode. Hence, a moderate cognitive positivity bias in ability will become a vast cognitive positivity bias in proclivity.

Predicted cognitive asymmetries. Four derived predictions about cognitive asymmetries are tested in the studies described below. Firstly, when given a directed-thinking, ability task specifically calling for a designated positivity type of thinking about a topic of thought (thus largely controlling for proclivity), the person will be

able to generate somewhat more affirmational than negational characteristics of the evoking topic (as tested in Experiments 1, 2, 3, and 4).
This prediction is derivable from at least four theories (discussed further in McGuire & McGuire, 1992c): our own distinctiveness theory
of selective attention (see chapter 8); a two-step theory of negation;
the storage of topic characteristics in a tree structure; or the contamination of linguistic markedness with undesirability. Secondly, it is
predicted that in free-association proclivity tasks such as those used in
Experiments 5 through 8, which leave the person free to think about
whatever topics he or she prefers, the person will generate a vast excess of affirmational over negational characteristics of the topics
thought about. Thirdly, as a child matures, situational demands will
have provided him or her with increasing practice in carrying out the
more difficult negational thinking, enhancing ability and confidence
in negational thinking. Therefore there will be an age-trend during
childhood and adolescence of an increasing ratio of negational to affirmational assertions in free descriptions of familiar stimuli (see Experiments 5 and 6). Fourthly, because the strong proclivity to positivity will have left people relatively out of practice in doing this slightly
more difficult and so usually avoided negational thinking, there will
be a practice effect such that use of negational thinking will tend to
catch up with affirmational during the session as practice continues
(see Experiment 2).

Predicted affective asymmetries.   As regards affective positivity–negativity asymmetries, we predict little difference in ability to generate
desirable versus undesirable characteristics of a topic as measured by
how well people carry out directed-thinking, ability tasks (see Experiments 3 and 4), because coping with their normal environment will often have required people to think of undesirable as well as desirable
characteristics of thought topics. Affective asymmetries are predicted
in proclivity situations where performance reflects preference as well
as ability, but they can go in either direction. In realistic thinking situations (those in which the person needs to cope with the external environment) an affective negativity bias is predicted, because it is more
adaptive and less disappointing to anticipate and prepare to cope with
undesirable characteristics or outcomes than to prepare to enjoy desirable ones (see Experiments 7 and 8). Conversely, in autistic thinking
situations (those in which the person is more concerned with hedonic
gratification in fantasy) an affective positivity bias is predicted, on the
assumption that the person derives more pleasure from thinking about

desirable than undesirable characteristics and outcomes (see Experiment 8; Fiedler, 1988; Peeters & Czapínski, 1990).

Outline of the empirical studies. Ten empirical studies are reported in three sets. Experiments 1 through 4 study cognitive and affective asymmetries in *ability,* minimizing the contribution of proclivity by using a directive task that prescribes whether positive or negative thoughts are to be generated. The second set of experiments, 5 through 8, investigate cognitive and affective asymmetries in *proclivity* that show up on nondirective free-association tasks that allow participants to think about either positive or negative aspects of the evoking topics. The dependent variable in these first eight experiments is thought fluency, the number of thoughts generated in one versus another positivity condition. The third set of experiments, 9 and 10, investigate how thinking in the 2 × 2 positivity conditions affects another dependent variable, evaluation of the evoking topic, instead of fluency in thinking about it.

Positive–Negative Asymmetries in Four Directed-Thinking (Ability) Experiments

Experiments 1 through 4 test the predictions described above about people's ability to generate on demand positive versus negative thoughts. Experiments 1 and 2 investigate the cognitive dimension only; Experiments 3 and 4, both the cognitive and the affective dimensions. Thought topics and task wordings were deliberately varied across experiments to enhance generalizability.

Experiment 1: Ability to generate cognitively affirmational versus negational self-characteristics. On successive pages of an experimental booklet, 64 college students were asked to describe themselves by listing what they are or what they are not. Three minutes were allowed for each task, and the order of affirmational versus negational tasks was alternated. The dependent variable, the number of self-descriptive characteristics that participants were able to generate in the two task conditions, showed, as predicted, a moderate cognitive positivity bias in ability: Participants produced a mean of 14.88 self-thoughts in the affirmational condition (listing characteristics that they had) versus only 12.48 self-thoughts in the negational condition (listing characteristics that they did not have), a 19% positivity ability bias (p < .05) in fluency. See also McGuire and McGuire, (1991a).

Experiment 2: Ability to generate cognitively affirmational versus negational national stereotypes. The second experiment was similar to the first, except that its eliciting thought topics were, not the self, but nine specified nations. This study additionally varied the time allowed to carry out the directed-thinking task. The 36 college students worked through a booklet, six of whose pages asked that thoughts be generated about six different nations. The tasks on these six pages constituted a 2 × 3 within-participant experimental design. The two-level variable was the affirmational versus negational directed-thinking task ("Write down as many things as you can think of that nation X *is*" versus "Write down as many things as you can think of that nation Y *is not*"). The three-level independent variable was the time (1 vs. 2 vs. 3 minutes) allowed for this thought-generating task. The nations, orders of tasks, and time allowances were systematically rotated from participant to participant. The dependent variable measure was fluency, the mean number of thoughts generated about nations in each of the six cells of the design. A slight cognitive positivity bias was found, as predicted: A mean of 7.32 national characteristics were generated in the affirmational condition versus 6.87 in the negational condition, an 8% positivity bias that just reached the .05 level of significance. The predicted rustiness effect, in the form of a positivity × practice interaction effect was also confirmed (p < .05), in that the cognitive positivity bias decreased steadily for each successive minute of practice.

Experiment 3: Cognitive and affective positivity asymmetries in ability to describe nations. The third and fourth experiments studied both cognitive and affective asymmetry in ability by using four generating tasks in a 2 × 2 design: (1) desirable characteristics that a designated nation has, (2) undesirable characteristics that another nation has, (3) desirable characteristics that still another nation does not have, and (4) undesirable characteristics that a fourth nation does not have. Task order and nations were counterbalanced among the participants. As predicted, a 22% cognitive positivity bias (p < .01) was found, in that participants were able to generate a mean of 6.38 characteristics in the two affirmational conditions versus only 5.24 characteristics in the two negational conditions. As predicted, there was no appreciable affective asymmetry, main or interaction effect.

Experiment 4: Cognitive and affective positivity asymmetries in ability to think about future events. This experiment is similar to the preceding one in hypotheses and methods but used different topics of thought, using eventualities that might occur rather than nations. Each of 96 students was given four tasks in a 2 × 2 within-participant design, each task calling for generating a different type of antecedent or consequence of a different eventuality. The four tasks included generating, for 3 minutes each: (1) desirable antecedents (or consequences) promotively related to a future eventuality, (2) undesirable antecedents (or consequences) promotively related to a second eventuality, (3) desirable ones preventively related to a third future eventuality, and (4) undesirable ones preventively related to a fourth eventuality. The order of the four tasks and the assignment of eventualities to tasks were rotated systematically. The dependent variable was fluency, the number of thoughts generated in 3 minutes for each of the four tasks. The asymmetries found in this 2 × 2 "eventualities" study are similar to the results in the preceding "nations" study. There was a significant 48% positivity bias (p < .01) in cognitive ability, with 3.99 promotive antecedents (or consequences) versus only 2.69 preventive. Again, as predicted, there was no appreciable affective positivity asymmetry in ability.

Conclusions about positivity asymmetries in thinking ability. All four directed-thinking abilities studies indicate a significant cognitive positivity bias such that participants were able to generate more thoughts when given the task of describing what the thought topic is, rather than what it is not – 15% more for thinking about nations, 19% more about the self, and 48% more about future eventualities. This positivity bias is comparatively large at the outset of the directed-thinking session but diminishes as the session continues, which may indicate that practice overcomes the person's rustiness on the negational task. As predicted, none of these directed-thinking ability tasks showed significant affective positivity asymmetry in that participants thought of similar numbers of undesirable and desirable characteristics, nor did these four ability studies show any cognitive × affective positivity interaction effects on fluency.

Positive–Negative Asymmetries in Four Free-Association (Proclivity) Experiments

A second quartet of experiments switch from ability tasks to proclivity tasks, testing predictions regarding positive–negative asymmetries in preferred modes of thinking when people are allowed to free-associate on a variety of topics. A much greater cognitive affirmational bias is predicted for proclivity in Experiments 5 to 8 than was just reported for ability in Experiments 1 to 4. As regards affective proclivity asymmetries, a negativity bias (more thoughts of undesirable than desirable characteristics) is predicted in situations calling for realistic thinking and a positivity (desirability) bias is predicted when the situation invites autistic, wishful thinking.

Experiments 5 and 6: Cognitive asymmetries in children's thinking proclivities.   These two experiments tested the predictions that children's preferred mode of thinking will exhibit a strong cognitive affirmational bias that will decrease somewhat as they grow older and develop increasing mastery over the more difficult negational thinking. Experiment 5 tested the oral responses of 560 schoolchildren, 70 boys and 70 girls at each of four age levels, 7, 9, 13, and 17 years. Each child was presented with four successive topic probes, order counterbalanced: "Tell us about yourself," "Tell us about your family," "Tell us about school," and "Tell us about the future," and was given three minutes to respond orally to each request. Experiment 6 tested 800 children who responded in writing, again for 3 minutes, to each of the same four probes. The 800 participants included 100 boys and 100 girls at each of four age levels, 11, 13, 15, and 17 years. Across all four topics (self, family, school, the future) there was a vast affirmational preference. In the oral-response replication, the proportion of affirmations versus negations were .84 versus .16, constituting a 525% cognitive positivity bias ($p < .001$); in the written response replication, the proportion of affirmations versus negations was .80 versus .20, constituting a 400% positivity bias ($p < .001$). (The affirmational proportions were almost identical when we consider data only from grades 7 and 11, the two grade levels that appeared in both oral and written studies.) Figure 9.1 shows that, as further predicted, the proportion of negational responses increased steadily with age in both oral and written replications.

Experiment 7: Cognitive and affective asymmetries in thinking about societal eventualities.   Experiments 7 and 8 used the free associations evoked by future eventualities to measure proclivity (preference) asymmetries on both the cognitive and affective dimensions. In Experiment 7, Yale introductory psychology students ($N = 96$) were asked to free-associate for 3 minutes on each of 36 varied eventuali-

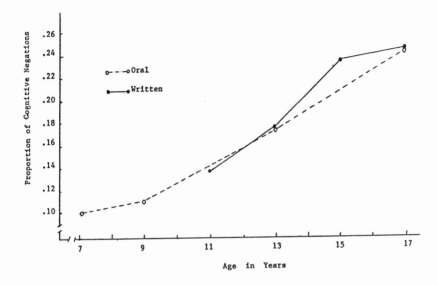

Figure 9.1
Increasing proportions of cognitive negations in 7- to 17-year-old children's free associations about familiar life domains (self, family, school, the future). Experiments 5 and 6.

ties (concerning politics, health, life-style, etc.) that might plausibly occur in society. A content analysis sorted the generated thoughts (with over 90% interrater agreement) into four categories: desirable antecedents (or consequences) promotively related to the eventuality, undesirable ones promotively related, desirable ones preventively related, and undesirable ones preventively related.

The 96 participants generated a mean of 5.34 thought segments per societal eventuality in the 3 minutes allowed, 79% of which were either antecedents or consequences. Both antecedents and consequences showed a vast cognitive positivity bias, with a mean of 3.65 of all evoked antecedents and consequences being promotively related versus a mean of only 0.58 preventively related to the evoking eventuality, a 629% excess (p < .001) of affirmational over negational thoughts. On the affective dimension there was a modest negativity bias among both the antecedents and the consequences generated. These impersonal societal eventualities evoked 2.36 undesirable versus only 1.87 desirable antecedents and consequences, a 27% affective positivity bias, significant at the .05 level but much lower than the 629% cognitive positivity bias.

Experiment 8: Asymmetries in preferred thinking about personal versus societal eventualities.   Experiment 8 is similar to the one just reported except that it introduced an additional independent variable by measuring thought systems evoked by personal as well as societal future eventualities. The societal eventualities pertain to happenings in the thinker's society in general (such as the occurrence of a major economic depression or the development of a cure for AIDS), whereas the personal eventualities pertain to possible happenings that might befall the thinker more personally (such as succeeding in one's chosen career or oneself suffering from a serious illness). Eight personal eventualities were matched in desirability and likelihood with eight societal eventualities. Each of 64 university students free-associated for 3 minutes on each of four eventualities. As usual, a content analysis sorted the evoked antecedents and consequences into the 2 × 2 positivity categories (desirable promotive, undesirable promotive, desirable preventive, and undesirable preventive).

The students' thought systems around the personal eventualities were richer (p < .001) than those around the societal eventualities: The mean number of thoughts evoked by the eight personal eventualities was 7.45 versus 5.59 by the matched societal eventualities. Of these 7.45 thoughts evoked per student per personal event, 5.70 (77%) were either antecedents or consequences. The antecedents and consequences evoked by the personal eventualities showed a vast 482% cognitive positivity bias (p < .001); as can be seen in Table 9.1A, 4.72 were affirmational (promotive) versus only 0.98 negational (preventive) in their relation to the evoking event. Of the antecedents and consequences evoked by the matched societal eventualities, Table 9.1B shows that 3.57 were affirmational versus only 0.68 negational, a similarly high cognitive positivity bias of 525%.

As regards affective positivity, Table 9.1A shows a positivity (desirability) bias in the antecedents and consequences evoked by the personal eventualities, in that 3.42 were desirable occurrences versus only 2.28 undesirable, a 50% excess (p < .01) of desirable over undesirable. The matched societal eventualities evoked, as predicted, an opposite negativity (undesirability) affective excess. As can be seen in Table 9.1B, 2.49 of the evoked antecedents and consequences were

Table 9.1

Cognitive and affective positivity asymmetries in the antecedents and consequences evoked by personal versus matched societal (impersonal) eventualities in Experiment 8.

A. NUMBER EVOKED BY PERSONAL EVENTS				B. NUMBER EVOKED BY SOCIETAL EVENTS			
Cognitive positivity	Affective positivity			Cognitive positivity	Affective positivity		
	Undesirable	Desirable	Total		Undesirable	Desirable	Total
Promote	1.98	2.74	4.72	Promote	2.26	1.31	3.57
Prevent	.30	.68	.98	Prevent	.23	.45	.68
Total	2.28	3.42	5.70	Total	2.49	1.76	4.25

A, on the left, shows number of antecedents and consequences evoked by personal events; B on the right, by societal events.

undesirable versus only 1.76 desirable, a 41% negative affective bias ($p < .01$). Hence, in this study of thoughts freely evoked by mention of personal versus societal eventualities, there emerged the usual powerfull 500% cognitive affirmational bias in predilection for both personal and societal eventualities, 10 times larger than the cognitive affirmational bias in ability. As regards affective asymmetry, there was the predicted reversal between the personal and the societal events: With the personal eventualities (where hedonic, wishful-thinking needs were assumed to loom larger) there was an affective positivity bias ($p < .01$); but with societal eventualities (where realistic thinking such as damage control would be more operative) there is an affective negativity bias ($p < .01$) – that is, more thoughts of undesirable than desirable consequences.

Cognitive and Affective Asymmetries in How Directed Thinking Affects Topic Evaluations

Experiment 9: Effects of directed thinking on evaluations of events. Whereas Experiments 1 through 8 investigate cognitive and affective positivity asymmetries as they affect fluency as the dependent variable, Experiments 9 and 10 investigate positivity as it affects evaluation of the evoking thought topics (which were future eventualities in Experiment 9 and the self in Experiment 10). In Experiment 9 the participants were presented with four societal eventualities (e.g., that more meals will be eaten at restaurants than at home) and asked to list as many as they could of a designated one of our usual four types of consequences of that event (desirable promoted, undesirable promoted, desirable prevented, and undesirable prevented). Eventualities and task order were rotated systematically. After completing the four directed thought-generating tasks, each on a different eventuality, participants evaluated the desirability of each eventuality on a 0 to 100 scale, to test whether the generating task's manipulating the salience of biased subsets of consequences had the hypothesized effects on the perceived desirability of the eventuality.

The main prediction was strongly confirmed, in that eventualities receive a mean evaluation of only 31.06 in the Table 9.2A down-and-to-the-right diagonal (after generating undesirable consequences that the eventuality promotes or desirable ones that it prevents), far lower (p < .001) than the 46.62 mean evaluation in the Table 9.2A down-and-to-the-left diagonal (after generating the desirable consequences that the eventuality promotes or undesirable consequences that it prevents). Hence, directed thinking about a topic has remote ramifications on its evaluation. As predicted, this effect operated symmetrically as regards affective positivity. It also operated symmetrically as regards cognitive positivity, disconfirming our affirmational-bias prediction that the promotive effect would be greater than the preventive effect.

Experiment 10: Effects of directed thinking on self-evaluation. Experiment 10 differs from Experiment 9 in using the self rather than future eventualities as the thought-evoking topic. College students (N = 64) were divided randomly into four subgroups, each given one of four tasks in a 2 × 2 design: generating desirable (or undesirable) characteristics that the self has (or does not have). Then each participant completed a 10-item self-esteem scale. We made the same predictions as in the preceding study regarding how the four directed thought-generating tasks would affect the participants' self-esteem.

The basic interaction prediction was strongly confirmed (as can be seen in the Table 9.2B diagonals). After generating desirable characteristics that they had or undesirable characteristics from which they were free, participants' mean self-esteem score of 98.02 was significantly higher (p < .001) than the 81.65 self-esteem mean for participants generating undesirable characteristics they had or desirable char-

Table 9.2

How thinking about a stimulus in terms of its cognitively and affectively positive-versus-negative characteristics affects subsequent evaluation of the stimulus

A. How thinking about desirable-versus undesirable consequences that a future eventuality promotes versus prevents affects the judged desirability of the eventuality (Experiment 9)				B. How thinking about the desirable-versus-undesirable characteristics that the self has versus lacks affects the thinker's subsequent self-esteem (Experiment 10)			
Cognitive positivity	Affective positivity			Cognitive positivity	Affective positivity		
	Undesirable	Desirable	Mean		Undesirable	Desirable	Mean
Promoted	30.47	43.91	37.19	Has	79.75	103.85	91.82
Prevented	49.34	31.66	40.50	Lacks	92.19	83.56	87.88
Mean	39.90	37.78	38.84	Mean	85.97	93.72	89.84

acteristics that they lacked. As predicted, there was no appreciable affective positivity asymmetry. Also as predicted, there was a cognitive positivity bias in that the self-esteem differentials, after generating desirable versus undesirable self-characteristics, were significantly greater (p < .05) in the "affirmational" than in the "negational" columns of Table 9.2B. Hence, Experiments 9 and 10 both show that the effects of cognitive and of affective positivity must be considered both separately and jointly to understand how manipulating the salience of contrasting positivity types of topic-relevant information will affect the evaluation of the evoking topics. In Experiment 10 people's self-esteem was raised or lowered, not by giving them new information about themselves, but simply by having them remind themselves selectively of things they already believed about themselves. The obtained cognitive positivity bias indicates further that people's self-esteem is lowered more when they remind themselves of undesirable characteristics that they do possess than when they remind themselves of desirable characteristics that they lack. It also indicates that people's self-esteem can be raised more effectively by making them aware of desirable characteristics they have than of undesirable characteristics from which they are free. Hence, cognitive positivity bias has clinical as well as theoretical implications (McGuire & McGuire, 1996b).

THE PSYCHOLOGICAL SIGNIFICANCE
OF SEEMINGLY ARBITRARY WORD-ORDER
REGULARITIES: THE CASE OF KIN PAIRS

[Adapted from W. J. McGuire & C. V. McGuire, 1992b, Psychological significance of seemingly arbitrary word-order regularities: The case of kin pairs, in G. Semin & K. Fiedler (Eds.), *Language, interaction, and social cognition,* pp. 214–236 (London: Sage).]

A second line of our research on thought and language asymmetries focuses on preferential word orderings, which are puzzlingly ubiquitous, extreme, and widely shared even though they are prescribed by no explicit rule and serve no obvious function. Examples abound within all parts of speech, although our research has focused so far on noun and adjective instances. Most commonly paired noun expressions (two nouns joined by "and" or "or") show asymmetrical ordering preferences, often quite extreme. In the familiar domain of kin pairs, when several hundred English-speakers were asked to write down "kin x and kin y" expressions, 75% of sibling pair mentions were in the "brother and sister" order, and 82% of the parent pairings were in the "mother and father" order. In the food-pair domain, 91% of joint occurrences are ordered "apples and oranges" and 95% "cream and sugar." In the domain of familiar objects, 100% of their co-occurrences are ordered "knife and fork" and 96% "hat and coat." Adjective series (two or more adjectives modifying a noun) also exhibit ubiquitous asymmetrical ordering preferences. When asked to write down "adjective *x,* adjective *y,* noun" expressions, English-speakers almost invariably listed size adjectives before color adjectives ("long white dress" rather than "white long dress") and color adjectives before materials adjectives ("white silk dress" rather than "silk white dress").

These word-order regularities are an attractive research tool for investigating thought because they are common and mysterious, and fluc-tuate reliably and provocatively with numerous situational and dispositional variables. The research reported here is limited to English-language data and uses the theoretically eclectic strategy of hypothesizing a wide range of independent-variable determinants, both semantic and phonological, to account for these ordering biases. This research is eclectic also as regards method, a wide variety of data and analyses being used.

Types of Word-Order Regularities

The seemingly arbitrary word-order regularities discussed here should be distinguished from four other, more purposive orderings that do not immediately concern us in this research program. (1) We are not concerned about cross-language universals between grammatical categories (e.g., subjects precede objects) that presumably reflect deep language constructing modes (Greenberg, 1966; Jakobson, 1966). (2) Nor are we investigating word orderings that affect meaning (e.g., "John loves Mary" versus "Mary loves John"). (3) We are not studying order regularities imposed by grammatical rules, however arbitrary (e.g., French grammar's meticulous but mysterious prescription of which adjectives precede versus follow the nouns they modify [Waugh, 1977]). (4) Nor are we considering esthetically prescribed word orders, as to maintain rhythm in metrical poetry. We are not studying any of these between-categories types of word orderings. Rather, we are studying the ordering of words within a grammatical category that most people observe spontaneously without obvious reason. Almost everyone says "shoes and socks" rather than "socks and shoes," and "flimsy wooden fence" instead of "wooden flimsy fence," but when asked why, they typically give near tautological or easily refuted explanations. These mysterious regularities, although ubiquitous, have received surprisingly little study (Cooper & Ross, 1975; Enkvist & Kohonen, 1976; Pinker & Birdsong, 1979). Some standardized word ordering is needed for efficient language acquisition if it is the case that children first learn the meaning of whole sentences and only later discriminate the component phrases and words as having separate atomistic meanings (Donaldson, 1987; Quine, 1987). The question here is which standardized order?

The Strategic Planning of Programmatic Word-Order Research: The Research Parallelepiped

In keeping with perspectivism's prescription (see chapter 12) that research be planned programmatically on the multi-experiment strategic level, we initially blocked out the total research space by defining the three orthogonal "edges" that define any domain to be investigated, including dependent variables × the theorized independent variables × available methods. As in many other problem domains, these three edges, shown in Figure 9.2, block out the domain in which word-order regularities occur.

Multiple domains of word-order regularities: The dependent variables. These arbitrary word-order regularities show up in all parts of speech, as partially listed on the vertical axis of the Figure 9.2 parallelepiped. Noun-pair asymmetries are prevalent across meaning domains, including kin ("husband and wife"), individual celebrities ("Victoria and Albert"), foods ("lettuce and tomatoes"), common objects ("needle and thread"), states ("in sickness or in health"), and abstractions ("good and evil"). Series of adjectives also show compelling regularities in ordering ("shiny new car"), as do commonly paired verbs ("stop and go"), and paired adverbs ("slowly but surely"). Even conjunctions have preferred orderings, "no ifs, ands, or buts about it." Our strategy is to study word orderings in two familiar but contrasting domains, noun pairs and adjective series, that we suspect have rather different determinants.

Further, within noun pairs we began with kin pairs and then went on to food pairs. Both kinship and food are central domains of human experience, with instances easily collected in natural speech samples. The kin domain has a manageably small vocabulary, which simplifies the initial explorations; and the food domain has a rich vocabulary that allows follow-up studies to resolve ambiguities. The present chapter is largely confined to results on word-order regularities in kin pairs; we shall mention food-pairs and adjective-series data mainly when they clarify an issue left ambiguous by the small vocabulary of the kin-pair data.

Multiple categories of hypothesized determinants: The theorized independent variables. On the second, horizontal edge of the Figure 9.2 research block are listed independent variables theorized to explain primacy in word ordering. We theorize eclectically that noun-pair primacy is accounted for by five broad categories of variables. Three are semantic in that they involve the meanings of the ordered concepts: (1) cognitive availability, (2) affective charge, and (3) sociocultural status. Two other categories involve phonological characteristics of the concepts' labels rather than the concepts' meanings: (4) on the encoding side, vocalization ease; and (5) on the decoding side, auditory recognizability. Category 1 (cognitive availability) determining variables include many partial definitions, such as frequency,

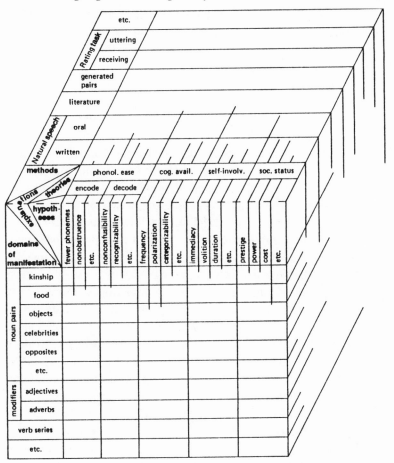

Figure 9.2
The research parallelepiped: Conceptual space within which a program of
research, such as that on word-order regularities, can be developed.

recency, meaningfulness, retrievability, categorizability, and polarization. Category 2 (affective charge) includes variables such as evaluation, closeness to self, relevance to current needs and to enduring values, and personal involvement. Variables in the social-status Category
3 include partial definitions such as power, cost, prestige, and ethical
status. As regards the two classes of phonological determinants, Category 4, vocalization ease, implies that primacy will go up with such
factors as the label's brevity, the nonobstruance of its phonemes, and its

articulatory simplicity. Category 5, auditory recognizability variables, includes factors such as the familiarity of the terms' phonemes, their nonconfusibility, and the distinctiveness of their features. These five categories are not independent and the variables in each have interaction as well as main effects on word-order primacy.

Multiple methods of data collection.   On the third edge of the Figure 9.2 research space, its depth dimension, are listed various methods of data collection such as reactive ratings, pair generation, concordances of canonical literature, and natural speech. The reactive rating method, the most efficient but also artificial of the four, presents the respondents with pairs of expressions varying only in the ordering of two kin terms (for example, "They like their aunt and uncle" versus "They like their uncle and aunt"), and the respondent is asked which of the two expressions sounds better or which is usually used. A second method, pair generation, yields productive rather than reactive data by asking participants to generate as many commonly paired kin terms as they can think of in the form "They like their kin x and kin y." Our third source of word-order data comes from the works of seventeenth- to twentieth-century English-language writers sufficiently canonical for a substantial portion of their work to have been made available in concordances in which each word used by the author is listed in alphabetical order in the context of the several preceding and following words, allowing easy calculation of, say, that author's number of "aunt and uncle" versus "uncle and aunt" usages. Because our authors span four centuries, these concordances allow us to trace historical changes in primacy in formal language production. Our fourth data-collection method analyzes word order in informal natural speech or writing samples. We have collected a data bank of thousands of naturally occurring kin-pair expressions in children's 3-minute free responses to a "Tell us about your family" probe.

Effects of Five Categories of Variables
on Kin-Pair Primacy

To conserve space, the effects of variables in each of the five hypothesized independent-variable categories will be reported only for kin-pair noun data obtained by reactive ratings. We shall mention results obtained by other methods (pair generation, natural speech, and concordanced literature) and other domains (food pairs or adjective series) only when these other data are needed for clarification.

Method in the reactive study. The kin-pair rating data were obtained by mailing a questionnaire to 650 persons selected at random from directories for four widely separated counties in the United States, of whom 163 returned by post the completed questionnaire (a 25% usable return rate). The questionnaire included 68 pairs of simple sentences, each pair made up of opposite orderings of a kin pair (for example, "Their niece and nephew like them" and "Their nephew and niece like them"). Half of the respondents rated which of the two paired expressions "sounds better"; the other half, which "you would usually say." The verb *like* was used in half of the sentence pairs and *know* was used in the other half. In half of the sentences the kin pair appeared as the subjects, and in the other half as the objects of the sentences. For half of the pairs the rater checked off the preferred sentence of the pair; for the other half the rater wrote out the preferred sentence. We shall report the effects of these counterbalanced method variables, and of dispositional variables like respondent's sex and age, only when they make a clarifying significant difference in the preferred ordering of the kin pairs. The 68 kin pairs that the respondents rated on the questionnaire (two of which were repeats for a reliability check) included all the 13 basic English kin terms (mother, father, . . . cousin) plus some generic terms (parent, spouse, relatives, etc.) and some compounds (grandfather, son-in-law, etc.).

Semantic variables affecting word-order primacy. Multiple variables in each of the three hypothesized semantic categories sizably affected primacy. Kinship-pair primacy correlated positively and significantly with a wide range of cognitive-availability measures, including frequency of English usage (Thorndike & Lorge, 1944; Kučera & Francis, 1967), the activity (but not the potency) score on the semantic differential (Osgood, Suci, & Tannenbaum, 1957), the Toglia and Battig (1978) categorizability score, and a meaning polarization score calculated across the latters' six cognitive scales.

The influence of the Category 2 affective-charge variables in increasing kin-pair primacy can be illustrated by the effects of two interestingly contrasting variables: genetic closeness and voluntariness of the relationship. Evolutionary theorizing suggests that attachment and therefore retrieval primacy should increase with genetic closeness. Among our 66 rated kin pairs, the members of 13 pairs satisfied the criteria of same-sex and differing genetic closeness. In 12 of these 13 relevant kin pairs there was a sizable ($p < .05$) preference for saying the pair with the genetically closer-related kin first (e.g., "father and grandfather" is preferred by 93% of the raters, "uncle and nephew" by 81%, etc.). (Here an ordering split more asymmetrical than .41 versus .59 is significant at the .05 level.) A second hypothesized Category 2 affective-charge variable, volitional choice in the relationship, presents an interesting contrast. Because between two kin terms the one involving closer genetic relationship tends to be said first, it might be expected that genetically related kin in general would have primacy over nongenetic significant others. On the contrary, in all 14 pairs that included a genetic and an unrelated (voluntarily chosen) significant other, the voluntarily chosen, genetically unrelated significant other (spouse, friend, etc.) came first by a wide margin, as in "friends and relatives" (62%) and "wife and son" (76%). One's spouse, while genetically unrelated to the self, is clearly the closest kin there is by the criterion of primacy (e.g., "wife and daughter" [94%], "husband and brother" [80%]). Volition's enhancement of primacy is much greater (in all six relevant pairs) for within-sex than for between-sex pairs (e.g., "wife and sister" [91%] vs. "wife and brother" [60%]), suggesting that for opposite-sex pairs the primacy choice may already have been made on the basis of sex, before voluntariness came into consideration. This and other findings reported below suggest that the primacy decision may be made on a stepwise variable-by-variable procedure rather than by a multivariable weighted decision process.

Category 3 (social status) variables' effects on primacy in kin pairs can be illustrated by age and sex. On the assumption that generational seniority confers status, respect, and power on a family member, we predicted that the older kin would have primacy of mention. For all 17 pairs in which members were of different generations but were related equally closely to the reference person, the older member was mentioned first, for example, "father and son" was preferred over "son and father" by 97% of the raters, "mother and daughter" (preferred by 93%), and "mother and son" (preferred by 93%). Seniority enhances primacy also outside the family, but not as strongly as within: "man and girl" (77%), "adult and child" (73%), "Mrs. and Miss" (67%), "Mrs. and Ms." (68%), suggesting that age confers status more strongly within the family than in broader society.

On the assumption that males dominate society and exercise more power within the family, a further Category 3 prediction is that there would be male primacy in kinship pairs. However, of the 21 pairs that satisfied the criteria of having members of the same generation and same degree of relationship but of different sexes, 12 were preferred with male first and 9 with female first. Although there was little male primacy overall, individual pairs did tend to manifest highly asymmetrical sex-primacy preferences in one or the other direction. There was pronounced male primacy within spouse, offspring, and sibling pairings, for example, "husband and wife" (87%), "son and daughter" (79%), and "brother and sister" (77%). However, there was a pronounced female primacy in parental and avuncular pairings, "mom and dad" (82%), "niece and nephew" (80%), and "aunt and uncle" (76%). Outside the family male primacy is more pronounced: "Mr. and Mrs." (98%), "male and female" (93%), "sir and madam" (74%). The broader society, more than the family, appears to be a man's world.

Phonemic variables affecting word-order primacy. Our Category 4 of theorized determinants, the label's vocalization ease, was suggested by Panini, the Sanskrit grammarian who first studied this word-order phenomenon two and a half millennia ago. Panini's "law" asserts that in such discretionary word pairs one tends to say the shorter first. Panini's law is supported by our obtained $-.31$ correlation ($p < .05$) between number of syllables and primacy among the kin terms that appeared on the rating questionnaire. However, the kin-pair domain is a poor one in which to test the role of word length because in the most frequently paired kin terms (except for avuncular pairs) labels of both members have the same number of syllables in English. The more length-varying food-pair comparisons show that shorter food terms tend to be said first (e.g., among vegetables, people say "peas and carrots" [92%] but "carrots and celery" [95%]). Other Category 4 ease-of-vocalization variables found to enhance primacy are labels starting with vowels rather than consonants, and starting with less obstruent and fewer consonants.

Category 5, auditory recognizability variables, are theorized to enhance word-order primacy for the adaptive reason that hearing the more recognizable label first provides a context that facilitates recognition of the less clear, later label. Recognizability's partial operational definitions include distinctiveness of the phonemes (as regards their formants, their places and manner of articulation, etc.), their nonconfusibility, and the familiarity of the label's sounds. In our kin pairs, recognizability-enhancing familiarity – such as English-language frequency of initial phonemes – did contribute to primacy. A challengeable theoretical complication is how variables from the five categories are interrelated. For example, as Zipf's laws would suggest, a label's frequency (a Category 5 variable) tends to be confounded with its brevity (a Category 4 variable). Needed next are factor analyses (probably oblique) to identify a small set of variables that efficiently map each of the five categories.

Research on Primacy Decision Processes and Interactions

A second phase of our research program investigates theoretically interesting ways in which variables in the five categories interact with one another and with situational or dispositional variables in determining word-order primacy. For variety we shall illustrate interaction effects mainly with data collected by the other three methods – generated pairs, natural speech, and formal literature.

Weighting models versus decision by aspect.   Needing clarification is the cognitive algebra operating in cases when several variables (from the same or different categories) vary simultaneously and push primacy between the pair's members in opposite directions. For example, when "spouse" and "parent" are paired, the Category 2 volitional variable predicts spousal priority, while the Category 3 age-seniority status variable predicts parental primacy. One combinatory possibility is a weighted regression model such that the effects of each of the determinants varying between the pair's members is factored in, each weighted by the members' difference on it and by currently relevant dispositional and situational conditions affecting the dimension's weighting (analogous to a full subjective-expected-utility decision model). Alternatively, there might be a stepwise decision process establishing primacy on one variable at a time until a sufficing criterion is reached (analogous to a simplified, one-aspect-at-a-time decision model). For example, Category 3 (sociocultural status) variables like age seniority may be determining in formal or abstract circumstances, and the Category 2 (affective charge) variables like volitional choice may be determining in more concrete, affectively involving circumstances. Supporting this prediction is that when abstract generic-category terms like "parent" and "spouse" are used, then age-seniority (Category 3) dominates primacy, with 73% preferring the "parent and spouse" ordering. However, when concrete terms focusing on individuals are used (wife, husband, mother, etc.) then the Category 2 volitional variable dominates primacy, with 60% of the respondents preferring "wife and mother." Likewise for parental terms: In informal situations where fond names are used, then the female parent, who scores higher on Category 2 affective charge, comes first (e.g., "mom and dad" [82%]); where in circumstances in which formal terms are used, "father and mother," the male parent comes first, reflecting his greater Category 3 socioeconomic status.

Nontransitivity and other logical peculiarities in primacy. Word-order data show intriguing departures from simple logical relations. Nontransitivity of kin-pair orderings is common in natural-language free descriptions of one's family, as illustrated by orderings of "mother," "father," and "sister." "Mother and father" is the preferred order in 80% of the parent pairings occurring in oral and written family descriptions, and "father and sister" is the order used in 79% of their pairings. Hence for transitivity one would expect "mother" to have a great primacy over "sister"; but, on the contrary, the reverse "sister and mother" order is used in 59% (p < .05) of the pairings. Comparable intransitivity is found in the mother-father-brother triad. Such nontransitivities may reflect a decision-by-dimension cognitive algebra, with the order of entering different determinants changing with contexts (in this example, when we go from different- to same-sex pairs).

A similar decisional process may be operating in the previously mentioned primacy of volitionally chosen over genetically given significant others. This volitional primacy is considerably stronger when the two kin are of the same sex (e.g., "wife and sister" is preferred in 91% of their joint uses); but when of the opposite sex (e.g., "wife and brother") it is preferred by only 60%. Similarly, in the same sex, the "husband and brother" ordering is preferred by 80% but "husband and sister" by only 53%. It may be that when there is a sex difference between members of the pair, speakers tend to make retrieval-primacy decisions on the basis of sex, paying little attention to the volitional variable; but when both members are of the same sex, the ordering decision is made on the basis of volition.

Interestingly, nontransitivities like this illustrative mother-father-sister case, although appearing strongly in informal natural speech samples, do not occur in the more deliberative formal literary data, where the concordanced literature shows a predominant (89%) "father and mother" ordering (reflecting a Category 3 status determination) as contrasted to the opposite 80% "mother and father" ordering in informal speech (reflecting the Category 2 personal-attachment determination over status determination). Hence, the mother-father-sister triad shows primacy transitivity in formal literature, in contrast to the pronounced intransitivity shown in spontaneous, uncensored informal oral or written accounts of one's family.

Another type of primacy asymmetry can be illustrated by word orderings of parents and siblings. In natural speech pairings the male parent has primacy ($p < .01$) over siblings ("father and brother" [72%], "father and sister" [79%]); however, siblings have primacy ($p < .05$) over the female parent ("sister and mother" [59%], "brother and mother" [58%]). This asymmetry, surprising in itself, is especially paradoxical because when the two parents are paired with one another in natural speech "mother" has strong (80%) primacy over "father," suggesting that any asymmetry should go in the direction opposite to that found. Such paradoxical reversals may reflect contrasting contexts in which these different kin pairs tend to be mentioned in natural speech.

Communicating by violating primacy conventions. Listeners probably infer little about a speaker's meaning when the utterance follows conventional word ordering but may draw inferences from violations of the usual ordering. For example, when polar opposite terms are paired, the socially desirable one is typically said first ("good and evil," "rich and poor," "life and death," etc.). Hence, when the sheriff's reward poster announces "Wanted: dead or alive," his nonstandard ordering may be communicating that he would prefer to receive the desperado in a moribund condition.

Obtained Interaction Effects

Methods interactions. In this research program each of our four supplementary methods of gathering kin-pair primacy data has been used with variations. For example, in the reactive rating tasks the kin pairs were used with cognitive and affective verbs ("know" and "like"); the generating-pairs task asked separately for frequently and infrequently paired terms; free descriptions involved responding in written versus oral modes; concordanced literature involved contemporary authors versus those from several centuries back. This multimethod approach provides both useful methodological information (e.g., whether simpler artificial data-collection methods may be safely substituted for more onerous natural ones) and also substantive information (e.g., how methods variables such as formality or historical period interact with variables from the five categories in determining primacy).

Primacy differences as a function of formality.   Primacy within the parental kin pair represents the resolution of conflicting determinants. Maleness, a Category 3 status determinant, would incline toward paternal primacy, "father and mother," whereas the Category 2 affective-attachment determinant would incline toward maternal primacy. The data show that the male-primacy (Category 3) status determinant is stronger in formal circumstances (as in "Honor thy father and mother"), while the maternal-attachment intimacy (Category 2) determinant will operate more powerfully with intimate terms where affection is more salient ("mom and pop store"). Four methods manipulated formality of context across four levels: (1) least formal usage was to score primacy in parental pairing occurring during oral or written natural descriptions of one's family; (2) a step more formal was to ask respondents to judge which sounded better between pairs of sentences containing contrasting orderings; (3) still more formal was the two parental orderings in modern (nineteenth- and twentieth-century) literature; and (4) most formal, the orderings in seventeenth- and eighteenth-century classical literature. Across these four levels of increasing formality, the proportion of parental pairs in the more formal "father and mother" paternal primacy ordering increased sharply and steadily ($p < .001$) from 20%, to 47%, to 82%, to 96%. A second confirmed formality prediction is that maternal primacy is higher ($p < .05$) when the affectionate "mom and dad" terms were used than with "mother and father" at each level of data-collection formality (e.g., in oral and written free accounts of one's family, 20% of all parental pairings using the formal terms are in the male primacy "father and mother" order, while only 12% of all pairings using the affectionate terms are in the male primacy "dad and mom" order).

Historical changes in word-order primacy.   On the assumption that family relations in England and the United States have grown more egalitarian over the past several centuries, we predicted that Category 3 status variables, such as male and age primacy, would be less determining in the literature of recent centuries than of earlier ones. Our concordance data on seventeenth- and eighteenth-century English-language authors versus nineteenth- and twentieth-century authors do show a reliable decline in male primacy. For example, the proportion of "father and mother" ordering has declined ($p < .05$) from 89% to 71%, and the proportion of "brother and sister" ordering is down from 86% to 64%. However, the literature concordance data show no decline in the age-seniority primacy (e.g., the "father and son" order remains constant at about 90% across these four centuries). The demographic changes underlying the youth culture may be too recent to be reflected in such modern literature as has entered the Establishment canon sufficiently to be availably concordanced.

Speaker characteristics as they affect word-order primacy. That word-order regularities stabilize early in life is shown by the finding that variation in speaker's age from 6 to 70 years has little effect on primacy within kin pairs. Speaker's sex produces a slight Category 2 egocentric, own-sex bias (e.g., the "mother and father" ordering is preferred by 58% of female raters and only 46% of male; and "mom and dad" is preferred by 86% of the females and 76% of the males). This own-sex primacy bias is stronger in actual-speech data than in rating data, perhaps because of better monitoring and purging the egocentric own-sex bias in one's reactive ratings than in one's spontaneous speech.

Future Directions

Future research on primacy in other word domains. Further word-order primacy issues and opportunities arise as we go from kin pairs to food pairs and especially to adjective series. Between kin pairs and the food pairs many of the determinants in the three semantic categories correspond analogously. For example, the Category 2 kin variable of affectionate attraction may correspond to the food variable of flavorfulness; the Category 3 kin variables of power and status may correspond to the food variables of nutritional value and price. Finding more abstract generic variables that embrace analogous variables from kin and food domains can advance one's grasp of the deeper psychological significance of each variable. Some variables can be studied better in the food than in the kin domain, for example, Categories 4 and 5 phonological variables, because commonly paired food terms vary more on phonological characteristics than do usually paired kin terms.

One can also investigate the operation of new factors with the food pairs. Ordinarily in food pairs meats are said before nonmeats ("ham and eggs," "franks and beans"); but if the nonmeat has been transformed by human effort, it may gain in primacy (e.g., "deviled eggs and ham," "baked beans and franks"). This could reflect either the operation of a Lévi-Straussian raw/cooked, nature/culture dimension, or a Ricardo/Marxist labor theory of value, between which we can test by cross-varying transformed versus nontransformed foods with cases where the transformation adds ("poached") versus subtracts ("overcooked") value. Other issues raised by food pairs include the need to account for the high primacy of fruits, the low primacy of vegetables, and the middling primacy of sweets.

Future research on primacy in adjective series. Primacy in adjective series, such as people's almost unanimous tendency to say "old oaken bucket" and "dirty old man" rather than "oaken old bucket" and "old dirty man," we theorize to reflect quite different thought processes from those which determine primacy in noun pairs. We find that primacy declines progressively across the six adjective classes of number, size, evaluation, time, sensory quality, and materials, as in "The agent sold three large dilapidated old white stucco houses." This abstract-to-concrete ordering seems a maladaptive communication strategy because starting with the most abstract adjectives aggravates their vagueness. The reverse ordering of saying the more concrete, imaginable adjectives first would have provided needed context for specifying later-coming abstract adjectives.

A possible explanation is that the hearer stores the successive adjectives in a push-down list until the noun arrives and then retrieves the adjectives for processing relative to the noun with a last-in, first-out ordering. This implies that the privileged position for adjectives is not primacy in vocalization but closeness to noun, and by implication that the preferred ordering of adjectives may reverse when they follow rather than precede the noun, for example, 74% of respondents prefer "The handsome young man escaped" ordering over "The young handsome man escaped." However, when the adjectives follow the noun they modify, the preference reverses, with 92% of the respondents preferring "The man, young and handsome, escaped" over "The man, handsome and young, escaped." This push-down stacking (with its last-in, first-out processing) may account also for other ordering oddities in communication, such as people's tendency to describe the location of an object in an inefficient inside-out sequence, as by saying

"You will find the scissors under some papers on the left side of the top drawer of the cabinet in the dining room," directions that are puzzlingly inefficient because the first-named clues provide little guidance until the later ones are heard. Such a communication strategy would be reasonable if such information were processed by temporary storage in a push-down list. In an organized research program, relations that start out as questions tend to become answers. This research began by asking which hypothesized variables affect word-order primacy; as answers become clearer, word-order primacy can be increasingly used to throw light on other processes.

AN OBSERVATION REGARDING THE
DIVERSITY OF MY LINES OF WORK

In this and other chapters I have urged psychologists to pay more attention to the strategic planning of whole programs of research rather than just to the tactics of planning the individual experiment; and chapter 12 describes a perspectivist psychology of science that facilitates doing such programmatic planning in place of jumping around from one isolated study to another. It may seem inconsistent that my lines of research, as described in this and the preceding chapters, have been quite diverse. Although it is true that engaging in diverse lines of work sometimes does indicate an unorganized jumping around from one isolated study to another, my approach has been to do an organized program of work on each of my lines of research. Perhaps symptomatic of my diversity-plus-depth style is that I have become a member of nine varied divisions of the American Psychological Association and have subsequently been elected a fellow in all nine of them, probably a rare (perhaps even unique) broadness of fellow-level contribution in the APA. Most of my colleagues who have been aware of one or two of my programmatic lines of work have not known that I carried out substantial programs of research in many other areas.

10

Psychology and History

More than most research psychologists, I have provided historical analyses and theoretical integrations of the topics I investigate. Such broad contributions are only moderately prized and can even be injurious to the health of one's reputation. Several members of the psychological *nomenklatura* have asked me why a smart guy like me bothers with this history and theoretical integration stuff. I have explained, if not excused, this predilection in terms of peculiar values inculcated by my atypical educational background. The tradition of the new has long been central to the mainstream American research university, shaping scholars hungry to publish unprecedented innovations. In contrast, the Catholic university of my youth inculcated the tradition of continuity, encouraging one to find adumbrations of one's insights in past contributions. An example is the distinctiveness principle, developed in chapter 8, that one notices not what is there but what is missing, so that complex stimuli like the self are selectively perceived in terms of their peculiar (unpredictable, information-rich, distinctive) features. I reported foreshadowings of this principle in other thinkers stretching from the Upanishads, through Duns Scotus, Nicholas of Cusa, and the Lurian Cabala, to Buber, Pavlov, Lashley, and G. A. Miller (McGuire, 1984a; see chapter 8 in this volume). My aberrant schooling encouraged the use of creativity to discover, not the uniqueness of one's insight, but its enriching connectedness. This chapter presents as examples my interpretive histories of social psychology and of political psychology, and then a discussion of the use of historical data in psychology.

THE VICISSITUDES OF ATTITUDES
IN SOCIAL PSYCHOLOGY

[Adapted with permission from W. J. McGuire, 1985a.]

The Prehistory of Attitude Research

Our moment in history has been given many names – just to start at the top of the alphabet, the atomic age, Atlantic age, automobile age, aspirin age, age of alienation, of anxiety, of affluence, and, most pertinent here, the age of advertising. Currently, tremendous efforts are being made to influence attitudes and actions via persuasive communication. Advertisers spend over $150 billion annually in the United States and political candidates over a half-billion more. Mammon and Caesar share the channels with God, with 14% of radio stations and a whole television network being devoted exclusively to evangelizing Christianity (Hadden & Swann, 1981). Ubiquitous public-service ads urge us to save our bodies as well as our souls by using seat belts or not using cigarettes, getting our grandchildren immunized against polio or our grandparents diagnosed for hypertension. Appeals are made even to our altruism, urging us at some personal sacrifice to save the wolf, the whale, or the sand darter, to conserve energy, eschew littering, desist from burning the forests or the Bronx, and to contribute to the United Fund or Amnesty International (Rice & Atkin, 1989).

Ever since the neolithic revolution gave rise to community and consciousness (Jaynes, 1977), skill in using words persuasively to resolve conflicts or to mobilize effort has been a useful human asset (Lasswell, Lerner, & Speier, 1980). The current clamorous cacophony might suggest that human society has always been this argumentative, but actually open societies like ours have been rare in the three millennia of European/Middle Eastern history (Popper, 1945). Persuasion has been the key mode of social control and effort mobilization in only four scattered centuries: the Periclean Hellenic period, the final century of the Roman Republic, the humanistic Renaissance, and our own mass-media century. Persuasion was commonly used at other times and places (Thompson, 1977), having been a prevalent aspect of Christianity since the preaching of Christ and Saint Paul (Wilder, 1964; Forman, 1979; E. Cohen, 1981). Oratory has flourished in several periods of Chinese and Indian history (Oliver, 1971; A. F. Wright, 1979) and in many preliterate societies (Bloch, 1975; Vincent, 1978). However, only in the four centuries mentioned has persuasion played so central an economic, social, and political role as to have become not just an art but an essential craft (in whose rules of thumb the elite youth were trained), and even a recognized science with a systemized body of empirical theory.

[Adapted with permission from W. J. McGuire, 1986a, The vicissitudes of attitudes and similar representational constructs in twentieth-century psychology, *European Journal of Social Psychology, 16,* pp. 89–130. Copyright © 1986 by John Wiley & Sons Ltd.]

After two-and-a-half millennia of prehistory as an art (carried out intuitively by gifted virtuosos), persuasion has in the past century evolved into a craft (practiced by technicians who have mastered rules of thumb during an apprenticeship) and even to a science (guided by hypotheses derived from explicit, tested theoretical principles). As a science, persuasive communication and attitude research have had three flourishings in the twentieth century: a 1920s and 1930s era concerned with attitude measurement, a 1950s and 1960s era studying attitude change, and a 1980s and 1990s era devoted to attitude systems. These three eras of social psychology were separated by the 1935–55 group dynamics interregnum and the 1965–85 social cognition interregnum.

If we take Wundt's founding of his Leipzig Psychologische Institut in 1879 as the marker event from which to date empirical psychology's birth as a separate discipline (Boring, 1929/1950; Farr, 1983, 1996), then social psychology is a generation younger than the parent discipline, born with the new century marked by Wundt's (1900–20) *Völkerpsychologie* and the concurrent appearance of the first two textbooks explicitly called *Social Psychology,* one by a sociologist (Ross, 1908) and the other by a psychologist (McDougall, 1908). Social psychological research developed rapidly, so that by the 1920s one of its major foci, attitude scaling, was recognized as a cutting edge across the whole spectrum of psychology. The section that follows describes the progress of social psychology over this succession of five overlapping periods.

The Attitude-Measurement Flourishing in the 1920s and 1930s

Social psychology catapulted into respectability during the 1920s and 1930s when methodologists such as Bogardus (1925), Thurstone and Chave (1929), and Likert (1932) developed scaling procedures to measure social propensities such as religiosity, ethnic prejudice, and political conservatism. Number manipulation evokes admiration and aversion, its difficult abstractions lending it an elitist cachet for the initiates while repelling arithmophobes. The use of social attitudes as the 1920s measurement models raised the scientific respectability of attitude study and of social psychology in general.

The measurement of mind. The 1920s attitude scalers, grappling with the problems and possibilities of measuring subjective states, sensitized perspicacious psychologists to the need for better measurement of variables to allow theories to evolve beyond impoverished null-hypothesis testing of simplistic rectilinear relations, although they fell short of suggesting the desirability of developing measures of the variables and of the relation between them simultaneously, within a single experimental design, as in later conjoint (Luce & Tukey, 1964) and functional (Anderson, 1982) measurement. A secondary focus of this first 1920s–1930s flourishing was on attitudes' relation to actions (LaPiere, 1934), the modesty of which relation has long been the scandal of social psychology.

By the end of the 1930s the creative momentum of this great leap forward in attitude measurement research was ebbing and social psychology's central enthusiasm was shifting from attitudes to group processes. Interesting advances have continued to be made subsequently on attitude measurement (e.g., Lazarsfeld's latent structure, Guttman's scalogram, and Coomb's data theory approaches); on multiple indices (S. W. Cook and Selltiz, 1964); on nonreactive measures (Webb, Campbell, Schwartz, & Sechrest, 1966; Sechrest & Belew, 1983); on internal and external validation (Campbell & Stanley, 1963; T. D. Cook & Campbell, 1979); on Fishbein's theory of reasoned action and Anderson's functional measurement; and on multiple paths and physiological pattern indices (Cacioppo & Petty, 1983, 1986). However, after the 1930s measurement issues never again dominated social psychology, or even its attitude subdomain.

Distinctive attitudes and collective representations. There is a witticism that psychologists have made two great discoveries, that all people are basically the same and that everyone is fundamentally different. It was exhibited in these early years by the simultaneous popularity of the Wundtian *Völkerpsychologie* and Durkheimian *représentations collectives* notions on the Continent, while the Spearman, Bogardus, and Thurstone individual-differences scaling work flourished in the Anglo-American offshore provinces. The two efforts are supplementary in that collective representationalists focus on within-group homogeneity and among-group contrasts, whereas individual-difference attitudinalists focus on variability both within and among groups. The Saussurian notion that perception basically involves making distinctions applies to both. Members of a culture tend to be unaware of their own shared representations until contrasted with an alternative representation shared by members of their outgroups, as in the maxim "The fish are the last ones to discover the ocean."

Causes of fluctuations in topic popularity: Internal factors cooling the old enthusiasm. This first attitude-measurement era, like the subsequent four social psychological enthusiasms, each waxing and waning over a 20-year cycle, declined due to forces both internal and external to the movement. Internal factors stifling the old enthusiasm tend to be virtues carried to excess, such as conceptual overelaboration, excessive practical application, and hyperquantification. Conceptual analysis is needed for clarity, but definitions and distinctions tend to be elaborated by initiates until the accumulation becomes a jungle of jargon to outsiders and a stultifying distraction to initiates. G. W. Allport's (1935) pages of conceptual analysis of "attitudes" in his handbook chapter are a scholarly tour de force, but also a moribund albatross that weighs down rather than gives flight to thought.

Practical application, a second excess, is also a Good Thing like 1066 and all that, but tends to play a zero-sum game with basic research in psychology. Attitude studies (or other intellectual activities) hardly constitute so popular a spectator sport that just watching our research virtuosity affords the public sufficient return for the taxes they are charged to support it. Nevertheless, as applications grow, a topic seems to lose panache for creative basic researchers and attracts instead entrepreneurial types gifted with political acumen rather than research talent. Basic researchers moved out of attitude measurement as political activists began to apply it to controversial variables such as birth control, atheism, conservatism, and racial hostility; then marketing and advertising researchers applied it to purveying goods and services; and finally, in the 1940s, Doctor Win-the-War (Stouffer, 1950; Lumsdaine, 1984) applied it to wars, first hot and then cold.

A third excess of virtue that dampened the 1920s–1930s attitude-measurement flourishing is the increasing quantification that encumbers researchers with tedious and intimidating analytical procedures.

Quantification was the prime purpose and a lasting legacy of this era, but the elegant precision with which attitudes came to be measured isolated them in a golden ghetto because few other psychological variables could be measured with a comparable elegance that would entitle them to enter into hypothetical relations with attitudes. Premature quantification is a common danger in disciplines with unevenly developing subfields. Poincaré has argued (but see Truesdell, 1980) that thermodynamics might have developed more rapidly in the nineteenth century had it been investigated on the qualitative levels that would have sufficed to resolve points then at issue; but the precise measurement standards to which mechanics and motions had accustomed physicists inhibited them from studying thermodynamics on the poorly quantified level that was feasible and sufficing, and so the field was neglected until precise measurement became possible. That the periodic focusings of the scientific Establishment on certain "high table" topics tend to bear within themselves the seeds of their own destruction is probably beneficial to the long-term progress of a discipline.

External forces shaping the new enthusiasm.   The transition of enthusiasms in a discipline involves, besides these internal factors (typically excesses of virtues) that bring down the old topic, also external factors (from other disciplines and general social conditions) that shape the new replacement enthusiasms. The earlier 1920s–1930s attitude measurement enthusiasm had occurred in response to the early century's massive immigrations to the United States from eastern and southern Europe, which provoked a felt need for assimilation, and by its intervention in the 1914–18 Great War, which sharpened realization of the diversity within a melting-pot society and heightened concern to find a public-opinion consensus that could give direction to the maturing society's energies.

The 1935–1955 Group-Dynamics Interlude

In the 1930s society became increasingly conscious of sin, a series of disturbing realities having destabilized Europe and America in the two decades that intervened between the World Wars. Nationalistic and class antagonisms intensified even to the removals and exterminations of peoples, and economies deteriorated into inflation, stock-market crashes, unemployment, and poverty, resulting in loss of faith in the old guidelines and decay of hope for a future in which loomed the foreseeable cataclysm of the 1937–45 war. Static attitude-measurement studies were shelved for the more urgent task of discovering ways to control and redirect social action. Shamed by the Marxian challenge, social psychologists became impatient with describing public opinion and took on the task of changing it. When the long-threatening war erupted with the 1937 Japanese invasion of China and the 1939 invasion of Poland by Germany and the Soviet Union, the need was made still more evident by the war's extensiveness and ferocity, with its undeclared incursions, unrelenting aerial attacks on massed civilian populations, brutal military occupations and their collaborationist and resistance reactions, and the obscenity of methodical mass murder in the death camps. The postwar survivors emerged in a state of stunned wonder about the group processes that had permitted and even promoted these recent horrors. The response had to await infrastructure reconstruction in the ravaged countries of Europe; but in the United States, which had been spared physical damage, social psychologists went to work soon after precipitous demobilization.

Social psychology's group-dynamics response. The group-dynamics movement that became social psychology's cutting edge in the decades around the 1937–45 war was an apt response to these external needs. Much of the excitement emanated from researchers associated with Kurt Lewin (Back, 1972), who himself switched from cognitive and developmental psychology to group-decision work in response to war needs. After the war and his early death in 1947, his interpersonal research was carried on by his disciples, including Festinger, Cartwright, Deutsch, Bavelas, Schachter, and Kelley, who made small-group dynamics the most exciting topic of social psychological research until well into the 1950s. These Lewinians, along with some non-Lewinians (Sherif, 1935; Newcomb, 1943; Asch, 1956), studied interpersonal processes such as shared norms, cohesiveness, conformity, productivity, leadership style, power, communication networks, social influence, cooperation and competition, and occasionally intergroup processes. Much of this group-dynamics research now appears banal conceptually and naive empirically; but after witnessing the terrible events that laissez-faire and authoritarian modes of social organization had failed to prevent, contemporary researchers did their best to find a way in which people could achieve self-realization within benign collectivist constraints.

Group-processes research was hegemonic in 1935–55, although good research was done during these years on other topics and good research on groups was done earlier and later. Even in these "group-dynamics" decades good research on attitudes (increasingly on their determinants rather than their measurement) was already being reported (Hovland, Lumsdaine, & Sheffield, 1949; Adorno et al., 1950; Smith, Bruner, & White, 1956). Worthwhile research had been done earlier on both "hot" and "cold" group processes, that is, effects both within dynamically interacting groups (G. Watson, 1928; Bechterev, 1928/1932) and effects involving mere copresence (F. Allport, 1920; Moede, 1920; Dashiell, 1935). After the 1935–55 group-dynamics hegemony respectable research has continued to be done on various group topics such as risky shift (Cartwright, 1971), minority influence (Moscovici, 1976; Papastamou, 1983), and jury decision-making (Hastie, Penrod, & Pennington, 1984). However, it was only during the 1935–55 period that group processes research held center stage as the main focus of social psychological attention. It is odd that a field called "social" psychology has so seldom focused on inter-group or interpersonal processes. Even Lewinians (e.g., Festinger and Schachter) soon shifted their research to intrapersonal processes.

Decline of the group-dynamics movement.   Forces dampening the enthusiasm for this group-dynamics research are similar to those that had led to the decline of the preceding era's attitude-measurement movement: (*a*) internal forces in the form of excesses of virtues such as conceptual clarification, practical application, and methodological elegance that brought down the existing group-dynamics movement; and (*b*) external factors that shaped the replacement, attitude-change research enthusiasm. The intricate refinements of terms like *cohesiveness, power,* or *leadership* by the group mavens are intellectual achievements, but mastering this vocabulary constitutes a formidable initiation fee for potential recruits. That the group-dynamics movement derived from the "practical theorist" Kurt Lewin (Marrow, 1969) gave it from the start dual basic and applied aspects (Back, 1972), but basic researchers in the Lewinian tradition kept their distance from NTL Bethel-type encounter groups and sensitivity training practitioners. There were intimidating advances also in methodology, such as graph theory analysis (Cartwright & Harary, 1956; Flament, 1963) and elegant apparatus to provide complex communication networks or individually tailored false feedback (Crutchfield, 1955; Deutsch &

Krauss, 1960), so that cutting-edge work began to require technical expertise and an equipment budget.

Origins of some present discontents. Mention should be made here of an interaction between time and place in the evolution of social psychology. In dating the group-dynamics era as extending from 1935 to 1955 I am referring to the North American setting; in Europe the enthusiasm lagged a decade behind. The devastation of the 1937–45 war left Europe with infrastructure rebuilding tasks far more urgent than revitalizing the social sciences. Losses due to intellectual emigration and the need to rebuild left the European social sciences susceptible to U.S. contributions, at first welcomed, but evoking understandable resentment in the long run. As the group-dynamics interest waned in the United States during the 1950s, its Lewinian promoters were seized by a missionary fervor to find European markets to which to export their insights. Meanwhile, the pioneers developing the new U.S. attitude-change enthusiasm were too preoccupied in the sellers' market at home to embark on foreign adventures. Thus the declining Lewinian movement gained uncontested control of funding sources for foreign proselytizing, mainly channeled through U.S. private-sector agencies such as the Ford Foundation and the Social Science Research Council (the latter was particularly prone to domination by narrow factions), and through the U.S. Office of Naval Research. Predictably, by the late 1960s the most favored European social psychologists who had at first welcomed the missionaries (or at least the gifts they bore) became embarrassed by their acceptance of this cultural colonization and disenchanted with the obsolescent models that had been foisted upon them. A number of European social psychologists of that generation endeavored in the 1965 to 1985 period to promote a more distinctively European social psychology, forged out of everything from a Marxist-Leninist historical materialism to a Durkheimian collective representational idealism (Israel & Tajfel, 1972).

This nationalistic reaction is understandable but carries a warning and a consolation. Critics overly sensitive to a *foetor Americanus* should be warned that intellectuals who become reactively caught up in opposing an exogenous system are in danger of ending up coopted by it, because they introject its assumptions to define themselves by contrast and to argue against it in its own terms. In the case of a Marx struggling against a Hegel, or a Sartre contending against a Kant, the tragedy is lessened in that the rebel is at least ensnared by a colossus;

but the revolting nationalists of reactionary European social psychology, too preoccupied with demonstrating their distinctiveness from an archaic Lewinian remnant, risk ending up hopelessly entwined with a Lilliputian. Overly concerned with establishing their distinctiveness from moribund U.S. work on group dynamics (or attitude change, dissonance, attribution, or whatever), these reactionary factions end up with trivial antitheses to the trivial theses from which they are trying to distance themselves. Rather than jousting against abandoned windmills they might better devote their talents to the third, structuralist, attitudinal flourishing in the 1980s and 1990s as it struggles to describe knowledge constructions of experienced life.

It may be some consolation to these reactionaries that, in being proselytized by U.S. Lewinian remnants in the 1950s and 1960s, Europe was being given back its own rather than being indoctrinated with a foreign gospel. The inspiration for group-dynamics research was not Lower-48 tribal secrets whispered by the last of the Mohicans to some Ann Arbor psychologists on the banks of the mighty Huron River. Rather, group research (like the Californian grape rootstock repatriated in 1900 to reestablish the stricken European vineyards) had been transplanted to the United States from Europe by oenologists and vinoculturists like Münsterberg, Sherif, Lewin, Heider, and others *gänz europäisch* psychologists who had earlier brought the good news to U.S. provincials. It was their North American converts who in the 1960s retold the same dull tales around the camp fires of European summer schools sponsored by the Ford Foundation, the U.S. Navy, or the SSRC. Fortunately, the newer generations of cognitive social psychologists from several continents seem more interested in getting on with the work than in fabricating national distinctiveness.

The Attitude-Change Flourishing
in the 1950s and 1960s

Societal factors underlying the attitude-change ascendancy.   The group-dynamics movement was succeeded by a 1950s and 1960s attitude-change era. The U.S. Army indoctrination and morale research during World War II (Lumsdaine, 1984) served as the fulcrum redirecting the attitudinal momentum from its earlier measurement flourishing into its second, attitude-change, ascendancy. The four volumes describing the U.S. Army wartime research includes one volume

(Stouffer, 1950) on wartime attitude-measurement work by Lazarsfeld, Guttman, and other second-generation scaling theorists, and another volume (Hovland, Lumsdaine, & Sheffield, 1949) on the persuasive effectiveness of the U.S. Army indoctrination films that initiated the new attitude-change era. These two volumes constituted a *vale atque ave* transition from the first to the second, from the synchronic to diachronic, attitude eras. The 1940s War Department funding of research on social influence via persuasive communication helped to create the new information/communication science discipline (Rogers, 1994; Dennis & Wartella, 1996).

Political developments gave purpose to the possibilities provided by scientific and technological advances. The United States emerged from the war in 1945 with world hegemony in economic productivity and military prowess, and even in moral stature and goodwill among the world's publics. Two major wars in a single generation had reoriented attitudes in the United States from traditional too-proud-to-fight isolationism to aggressive interventionism. Being perceived as a colossus astride the world paradoxically evokes a sense of danger, because such hideous strength of one party tends to polarize others into an oppositional coalition lest the hegemony become insurmountable. This paradoxical combination of felt strength and felt peril intensified when in the 1950s the United States became caught up in a cold war with a sizable segment of the Western European intellectual elite and with a Soviet Union that seemed menacing and formidable to this elite, its demographic and economic weaknesses being not yet widely appreciated. This 1986a article of mine was a rare recognition that the USSR was a Potemkin village beset by health and productivity deterioration. As a result, the fearsome and fearful U.S. giant became desperate to find words for its loud but tremulous voice, words that would justify its ways to the classes and win the hearts of the masses.

United States social psychologists responded to the cold war situation with a "massive detergence" policy that if we can sell soap we can sell antitotalitarianism. Support for attitude-change research came from private foundations such as Rockefeller and Ford, corporations such as Bell Labs and General Electric, and, most munificently, from governmental agencies such as the Office of Naval Research, the National Institutes of Mental Health, and the National Science Foundation. Thus programmed and fueled, attitude-change research took off and flew high over the field of social psychology during the 1950s and 1960s.

The first, convergent-style decade of the attitude-change era. This 1950s and 1960s flourishing of attitude-change social influence processes went through two phases: an earlier topic-focused "convergent" style of work typified by Hovland and his Yale group, who dominated the 1950s, and then a theory-focused "divergent" style exemplified by Festinger and his Minnesota/Stanford group, who dominated the 1960s. The 1950s convergent stylist typically started off with a hypothetical relation to be explained (e.g., primacy versus recency effects in persuasion), on which was brought convergently to bear a wide variety of explanatory notions. The Hovland/Yale group was eclectic as to theory and decentralized in work style (McGuire, 1996a), including stimulus-response theorist Hovland, contiguity theorist Sheffield, psychoanalytic Janis, Lewinian Kelley, Gestalter Luchins, and reference-grouper Sherif. Convergent stylists' topic-centered, theory-eclectic proclivities shape their empirical work (McGuire, 1983a), which is characterized by inclusion of multiple orthogonal independent variables, superficial manipulations of independent variables, careful dependent variable measures, use of large samples with each participant serving in multiple conditions, across-issues replications, and relatively sensitive and parametric inferential statistics such as analysis of variance. This convergent style has strengths and weaknesses. As regards hypothesis generating, its tenacious grappling with a specific relation has the merit of keeping it focused on worthwhile issues; but its theoretical eclecticism makes it seem wandering, unfocused, and devoid of grand explanatory notions. As regards hypothesis testing, its procedures enhance efficiency, power, and replicability, but at the costs of artificiality and superficiality.

The second, divergent-style decade of the attitude-change era. By the 1960s the popular approach to attitude-change research had shifted from the convergent to the divergent style typified by the Festinger dissonance group. A divergent stylist starts off with a guiding-idea theory (McGuire, 1985a; chapter 5 in this volume), a partial view of the person such as dissonance or attribution, and applies it divergently across a series of studies to a variety of (attitude) phenomena (e.g., to selective avoidance, postdecisional readjustments, effects of counterattitudinal advocacy, etc.). The divergent stylist hopes to account for a small amount of covariance in each of a wide variety of relations, a hit-and-run ("have theory, will travel") progress that has been criticized as a fun-and-games approach (Ring, 1967; but see McGuire, 1967 and chapter 11 in this volume). Staying with a single theory rather than a substantive issue as its focus and using the favored theory to account for a small amount of variance in each of a variety of phenomena are central to the divergent style, leading to its use of simple designs with few independent variables that are carefully manipulated in elaborately contrived situations; on the other hand, the dependent variable is often measured precariously, perhaps by a dichotomous choice between two booklets or between waiting in an empty versus an occupied room. The elegantly contrived experimental situation often requires participation by one person at a time, which, along with the gross scaling of the dependent variable, makes it difficult to test interaction predictions, or study large samples, or use sensitive inferential statistics.

The convergent or divergent style each imposes a useful focusing of attention and guides a sustained course through a complex explanation space, but each imposes tunnel vision that obscures much of the surrounding reality (McGuire, 1983a). Researchers differ in the style with which they best resonate, and different styles may be particularly apt for given topics. Mixing styles within a single research program risks losing the focus and direction that each provides for explaining an intimidatingly complicated process like attitude change. Both the convergent and the divergent approaches are linear styles that may be replaced by the systems styles discussed more fully later in this chapter.

The 1950s and 1960s era witnessed a vast outpouring of attitude-change research by each style, but social psychologists' infatuation with attitude change eventually cooled due to internal and external factors of the types described above as causing the declines of previous enthusiasms. Good work on attitude change had been done earlier (Peterson & Thurstone, 1933) and continues to be done up to the present, as reviewed by McGuire (1985a, 1994b; see chapter 4 in this volume) and Eagly and Chaiken (1993), but only during the 1950s and 1960s did attitude-change research constitute the main force of social psychology advance.

The 1965–1985 Social Cognition Interlude

By the early 1970s boredom with attitude-change relations, annoyance with the "fun-and-games" ambience, and embarrassment over low attitude-action correlations had reached the point where it was debated whether the concept of attitudes is at all useful (Wicker, 1971; Abelson, 1972; Needham, 1973; Kelman, 1974). In its place the social cognition movement that would dominate the 1965–85 period could be observed slouching toward the trendy doctoral programs to be born.

General characteristics of social cognition research   Social cognition theorizing tries to account for the transformations of the known into knowledge (mis)representations, including (1) abstraction operations that result in cognitive reduction or "underrepresentation" of the known; (2) inference operations that result in cognitive elaboration and extrapolation types of "overrepresentations"; and (3) translation operations that result in alterations, or "malrepresentation." The reductional aspects involve abstracting a small proportion of the information registered by the senses (which themselves screen out most of the information contained in the actual situation) and assimilating this subset of information to preexisting cognitive categories, thus yielding a manageably oversimplified representation of the present reality. The elaborational aspects of cognitive representation involve extrapolating beyond the information received to additional assumptions (ontogenetically or phylogenetically acquired) about the reality represented. Each of these opposite cognitive processes aids coping, although psychological discussions tend to overemphasize rather the error-causing side effects of these transformations, perhaps because it is productive as a research tactic to study erroneous rather than correct responding. (See chapter 12 for discussion of these, and of the third type of knowledge distortions, cognitive malrepresentations.)

What is "social" about social cognition.   It has become fashionable to prefix the adjective "social" to knowledge operations such as "social cognition" (Forgas, 1981; Fiske & Taylor, 1984; Wyer & Srull, 1984), "social representation" (Farr & Moscovici, 1984) and "social inference" (Hastie, 1983). *Social* is used with at least six different meanings, resulting in confusion because a cognition's being "social" by one of these criteria says little about its being "social" by others of the five. A defensible but uninteresting use of the *social* modifier is to label the subset of cognitions that deal with social objects – for example, perceptions of other people, of interpersonal relations, of human institutions, and of cultural values. A more common usage is to use *social* to specify cognitions that are shared by members of a specified society, as in Durkheim's (1898) notion of "représentations collectives," in contrast to heterogeneous attitudinal positions that differentiate members of a group. A third usage of *social* refers to the extent to which the cognition originates, not in the knower's genes or private experiences, but through interacting with other people, as in Blumer's (1969) symbolic interactionist extensions of Mead's (1934) Chicago school of social behaviorism. In a fourth usage *social* refers to the extent to which cognitions are interpersonally communicable (by being phenomenologically accessible and verbally expressible) rather than being implicit deep structures that may guide the person's experiences and actions even though he or she is unaware of them or can picture or feel them, if at all, only as unverbalizable images. A fifth use of *social* is to distinguish those cognitions which serve to maintain the current social system and cultural forms (e.g., systems justification, false consciousness, stereotypes, etc.) from those not serving to bolster the status quo. A sixth usage of *social* is for imputing an emergent transcendental quality to cognitions such that they have an existence outside of individual heads, as in language structures, institutions, or bureaucracies that transcend the individual.

None of these half-dozen usages of *social* is unreasonable in itself, but not making clear to oneself and others which meaning one intends can be confusing. For example, representations may be social in the sense of being shared by most members of a group without being interactional in origin; indeed, its universality suggests that, on the contrary, the cognition may derive from the genes rather than from interpersonal experience. Or again, because a cognition is widely shared does not imply that it is conscious and communicable; on the contrary, what is accepted by all may go without saying and without even entering awareness. The "shared" meaning (Jaspars & Fraser, 1984) tends to confuse heterogeneity among societies with homogeneity within societies.

Cognitive representational selectivity.　　Selectivity processes (discussed more fully in chapter 8) occur both in encoding (intake) and in decoding (output) aspects of cognition. Encoding selectivity screens out much of the incoming information, preventing overload; the selected elements are assigned to preexisting categories, allowing the situation to be recognized and labeled. Decoding selectivity inhibits most of the person's response repertory as situationally inappropriate (thus avoiding paralyzing indecision) and provides a template for guiding the pattern of action through a sequence of responses keyed to the circumstances. Constructs like "rules," "schemata," and "assimilation" involve decoding selectivity, as does "implicit (tacit) theory" research, such as conceptualizing the person as implicit biologist and as implicit economist (McGuire, 1985a).

Discussion of decoding selectivities in cognition goes back at least to Dilthey's *Verstehen* notion as popularized by Max Weber, to Tolman's (1932) notion of cognitive maps that channel behavior, and to Bartlett's (1932) schemata notion of how a person's available narrative structures guide transformations of experience in perception and memory. An aura of vitalism and teleology had inhibited psychologists' use of these guiding-template notions as long as the preferred hard-hat analogue for the human brain was the serial-path metaphor suggested by Sherrington's (1906) reflex arc, although Hebb's (1949) cell-assembly and phase-sequence notions were efforts to cope with this limitation, and Brentano's act psychology was an inspired anticipation. The mid-twentieth-century introduction of the computer metaphor for the brain (Ashby, 1952; Von Neumann, 1958) makes it easier to imagine behavior in terms of acts rather than movements without abandoning the prescribed materialistic metatheory (McGuire, 1986a).

Cognitive inferential extrapolation.   The 1965–85 social cognition era includes (besides the just mentioned research on selective, simplifying representational processes) studies of elaborational processes that enable the person to extrapolate beyond the immediately received information by generating inferences that enhance the information's relevance to his or her purposes and possibilities. Three main strands of social inference research – meaning attribution, person perception, and cognitive ramifications – exploit the assumption that acts of knowing involve melding sensory intake with available content and structures already within the knower. Beyond this unifying assumption, social inference theorists disagree on several issues. Some concur with Helmholz's and Michotte's postulate that inferential extrapolations from the externally presented information are as immediate and automatic as are the sensations themselves, while others maintain that such inferential elaborations occur only after some extrinsic motivation arises, such as an environmental demand (Bem, 1972) or a self-esteem need (Feldman, 1966; Aronson, 1969; Wicklund & Frey,

1981). Theorists differ also as regards the postulated structure of inferences: Person-perception researchers typically assume parallel converging structures made up of inferences about what traits go together and about what cognitive algebra is used for information integration; on the other hand, meaning attributions and cognitive ramifications researchers usually assume agenda or script structures with sequential organization, as from premises to conclusions (McGuire, 1960a) or from perceived effects to causes (Jones et al., 1972). Cognitive extrapolation work on all three topics (meaning attribution, person perception, and cognitive ramifications) is discussed more fully in McGuire (1986a).

The Attitude-Systems Flourishing in the 1980s and 1990s

Describing the emerging attitude-systems enthusiasm requires turning from the intimidating task of interpreting the past to the still more perilous project of predicting the future. This third attitudinal flourishing calls for grappling with structure on three levels that will be discussed in turn: the structure of individual attitudes, of systems of attitudes, and of attitude systems in relation to other systems within the total person.

Structure of individual attitudes. The most popular model of the individual attitude is the tired tripartite thought-feeling-action analysis that seems arbitrary but may resonate with some deep structure of Indo-European thought because it appears in Hindu, Zoroastrian, and Hellenic psychology (McGuire, 1985a) and may be related to the brain's three evolutionary layers – the cerebral cortex, limbic systems, and old brain. Since being revived by von Wolff as part of the eighteenth-century reprofessionalization of European philosophy, this triadic analysis has been routinely used from Kant to Krech (Bagozzi, 1978; Hilgard, 1980). Measures of the three components are deficient in discriminant validity, submeasures often correlating as highly across as within components, but this may be an artifact of psychologists' obsession with the evaluative dimension, which leads them to reduce information in each of the three dimensions to its evaluative aspect.

A second heavily worked model analyzes individual attitudes into attribution $\times$ evaluation components (also called the expectancy $\times$

values, instrumentality × goals, expected value, utility maximizing, subjective expected utility [SEU], rational choice, etc., approach). Its popularity derives from its being plausible (to the border of banality) and sufficiently quantifiable (Edwards, 1954; Savage, 1954) to allow investigation of controversies such as the additive versus averaging models of information integration (Anderson, 1981). It is expandable by the addition of other variables (Fishbein & Ajzen, 1975; Triandis, 1980). It was particularly popular at mid-twentieth century and since then has been promoted by the Michigan-Illinois school, particularly Fishbein (1963; Fishbein & Ajzen, 1975), and by marketing researchers (Bagozzi, 1982). This model requires an implausibly labor-intensive process of estimating each alternative's subjective expected utility by making many judgments, complexly combined. Even a peculiarly deliberative person making an unusually important decision is unlikely to go through so onerous a procedure (although personal computers could provide programs that would perform much of the labor). Continued work on this analytical model seems inevitable, the most promising paths to progress being along the lines of Anderson's (1981) functional measurement, information-integration work, and Bagozzi's (1982) use of structural equation models to identify multiple causal pathways.

A third, construction-by-characteristic, model of individual attitudes serves as a simpler approximation of the full SEU model just described. It calls for rating the alternatives on one dimension at a time, starting with the most available dimension and eliminating all alternatives that do not meet a sufficing cutoff point on it. The survivors are then judged as to whether they meet the sufficing level on each of the successive characteristics in turn. This shortcut analysis usually results in an easily obtained preference ordering similar to that yielded tediously by the full attribution × evaluation SEU model; but conditions are easily rigged in the laboratory so that it leads to a nonoptimal preference ordering. Evidence that people overestimate the number of characteristics they use to make choices suggests that this simpler analytical model may better fit actual attitudinal processes. Useful lines of pursuit would be to identify dispositional and situational variables that determine the order in which characteristics or values are considered, and what determines the acceptability cutoff point on each characteristic.

A fourth model for the structure of the individual attitude, the subject-verb-object analysis popularized by Osgood, Suci, and Tannenbaum (1957), regards an attitude as an assertion that some subject concept (e.g., the person whose attitude is under consideration or a topic valued by that person) is in some relation (as specified by verb concepts such as "is conducive to" or "dislikes") to some object concept. Among provocative issues deserving further research are the partition of verbs into subsets among which different laws obtain (see chapter 7 in this volume) and which component is of greatest psychological importance when such S-V-O structures are analyzed into orthogonal main and interaction components (Wyer & Carlston, 1979).

A fifth model of an attitude's structure is as a proposition that assigns a topic of meaning to some location on a dimension of judgment, as discussed more fully in McGuire and McGuire (1991c) and in chapter 6 in this volume. Research is needed on what dimensions of judgment are salient in one's meaning space (Kreitler & Kreitler, 1984) and on what determines the axes on which they align (e.g., are a person's judgments of female beauty made on dimensions whose locations are set in infancy by the distinctive facial characteristics of one's mother?). Do attitudes function differently depending on which transcendental dimension of judgment is involved (e.g., desirability vs. likelihood)? Also inviting is work on the metaphoric and other rhetorical extensions of circumscribed dimensions (see chapter 7).

A sixth way of analyzing individual attitudes is into a basal component firmly rooted and resistant to ordinary persuasive communications (Anderson, 1959; Lazarsfeld, 1959; Jaspars, 1978; Kelman, 1980) versus a peripheral component easily changed (Anderson & Farkas, 1973), oscillating widely (Kaplowitz, Fink, & Bauer, 1983), with a considerable latitude of acceptance (Sherif & Hovland, 1961) and loose-linkage (McGuire, 1968d), whose changes tend to be elastic (Cialdini, Levy, Herman, Kozlowski, & Petty, 1976), snapping back into accord with the relatively immobile basal component once the social influence pressure is removed (Nuttin, 1975; Cialdini et al., 1976; Hass & Mann, 1976).

A seventh structural analysis of individual attitudes calls for identifying characteristics in which attitudes differ from one another as regards either dimensions of judgment or topics of meaning, for example, the Kreitler and Kreitler (1976, 1990) analysis in terms of individual differences in meaning-assigning tendencies. Analyzing attitudes into types on the basis of their topics of thought is due for a revival of interest (Tetlock, 1983; Kreitler & Kreitler, 1990) after having lain dormant for several decades following its popularity around

1960 when Zajonc (1960) distinguished attitude topics on such dimensions as differentiation, complexity, unity, and organization; Katz (1960) on generality, differentiation, and unity; Rokeach (1960) on centrality and permeability; and O. J. Harvey, Hunt, and Schroder (1961) on inclusiveness, internal structure, and external relatedness. In several eras such dimensionalization has seemed promising but ultimately proved disappointing.

Structure within minisystems of attitudes.   Broader than the structure of individual attitudes is the structure of systems of attitudes. My preferred definition, that the individual attitude is a response that locates a topic of meaning on a dimension of judgment (see chapter 6), implies that structure can arise within a system of attitudes on several levels: (*a*) in minisystems involving several topics of meaning projected on a single dimension of judgment (as in propositional reasoning), or a single topic of meaning projected on several dimensions of judgment (as in person perception); or (*b*) in mesosystems involving multiple interrelated topics of meaning projected on several dimensions of judgment (as in our research reported in chapter 6); or (*c*) in maxisystems (ideologies) involving many topics of meaning located on multiple dimensions of judgment.

Minisystems of the first type, made up of multiple topics of meaning projected on a single dimension of judgment, are illustrated by the probabilogical model developed over the years by McGuire (1960c, 1968d, 1981a, 1991c) and Wyer (Wyer & Goldberg, 1970; Wyer & Carlston, 1979). It has given rise to four interesting lines of research, described in chapter 6 of this volume. A second type of attitude minisystems, those made up of a single topic of meaning (e.g., a person) judged as regards their positions on multiple dimensions of variability, has been most astutely studied in Anderson's (1981, 1982) information-integration research program using functional measurement to test a weighted-averaging model of cognitive algebra. His social judgment approach simultaneously provides interval-scaled measures of the topic's locations on the dimensions and tests the hypothesized relations among the dimensions providing that specified assumptions are met. Anderson uses the parallelism theorem in the weighted-averaging additive case and the fan theorem in the multiplicative case. This Anderson work sets a methodological standard for the study of attitude systems by its elegant designs, simultaneous measures of the variables and the relations between them, careful data collection, sophisticated theoretical models of cognitive algebra, use of good-ness-of-fit rather than gross correlation to test among models, and wide range of stimulus materials (although it would be desirable to extend its testing procedures and response tasks beyond artificial lab-oratory situations). Somewhat more complex mesosystems of atti-tudes are described in chapter 6 of this volume.

Structure within maxisystems of attitudes (ideologies). Maxisystems of attitudes, sometimes called "ideologies," consist of many topics of meaning projected on multiple dimensions of judgment. Conventional wisdom takes it for granted that people have organized persisting ide-ologies manifested over a wide spectrum of beliefs and behaviors. However, many lines of disillusioning empirical evidence have led some survey researchers to conclude that the public's attitudes are so shallow, fickle, and randomly interrelated as to put in doubt whether people have organized ideologies. Lines of evidence against the exis-tence of ideology (McGuire, 1985a, 1989a) are that people frequently have no reportable opinion on issues vitally affecting them, can give no reasons for holding the opinions they do, give erroneous reasons or reasons that support a contrary opinion or conflict with their obvious self-interest. Also, the person often expresses very different opinions on an issue when the wording is changed only slightly or even when a preceding question is changed. Even when the wording remains iden-tical, the person often expresses opposite opinions on successive oc-casions. Also putting ideologies in doubt is the fact that people hold opposite opinions on related manifestations of the same principle, or hold an opinion on a general principle that is opposite to those held on most of the specific instances on which the generalization would seem to be based. This end-of-ideology conclusion by survey researchers is in agreement with the recent emphasis by basic researchers on situa-tional rather than dispositional determination of behavior, on the sep-arate storage of affect and information about topics of meaning, on one's dependence on self-observation of one's external behavior to as-certain one's own beliefs, and on the experiencing of affective reac-tion to a topic even before one recognizes what the topic is.

Revisionists have offered excuses to defend the existence of ideo-logical coherence despite these numerous lines of contrary evidence. Some of these salvaging excuses are methodological, such as the claim that ideological organization would be found if individual atti-tudes were better measured (more unidimensionally, with more reli-

able, continuous, ratio scales, and with refinements of the "unde-
cided" responses), thus correcting the attenuation of the obtained relations among attitudes due to unreliable measurement of the individual
attitudes. Another type of fall-back position is to admit that organized
ideologies are lacking in the general public but might be found at least
within circumscribed subpopulations such as among the elites, or
single-issue zealots, or in especially contentious and polarized times
and places, or within particularly vital or familiar domains. However,
it must be admitted that none of these lines of inquiry to salvage ideology has so far yielded strong evidence of highly organized ideological
systems. Perhaps ideological coherence will be found, not along conventionally recognized dimensions such as liberalism-conservatism
(whether that be treated as a bipolar single dimension or as two orthogonal dimensions), but along deep structural polarities such as
Lévi-Straussian raw-cooked, or Jungian animus–anima, or hard-to-
verbalize imagery dimensions. Also likely to be investigated heavily
during the 1980s and 1990s is the search for ideologies in the form
of miniature belief modules currently attracting attention under such
labels as schemata, implicit theories, scripts, frames, agenda, and
rules. These various possibilities are discussed further in McGuire
(1985a, 1989a).

*Structures relating attitude systems to other systems in the per-
son.* The most complex level of attitude structure involves linkages
between affective attitudinal systems and other systems within the total person, especially the person's information systems and behavioral
systems. As regards linkages between affective attitudinal systems
and informational systems, four approaches have found only limited
correspondence (see reviews by T. D. Cook & Flay, 1978, and
McGuire, 1985a). (1) The simple static approach of relating liking for
a set of topics to the contemporaneous net excesses of favorable over
unfavorable information about it often yields positive correlations
reaching the .05 level of statistical significance but modest in size.
Several more dynamic approaches also detect low degrees of structure: (2) Slight increases and decreases of liking often occur when the
person acquires new favorable or unfavorable information about the
topic; and (3) as time passes, temporal decay of this enhanced liking
occasionally shows some slight correlation with forgetting of the acquired information. (4) Variables that enhance message comprehensi-
bility tend to enhance the message's affective impact. The slight posi-

tive correlations between affect and information found by these four approaches suggest that there are some structural connections between affect and information systems but that the two are largely independent.

Several issues regarding this elusive information-affect correspondence seem especially ripe for investigation during the attitude-structure flourishing. To complement the usually assumed direction of causality from information to affect (Lazarus, 1984), more work is needed on how manipulating mood or other affect influences information availability (Zajonc, 1984). Also deserving of study is how changes in affect can be induced, not only by introducing new information from an outside source, but also by enhancing the salience of information already within the individual's cognitive repertory, as by the Socratic question-asking or directed-thinking tasks (see chapter 6 in this volume). Self-generated information may change affect more than does information absorbed from an outside source (Greenwald, 1968; Calder et al., 1974; Higgins & Rholes, 1978; Sherman et al., 1983). Additional research attention should also be given to two multiple-paths issues: alternative paths to attitude change (e.g., a direct information-skirting path in low-involvement contexts and a path via the information system in more important or uncertain situations). A second two-paths issue involves the possible separate storage in memory of the induced attitude change and of the new information; initially the new information may be needed to induce the change, but once induced, the attitude change becomes functionally autonomous from retention of the new information.

The second type of intersystems structure, that between affective and behavioral systems, has been studied even more frequently than the just-discussed linkages between information and the affective systems by a similar variety of static and dynamic approaches, and with an even more discouraging outcome. Indeed, the low correlation of the affective and cognitive components of attitudes with actual behavior has been the perennial scandal of attitudes research (LaPiere, 1934). The empirical work suggests some weak linkage between beliefs and behavior, statistically significant under certain conditions but even then accounting for a disappointingly low proportion of covariance.

Hope against hope having survived a half-century of disappointing findings, we can expect stubborn explorations in search of the elusive attitude – action link to continue during the third, structural flourishing of attitude research and so some hopeful approaches will be mentioned here. The unreliability attenuating of the relation between the two systems may be reduced by improved measures of both attitude and action by using multiple items, tapping multiple dimensions of each (particularly interpersonally shared dimensions) and measuring each more similarly and under low levels of situational constraint. Other proposed measurement revisions are more superficial in that they enhance the obtained correlation only at the cost of losing ecological generalizability (e.g., by the use of laboratory rather than field settings, of within- rather than among-subject designs, of shorter intervals between the measures, or of self-reported behavior or behavioral intentions rather than actual behavior). Instead of searching for close attitude-action correspondence in the overall domain, a fallback position is to seek correspondence in especially promising subdomains (e.g., with more familiar, salient, and important attitudes and actions, and among people with higher self-esteem, maturity, self-monitoring, and felt responsibility).

More generally, progress in clarifying information-affect-action correspondence calls for using the systems style of research (McGuire, 1986a), which introduces more variables into the research design, measures them by permissive and revealing open-ended methods, lets each vary naturalistically, and analyzes time-series data by causal models that detect multiple paths of influence among variables, two-directional causal links, and feedback loops. Admittedly, the systems style is labor-intensive, but it provides new information on structural issues. It is needed to supplement the two rectilinear styles, the convergent and divergent, described earlier in this chapter as characterizing the second, attitude-change era in the 1950s and 1960s. McGuire (1989a) makes the subtle suggestion that the modesty of the demonstrated information-attitude-action correspondence results from the researchers' seeking for molecular one-to-one relations when the actual correspondence is molar.

The Secular Trend toward Complexity in the Progress in Attitude Research

Attitudes have been a perennial, and often the paramount, topic of social psychological research. The three successive waves of enthusiasm for the topic that have swept across the discipline since the 1920s have dealt with progressively more sophisticated issues. The first

1920s–1930s flourishing involved the static issues of the measurement and relation to behavior of individual attitudes; the second 1950s–1960s flourishing focused on inducing dynamic changes in individual attitudes. The third flourishing in the 1980s and 1990s has moved up from the study of static and dynamic relations of single attitudes to issues having to do with the structure and functioning of systems of attitudes.

THE POLY-PSY RELATIONSHIP: THREE PHASES OF A LONG AFFAIR

[Adapted with permission from W. J. McGuire, 1993b, The poly–psy relationship: Three phases of a long affair, in S. Iyengar & W. J. McGuire (Eds.), *Explorations in political psychology,* pp. 9–35 (Durham, NC: Duke University Press, copyright © 1993).]

Interdisciplinary cross-fertilization, never above a modest level, has been as sustained between political science and psychology as between any two social sciences, which is surprising considering that each discipline has longer common borders with other fields – political science with history and economics, psychology with sociology and anthropology. The collaboration has persisted through three successive 20-year eras differing in preferred topics of study, *nihil obstat* theoretical explanations, and high-table approved methods. For clarifying uniformity, each era will be labeled here by its popular topics of study: Thus the first 1940s and 1950s interdisciplinary flourishing will be called the "personality and culture" era; the second, 1960s and 1970s wave, the "attitudes and voting behavior" era; and the third flourishing, which dominated the 1980s and 1990s, the "ideology and decision" era. Labeling each of the three by its preferred topic is convenient but should not obscure the fact that in some eras a shared theory or a shared method constituted a stronger bond than a shared topic.

Contributions were made during each of the three eras by both humanistic and scientific approaches, within each on both micro- and macrolevels. "Humanistic" research uses insights idiographically to account for peculiarities in the thick texture of complex concrete cases, whereas "scientific" research uses these insights nomothetically to study an abstract general relation as it manifests itself across a wide range of cases whose peculiarities tend to cancel each other out. The idiographic humanistic approach brings theory into confrontation with empirical observations better to understand the specific case; the nomothetic scientific approach confronts them better to develop the theory. Each has its uses. Within each approach some work is at the microlevel, investigating the variables of interest as they relate across individual persons as the units measured; other work is at the macro level, investigating these relations across collectives (e.g., nations, social classes, historical epochs) as the units measured.

Table 10.1 gives an overview of this half-century of interdisciplinary collaboration. Its three rows list the three successive 20-year eras focusing on personality, on attitudes, and on ideology, in turn. The seven columns define each era: The three leftmost columns give a connotative definition of each era in terms of its characteristic topics, theories, and methods; and the four rightmost columns provide a denotative definition of each era by citing some of its important contributions, partitioned first between the idiographic humanistic versus the nomothetic scientific approaches, these two each then subdivided between studies on the micro- versus macrolevels. My description is provocatively symmetrical, imposing sharp contours on an amorphous body of research that in actuality had more continuity and less direction than are represented here. Intellectual history (and any representational knowledge) must highlight regularities and sharpen distinctions if it is to detect faint signals masked by background noise, as is discussed more fully in the chapter 12 exposition of my "perspectivist" epistemology (McGuire, 1982a, 1986b, 1989b). Hence, my history here of political psychology should be supplemented by others, especially those more fully reflecting political psychological work done outside North America.

The 1940s–1950s Personality and Culture Era

In the first, personality and culture, era the main common ground among researchers was a shared theoretical enthusiasm for explaining political thoughts, feelings, and actions in terms of environmental (versus hereditary) determinants, using explanatory concepts drawn from psychoanalysis, behaviorism, and Marxism, in declining order of importance, often emphasizing childhood-experience determinants. I shall describe this personality and culture era, first connotatively in terms of its theoretical, topical, and methodological distinctive characteristics; then denotatively, in terms of significant research contributions in each of four approaches, the micro- and macrohumanistic and the micro- and macroscientific.

Connotative definition of the 1940s–1950s personality-culture era: Preferred theories. A unifying assumption behind this 1940s–1950s interdisciplinary flourishing is that political personality and the behavior of leaders and masses are formed by ontogenetic socialization experiences, especially those emphasized by the environmentalistic metatheorizing of psychoanalytic, behavioristic, and Marxist theorizing. The era's environmentalism was an exaggerated antigenetic reaction to the excesses of social Darwinism by Spencer and others earlier in the century, and held the hope of ameliorating the disturbed economic and political conditions left by the 1914–18 war. Another shared ideological orientation was a loathing for the fascistic personality, a syndrome hard to define but (at least in those days) one knew it when one saw it. These revulsions against social Darwinism and fascism were probably related (Hofstadter, 1944; Stein, 1988).

Psychoanalytic theory had great impact on western European and North American social science during the middle part of the twentieth century. Behind the 1930s introjection of Freudianism by many students of politics looms the father figure of Harold Lasswell (1930, 1935), who popularized use of Freudian notions of unconscious erotic drives (but typically suppressing the thanatotic), of defense mechanisms that adaptively channel the expression of these drives, and of Freud's psychosexual developmental notions of how oral, anal, and phallic frustrations of early childhood shape the id, ego, and superego aspects of personality. These rich notions provoked a gold mine of hypotheses about the development and operation of politically relevant thoughts, feelings, and actions in public and in their leaders, although a few critics at the time (Bendix, 1952) objected to the reductionalism of such psychologizing.

Environmental determinism in this 1940s–1950s political-personality theorizing derived also from Marxist historical materialism in attributing a society's political consciousness to its social and political institutions, shaped in turn by its modes and relationships of production, and these by physical realities. Marxists accepted Engels's (1884/1972) low opinion of the bourgeois family (the *Communist Manifesto* [1848] called for its abolition), but unlike the Freudians they did not detail the baleful effects of the early childhood home on adult political personality. S-R (stimulus-response) behaviorism or

Table 10.1.

Connotative definitions (distinguishing features) and denonative definitions (notable examples) of the three successive eras of collaboration between political science and psychology

	Connotative Definition: Distinguishing Characteristics		
Eras	Preferred topics	Preferred Theories	Preferred methods (and statistics)
1. 1940s & 1950s	Political personality (in leaders and in masses)	Environmental determination (psychoanalysis, S-R behaviorism, Marxism)	Content analysis of records and interviews (contingency coefficients and chi-squares)
2. 1960s & 1970s	Political attitudes and voting behavior	Rational person (subjective-utility maximizing, cognition → affects → action)	Questionnaires in survey research; Participant observation (correlation coefficients and ANOVA)
3. 1980s & 1990s	Political ideology (content and processes of belief systems)	Information processing (cognitive heuristics, decision theories)	Experimental manipulation: (Computer flowchart; Structural equation models)

Table 10.1 (continued)

Denotative Definition: Notable Contributions within Each of Four Approaches			
Humanstic approaches (ideographic, synthetic)		Scientific approaches (nomothetic, analytical)	
Micro	Macro	Micro	Macro
Psychohistory, psychobiography: Fromm (1941) Langer (1972) George & George (1956) Erikson (1958)	National character: Benedict (1946) Mead (1942) Gorer (1948) Riesman (1950)	Dollard et al. (1939) Adorno et al. (1950) Smith, Bruner, & White (1956) McClosky (1958)	Sorokin (1937–41) Kluckhohn & Murray (1948) HRAF (Murdock, Ford) Whiting & Child (1953)
Lane (1959, 1962) Goffman (1959, 1961)	Ariès (1960) *Annals* (Block) Foucault (1961, 1984)	Election studies Campbell et al. (1954, 1960, 1966) Roper Center	Lipset (1960) McClelland (1961) ICPSR (1962) Rokkan (1962) Almond & Verba (1963) Russett et al. (1964) Inkeles & Smith (1974)
George (1980) Larson (1985) Doise (1986)	Lebow (1981) Jervis et al. (1985, 1986) Radding (1985)	Tetlock (1981) Simonton (1984)	Archer & Gartner (1984) Tetlock (1985)

learning (reinforcement) theory also provided inspiration for the political-personality movement, particularly through the circle of interdisciplinary workers around Clark Hull at the Yale Institute of Human Relations. These theorists seasoned a "liberated" behaviorism with a generous sprinkling of psychoanalytic theory and a pinch of Marxism, as illustrated by their work on frustration and aggression, social learning, personality, and psychopathology (Dollard et al., 1939, 1950; Miller & Dollard, 1941).

Preferred topics in the personality and culture era. A secondary unifying focus of these interdisciplinary researchers in the 1940s and 1950s was a shared subject-matter interest in personality as a mediating explanatory variable, how it is affected by the individual's cultural experiences, and how it in turn affects the politically significant thoughts, feelings, and actions of the masses and their leaders. "Personality" was used broadly to include motivations and values, perceptions and stereotypes, cognitive and interpersonal styles, and characteristic modes of coping. Popular independent variables to account for these mediating personality variables were the culture's early childhood socialization experiences, singled out by psychoanalytic theory as crucial. Other popular independent-variable determinants, reflecting the behavioristic and Marxist materialism of the era's theorists, were the institutions of society in regard to the stimuli they presented, the response options they left available, the drives they aroused, and the schedules of reinforcement they administered. For example, the aggressive foreign policy of a national leader or the bellicosity of a population might be attributed: (*a*) to the culture's displacement of oedipal ambivalence regarding one's father to outgroup targets; or (*b*) to frustration caused by economic deprivation (absolute or relative to others' or to one's own rising expectations); or (*c*) to felt loss of control due to bureaucratization; or (*d*) to alienation of workers from the products of their labor; or (*e*) to social modeling and reinforcing of aggressive responses in childhood.

Preferred methods in the personality and culture era. Researchers in this first era were not as self-conscious about methodologies as were workers in the next two eras. Scholars in its humanistic branch used secondary analysis of the textual record, occasionally supplemented by participant observation, interviews, and analysis of artifacts. These procedures continued to be popular in the humanist branch during the next two eras as well; methodological variations among the three eras are less pronounced in the humanistic than in the scientific approaches. Scientific workers in this first era characteristically used data from questionnaires or from content analyses of archival data. Their preferred descriptive statistics were measures of simple association such as contingency coefficients, adequate for their purposes but inefficient for the study of nonmonotonic, mediational, and interactional relations.

Denotative definition of the 1940s–1950s personality-culture era: Microhumanistic studies. The connotative definition given above of the culture and personality era in terms of its characteristic topics, theories, and methods can be supplemented by giving its denotative definition in terms of its major published contributions in each of four approaches, micro- and macrohumanistic and micro- and macroscientific. Political science, despite its name, has always depended largely on humanistic approaches, using "thick" descriptive analyses (Geertz, 1973, 1983) to demonstrate how some theory or combination of factors can account in depth for a concrete case. Humanistic studies on the microlevel use individual persons as the units of observation, and on the macrolevel use collectives (such as nations or historical epochs). The microhumanistic branch in this political-personality era has come to be known as "psychobiography" or "psychohistory," and its macro branch has been labeled "national character" study.

   The master himself contributed one of the earliest microhumanistic psychobiographies in his analysis of Leonardo da Vinci (Freud, 1910). Psychobiographies are occasionally done on nonpolitical personages such as Martin Luther (Erikson, 1958), but political leaders have become the most popular subjects (Greenstein, 1969; Glad, 1973; Runyan, 1993). A seminal contribution was the George and George (1956) analysis of how Woodrow Wilson's boyhood experiences with a demanding father laid down a personality style that led to his fractious behavior in later authority situations, as illustrated by his recurring problems in dealing with the Princeton University trustees, the New Jersey legislature, and the U.S. Senate. Freud himself purportedly coauthored a Wilson psychobiography, if the "Freud and" Bullitt (1967) hatchet job is authentic (Erikson & Hofstadter, 1967). Neo-Freudian, Marxist, and ego-psychological theorists contributed political psychobiographies of Hitler (Erikson, 1950; Fromm, 1973), Cardinal Richelieu (Marvick, 1983), and Atatürk (Volkan & Itzkowitz, 1984). This movement gained status among policymakers by its World War II use, as illustrated on the micro side by Langer's (1972) psychobiography of Hitler and on the macro side by Benedict's (1946) analysis of the Japanese national character.

Macrohumanistic national character studies of culture and personality. The macro branch is illustrated by such influential studies as Benedict's (1946) depiction of Japanese national character and Riesman's (1950) depiction of personality orientation as evolving from tradition-directed, through inner-directed, to other-directed. Most of the 1940s national-character research in the macrohumanistic line was more explicitly psychoanalytic than Benedict's, even in regard to her own area of Japanese modal personality. Psychoanalytically oriented theorists demonstrated that the Japanese national character was oral (Spitzer, 1947), and anal (LaBarre, 1945), and phallic (Silberpfennig, 1945), illustrating the protean quality, at once admirable and worrisome, of psychoanalytic theory. Concurrent analyses of American national character tended to be less Freudian (Mead, 1942; Gorer, 1948).

Notable work in the humanistic tradition has continued beyond its 1940s and 1950s prime, particularly in its micro, psychobiography branch, as reviewed by Runyan (1982, 1988, 1993) and Cocks and Crosby (1987). The challenge presented by Richard Nixon's personality (Brodie, 1981) by itself could have sufficed to revive the enterprise. The macro branch has been quiescent (Patai, 1973, 1977) after its 1940s and 1950s popularity, perhaps because ascribing distinctive characteristics to national or other groups can be politically dangerous, as illustrated by hostile reactions to Oscar Lewis's (1961) well-intentioned use of the "culture of poverty" concept. The cautious scholar builds a fence around the law to avoid being tarred by the racism brush (Bendersky, 1988). The shokku of Japan-Incorporated has evoked a flood of books on Japanese culture and character, subspecies Homo economicus. The shock to Europe and North America by the revolting youth in the late 1960s popularized macroanalyses of epoch personality of successive brief waves of youth cohorts, assigned acronyms and other picturesque labels such as teddy boys, skinheads, beats, flower children, punks, baby-boomers, yuppies, dincs, yucas, and generation X, showing that the concept of adolescent political generations is a tenacious one (Mannheim, 1923/1952; Jennings & Niemi, 1981; Jennings, 1987). New youth generations are probably even now slouching toward Bethlehem (perhaps somewhere in California) to be born (Peabody, 1985).

Microscientific studies of culture and personality. Scientific approaches involve sampling cases from a designated universe to which one wishes to generalize and measuring each case both on the independent variable (in this first era, often on some psychoanalytically relevant dimension of early childhood experience) and on the dependent variable (here, usually some politically significant dimension of personality). Then the relation between distributions of scores on independent and dependent variables is calculated across cases (units of observation), which are individual persons on the microlevel and multiperson social composites (e.g., nations or epochs) on the macrolevel.

Both micro- and macroscientific examples are reported in the era-inaugurating Dollard et al. (1939) frustration-aggression volume with its Freudian underpinnings, although it does not fully exploit the richness of Freud's three theories of aggression (Stepansky, 1977). Microstudies in the Dollard et al. volume systematically manipulated the frustration levels of individual rats and then measured these rats' aggressiveness toward available targets not associated with their frustration; the volume's macrostudies (Hovland & Sears, 1939) correlated annual fluctuations in U.S. economic frustration (measured by gross national product or price of cotton) with annual scapegoating scores (measured by yearly numbers of lynchings in the United States).

A comparably important microscientific study in the political-personality era was the Adorno et al. (1950) authoritarian personality research deriving from Freudian and Marxist orientations, which postulated that the authoritarian (fascist) personality syndrome (characterized by hostility to Jews and other out-groups, along with idealization of high-power individuals and groups) resulted from an oedipal situation in which a boy's punitive father severely punished any hostility directed at him, resulting in the boy's growing up rigorously repressing aggressive feelings toward his father (and, by extension, to other authority figures) by the use of the reaction-formation mechanism of idealizing the father (and other authority figures) and releasing the pent-up hostility vicariously toward out-groups whose demographics or life-styles place them in opposition to, or at least outside, the Establishment's power structure. Other microscientific studies in the era included Almond's (1954) on the appeals of communism, Srole's (1956) on anomie and prejudice, Smith, Bruner, and White's (1956) on the functional bases of political attitudes, and McClosky's (1958) on political conservatism and personality.

Macroscientific studies of culture and personality. Early scientific macrostudies (discussed later in this chapter) were Sorokin's (1937–41) formidable analysis of Western civilization over millennia and Richardson's (1960) posthumously published work on the statistics of deadly quarrels, also discussed later in this chapter. These pioneers had to do Stakhanovite labor (before the availability of large research grants or computers or interuniversity data-bank consortia) to assemble personally, with a little help from their friends and students, large-scale historical data archives. Macroempirical research on personality was given a major impetus in the 1940s by the development of social-data archives, beginning when the Yale group set up the anthropological Human Relations Area Files of cross-cultural data (Kluckhohn & Murray, 1948; Whiting & Child, 1953).

In summary, this 1940s–1950s personality and culture era was an exciting time during which a small invisible college of interdisciplinary researchers, sharing overlapping explanatory targets, grew to a critical mass. Operating across disciplinary frontiers, using psychoanalytic (supplemented by behaviorist and Marxist) theorizing, they studied how a society's child-rearing practices or dominant socioeconomic institutions affect politically relevant personality syndromes, with politically significant consequences. Participants came from beyond psychology and political science (e.g., Benedict and Whiting were anthropologists and Adorno, a philosopher and musicologist). Cross-disciplinary research tends to be an exciting participatory sport, but it is a young person's game, drawing few spectators and fewer participants from the parent disciplines' established leaders who tend to be preoccupied by the traditional topics with which the discipline has become fairly comfortable. Because workers at interdisciplinary borders are relatively few, their focusing narrowly in any one era as regards topics, theories, and methods may be necessary if they are to attain a critical mass of mutually stimulating work. Such within-era narrowness tends to be corrected by sizable shifts of focus from one era to the next.

The 1960s–1970s Attitudes and Voting Behavior Era

In the second, 1960s and 1970s, interdisciplinary flourishing of political psychology, the topical focus shifted from political-personality and behavioral pathology to political attitudes and voting behavior. As shown in the second row of Table 10.1, this second era, like the first, had its preferred topic, theory, and method, but the relative emphasis on the three characteristics reversed between the two eras. The primary commonality among these 1960s and 1970s political attitude workers was a shared methodological enthusiasm for survey research; a secondary bond was a shared topic preoccupation with political attitudes and voting behavior; while theory, in the form of a self-interest, rational-choice, Subjective-Expected-Utility, benefits/costs maximizing view, supplied only a weak tertiary bond, often used only implicitly. I shall describe this second, political attitudes era first connotatively and then denotatively.

Connotative characteristics of the 1960s–1970s attitudes era: Preferred theories. The interdisciplinary researchers in this political-attitudes, second era were not doctrinaire about their own theoretical explanations, nor did they impute highly organized thought systems to the public (Converse, 1964), as befits an "end-of-ideology" era (Namier, 1955; Mills, 1959; Bell, 1960), even if it now appears that ideology was not dead but hiding out in Paris and Frankfurt (Skinner, 1985). Underlying much of the research was an implicit assumption that persons operate hedonistically in accord with the self-interest, subjective-utility maximizing model described earlier in this chapter (Feather, 1982).

Supplementing this expected-utility conceptualization was another rationality assumption, the "cognitive→ affective→ conative" concept of the person as having beliefs that shape preferences that channel actions (Krech and Crutchfield, 1948). A third underlying assumption was the "reference group" consistency concept that the person maximizes in-group homogeneity and out-group contrast by adopting attitudes and behaviors normative and distinctive to his or her demographic or social groups (Newcomb, 1943). These three rationality postulates of the 1960s and 1970s political-attitudes era went almost without saying, in contrast with the belligerent assertiveness of the psychoanalytic, behavioristic, and Marxist theorizing during the earlier 1940s and 1950s political-personality era. An environmental determinism bridged both eras; the reawakening appreciation in the biological disciplines of the evolutionary and genetic contributions to human proclivities had as yet little influence on these researchers in politics and psychology.

Preferred topics in the attitudes/voting era.   At least as much as psychologists and political scientists, sociologists like Lazarsfeld at Columbia, Berelson at Chicago, and Lipset at Berkeley played major roles from the outset in studying how voting behavior and attitudes toward political issues, parties, and candidates are predictable from group memberships, personal interactions, and mass media. Before the 1930s depression political elections had been regarded as a great American game (Farley, 1938), an interesting, uncouth spectator sport like prizefighting and baseball. Brahmin scholars, both in the academy (e.g., Frederick Jackson Turner) and outside it (e.g., Henry Adams), were willing to leave its practice to the upwardly mobile hinterland provincials and immigrant urban proletarians. As some of these outsiders shouldered or sidled their way into academic halls (Orren, 1985), and as the Great Depression and the agitprop of international socialism and the terrors of National Socialism riveted scholars' attention on politics, the study of political attitudes and voting behavior became respectable in the relatively democratic nations. Turn-of-the-century political scientists (e.g., Acton, 1907) had found power distasteful, but by midcentury students of politics had become comfortable, even fascinated, with power and its study (Leighton, 1945; Lasswell, 1948; Hunter, 1953; Dahl, 1961; Winter, 1973; McClelland, 1975), perhaps because of seeing governmental power exercised both to perpetrate genocide and to defeat the perpetrators in a war that incidentally caged the big bad wolf of economic depression. Indeed, many of these post-1940 students of politics had played participatory Dr. Win-the-War roles.

Preferred methods in the attitudes/voting era.   It was their shared "Do surveys; will travel" methodology that especially united these 1960s–1970s political attitudes and voting researchers, more than did their shared rational-person theoretical orientation, or even their shared topical interest in political attitudes and voting. They designed questionnaires asking a sample representative of some population about their demographics, media consumption, political information, or other personal characteristics (as independent variable measures) and about their political attitudes and voting intentions or behaviors (to measure political partisanship and participation as mediating and dependent variables). Such formal survey-research methods characterized the scientific branch of political-attitudes work, while the humanistic branch often used less formalized depth interviews that allowed open-ended responses to general probes. Secondarily, participant observation passed from anthropology to sociology, with fertile use by Whyte (1943, 1949) in his studies of street-corner and restaurant societies, and by Goffman (1959, 1961) in his analyses of self-presentation in varied settings (e.g., gambling casinos and asylums).

Denotative mapping of the 1960s–1970s attitudes era: The microhumanistic approach. To provide a denotative definition of this 1960s and 1970s political-attitudes and voting behavior era, prototypical contributions will be described in each of the four approaches. Throughout the century of progress following Henry Mayhew's (1861) microhumanistic interviews of the poor in early Victorian London, to the current sophisticated survey-research training programs at universities such as Michigan and Chicago, students of society and mentality have made thoughtful use of the interview method, developing it from an art to a craft, if not yet quite a science. As an art, it calls for virtuosi such as Henry Mayhew and Studs Terkel (1967, 1970), who use intuitive techniques difficult to verbalize. Interviewing evolved to craft status as its experienced practitioners became able to articulate rules of thumb teachable to apprentices. It is only beginning to develop to the status of a science with an organized body of theory from which new testable relations can be derived and that can evolve by assimilating new findings. Robert E. Lane (1959, 1962) made early contributions of this type in his investigations of attitudes associated with political participation and then of the origins of these attitudes. Oral history archives promise to expand the collection and availability of useful bodies of interview materials for scholars in the future. Thoughtful standardization of these archives would be useful.

Macrohumanistic studies of attitudes. Precursory to macrohumanistic studies of collectives was Myrdal's (1944) analysis of an American dilemma, constituted by egalitarian attitudes at odds with racially discriminatory behavior. Regional studies, often centered on an archetypical community ("Jonesville," "Yankee City," "Middletown," etc.) depicted the political minds of the South, of New England, and of the American heartland; only the Far West was neglected (perhaps because in those pre-jet days academic researchers were loathe to travel three thousand miles from the ocean to make their observations). Paradoxically, this macrohumanistic research, originally preoccupied with the minutiae of overt behavior and objective physical data, metamorphosed into a depiction of modal group mentality. This occurred among both U.S. participant-observers and the French *Annales* group. Participant observers such as Goffman recorded external gross behavior as data, but their interpretations often depict mentality more than do accounts by the survey researchers, even though the latter's verbal interview material promises more direct access to the subjective worlds of the respondents. A similar paradox appears in the earlier-born, more formidable *Annales* school stemming from Block and Febvre (Le Roy Ladurie, 1978/1981).

Microscientific studies of attitudes and voting.   Prototypical of the microscientific research on political attitudes were the early voting studies by Lazarsfeld, Berelson, and their colleagues (Lazarsfeld et al., 1944; Berelson, Lazarsfeld, & McPhee, 1954) associated with Columbia University and the University of Chicago. The most sustained program of such research has been at the University of Michigan, involving A. Campbell, Converse, Miller, and their colleagues (Campbell et al., 1954, 1960, 1966). The 1960s and 1970s were the great decades of this microscientific research on political attitudes and voting, as summarized by Kinder and Sears (1985), but interest has remained high due to the practical importance of the topic.

Macroscientific studies of political attitudes.   Macroscientific studies using conglomerates (nations, epochs, etc.) are rarer than microscientific studies. A macroscientific study transitional between the 1940s and 1950s political-personality era and the 1960s and 1970s political-attitudes era is McClelland's (1961) research on how societies' child-rearing practices affect and are affected by their citizens' achievement, power, and affiliation motivations, and how these in turn affect the rise and fall of the societies' political dominance, their cultural influence, and their economic affluence. McClelland's motivational mediators have elements both of the first era's personality and this second era's attitudinal mediators.

Because nations had been scored more frequently in regard to modal actions than modal attitudes, many macrostudies have focused on overt behaviors such as voting or violent acts rather than on the attitudes presumed to underlie them (although growing accumulations in social data archives are gradually facilitating work on the latter). Much of the macro work in the 1960s concentrated on politically disruptive behavior such as war, revolution, and crime (Davies, 1962; Feierabend & Feierabend, 1966; Gurr, 1970; Singer & Small, 1972; Naroll, Bullough, & Naroll, 1974). Other macroscientific studies focused on constructive characteristics, for example, Lipset's (1960) on political stability, Rokkan's (1962) and Almond and Verba's (1963) on cross-national differences in attitudes and political participation, Inkeles and Smith's (1974) on modernization attitudes, and Cantril's (1965) and Szalai and Andrews's (1980) on cross-national differences in felt quality of life and uses of leisure. The feasibility of such studies will increase as social data archives grow and multivariate, time-series causal analysis improves.

The 1980s–1990s Political Cognition and Decision Era

Characteristics of the 1980s–1990s political ideology era. The preferred interdisciplinary border-crossing has now shifted to a third frontier, political cognition, again with its distinguishing subject matter, method, and theory. It is best defined by its distinctive subject-matter focus, the content and operations of cognitive systems that affect decision-making in the political domain. Shared theoretical and methodological orientations provide only weak bonds in this third era, and are largely confined to using the computer as metaphor and tool. Depicting the person as an information-processing machine is a dominant theoretical model, with specifics drawn from cognitive science assumptions regarding how information is stored in memory and from decision theory assumptions regarding the heuristics of selective retrieval and weighing of information to arrive at a judgment (Axelrod, 1976; Tversky & Kahneman, 1983). Hastie (1986) summarizes aspects of cognitive science theorizing particularly pertinent to political psychology. Symptomatic of the computer inspiration of this third era is the use of computer flow charts to depict the person's ideology and decision processes (Janis, 1989).

The need to depict complex cognition systems and processes in this third era is likely to require more use of manipulational laboratory experimentation (Lodge & Hamill, 1986; Beer, Healy, Sinclair, & Bourne, 1987; Masters & Sullivan, 1993) than did the first two eras, but most data will continue to be collected in the natural political world (Tetlock, 1993). The complexity of using these natural-world data to clarify the structure and operation of ideology will require increasing use of path analysis, structural equation modeling (Hurwitz & Peffley, 1987), and computer simulations (Ostrom, 1988).

Notable contributions in the 1980s–1990s political ideology era. It would be premature this early in the third, political ideology, era to define it denotatively by a definitive listing of its major monographic contributions, but illustrative contributions are discernible in each of the four approaches. As regards the microhumanistic approach, noteworthy is Larson's (1985) use of cognitive heuristics to analyze the origins of the U.S. containment policy toward the Soviet Union during the early years of the cold war. George (1980) describes the effective use of information in presidential foreign-policy decisions. Purkitt and Dyson (1986) analyze the role of cognitive heuristics in affecting recent U.S. policy toward South Africa. Jervis (1986, 1993) analyzes how processes found in the laboratory (e.g., decision-makers ignoring base-rate information) may not operate in actual foreign-policy decision-making. Illustrative of the new cognitive psychobiography approach is Doise's (1986) analysis of how Mussolini's political ideology, derived from his study of Le Bon, Orano, and Sorel, affected his political policies and tactics. Depth interviewing is used to study the development of political consciousness and ideology in children by Coles (1986) and in adults by Reinarman (1987).

Macrohumanistic studies in the cognitive era, with nations as the units of observation, typically use case-history analyses such as those by Lebow (1981) on brinkmanship crises; by Jervis, Lebow, and Stein (1985) on the efficacy of a deterrence policy for averting war; and by Frei (1986) on cognitive barriers to disarmament. Popkin (1993) describes cognitive distortions that affect arms policies. Neustadt and May (1986) review the use of case histories by political decision-makers. A macrohumanistic study using epochs as the units of observation is Radding's (1985) application of Piaget's theory of cognitive development to account for a purported transformation toward abstractness in the mentality and society of western Europe from 400 to 1200 C.E.

The microscientific approach is illustrated by Suedfeld and Rank's (1976) and Tetlock's (1981, 1993) analyses of the kind of cognitive complexity required by revolutionary leaders if, like Fidel Castro, they are to avoid the classic Robespierrean trajectory of being consumed by their own revolution. These survivors need single-minded fanaticism to win the revolutionary struggle, but also flexibility to use compromise and accommodation in governing the postrevolutionary regime. Simonton has done intriguing microscientific studies of social factors affecting the productivity and processes of political and cultural leaders.

Illustrative of the nation-as-unit macroscientific approach to political psychology are Archer and Gartner's (1984) account of cross-national differences in violence in terms of social conditions on the national level that affect the cognitive salience of aggression as a mode of coping; Reychler's (1979) analysis of national differences in patterns of diplomatic thinking; and Tetlock's (1985) discussion of complexity in Soviet and U.S. foreign-policy rhetoric. Peripherally related are Martindale's (1981) cross-epoch analysis of the evolution of stylistic consciousness in art and Reiss's (1986) cross-cultural analyses of societal-level factors affecting the conceptualization of sexuality.

Future Directions

The politics and psychology relationship has been lively and long-lasting as interdisciplinary affairs go, its longevity fostered by frequent shiftings of its popular topics, methods, and theories. The fluidity has made participation both exciting and precarious, offering novelties that lure new recruits and facilitating the weeding out of tried-and-trivialized old constructs. The obverse of this tradition of novelty in interdisciplinary research is painfully rapid obsolescence. Earlier, the depth analysts of the political-personality era were edged out of the fast lane by the survey researchers of the political attitudes era, well-funded to study U.S. presidential elections; now these second-era survey researchers are finding the third era's cognitive science mavens tailgating to edge them out of the passing lane into cyberspace.

Participants in this interdisciplinary work. Recruitment of workers for the successive eras has been accomplished more by replacement than by retooling. A few (e.g., Lasswell, George, Lane, Converse, etc.) have moved with the changing interests of successive eras. More typically, researchers who initially created each era have continued to do good work in that old line after the new generation has moved a replacement enthusiasm to center stage. Over the three eras the participating subdiscipline from within psychology and the auxiliary field have shifted from personality psychology and psychiatry, to social psychology and communication, to cognitive psychology and computer science; however, the political scientists in all three eras have come mainly from its politics subdiscipline, plus, recently, students of international relations (Sears & Funk, 1991).

There has been a shift across the three eras also in regard to which third, auxiliary disciplines have contributed most to this collaboration. In the first, the political-personality era, outside help came primarily from psychiatrists and anthropologists (Stocking, 1987). In the second, the political-attitudes and voting behavior, era, the main outside collaboration was from sociologists and communication theorists; indeed, the sociologists' contributions to the study of voting behavior may have exceeded that of the political scientists or the psychologists . . . but who's counting? In the third, the political ideology era, cognitive scientists and decision theorists are the main auxiliary collaborators. Historians, particularly the cliometrics branch not always welcomed by more orthodox humanistic historians (Barzun, 1974; Bogue, 1983), have also contributed substantially (McGuire, 1976c).

A possible fourth era.   Past trends allow projecting, at least through a glass darkly, a fourth flourishing of political science/psychology collaboration that might follow the current 1980s and 1990s political ideology era. The past three eras have focused largely on intrapersonal topics (personality, attitudes, ideology), albeit as they are affected by social factors and as they in turn affect society. The fourth era is likely to switch, not again simply to another intrapersonal topic, but to interpersonal (and even intergroup) processes. The shift is adumbrated in the current work on how stereotypical perceptions and selective-information encoding affect international relations (Jervis, 1976), on jury decision-making (Hastie, Penrod, & Pennington, 1983), and on intergroup processes (Turner et al., 1987; Jervis, 1993; Sidanius, 1993).

If interest does move to interpersonal and intergroup processes, the union local of the psychological participants is likely to shift again, this time to group dynamics and organizational psychology; and participants from within political science are likely to come more often from foreign-policy and international relations as well as politics (Tetlock, 1986); the third-party collaboration is likely to come from historians and area specialists. Macroresearch is likely to grow relative to microresearch due to growing interest in intergroup issues. Both humanistic and scientific branches are likely to flourish: the humanistic, because the complexity of group processes invites the idiographic descriptive case-history approach; and the scientific, because increasing availability of social data archives and growing technical capacity for collecting and causally analyzing multivariate time-series data will make systems styles of research more possible. It would take more hubris than is pardonable to prognosticate in fuller detail the shape of this fourth flourishing in the new millennium.

HISTORICAL COMPARISONS: TESTING PSYCHOLOGICAL THEORY WITH CROSS-ERA DATA

[Adapted with permission from W. J. McGuire, 1976c, Historical comparisons: Testing psychological hypotheses with cross-era data, *International Journal of Psychology, 11,* pp. 161–183. Copyright © 1976 by the International Union of Psychological Science.]

Comparative (or Macro) Approaches in General

Here I turn from the history of psychology to the psychology of history, specifically to the use of cross-era comparative data on psychological variables to advance historical or psychological knowledge. Using cross-era data is only one (and a rather rare) species of current comparative approaches. Actually, the term *comparative research* as commonly used is inappropriate, not because it fails to fit the approaches so designated, but because it also fits most other research approaches. Almost all hypothesis testing is comparative in that one studies covariations across groups or individuals. What distinguishes the approaches under consideration is that comparisons are made among groupings larger than individual persons. Hence, a more apt term for the approaches discussed here (comparative anatomy, comparative literature, etc.) is the "cross-group" or "macro" approach. Use of macro units of observation raises philosophical worries like reductionism and the emergent properties of groups, but such problems turn out to be more apparent than real. Workers in the area readily appreciate the distinction between, say, differences in the relative ages of societies per se and differences in the mean age of the societies' members.

Organisms can be partitioned into subsets on many different bases, for example, into cross-species studies to yield "comparative anatomy," or into males versus females, giving us the study of sex differences; or we can partition humans on other bases to yield cross-national, cross-class, cross-cultural, cross-religion, or cross-era studies. It is on the latter that I focus here. Whether there are common themes that unite these various macrocomparative partitionings is a question that I and a few colleagues at the University of California, San Diego, discussed years ago. We considered whether a center for macrocomparative studies might be useful and whether a technique developed in, say, comparative anatomy might be useful in comparative literature and comparative psychology. We proposed to begin modestly with a graduate seminar that might interest a small number of students from our diverse departments. If that proved useful, we planned to take more ambitious steps and eventually write a proposal for establishing a grandiose center of comparative studies with seminars, research funds, and predoctoral and postdoctoral fellowship support. Political realities derailed our plans, but the idea deserves further consideration.

Past Utilizations of Historical Data to Test Psychological Hypotheses

The use of historical data has not been popular in psychology, but there has been enough passage along this historical side road to warrant mention of examples covering a half-century of research (McGuire, 1976c, 1994a).

Sorokin's cultural dynamics.   Pride of place as regards pioneering and energy level goes to Sorokin's (1937–41) four-volumed *Social and Cultural Dynamics,* in which he used historical data stretching over a millennium to develop his theses that culture in any era reflects a dominant Weltanschauung in all of its various manifestations – philosophical, political, artistic, scientific, and economic – and that the Weltanschauung evolves through three dominant themes, the sensate, the ideational, and the idealistic. Before government agencies provided funds, this unusual researcher managed to score a millennium of human history, decade by decade, on such variables as the personalities of its rulers, topics of its literature and painting, themes in its philosophical and religious thought, number of its scientific discoveries, and frequency and deadliness of its internal and international conflicts. Questions can be raised about some of his conclusions (Simonton, 1984), but Sorokin's time-series data remain a valuable social archival resource and a monument to what could, before the current research-grant era, be accomplished by a Stakhanovite laborer with a little help from friends and students.

J. Richardson's and Kroeber's analysis of women's dress fashions. Quantitative analysis by Jane Richardson and Kroeber (1940) of fluctuations in women's dress styles over the past two centuries reported a periodicity paralleling fluctuations in social unrest. They found an asymmetrical dress-style cycle whose dominant phase (constituting 75% of the cycle) was characterized by long and full skirts, with waists constricted and located at the anatomically appropriate place, and perhaps a large cutout at the neck. This long stable phase of the dress cycle was accompanied by a quiet, stable society. Periodically dress style swings briefly to the opposite phase (shorter and narrower skirts and waists that are higher or lower than is anatomically appropriate). This briefer phase of the cycle shows considerable stylistic fluctuation and is accompanied by social unrest.

L. Richardson's statistics of deadly quarrels.   Collecting and analyzing statistics on deadly quarrels was psychologist-turned-meteorologist Lewis Richardson's pioneering avocation for many years, although his books were published only posthumously (L. Richardson, 1960). He collected data on all violent deaths anywhere in the world over a 130-year period, these accounting for 1% of all deaths, occurring mostly in very small or very large conflicts. Discouragingly, wars seem to occur at a constant rate, breaking out and ending at intervals approximating a chance Poisson distribution. Nevertheless, Richardson investigated how frequency of war related to religion, language, contiguity, familiarity, economics, ideology, and the desire for revenge. In the process he also developed his unilateral disengagement approach to arms reduction.

McClelland's achieving-society research.   McClelland (1961) and his coworkers developed and tested their theory of how successive generations' inculcation of achievement, affiliation, and power motives in a society's children affects later economic, political, and cultural growth. They used historical data that ranged from half a millennium B.C.E. of the Hellenic experience, through several post-1500 C.E. centuries of Spain's and England's waxings and wanings, to the economic development of dozens of nations in the period between the two world wars. McClelland showed considerable ingenuity in defining and scoring across the centuries variables ranging from subjective motivational states to economic growth.

McGuire's historical archive of famous persons. In the early 1960s I began to assemble a historical archive of cultural data intended ultimately to include information on a wide range of culturally significant variables for most regions of the developed world for each quarter-century over several thousand years, and so to expand the temporal narrowness of the contemporary social indicator movement (Parke, 1976). Development of causal models, beginning with Donald Campbell's work on cross-lagged panel designs and then structural-equation models, promised powerful analyses. I began with a bottom-up historical materialism theory that natural resources and challenges were the driving forces in cultural evolution. My most basic independent variable was climate (global and micro) as history's fluctuating-variable driving engine. Climatic variations were hypothesized to affect, in turn, surplus labor, technical advances, institutional structure, and psychological differences in complex causal interrelations. I could have proceeded systematically by collecting time-series data on a broad spectrum of variables such as climatic changes, familial and other social organization, population fluctuation, economic and technological advances, artistic and cultural manifestations, and philosophical and religious orientations. Instead, I chose a more focused approach by collecting time-series data on just a few variables of obvious social scientific interest. I judged it more efficient if I and other historical archivists each began independently by collecting narrow bands of time-series data, each of us on variables that particularly interested us, while leaving until later the melding of these individual efforts and filling in the gaps.

My choice was to begin by developing a historical archive of data on eminent people of all times and places. Notable-people data are appealing because the topic is intrinsically interesting, because information tends to remain about noteworthy people even after little else is retained in historical memory, and because these data have been as-

C.E

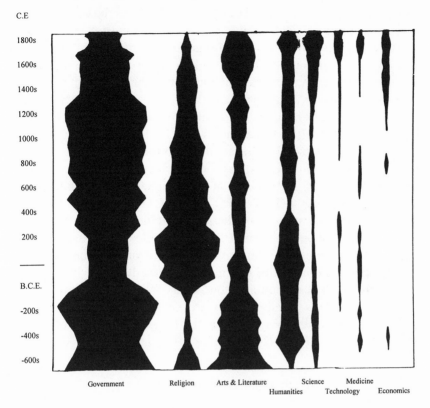

Figure 10.1
Variations from century to century in fields of endeavor in which fame was
attained. Width of each column indicates portion of all people eminent in
the row century who attained eminence in the column field.

sembled and preprocessed in forms easy to code. During the early
1960s Claire McGuire and I (with the help of undergraduate students from Columbia and Barnard College) assembled a historical
data archive containing basic information on 37,000 famous people of all times and places. Figure 10.1 shows the proportion of famous people in successive centuries of the past 2,500 years who
attained their fame in each of eight broad fields of endeavor (e.g.,
government, literature and art, business, etc.), fame being defined
as being named in *Webster's Biographical Dictionary.* These eight
broad fields of endeavor were broken down into three further levels of subdivision.

Other contemporary work. The growing interest in the historical approach of testing psychological hypotheses on the basis of quantitative cross-era data owes more to historians than to psychologists, especially to cliometricians such as Aydelotte, Benson, Fogel, and Tilly. Not everyone agrees that this quantitative history movement is a great leap forward, but any enterprise that is so vehemently condemned by Barzun (1974) can't be all bad. Contributions to two opposite, destructive versus constructive, topical areas have been particularly rich. One area is research on social conflict, foreshadowed by Wright (1942) and L. Richardson (1960). A number of researchers (Feierabend & Feierabend, 1966; Davis, 1971; Gamson & Modigliani, 1971; Naroll, Bullough, & Naroll, 1974; Tilly, 1975; Archer & Gartner, 1984) have developed social data archives on domestic and international violence to test hypotheses about war, crime, and modes of conflict resolution, including but going beyond the "revolution of rising expectation" theorizing. Contrasting with this research on destructive behavior is a parallel line of inquiry on cultural flourishing, following the trail blazed by Sorokin (1937–41) and paved by McClelland (1961), as previously described, often using biographical data (Jensen, 1970; Naroll et al., 1971; Simonton, 1975, 1976; McGuire, 1976c).

Methodological Challenges in Using Historical Data

Using historical data raises challenging problems in each phase of research: hypothesis generating, hypothesis testing, and communicating and utilizing the findings.

Creative hypothesis formation with historical data. The always challenging problem of generating interesting hypotheses may be especially demanding in a neglected approach like using cross-era data. A few of the creative heuristics described by McGuire (1973c, 1997b; see Table 11.1 in this volume) seem especially useful for hypothesis generation in cross-era research. (1) The case-study technique is appropriate in that certain historical moments serve as archetypical episodes that have been assimilated into many aspects of our common cultural heritage and have attained mythical status. Some involve quasi-historical personages such as Job, Oedipus, or Hamlet; others are actual historical episodes such as the French Revolution, the Cuban missile crisis, the industrial revolution, and diverse "media events" (Katz, 1980). Historical scholarship can constitute a refining process for bringing to the surface such hypothesis-provoking nuggets. (2) The paradoxical-incident technique involves recognizing the challenge of unexpected or implausible incidents rather than conditioning ourselves to ignore aberrant events that do not fit into our preconceptions or the general secular trend. For example, a moribund fin de siècle Vienna, semicapital of a decaying Hapsburg society, unexpectedly gave rise to a broad spectrum of cultural flourishing (e.g., Freud and the psychoanalytic movement, Mahler and Schönberg's musical innovations, Herzl and the other Zionists and kibbutz theorists launching their venture in Utopia, and innovators at the foundations of mathematics, philosophy, and science like Mach, Carnap, the Vienna circle, Wittgenstein, etc.). The attempt to account for this unexpected late Hapsburg flourishing, even in retrospect, is a provocative challenge. (3) Analogy as a technique of creative thinking involves extrapolating from relations between variables in a more familiar area to hypothesized corresponding relations in another area. In cross-era hypothesis generating a popular analogy is that between the growth of organisms and the history of societies, as is found in Toynbee (1946–57). From one's grasp of forces that affect the more familiar and briefer development of the individual, one makes analogies regarding the longer-term growth and decay of a civilization. This organism–society analogy is suspected to be linked to totalitarianism (Hofstadter, 1944), but its political incorrectness should not frighten one away from using a creative technique.

(4) Creative use of practitioners' rules of thumb involves the researcher's learning from the practitioner. For example, a conflict resolution theorist might examine the memoirs of diplomats to accumulate a propositional inventory of their dogmatically asserted principles or anecdotes about treaty negotiations, these propositions to be refined and tested empirically. (5) Analyses of conflicting observations in past studies or between past eras can be provocative in suggesting how the appearances can be saved (e.g., by redefining one's variables, adding restricting interaction assumptions, etc.). For example, in looking for an early warning signal of social unrest we may notice the prevalence of bearded men in twentieth-century cartoons depicting revolutionaries, suggesting as a first hypothesis that increasing (male) hairiness presages social upheaval. However, we then notice that prototypical French revolutionaries suggest the opposite hypothesis, that the Parisian aristocracy should have fled for their

châteaux when Robespierre, Sainte-Juste, and other young provincials began turning up in the bearded urban milieu with clean-shaven faces. Perhaps what is crucial is the first derivative – not whether males increase or decrease their hairiness absolutely, but whether there is a difference in hairiness between generations, sexes, or social classes. Other creative, hypothesis-generating heuristics are mentioned in McGuire, (1983a, 1997b), and in Table 11.1 in this volume.

Challenges in testing hypotheses with cross-era historical data. After one's psychology-of-history hypotheses have been formulated, special methods problems arise in the empirical-confrontational aspects of cross-era research having to do successively with devising the test, collecting the data, dealing with artifacts, and statistical analysis. Selecting units of observation can give rise to special problems in cross-era research. In my historical analyses of the proportion of all the eminent people who came from specified areas, the problem often arose that the geographic expanse of a country or province varied greatly from era to era: Poland and Lithuania at different times have each covered locations that are virtually nonoverlapping. Should we define political macro units of observation by political labels or by fixed geographic coordinates?

Operational definitions of historical variables pose special problems, even when archival time-series data are available in reference books such as the U.S. Bureau of the Census's *Historical Statistics of the U.S.* (1975) that give adjusted time-series data (e.g., adjusting costs or wages for inflation), but further tedious adjustments are often needed. With ingenuity, even the subjective states of societies in the remote past can be measured by content analyses of the literary corpus, as in the McClelland (1961) measures of achievement, affiliation, and power needs in classical Hellas from the ninth to the second centuries B.C.E. Even pictorial remains may serve, as illustrated by McClelland's (1961) use of a two-step analysis, starting with doodles diagnostic of current students' need for achievement, from which he inferred pre-Inca achievement needs from "doodles" on vase paintings.

Data collecting in cross-era research tend to be highly demanding of ingenuity, funds, and time. The solution is to enjoy the work oneself, develop a very high energy level, and have a family resigned to being neglected (or, better still, to pitching in on the task). One should also be willing and able to train others in these procedures, even where it involves a considerable amount of detailed instruction and prolonged supervision. Undergraduates tend to be more interested and interesting than graduate students, who are often too committed to mainstream approaches to tolerate the risks and tedium involved in offbeat comparative research (C. P. Smith, 1992). Like other special techniques, content analysis is not for everyone and should not be a required part of the curriculum, but should be available as an option in more graduate programs.

Artifacts such as bias by data loss tend to be prevalent in historical time-series data. It is not only that history is written by the victors but also that some domains are intrinsically more recordable than others (e.g., governmental and religious figures are better recalled by posterity than are business people and technological innovators, and artists better than scientists). More complex interactional selectivity arises when histories of contrasting fields are written by scholars of different nationalities or disciplines. We drew samples of famous people from two "universal" biographical dictionaries, one British (Thorne, 1962) and one American (Webster, 1972), and scored the biographies for birthplace, birth year, and field of work in which fame was attained. The scores from the British and U.S. sources correlated almost perfectly regarding what proportion of all eminent people were contributed by successive centuries (r = 1.00) and by eight broad fields of work (r = .97), but were more modestly correlated (r = .79) for the proportions contributed by broad geographic regions. Specifically, each nation's sourcebook exaggerated the contribution of its own geographical region. If we leave out the two dictionaries' own nations, the r =.79 across-dictionary reliability index for geography rises to r = .99. Selectional biases can be reduced by ipsatizing. More sophisticated adjustments are needed to handle more complex, interactional biases (e.g., if a biographical dictionary is overinclusive of Japanese artists while neglectful of Japanese authors). A distortion in cross-era research is that progress may speed up (e.g., Henry Adams's 1919 theory that historical change is accelerating exponentially). Corrections by scale transformations aggravate postfactum capitalization on chance and increase the need for cross-validation.

Two pervasive problems in cross-era research are that one is typically dealing with many factors covarying and with correlational data without the luxury of being able to use experimenter manipulation to help identify causal directions. Fortunately, there has been a great leap forward recently in multivariate analysis and on the causal-direction problem, even with the poorly scaled data typically available in cross-era research (Heise, 1976). It is not necessary that all students master such techniques, but the option to do so should be made widely available.

Problems in communicating and utilizing the results.   Because cross-era researchers are few and scattered, they should be especially attentive to one another's existence, exchanging letters and e-mail, and organizing symposia at conventions, until interest is stirred up sufficiently to support a newsletter, an internet bulletin board, and summer workshops, thus producing the level of social support, mutual stimulation, and training that many researchers need to do their best work.

The unfamiliarity of the cross-era approach poses problems also for publishing one's completed studies. Few editors are familiar with this type of manuscript, and the usual reviewers are inexperienced in evaluating and appreciating such work. Authors submitting cross-era manuscripts should be prepared for slower reviews, less useful critiques, and higher rejection rates. However, it is my impression that neither journals nor granting agencies are prejudiced against the use of unorthodox techniques such as the cross-era approach, and indeed are often attracted by such novelty if the study is solid.

There are special problems in using cross-era research to enrich psychological theorizing because its novelty makes it difficult for basic researchers to appreciate its relevance. The cross-era researcher should present the results in a way that will make it easy for readers accustomed to other approaches to incorporate the findings into their own theorizing. Special problems interfere with utilization of the results of cross-era research by theoreticians in other disciplines. Historians are typically humanistically oriented and gaze with something between fear and loathing upon data-mongering cross-era psychological research. It may be too late to convert humanistically oriented senior historians, but there are now journals of interdisciplinary history and an appreciable number of historians who are making highly sophisticated use of quantitative methods. Indeed, psychologists using historical data may find more welcome from cliometricians than psychologists.

As regards utilization by policymakers, again there are special problems for cross-era research. There are few bridges in the form of liaison people or institutions between the cross-era researcher and the practitioner, with the result that certifying the adequacy of specific cross-era studies is difficult. On the positive side, psychologists using historical data have the advantage of dealing with naturalistic and patently relevant content, due to testing hypotheses in real settings, which makes the subject matter more graspable by the practitioner than is research employing laboratory simulations. My focusing here on problems in cross-era research should not be discouraging, as these problems present interesting challenges for which solutions are becoming increasingly available.

11

Winters of Our Discontents: Crises in Social Psychology

[Adapted with permission from McGuire, 1973c, The yin and yang of progress in social psychology: Seven Koan, *Journal of Personality and Social Psychology, 26,* pp. 446–56. Copyright © 1973 by the American Psychological Association.]

Dissatisfactions are frequently expressed regarding experimental social psychology's Establishment paradigm of testing theory-derived hypotheses by laboratory manipulational experiments. These dissatisfactions are not fully met by the suggested variant of doing field experiments. A more radical departure is needed that would investigate programmatically systems of variables rather than simplistic independent-dependent variable relations. On the conceptual side an adequate replacement would derive hypotheses from a systems theory of social or cognitive structures that takes into account multiple and bidirectional causal links among the variables. On the empirical side, the new paradigm should test hypotheses in multiexperimental programs of research using multivariate correlational designs with naturally fluctuating time-series variables. Some steps toward this needed paradigm were described (McGuire, 1973c) in the form of seven koan (the East Asian allusions reflecting this paper's having originated as an invited address at the Tokyo 20th Congress of Scientific Psychology in 1972).

A half-dozen years earlier, at the Moscow Congress, and even three years before, at the London 19th Congress, social psychology appeared to be in a golden age. It was a prestigious and productive area in which droves of bright young people, a sufficiency of middle-aged colonels, and a few grand old generals were pursuing their research with a confidence and energy found in those who know where they are going. Any doubts we had involved anxiety that we were not doing our thing well, rather than uncertainty as to whether it deserved doing at all. The image of these golden boys (and too few golden girls) of social psychology, glowing with confidence and chutzpa only six years earlier at the Moscow Congress, blissfully unaware of the strident attacks that were soon to strike confusion into their ranks, can be described by a beautiful haiku of Buson:

> On a temple bell
> Resting, Resplendent,
> A butterfly.

The peaceful temple bell on which we were then displaying ourselves has now rudely rung. During the past half-dozen years, vibrations only vaguely sensed at the time of the Moscow meeting have gathered force. Now the temple bell has tolled and tolled again, causing turbulence in the stream of experimental social psychological research and shaking the confidence of the experimenters. Researchers inside the field and outside observers both seem to experience a sense of crisis. The rest of this chapter analyzes and describes some sources of this uneasiness with an obsolescent paradigm and some undercurrents that may be gathering force for the wave of the future that will eventuate in a new paradigm leading to further successes, after current crises are surmounted. I shall discuss the laboratory-artificiality crisis, the fun-and-games crisis, the banality crisis, the funding crisis, and the ethical crisis, all of which have beset social psychology.

Times of trouble are distracting but exciting periods in which to work. They are contentious periods when everything is questioned, when "the best lack all conviction, while the worst are full of passionate intensity." Crisis after crisis leads to the feeling that this is a time calling for the vulture that "devours death, mocks mutability, has heart to make an end, keeps nature new," until some "rough beast, its hour come round at last, slouches toward Bethlehem to be born." I used Buson's beautiful image of the sleeping butterfly to describe the proud and placid pre-crises social psychology, just before the bell began to toll. An image of the new social psychology struggling to be born evokes the variant on Buson's haiku written by his disciple, the angry young man Shiki:

> On a temple bell
> Metamorphosing, smoldering,
> A firefly.

THE RELEVANCE CRISIS: UNTANGLING
INDISTINCT DISTINCTIONS

[Adapted with permission from McGuire, 1969b, Theory-oriented research in natural settings: The best of both worlds for social psychology, in M. Sherif & C. Sherif (Eds.), *Interdisciplinary relations in social science,* pp. 21–51 (Chicago: Aldine de Gruyter, copyright © 1969).]

The Establishment has long identified good social psychological research with laboratory manipulational experiments, copying the preferred method of the older fields of scientific psychology such as psychophysics and learning. I am neither urging nor predicting the abandonment of this method, nor even its subordination. It is probably the most efficient and powerful single weapon in our social psychological research armamentarium. However, organisms tend to over-congregate at optimal points, so those of us able to stand alone should foster evolution and progress by exploiting neglected, nonoptimal niches. We should correct the current, almost exclusive emphasis on the laboratory experiment by supplementing it, occasionally testing our theoretically derived hypotheses by correlational research in natural field settings. I am not asserting that we should stop acting like physicists but that we should act occasionally like astronomers.

Some Distinctions Regarding Distinctions
in Research

Distinctions, along with definitions, promote conceptual clarity but can add confusion when one fails to untangle several of them that are obliquely related to one another, as in the case of several overlapping distinctions often confused in social science methodology. A first of these distinctions is between the creative and the critical aspects of scientific research, between hypothesis generating and hypothesis testing and refinement. The two processes tend to intermingle: Even while creatively generating hypotheses, we are often critically censoring and qualifying them by conceptual confrontations; and the empirical confrontation of a hypothesis is heuristically provocative of new creative insights rather than being simply a test of some fixed a priori hypothesis. However intermingled the two processes are or ought to be in practice, they are conceptually distinct, and the total scientific process involves both generating and evaluating hypotheses.

A second, related but different, distinction is between basic and applied research, that is, between theory-oriented versus action-oriented research. In terms of my previous distinction, this basic-versus-applied distinction is pertinent to the creative, hypothesis-generating aspect of research. The scientist is engaged in basic research to the extent that, in the creative, hypothesis-generating process, he or she derives predictions from theoretical conceptualizations with the aim of clarifying, testing, and developing the theory. One is involved in applied research to the extent that he or she derives predictions during creative hypothesis generation from the practical need to make an informed decision in a policy situation requiring action. In either basic or applied research considerable creative ingenuity is needed if the research is to provide valid new information.

Still another distinction, that between field and laboratory research, arises in the critical, hypothesis-testing aspect of research. One is engaged in field research to the extent that one tests one's hypothesis in natural settings, in a world one never made. One is engaged in laboratory research to the extent that one tests one's hypothesis in artificial situations of one's own contrivance, acting like Daedalus as a skilled artificer forging conditions in which to test the hypothesis. There are gradations of naturalness and artificiality. This laboratory–field distinction pertains to the a posteriori, empirical aspect of research and thus is in principle orthogonal to the preceding distinction between basic and applied research, which pertains to the a priori, conceptual aspect of theory development. Either basic or applied research can be conducted in the laboratory or in the field.

A fourth distinction, pertaining to the a posteriori empirical aspect of hypothesis development, is that between correlational and manipulational research. Correlational research is involved when the researcher, in testing the hypothesis, does not manipulate the independent variable but capitalizes on nature's having already varied the units of observation (usually people) on it. Manipulational research involves hypothesis testing when the researcher determines the participants' levels of the independent variable, assigning them at random (or by some matching procedure) to different levels. This distinction is orthogonal to the previous one of testing hypotheses in natural settings versus in the laboratory, but, unfortunately, methodologists sometimes talk as if research in field settings confines one to the correlational tactic and laboratory research to the manipulational tactic. Manipulational research can be done either in the field or in the laboratory, as can correlational research.

Apotheosis of "The Experiment"

Although *experimental* is often used to refer narrowly to laboratory research (or to manipulational research, whether in laboratory or field), its etymologically correct usage is in the broader sense of "testing." One is experimenting whenever one tests an explicit hypothesis, whether in the laboratory or in the field and whether by manipulation or preselectional variation of the independent variable. Charity, as well as etymological correctness, calls for using *experimental* broadly, because ever since the 1960s the term has come to be used almost ritualistically as a PC adjective in any social psychology undertaking, including its periodicals (e.g., *Advances in Experimental Social Psychology* since 1964; the *Journal of Experimental Social Psychology* since 1965) or its associations (such as "The European Association of Experimental Social Psychology" since 1963; and, contemporaneously, "The Society of Experimental Social Psychology"). To restrict *experimental* to manipulational research would exclude much respectable work from the approved canon.

Controversies arise periodically regarding where the balance of our research effort should shift between basic and applied issues, or between laboratory and field settings, or between manipulational and preselectional variation on the independent variables. I am arguing here that these three choices raise quite different issues, often confused in the asking and answering. When each is unconfounded by the others, the appropriate answer tends to be that both poles on each dimension offer opportunities. Scientists tend to overcongregate at optimal points and therefore imbalances arise periodically that call for corrective shifting of effort toward the neglected pole, a shifting that usually eventuates in overcorrection.

THE SOBRIETY CRISIS: FUN-AND-GAMES VERSUS PURITANISM

[Adapted with permission from McGuire, 1967, Some impending reorientations in social psychology, *Journal of Experimental Social Psychology, 3*, pp. 124–39. Copyright © 1967 by Academic Press.]

Social psychologists' overemphasis on theory-oriented, laboratory manipulational research has had a by-product that some find particularly objectionable, namely, the emergence of a fun-and-games coterie who derive gratification from their clever deceptions, outrageous laboratory or field manipulations, and flashy gimmicks more than from either advancing psychological theory or providing directives for action. The charge has merit and the spectacle is gross. However, the fun-and-gamesters seem to evoke criticism, not only for their worrisome manipulations and outrageous deceptions per se, but also for their deriving pleasure from their flamboyant happenings. The indignation they arouse reminds me of H. L. Mencken's description of puritanism as the haunting fear that someone, somewhere, may be enjoying himself. One might wish that these fun-and-gamesters were motivated by some human impulse nobler than play, but if fun induces them to work then let the play go on.

Einstein has written that worshipers come to the temple of scientific research for many motives – financial gain, a pleasant life, social recognition – but few out of sheer love for the advancement of knowledge. I fear that such devotees are as rare in psychology as in physics. However, we should be tolerant of the motivations that bring laborers to the vineyard. If a researcher is at work it might be best to refrain from asking whether he or she is doing it to develop theory, to solve the world's problems, to make a living, to stay out of the army, or to outrage the bourgeoisie. If the yield is worthwhile, we can be permissive about motivation. At the U.S. Infantry School at Fort Benning, Georgia, they used to teach us, as a default tactical decision, "If in doubt, do anything, but do something." If there are some social psychology gamesters who do their work mainly because of its play aspect, then let us say to them, racket under arm, "Social psychology, anyone?"

Wrath against the fun-and-gamesters may derive in part, not from puritanism, but from fear that a Gresham's law might operate such that the fun-and-gamesters will corrupt or drive out the sterling youth by insinuating that serious social psychologists are floundering around in unimaginative, obvious research while the funsters alone are doing exciting, creative, counterintuitive work. However, I am confident that flashy work will not long lure students from high-quality programmatic research. I keep the faith that in the free market of ideas the best work wins out in the end and the best workers receive the most emulation. Arguing with the gamesters only strengthens their stubborn attachment to frivolities; if we allow them to work in peace we give them space to grow out of the gamester approach. Furthermore, the notion that good research has to be dull is no more compelling than that only flashy research is good. Researchers dismayed by the gamesters might echo De Gaulle's Delphic utterance to the revolting colonists of Algiers, "Je vous comprends," and like him proceed with their own agenda. I make a Pascalian wager that, in the long run, class will tell.

In this fun-and-games conflict, as in many others, there is much to be said on both sides. To every complex problem there is always a simple solution – and it is always wrong. This is not to say that we must be neutral between good and evil but that we must make a measured response: As one or another trend becomes overemphasized, some of us must provide the corrective counterweights. It is not to be expected that the corrective pressure needed in one decade will be the same as that needed ten years later. I am unworried either by the overemphasis of laboratory manipulational studies or by the visibility of the fun-and-games approach because correctives are already on the horizon, now no bigger than a person's hand, but likely to swell to an overcorrection that itself will call for counterpressure. Some of us should adopt Simone Weil's counterbalancing intellectual position: that there are those of us whose vocation it is, when two forces are in contention, to jump onto the scale on the weaker side and hope that the occasional error of our choice will be excused by the purity of our motives. The best policy may be to impute the highest purity of motives to those who are working with us (or even against us). The researcher, altercast by being attributed the purest of motives, tends to introject the noble imputation as reality and acts in keeping with it. By imputing to both fun-and-gamesters and their attackers the purest of motives we may create a moral climate that will permit a rapprochement and an escalation in the quality of research done by both parties.

THE CREATIVITY CRISIS: ONE HAND CLAPPING, WITH THE WRONG HAND

[Adapted with permission from McGuire, 1983a, A contextual theory of knowledge: Its implications for innovation and reform in psychological research, in L. Berkowitz (Ed.), *Advances in experimental social psychology,* Vol. 16, pp. 1–47 (New York: Academic Press, copyright © 1983). See also McGuire, 1997b.]

Researchers generally agree that the research process includes generating as well as testing hypotheses and probably agree also that the generating is the more important because a hypothesis must be formulated before it can be tested. That scientific methods courses and text-books focus almost exclusively on hypothesis-testing topics (e.g., experimental design, measurement, inferential statistics) and ignore the creation of hypotheses probably reflects, not failure to appreciate its importance, but beliefs that it is limited by the inborn creativity of the researcher and that it can hardly be described, much less taught. At most, a mentor may encourage the student to read publications by or work as an apprentice with creative researchers, on the chance that a knack for generating interesting hypotheses may be absorbed by some kind of intellectual osmosis.

The perspectivist view of knowledge (McGuire, 1989b; and chapter 12 in this volume) as (mis)representation of the known, whose validity varies with viewpoint and context, implies that creativity is commonplace, because even everyday acts of knowing involve considerable creativity (or "error") in the form of selectivity, extrapolation, and transformation. On the societal level, institutional arrangements can be designed to establish research settings that encourage scientists to produce creative theoretical representations (Pelz & Andrews, 1976; Andrews, 1979; Latour & Woolgar, 1979; Goodfield, 1981). On the microlevel, the individual researchers can be trained in the use of heuristics that facilitate creative hypothesis generating (Stein, 1974; Amabile, 1983). That the creative process can be described and taught is shown by the dozens of creative heuristics for which I have provided descriptions and training programs (McGuire, 1997a). In chapter 10 of this volume a half-dozen of these tactical heuristics are described as they are used for generating hypotheses in the special area of the psychology of history. For a description and organization of several dozen of these heuristics, see McGuire, 1973c, 1980c, 1983a, 1997a, 1997b as sketched in Table 11.1. Creative techniques on the broader strategic level of programmatic research are considered in chapter 12.

THE FUNDING CRISIS AND THE RICHES OF POVERTY

[Adapted with permission from McGuire, 1973c.]

The industrialized countries that finance most of the psychological research periodically suffer economic growing pains, which, if they do not quite reduce the total funds appropriated for scientific research, do reduce the rate at which this research funding has been growing.

384 Constructing Social Psychology

Table 11.1.

Types of creative heuristics used to generate psychological theories and hypotheses

I. Heuristics Simply Calling for Sensitivity to Provocative Natural Occurrences
   A Recognizing and Accounting for the Oddity of Observed Phenomena
      1. Accounting for deviations from the general trend
      2. Accounting for the oddity of the general trend itself
   B. Introspective Self-Analysis Heuristics
      3. Analyzing one's behavior in like situations
      4. Role playing: imagining oneself in a like situation
   C. Retrospective Comparison Heuristics
      5. Extrapolating from like problems already solved
      6. Confronting opposite problems to suggest reciprocal solutions
   D. Sustained, Deliberate Observation
      7. Intensive case studies
      8. Participant observation
      9. Assembling propositional inventories
II. Heuristics Involving Simple Conceptual Analysis (Direct Inference)
   E. Simple Conversions of a Banal Proposition
      10. Accounting for the contrary of a trite hypothesis
      11. Reversing the plausible direction of causality
      12. Pushing a reasonable hypothesis to an implausible extreme
      13. Imagining effects of reducing a variable to zero
      14. Conjecturing interaction variables that qualify a relation
   F. Multiplying Insights by Conceptual or Linguistic Division
      15. Linguistic explorations
      16. Alternative manipulations of the independent variable
      17. Dividing the dependent variable into distinctive subscales
      18. Analyzing output steps into a sequence
   G. Jolting Conceptualizing Out of Its Usual Ruts
      19. Shifting attention to the problem's opposite pole of the problem
      20. Alternating preferred/nonpreferred search styles
      21. Expressing one's hypothesis in multiple modalities
      22. Disrupting ordinary states of consciousness
III. Heuristics Requiring More Complex Conceptual Analysis (Mediated Inference)
   H. Deductive-Reasoning Heuristics
      23. Generating multiple explanations for a relation
      24. Alternating induction and deduction
      25. Identifying forces hiding an obvious relation
      26. Hypothetico-deductive sets of postulates

Table 11. 1 *(cont.)*

    I. Heuristics Using Thought-Diversifying Structures
       27. Using an idea-stimulating checklist
       28. Constructing complex generating structures
       29. Formalizing explanatory accounts
    J. Heuristics Using Metatheories as Thought Catapults
       30. Evolutionary functional (adaptivity) analyses
       31. Transferring conceptualizations analogously
       32. Quixotic defense of a theory
IV. Heuristics Demanding Reinterpretations of Past Research
    K. Delving into Single Past Studies
       33. Accounting for irregularities in obtained relations
       34. Decomposing nonmonotonic into simpler relations
       35. Deviant-case analysis
       36. Interpreting serendipitous interaction effects
    L. Discovery Tactics Involving Integrating Multiple Previous Studies
       37. Reconciling conflicting results and nonreplications
       38. Bringing together complementary past experiments
       39. Organizing current knowledge on a topic
  V. Heuristics Necessitating Collecting New or Reanalyzing Old Data
    M. Qualitative Analyses
       40. Content-analyzing open-ended responses
       41. Participating actively in the research routine
       42. Exploring a glamorous technique
       43. Including fertile, low-cost interaction variables in the design
       44. Pitting confounded factors against one another
       45. Strategic planning
    N. Quantitative Analyses
       46. Multivariate fishing expeditions
       47. Subtracting out the effect of a known mediator
       48. Computer simulation
       49. Mathematical modeling

Note: See McGuire, 1997b, for details.

With Dr. Pangloss optimism I insist that things are going to turn out well, and I even engage in gallows humor by saying that what psychological research needs is a good Depression. In periods of affluence, when government funds for psychological research can be had almost for the asking, the discipline develops some fat, bad habits and distorted priorities. Although corrections could theoretically be made without enforced poverty, at least we can make a virtue of necessity by using periods of budgetary retrenchment to cut out some of the waste and distraction so that we shall emerge from periods of retrenchment leaner but keener than we entered it.

Easy research money tends to induce frenzies of expensive and exhausting activity. In hiring more research assistants we often have to dip into less creative populations. To keep them busy, the easiest thing to do is to have them continue doing pretty much what they have been doing already, resulting in a stereotyping of research and a repetitious output. It also motivates researchers to churn out one little study after another, leaving little opportunity for the long view or blocks of time for programmatic planning of sequences of studies and for the more solitary and reflective intellectual activity of integrating isolated findings into more meaningful big pictures.

Affluence also encourages complex research organization, which diverts the senior scientist from observing the phenomena to observing the data. In research programs flush with research funds, the primary observation is typically done by graduate assistants and research associates, who often delegate the actual observations and data processing to undergraduates or hourly help. The data collected are fed into routine computer analysis programs whose output goes to research associates, who might call some of the more meaningful pages of relations to the attention of the senior researcher, who may be too busy meeting the payroll to control the form of the printout or look diligently through it when it arrives. A cutback in research funds might divert these assistants into more independent, productive, and satisfying work, while freeing the creative senior researcher for observing the phenomena instead of meeting the payroll.

Budgetary cutbacks could save us from running ever faster on the Big-Science treadmill. Instead, we could make the best of our fiscal adversity by changing our research organization, modes of working, and priorities. Rather than fighting for a bigger slice of a diminishing financial pie, established scientists might redirect their efforts and rediscover the gratification of personally observing the phenomena themselves and experiencing the freedom from administering a research empire. Time would become available for interpreting and integrating the empirical relations that have been turned up by the recent deluge of studies, rather than simply adding new, undigested relations to the existing pile.

THE ETHICAL CRISES

There are ethical aspects to most controversies, including those already mentioned in this chapter such as the basic-versus-applied approaches, the fun-and-games style of conducting research, and funding competition. In this section I shall deal with two issues whose ethical dimensions are especially central. One issue concerns persuasion, its use in society and its study by researchers; the other issue involves participants' right to privacy as it conflicts with the researcher's zest to discover and disclose.

The Social and Moral Significance of Persuasion and Its Study

[Adapted with permission from McGuire, 1985a.]

Great ages of persuasion.   The isolated periods of history when persuasion flourished as a major instrument for social mobilization and control (e.g., the Hellenic century, 427–322 B.C.E.) have been times of social disruption brought about by expanding economic and cultural experiences that presented new problems and challenges, sharpened cleavages among factions too numerous, divided, or evenly matched for any one to maintain hegemony, and that called into question traditional verities and accustomed modes of social mobilization and control. At such periods persuasive communication was especially needed to rally one's own faction, forge alliances, and woo the masses into temporary policy consensus. Such periods have been exciting but uncomfortable times of social mobility and instability, rich in cultural, artistic, and life-style novelties but with an accompanying vulgarization of taste, decay of ritual and liturgy, and decline of social amenities and polite conventions. The public contentiousness of these eras usually appalls the traditional elites, not only the political and religious Establishments but also the intelligentsia. Just as today's cultural elites express distaste for advertising and disdain for television programs, so the Platonic Academy loathed the sophists and so the Roman senatorial class despised the oratorical schools of Rhodes and Athens to which the rising commercial equites class (and not a few senators) sent their sons (G. A. Kennedy, 1980; Marrou, 1981).

Such vulgar contentiousness and hucksterism have not long to be endured. The three earlier great ages of persuasion (the 427–322

B.C.E. Hellenic, the 133–43 B.C.E. Roman, and the 1470–1572 C.E. Renaissance), have been nasty, brutish, and short interludes of social change that only briefly disturbed history's chronic sleepwalking. In each such age agitation and propaganda have soon been replaced by sterner means of social control (Lind, 1983). The tragic vanity of thinking that the word is mightier than the sword is exhibited by the fates of the rhetorical masters of each of the three previous centuries of persuasion: Demosthenes, done in by poison under the Macedonians his philippics had failed to halt; Cicero, by the knives of the triumvirs at whom his later philippics were aimed; and Ramus, dispatched in the St. Bartholomew's Day massacre – each silenced by his inarticulate targets, whose brutally effective responses proved that the rhetorician had spoken against them wisely but not too well. Contentious interludes like our own soon revert to the long torpor of history when structural means of social control repress the internal contradictions of society under state authoritarianism, religious orthodoxy, or the smothering conventionalities of village morality and political correctness.

The ethics of the study of persuasion.   The deliberate study of persuasion strikes some sensitive people as distasteful and even immoral (R. K. White, 1971; Andrén, 1980; Goodin, 1980). Plato, in *Gorgias*, used his certainty theory of knowledge and truth to argue that because rhetoric deals with probabilities, it inevitably spawns error; Aristotle, in *Rhetoric,* characteristically hedged by judging persuasion an ambivalent means that can serve either truth or error; but he regarded it as yielding at best an inferior type of truth (G. A. Kennedy, 1963). Current elites worry that advertising hucksters are creating new and insatiable wants, that political candidates are selling images without ideology, and the raucous rabble-rousers are making the masses less accepting of the discomforts to which they had become fairly accustomed. Conversely, but to the same effect, advocates of change complain that persuasive talent is coopted by the dominant factions to maintain the economic, cultural, political, and religious status quo (Goodin, 1980; E. Katz & Szecsko, 1981). We researchers who study persuasion should wrestle with these charges.

Persuasion does have its defenders. There is the romantic possibility that a lost cause, an innovative idea, or an individual at risk can gain a hearing and perhaps even prevail if advocated with sufficient eloquence. Although often used for oppression, persuasion more than other modes of social control can also become a source of release or innovation. Isocrates, in defending the sophists against Plato, argued that rhetoric is what distinguishes humans from beasts and is what has allowed the otherwise poorly endowed human species, lacking in tooth and claw, to form functioning communities within which they can endure and score their occasional triumphs. The hucksterism of our present persuasive interlude may be remembered with nostalgia after its suppression produces a quieter society within which each knows his or her place and there are few options to be argued. At those more normal times, a few aberrant young who see visions and old who dream dreams may discern that persuasion is the worst mode of social mobilization and conflict resolution – except for all the others.

Disclosure and Privacy: A Researcher's Dilemma

[Adapted from McGuire, 1980e, The value of privacy versus the need to know, in W. C. Bier (Ed.), *Privacy: A vanishing value?* pp. 331–347 (New York: Fordham University Press, copyright © 1980).]

An internal contradiction for intellectuals – producers and consumers of words – is that we tend to be very private people, cherishing our own privacy and solicitous after that of others but at the same time engaging in the zealous search for truth, for making known the hidden things of this world. Our personal attachment to privacy seems to conflict with our professional conviction that discovery will make us free, a dilemma that may lead to confusion and evasion or may provide the impetus for a higher ethical synthesis. As a member of a six-person American Psychological Association task force, I developed a code of ethics for the treatment of human participants in research (Cook et al., 1973), a code that devotes eleven of its hundred pages to discussing how participants' privacy should be protected. Of course, the task force affirmed that information about individual participants obtained during the course of research is confidential, and that when the possibility exists that others may gain access to such information this risk should at least be disclosed on the consent form. Recognizing that some people feel a greater need for privacy than do others and that some kinds of information are especially deserving of confidentiality, the researcher must take a conservative stance in keeping private anything learned about the participant where there is reasonable suspicion that a participant may prefer that it not be disclosed. Beyond this, our task force wrestled with hard cases, some of which will be mentioned here.

Obligations to violate one's commitment to privacy. The researcher's obligation to maintain the confidentiality of information obtained about the participant must sometimes be weighed against other moral considerations that permit or indeed compel disclosure, even when there has been an explicit promise of confidentiality. The participant's responses may disclose impending self- or other-destructive behaviors such as child abuse. These incidents are "hard cases," which the researcher must decide on an ad hoc basis. Evidence tends to be ambiguous and values to conflict. One's decisions not to disclose should be examined especially closely, because nonaction tends to be the easier choice for the researcher and so must stand scrutiny that it was not selected for the researcher's convenience rather than for the general good. Another hard case (McGuire, 1980e) is whether the participant has the right to privacy from the self: Did Milgram's (1974) obedience-to-authority studies deprive the participants of their right to remain ignorant of disturbing information about the self? A nontrivial proportion of potential recruits might choose not to participate if forewarned of the possibility of such stressful self-disillusionment.

The right to categorical privacy.   Still another hard case is whether the researcher's confidentiality obligations extend beyond the participants' individual privacy to his or her collective (or "categorical") privacy. For example, to test the hypothesis that Catholics, particularly those who have attended parochial schools, are more anti-Jewish than Jews are anti-Catholic, the social scientist (Greeley, 1977) may carry out survey research that not only fails to confirm the hypothesis but indicates the opposite: that Catholics are less anti-Jewish than Jews are anti-Catholic, and that Catholics who attended parochial school are particularly low in anti-Jewish feelings. It would, of course, be an ethical violation to report an individual participant's anti-Jewish or anti-Catholic attitude scores. The more subtle "disclosure by category" issue is whether it is an unethical violation of the privacy of the Jewish (or Catholic) participants to reveal that their religious group is the more prejudiced, a revelation that might disturb some participants and expose their group to abuse. One might reasonably suspect that some Jewish or Catholic respondents, had they foreseen disclosure of information damaging to their group, might have refused to participate.

Rather than forgo a socially important investigation the researcher could, in keeping with the informed-consent and privacy principles, reveal to the participants in advance the issue under study and the possibly embarrassing outcome, thus allowing those who do not wish to have their membership group's prejudiced feelings revealed to decline to participate. Unfortunately, forewarning is likely to result in selective refusals to participate and to activate a social-desirability sensitization that would distort the answers provided by those who did participate.

In this dilemma, the researcher might decide that society's need to know justifies a violation of the informed-consent and privacy principles, prejudice being so important a social problem and so basic a theoretical issue. The researcher might complain belligerently that if these individuals are so ashamed of their prejudices, then rather than hiding them they should change them. However, one purpose of our imposing on ourselves explicit ethical codes, outside reviewers, and other restrictions is to give us pause when our initial decision in a moral dilemma is in accord with our self-interest. Also, the principle of informed consent seems to confer on the participant the privilege of deciding which aspect of the research is relevant to his or her decision to participate and the right to be informed regarding this aspect. The person has the right to decline to participate even for what a researcher regards as a mere side issue or as none of the participant's business (e.g., who is sponsoring the research, what is being investigated, or intended uses of the results).

Research as intrinsically reducing the domain of the private. A function of psychological research is to lay bare hidden things about significant aspects of people and their environment, making these relations understandable, perhaps predictable, and even controllable. Research inevitably reduces the realm of the private, especially disturbing in the social and behavioral sciences whose revelations expose the person and human culture.

Are there some topics which are best left unstudied? This question might seem, in this age of inquiry, to have an antique sound, but Popper (1972) has reminded us that only in the last two centuries in western Europe, and perhaps in a century of Hellenic civilization, could thinkers inquire into the nature of the universe without risking charges of impiety (and even in these few inquiring centuries of history, questioners like Thales, Socrates, Darwin, and Bertrand Russell have been rebuked for their inquiries). The Judeo-Christian tradition of the fall of humanity is described in Genesis, chapter 3, as originating in inquiry that revealed shameful knowledge. Even in science-oriented nations of our own day, theorizing on topics as harmless as cosmogony and linguistics has been injurious to the health of the inquirer. That history reveals so few inquiring societies raises the worry that research may be maladaptive to the evolution, comfort, or even survival of human communities.

Western society today has so pronounced a respect for inquiry that it would be perverse to propose seriously that it is generally desirable to leave matters unexamined, respecting the privacy of all existence and leaving the world as we find it without putting questions to nature. However, it is still reasonable to ask whether there are some things, particularly within the subject matter of the social and behavioral sciences, that are best left unstudied. Even professional researchers often maintain in their private lives that some things are best left unclear, preserving benign ambiguities about their own and others' strengths and weaknesses, feelings, and fate in order to make life more bearable and human relationships more harmonious.

Privacy issues: Ethics or esthetics?   Perhaps I am here raising issues of taste or esthetics rather than of morality, a possibility suggested by the wide swings of fashion on this privacy issue. The older among us belong to a generation who, like Conrad's Kurtz or Marlow, have seen the Heart of Darkness in some personal Congo, so that even the stately Thames reminds us that "this also has been one of the dark places of earth," causing us to shudder and pull back. Younger-aged cohorts, not having experienced the horror, may resonate with Jerry Rubin and the 1960s Yippies' motto, "Let it all hang out." Predilections that a generation or two ago dared not speak their names now assault our ears with constant cacophonous clamor. Esthetic feeling, though it may be an origin or a partial test of the ethical, serves only as an oscillating compass.

Psychologists may have difficulty on occasion in reconciling two opposing obligations: to seek the truth by expanding the domain of knowledge versus to avoid embarrassing revelations by preserving those saving ambiguities and personal privacies which make life more tolerable. In carrying out their professional work researchers usually have little trouble resolving this dilemma. Having chosen an intellectual vocation, they tend to put high value on the discovery and communication of truth; rarely, if ever, do they decide that some domains are best left private; and if such decisions are made, it is probably in their private rather than professional activities. My personal position is that in our private life we should preserve a large domain for privacy and ambiguity. In our lives as professional researchers, in contrast, we should inquire zealously. There are some topics which I myself could not bear to study, but I would be hard put to name any topic which I feel to be so intrinsically private that I would put its study ethically off-limits or forbid its study by those with stronger stomachs, however much I might be revolted by their taste.

Several principles underlie my prejudice that conflicts between discovery and privacy should always be resolved in favor of discovery, even when the research topic concerns the person and human society. One excusing principle is that truth, like goodness, is a transcendental attribute of being, so ultimately the expansion of knowledge recovers the good. Knowledge becomes good by definition, so that conflicts between revelation and concealment should invariably be resolved in favor of discovery and communication. The researcher's professional imperative is that it is best to know, at least in the long run (even granting that in the short run the truth may hurt and that in the long run we shall all be dead).

So while remaining a very private person outside my professional vocation, when as a researcher I am confronted with difficult questions as to whether some things are best left uninvestigated, I invariably condone the inquiry (admittedly, sometimes with fear and trembling and often cringing with distaste at the Noah who can "bear to see the towns like coral under the keel"). This choice of discovery over privacy is obviously tainted by professional self-interest, but it puts me in harmony with the paean to knowledge found in the Book of Wisdom (Wis. 7:7–14) and that appeared in the Tridentine liturgy, appropriately, as the lesson in the mass for Saint Thomas Aquinas:

> I sought and understanding was given to me:
> I entreated, and the spirit of wisdom came upon me.
> And I preferred her to kingdoms and thrones;
> Compared to her, I held riches as nothing.
> I found no jewel to be her peer,

For compared to her, all gold is a pinch of sand,
And beside her silver ranks as clay.
I loved her more than health or beauty,
I preferred her to the light,
Since her light never fails.
In her company all good things came to me,
At her hands came riches without number.
In all of these things I rejoiced, since wisdom brings them,
Even when I did not know that she was the mother of them all.
What I have learned without envy I communicate without guile;
I shall not hide her riches.
For she is an inexhaustible treasure to all,
Which those who use become the friends of God,
Commended to Him by the gifts of wisdom.

12

A Perspectivist Epistemology:
Knowledge as Misrepresentation

[Adapted with permission from W. J. McGuire, 1986c, A perspectivist looks at contextualism and the future of behavioral science, in R. Rosnow & M. Georgoudi (Eds.), *Contextualism and understanding in behavioral science: Implications for research and theory*, pp. 271–301 (New York: Praeger, copyright © 1986). An imprint of Greenwood Publishing group.]

Each generation of intellectuals has a characteristic mode of wonder: Mine is an epistemological generation, whereas the preceding one was fascinated by cosmogonal issues, and the more recent generation by issues of power and publicity. I had the delight of entering psychology in an epistemological age: To paraphrase Wordsworth's *Prelude,* "Bliss it was in that dawn to be (a psychologist) but to be (a cognitive social psychologist) was very heaven." Most of my varied lines of research have been pursued with the metamotivation of grasping what it is "to understand." The descriptive and prescriptive principles for the advancement of behavioral science knowledge outlined in this chapter derive from my tragic view of knowledge called "perspectivisim," which recognizes knowledge as a necessary but essentially flawed mode of representational coping with an overly complex self and environment.

My epistemologically oriented cohort that entered psychology around midcentury was concerned with the nature of knowledge – its internal structure, its relations to the world it represents and to the language in which it is expressed. In this preoccupation we were heirs of early-twentieth-century philosophers like Peirce, James, Dewey, and the pragmatists; Wienerkreis affiliates such as Schlick, Carnap, Hempel, Feigl, Bergman, and Popper; Russell, Whitehead, Wittgenstein, and a gaggle of British or other word quibblers. This twentieth-century preoccupation with the nature of knowledge and the language in which it is expressed is a departure from the nineteenth-century preoccupation with cosmogonal issues regarding the evolution of the physical and biological worlds. The great leaps forward in amassing and organizing environmental information made by Darwin, Marx, Spencer, Mendeleev, and others had in the nineteenth century allowed turning from collecting to analyzing knowledge. The generation before mine was preoccupied with origins, whether evolution of the species or habit acquisition by the individual organism; the generation after my midcentury epistemological generation has been followed by one preoccupied with power, in actuality or in image. The elderly Yeats, in his poem *Politics,* poked gentle fun at Thomas Mann's assertion that the destiny of man now presents its meaning in political terms, but Mann was prescient. Although a few topics dominate each generation, certain basic issues do receive some attention from every age cohort, so that even in the current political age there is an audience for my epistemological wonderings, as in this chapter and in chapter 8. I shall first describe the epistemological underpinnings of my "perspectivist" psychology of science, and then its operationalizing in the strategic planning of programs of research.

THE EPISTEMOLOGICAL FOUNDATIONS OF PERSPECTIVISM: KNOWLEDGE AS MISREPRESENTATION

Knowing is the heart of the process and product of science, so that insights into the scientific enterprise can be gained by examining what it means more broadly to know, "Was ist das – das Wissen?" to paraphrase Heidegger. Hence, I shall consider the evolutionary functions, nature, and limitations of knowing, and then identify a wide range of intrinsic and extrinsic criteria for evaluating knowledge, with stress on the historical development of science's empirical-confrontation criterion.

The Nature of Knowledge

[Adapted with permission from W. J. McGuire, 1989b, A perspectivist approach to the strategic planning of programmatic scientific research, in B. Gholson, W. R. Shadish, Jr., R. A. Neimeyer, & A. C. Houts (Eds.), *The psychology of science: Contributions to meta-*

science, pp. 214–245 (New York: Cambridge University Press, copyright © 1989).]

Fields of knowledge, like other complex stimuli, are selectively perceived in terms of their distinctive features (McGuire, 1984a; see chapter 8 in this volume), and so descriptions of science emphasize (and perhaps overemphasize) its empirical, hypothesis-testing aspect because that is the defining feature that distinguishes science from other approaches to knowledge. A specific insight about people may be arrived at by an artistic novelist, a humanistic scholar, an enterprising entrepreneur, or a scientific psychologist; where these different specialists then diverge is in the use to which they put this insight. The novelist might use it by depicting how it operates in a poignant interpersonal episode; the humanistic scholar might show how it relates to Spinoza's theory of the emotions; the entrepreneur might use it to improve a marketing campaign; and the scientific psychologist might use it to construct a broad theory whose further derivations would then be put to empirical confrontations.

That science is thought of primarily in terms of its distinctive empirical-confrontational aspect is not only understandable but desirable, because attending selectively to distinctive (peculiar, unpredictable) features of complex stimuli is an efficient form of information processing, as discussed in chapter 8. However, like other generally cost-effective approximations, this heuristic is imperfect and sometimes results in researchers' overcongregation at optimal points, losing sight of important aspects of scientific methods other than this distinctive empirical-confrontation aspect. One unfortunate effect is that courses on scientific method typically cover only topics having to do with this distinctive hypothesis-testing aspect, to the neglect of the creative hypothesis-generating aspect (see chapter 11, especially Table 11.1). Another unfortunate effect is that methodology courses overemphasize tactical testing issues within single experiments, ignoring strategic, programmatic issues of how one progresses from experiment to experiment. The critical and tactical aspects of the scientific process deserve attention, but not to such neglect of its creative and strategic aspects.

The perspectivist epistemology discussed in this chapter reverses the customary imbalance in two ways. First, I focus on the hypothesis-generating more than the hypothesis-testing aspect of the scientific process, describing (and to some extent prescribing) how creative knowledge generating can be carried out, both in the a priori conceptual-confrontation phase of research and in its a posteriori empirical-confrontation phase. Secondly, I focus on the strategic aspects of developing multiexperiment programs of research beyond the usually emphasized tactical aspects of devising the individual experiment.

The origins of knowledge.   Knowing probably arose because organisms with fluctuating needs and response options are dependent on environments whose potentialities and threats vary over time and space. Humans, like many species, have developed capacities to monitor and coordinate selected aspects of these varying self and environmental states that particularly facilitate coping and constitute knowledge. Knowing entails the organism's distinguishing variations in crucial aspects of self and environment, perhaps by modifying representational organs (such as receptor orientation, neural circuits, brain chemistry and electrical activity, postural readiness, etc.) into some analogous correspondence to the fluctuating energies being monitored.

Evolving capacity for such representation is costly, as illustrated by the high metabolic and histological demands of the human brain and the long period of dependency in human development. Conceivably, species might have avoided the costs of developing and operating representational knowledge systems by evolving with an economy that ignores fluctuations in self and environmental states, inexorably following preprogrammed or random patterns of behavior. However, humans, like most organisms, have evolved with a noetic economy that devotes sensory and motor resources, as well as massive central processes, to taking into account critical aspects of the current states of self and environment. The costliness of representation requires that knowledge monitoring be highly selective, keeping the organism in touch with only a few crucial aspects of the environment while leaving unmonitored a vast range of aspects that are less relevant to the organism's needs and capacities (e.g., over the vast expanse of the electromagnetic spectrum, human sense organs can monitor directly only the tiny visible band between wave lengths 390 to 760 millimicrons). Knowledge involves representation, but only selective representation.

The tragedy of knowledge.   This functional sketch of the origins and nature of knowledge suggests that the person's representations are necessarily misrepresentations due to three types of inevitable errors: underrepresentation, malrepresentation, and overrepresentation. (1) Most obviously, underrepresentation results from the economical selectivity of knowledge, just described. (2) Malrepresentation results from the inevitability that representations are shaped by characteristics of the knowing apparatus as well as those of the known. Knowing probably involves some kind of modification of the knower's cognitive apparatus that keeps it in an analogous one-to-one correspondence with fluctuating critical features of the known. For example, two of my cognitive representations of the known desktop on which I write – my phenomenal representation of it as a hard continuous surface and my atomic physics representation of it as a mostly empty space with occasional electrons or other particles – are dramatically different from one another, but each is probably more different still from the known itself, the desktop per se. (3) A third source of error, overrepresentation, results because, if knowing is to be useful, it must involve extrapolations beyond the given by making inferences, potentially erroneous, regarding need-satisfying actions. Knowing without overrepresentation would not be worth the candle, as is suggested by Thomas à Kempis's remark that the eye is not fulfilled by seeing. This triple faultiness of knowledge does not imply that it is so defective as to be basically maladaptive. The evolutionary success of knowing species and individuals suggests that the maladaptiveness of knowing tends to be exceeded by the maladaptiveness of ignorance. The inherent under-, mal-, and overrepresentations of knowledge are all excesses of virtue, each being a cost-effective tendency selectively acquired during species evolution and individual development that is economically advantageous in the ordinary conditions that have obtained during the species' phylogenetic and the individual's ontogenetic history.

The proneness to error of knowledge representations becomes aggravated as they deal with less familiar and less concrete topics and dimensions. Knowledge representations of one's ordinary concrete situations (such as one's perception of the immediate physical environment through which one must locomote) have selectively evolved to be highly dependable, though not quite perfect. However, misrepresentations in knowledge are greatly aggravated in sophisticated abstractions like "justice," "attitudes," or "cause," which have been occasionally popular with the Mediterranean-European intelligentsia since the Ionian pre-Socratics and are quite pronounced in the abstractions of modern sciences. The tragedy of knowledge is not that it is intrinsically erroneous, but that, erroneous as it is, it is indispensable: We must do what we cannot do well.

Although scientific knowledge is necessarily flawed, abandoning it would be more maladaptive than using it, judging by the relative material and cultural success of societies in which scientific and technological explorations have been encouraged. Its imperfections call, not for the rejection of scientific theorizing, but for the use of compensatory measures such as generating multiple (even contradictory) explanations that reveal the variety of reasons for which, and the contextual limitations within which, any hypothesized relation obtains. The perspectivist's working premise, that all knowledge representations are imperfect but all catch some aspect of the known, implies that the a posteriori empirical confrontation as well as the a priori conceptual confrontation aspects of the scientific process are best used, not as a test of a fixed knowledge representation, but as a continuous process of creation that gradually discloses a representation's fuller meaning.

Criteria for Evaluating
Knowledge Representations

Because perspectivism stresses the multiple shortcomings of all knowledge representations and the needs for complementary depictions and explanations and for an appreciation of their contextual limitations, it follows that judging the value of knowledge representations will call for many varied criteria, even including mutually contradictory ones. All knowledge representations are imperfect but differ in type and degree of imperfection. Which is the least imperfect depends on the use to which the knowledge is put, so the relative weights of various criteria vary across circumstances. I shall mention eight intrinsic and ten extrinsic criteria for evaluating any explanatory account. Intrinsic criteria concern characteristics of the knowledge representation itself, and extrinsic criteria involve factors outside the representation, although the line between the two sometimes fades. These sets of diverse criteria are proposed both prescriptively and descriptively, each actually being used at least implicitly in the practice of science and rightly so, even though some of these criteria are disdained by purists and some pairs are mutually contrary.

Intrinsic criteria for evaluating knowledge. An intrinsic desideratum of knowledge representations so familiar that it needs no explanation or defense is an internal consistency such that none of its implications are mutually contradictory. A second intrinsic desideratum is, paradoxically, the opposite characteristic of internal contradiction, which is an asset from the Hegelian/Marxist dialectical viewpoint that intrinsic contradiction between thesis and antithesis is ubiquitous in the *Ding-an-sich* that is being represented, and that contradictions can be a creative force toward synthesis in the actuality itself and in the knowledge representation of it. Third and fourth criteria, novelty and banality, likewise constitute a contradictory pair. Obviously, a theory's being novel rather than just a variant on a hackneyed theme increases its yield of provocative new insights. However, banality is also an asset, in that a theory has little impact within the scientific Establishment unless it fits within the current metatheory (paradigm) by using orthodox explanatory constructs. The Establishment may consider sympathetically a physiologizing explanation of a cognitive relation but will reject a telepathy explanation. Fortunately, what is acceptable to Establishment science changes over time, as illustrated by the recent weakening of the demand for gradualism in scientific explanation: at midcentury, scientists laughed at Velikovsky's cataclysmic theory of petroleum deposits although more recently they are giving serious consideration to Alvarez's cataclysmic asteroid theory of late cretaceous dinosaur extinction.

Fifth and sixth desiderata, parsimony and extravagance, are also sufficiently opposed to require a trade-off. Parsimony (as in Occam's razor or Lloyd Morgan's canon) is measured in terms of how few variables (or, more important, few relations) are needed to explain a given domain of covariations. On the other hand, the opposite sixth criteria of rococo exuberance in a theory has its charms; for example, abstruse formulations such as Neoplatonism, the Ptolemaic system, cabalism, alchemic theory, and astrology, seem to attract interest because of their arcane qualities rather than in spite of them. A seventh intrinsic criterion is elegance, the extent to which the theory is harmonious or esthetically pleasing by the symmetry, simplicity, monotonicity, rectilinearity, and so on, of the relations it uses to account for the observed covariance. The desirability of and actual frequency of using such esthetic criteria are probably underestimated by outside observers and even by science professionals. Aphoristic, oracular style is an eighth desideraturm whose appeal is illustrated by the influence of Nietzsche's and Blake's pithy writings or the compelling quality of proverbs or apt lines of verse.

Extrinsic criteria for evaluating knowledge. Firstly, derivability of a knowledge representation from an accepted set of principles is an often used external evaluative criterion, as when a geometric theorem is judged to be acceptable if and only if it can be derived from Euclid's or some other set of axioms, or when a theory on the origin of the universe is judged acceptable to the extent that it agrees with Genesis. Secondly, a theory may be judged by the status of its author, which may sound like a distasteful authoritarian imposition of an orthodoxy, but even in science an implausible theory does (and perhaps should, despite calls for blind review) gain added consideration when one learns that it was proposed by someone with a proven track record. A third extrinsic criterion is the theory's acceptance by the Establishment or in high-table science. Learning that a preprint report that at first glance had seemed implausible has been accepted for publication in a prestigious refereed journal or funded after discriminating peer review may reasonably renew one's interest. An opposite fourth desideratum involves a contrarian stance of preferring counterintuitive hypotheses, even to the extent of asserting the contrary of commonsense obvious hypotheses and imagining circumstances in which this contrary obtains, as discussed below in the perspectivism approach.

Fifth and sixth criteria introduce opposite political criteria. The fifth is the contention that a theory is accepted to the extent that it supports the status quo, as in the Marxist notion of false consciousness or Freud's notion of ego-defensive rationalization. Such a criterion might be warranted by evolutionary theory. An opposite, sixth, criterion is that a theory be accepted to the extent that it shocks the bourgeoisie. Some anti-Establishment thinkers in circles where heterodoxy has become institutionalized are attracted to theories to the extent that they annoy the authorities and even frighten the horses. One's own subjective reaction to a knowledge representation is a seventh reasonable extrinsic criterion. Plato's felt certainty, Descartes's clear and distinct ideas, Archimedes' eureka, and Bolyai's shriek may seem idiosyncratic and vague as standards, but many scientists (Greenwald, Pratkanis, Leippe, & Baumgardner, 1986) will remember occasions when they clung tenaciously to a theory in the face of discouraging early results because of a feeling that it deserved to be true, confident, like Brigham Young, that "This is the place." The extent to which such subjective experiences correlate with ultimate vindication needs and deserves further study.

More often mentioned is an eighth, pragmatic, criterion that a knowledge representation is acceptable to the extent that it proves useful for the attainment of valued human goals such as explaining intriguing puzzles or increasing productivity. Such usefulness (e.g., of irrational numbers for designing electric circuitry or counterintuitive non-Euclidean geometries for cosmology) may even excuse a theory's violation of other criteria by, for example, its internal contradictions, implausible assumptions, or imprecision. A ninth criterion is heuristic provocativeness: A knowledge representation (e.g., psychoanalytic theory) often enjoys acceptance and general use because it suggests new insights even though it scores poorly on testability and other criteria listed here. A tenth extrinsic criterion for acceptance of a theory is that derivations from it survive the jeopardy of an empirical confrontation. This testability criterion is the one most often mentioned currently in discussions of scientific method, perhaps because it focuses on the most peculiar (and therefore most salient) aspect of the scientific approach, namely, putting the question to nature in some kind of empirical confrontation. Perspectivism, in urging the generation of multiple explanations because of the limitations of any one explanation, suggests that the heuristic provocativeness criterion may deserve more weight than this orthodox empirical testability criterion.

The Evolution of Empirical Confrontation as a Criterion for Validity

[Adapted with permission from McGuire, 1986c.]

Underlying the criteria that have successively exerted hegemony in Western thought is the notion that there is a corpus of knowledge and validating procedures so accepted by the Establishment that the adequacy of any further knowledge representations can be tested by the extent to which they and their implications conform to (or at least do not contradict) this shared canon. During the past two millennia of Western intellectual development this empirical, intersubjective criterion of legitimacy has gradually evolved with regard to the nature of the accepted corpus against which all knowledge representation can be tested and of the operations by which such a test is to be applied. In each cultural period one criterion tends to be hegemonic, though not interdictively so, within the Establishment. As Western culture evolved the epistemological hegemony passed successively through five stages: dogmatism, rationalism, positivism, logical empiricism, and perspectivism (although with lags among different domains of inquiry).

Dogmatism. The dogmatic criterion for judging the acceptability of a theory is its agreement with a corpus of accepted propositions revered for qualities such as source, antiquity, reasonableness, or eloquence. Any proposition that conflicts with this body of dogma is rejected, and any that is independent of it is considered suspect. Dogmatism was the Establishment epistemology in Mediterranean and western European society during the first millennium of the common era, at least from the Christianization of the Roman Empire. The dogma during this era included Judeo-Christian scriptures, patristic writings, codes of canon and civil law, as interpreted by the teaching office of the Church, by Talmudic rabbis, by courts and lawyers, or by the individual reader. Illustrative of skilled users of the dogmatic criterion were Athanasius, Augustine of Hippo, Gregory, Rashi, and al-Bukhari.

Early in the common era's second millennium the dominant criterion shifted to rationalism, but dogmatism continues to be accepted by special sectors of society such as constitutional jurists, religious fundamentalists, Marxist-Leninists, and Freudians of the Strict Observance. Dogmatisms risk rigidity but, just as a theory is an ambiguous representation of the known, so the corpus of dogma is ambiguous, allowing leeway for evolution as new needs or new options arise. Also, continuing revelation may be allowed (as in the Church of Jesus Christ of Latter-day Saints) to supplement or even reverse the dogmatic contents.

Rationalism. A more serious problem with dogmatism, one that led to rationalism's supplanting it within the European intelligentsia around 1000 C.E., is that the revered corpus of criterial truth usually contains principles that vary greatly in plausibility or are mutually inconsistent, yet all claim equal acceptance; Sikh scripture boldly asserts that if any two passages contradict one another, both are true. Advances in material life in western Europe during the 900s, after absorption of the disruptive Viking and Magyar incursions, opened the way to belated exploitations of "dark age" technical innovations such as the scythe, the shoulder harness for the horse, the heavy-wheeled plow, the stirrup, and three-field crop rotation in the early medieval period. These innovations provided the motivation and surplus production that led to intellectual ferment. When in this era Anselm was challenged by his monastic students to derive the whole body of Christian doctrine just from rational principles that would have been available to a noble pagan without access to Scripture, he responded with his *Monologium* (1077 C.E.). Within a generation Abelard's *Sic et non* went further by demonstrating that dogmatism is not only unnecessary but insufficient for judging the truth of knowledge propositions – unnecessary because rational analysis can be substituted for Scripture to derive Christian truths, and inadequate because the dogmatic corpus of Scripture includes contradictory statements even on basic issues and so does not offer a clear criterion for judging alternative formulations about these issues.

Each criterion tends to popularize new methods; in the case of rationalism, it was deductive reasoning. The rationalist starts with axioms that seem intrinsically convincing (e.g., that an effect cannot be greater than its cause) or seem well established by observation (e.g., that all life comes from life). Any proposition is evaluated by ascertaining its logical derivability from such basic postulates. In the hands of brilliant and indefatigable polemicists such as Averroes, Maimonides, Thomas Aquinas, Duns Scotus, Nicholas of Cusa, and William of Occam, this rationalist criterion and the deductive method it suggested contributed significantly to the advancement of knowledge. The intellectual palaces constructed by these rationalists were as impressive as their contemporaneous cathedrals of lacy stone and stained glass, their vaults of thought as elegant and supportive as flying buttresses. Rationalism represents an advance over dogmatism in that its initial propositions are accepted more for their observed or intuitive plausibility than for their givenness, and because its deductive test of fit for any knowledge representation is more logically formalized.

Positivism. The shift from rationalism to positivism was more dramatic than the preceding shift from dogmatism to rationalism, which simply involved a more sophisticated selection of one's initial premises and a more explicit test of fit for new knowledge. The positivist succession more radically stands rationalism on its head: The rationalist proceeds deductively from generalities to specifics, whereas the positivist goes inductively from specifics to the general. This reversal worked itself out from the fourteenth to the seventeenth centuries, from Roger Bacon through William of Occam and Robert Grosseteste to Francis Bacon's *Novum Organum* in 1620. By the seventeenth century positivism and its attendant inductive method had become the Establishment epistemological criterion, with advocates such as Locke, Voltaire, Hume, Diderot, and the British empiricist and Enlightenment movements, though it was not until the nineteenth century that Comte popularized its "positivism" label.

Logical empiricism. In the twentieth century, logical empiricism and the related falsification movement transcended its predecessors in a particularly sophisticated way by synthesizing the opposite insights of the two preceding hegemonies, the rationalist deductive thesis and the positivist inductive antithesis. Proponents such as Schlick, Carnap, Hempel, Feigl, Bergman, and Popper proposed criteria for scientific meaning that embraced both the rational deductive a priori and the positivistic inductive a posteriori. Logical empiricists maintain that knowledge representations should, on the a priori side, be validly deducible from broader, empirically anchored theory and, on the a posteriori side, should survive jeopardy of disconfirmation by the observations yielded by an empirical test.

By midcentury logical empiricism had become the dominant epistemology of scientific psychology, prescribing that an investigator begin with a hypothetico-deductive theory whose general principles derive from prior scientific work and imply new hypothesized relations between operationally defined independent and dependent variables, which are then subjected to empirical testing. If the test results confirm the derived hypothesis, it and the theory from which it is deduced can be held more confidently; if the hypothesized relation is disconfirmed, then the hypothesis and the theory from which it was derived are to be rejected. The past two generations of psychologists have conceptualized research within this prescription.

Perspectivism. I have been proposing (McGuire, 1973c, 1983a, 1984c, 1989b) that although logical empiricism's brilliant synthesis helped scientists to exploit both a priori theory and a posteriori controlled observations, it has shortcomings that threaten to corrupt the conduct of psychology and to alienate psychologists from their work. These defects of logical empiricism will be discussed in the next section, along with perspectivism's alternatives.

Perspectivism in Relation to Logical Empiricism: Extensions and Departures

My perspectivist psychology of science can be clarified by mentioning four important innovations of logical empiricism and then considering how perspectivism builds upon some and departs from others of these *Wienerkreis* advances. Logical empiricism's great leap forward in the 1920s and 1930s can be summarized for present purposes in four of its positions, two regarding the a priori conceptualizing aspects of the scientific process and two regarding its a posteriori empirical aspects. For each pair, perspectivism builds upon and extends one position and radically departs from the other.

Innovations regarding the a priori conceptualization aspect of science.   Firstly, on the a priori side, logical empiricism emphasizes the importance of having an explicit hypothesis, preferably embedded in a broader theoretical formulation, to guide empirical observation. Secondly, it maintains that one (at most) of conflicting hypotheses and theories is true. The perspectivist epistemology proposed here (McGuire, 1983a, 1989b) agrees with logical empiricism on the first position, that it is desirable to have an a priori theory-embedded hypothesis to guide observation and organize data (as opposed to a naive positivism that the scientist should proceed by induction, passively observing occurrences to induce regularities). Perspectivism goes further in advocating (a) that the initial hypothesis be accounted for by multiple theories and (b) that the scientist should posit also the contrary hypothesis, along with multiple theories from which it can be derived.

Perspectivism departs even more radically from logical empiricism's second a priori assumption that among conflicting hypotheses and theories one at most is true and the others false. Perspectivism maintains, rather, that all knowledge representations (all hypotheses and all theories) are false because all are essentially flawed by underrepresentation, malrepresentation, and overrepresentation. Perspectivism goes on to argue, more outrageously, that because every proposition is generally wrong so also is its contradictory, and therefore every proposition is occasionally true, at least in certain contexts viewed from certain perspectives, as epitomized in Blake's proverb "Everything possible to be believed is an image of truth." Neils Bohr has argued that there are trivial truths and great truths, with the opposite of a trivial truth's being plainly false and the opposite of a great truth being also true. This postulate, that all knowledge formulations are true, is perspectivism's pons asinorum, its hardest-to-accept principle. Perspectivism maintains that the task of science, in its a posteriori as well as a priori aspects, is not the dull and easy job of showing that a fixed hypothesis is right or wrong in a given context. Such a modest project is suggested by Popperian inversion of the null hypothesis and his inadequate understanding that the task of current science is to account for covariance rather than, as in antiquity, to establish category membership. Science has the more exciting task of discovering in what senses the hypothesis and its theoretical explanations are true and in what senses false.

Innovations regarding the a posteriori empirical aspect of science.   On the a posteriori side, two basic positions of logical empiricism are, firstly, that a knowledge representation should be subjected to empirical confrontation; and secondly, that the purpose of the empirical confrontation is to test whether the fixed knowledge representation is true. Perspectivism agrees with the first postulate that empirical confrontation should be a part of the scientific process, but goes further in advocating that the empirical confrontation extend beyond the tactics of a single experiment to a planned strategic program of research.

Perspectivism departs more radically from logical empiricism's second a posteriori position that the purpose of the empirical confrontation is to test whether the hypothesis and its theoretical explanation are true. Perspectivism assigns a higher purpose to the empirical confrontation, that it continue the discovery process, creating new knowledge by revealing, not whether one's fixed a priori hypothesis is correct or not, but what that hypothesis means, namely, the pattern of contexts (constituting interacting variables) in which it does and does not obtain, and the mix of reasons for which it obtains in any one context.

The Myth and Reality of Scientists' Use
of Empirical Confrontation

The prevailing myth in science that empirical confrontation is a test ("experiment") of a fixed a priori hypothesis and an explanatory theory that is used to account for it leads scientists to report their research as if what they did was to derive a hypothesis from a theory, design a representative experimental test of it, carry out the test, analyze whether the obtained data support the hypothesized relation, and then report whether or not the predictions are disconfirmed.

The way we live now. The actualities of the scientific process are quite different. A well-socialized contemporary scientist typically starts off, as the myth depicts, with an explicit hypothesis housed in a theory. However, before proceeding to a formal test of this hypothesis the responsible scientist usually does some thought experiments, thinking through alternative conceptualizations of the variables and of procedures and contexts for testing the hypothesized relation among the variables, winnowing out many of the considered alternatives as unpromising. When a promising approach is eventually selected on the basis of such thought experiments and discussions with colleagues, the careful scientist may carry out prestudies to try different manipulations of the independent variables, alternative dependent-variable measures, various subject samples and procedures, and so on, until she or he develops sufficient feel for the relevant parameters to choose appropriate procedures for a formal experiment, which is then carried out. If its results do not confirm the hypothesis, the scientist is more likely to reject the experiment than the hypothesis. Typically, the scientist ponders what went wrong with this experiment that caused it not to "work" and mulls over what is needed for confirmation (e.g., a more appropriate or bigger participant sample, a stronger independent variable manipulation, better control of extraneous factors, a more sensitive dependent-variable measure, etc.). The hypothesis also may be modified by redefining one of the variables or, more drastically, by conjecturing that there is an interaction effect such that the originally predicted main effect obtains only in certain contexts and in other contexts may even be reversed. The researcher may then design a new and improved experiment. If this new and improved experiment "works" by coming out right (confirming the hypothesis), then a report is written for publication based mainly on this final experiment, with hardly a mention of the initial thought experiments, the exploratory research, or even the preceding formal experiments that did not work, suppressing revelation of contexts in which the relation demonstrated in the report does not obtain. Should the researcher's manuscript report these "preliminaries," the editor is likely to ask that the account of these initial inconclusive flounderings be condensed or eliminated as not affordable in the page-scarce journal.

The perspectivist position endorses this preliminary thrashing around as quite proper; what is improper is doing it carelessly and then sanitizing the final report by expunging the formidable information it reveals. When trying to fit the hypothesis-testing myth, scientists often suppress revelations yielded by these preliminary thought experiments and other explorations and, as an anticlimax, report only the final confirmation obtained in the well-manicured demonstration experiment. What the empirical confrontation should be establishing is, not whether the original hypothesis can be shown in at least one context to be true, but what it means – namely, the pattern of contexts in which the hypothesized relation does and does not obtain, and for which reasons. The current hypothesis-testing myth restricts publication primarily to the well-formed final experiment, which yields little information beyond demonstrating the obvious: that a sufficiently ingenious, persistent, and well-financed researcher can finally come up with some laboratory or field context in which any hypothesized relation (or its contrary) obtains. An unfortunate effect of the hypothesis-testing myth is that it prevents the scientist from sufficiently appreciating and exploiting the rich information yielded by current meandering "preliminaries" that lead up to the final confirming experiment. These preliminaries, when programmatically planned and recorded, reveal the rich meanings of the original hypothesis, namely, the contexts in which it and alternative relations do and do not obtain for a diversity of reasons. What is wrong about these preliminary explorations is not that they are carried out, but that most of their information is lost because the hypothesis-testing myth blinds the researcher to their full potential. These preliminaries should be carried out in a more organized fashion, guided by a systematic strategy, considered priorities, more adequate data recording and analysis, and a full interpretative report.

[Adapted with permission from McGuire, 1983a.]

Corrupting effects of the hypothesis-testing myth. The Establishment fiction that empirical confrontation serves the narrow, negational function of testing an a priori hypothesis and a theory in which it is housed – and so simply tells one whether or not one's fixed a priori formulation had been right in the first place – has unfortunate effects on the way in which research is taught in the classroom, done in the laboratory or field, reported in the journals, and applied in society. What gets published is a sanitized version of research, the well-done demonstration that confirms the hypothesis, while leaving hidden the main underlying portion of the great iceberg of empirical information.

This misleading publication style is the end product of the current preperspectivist mode of research training that emphasizes hit-and-run, one-experiment-at-a-time research planning derived from the misconception that the empirical confrontation serves as a test of a fixed hypothesis. Students have been encouraged to muddle through exploratory prestudies with tunnel vision, diligently modifying conditions as needed to contrive a demonstration experiment that confirms the hypothesis. The perspectivist advance is to teach students to organize systematically the thought experiment, prestudy phase into a program of studies that will chart the pattern of contexts that modify the hypothesized relation. Currently, the most respected doctoral programs strive to turn out good "stage managers" with a knack for setting up hypothesis-testing experiments that come out "right" (McGuire, 1967, 1973c). Departments gain repute by attracting bright students and converting them into adept stage managers, enhancing their impresario skills by apprenticing them to past masters or mistresses of the theatrical art and craft of experimental stage setting. At an earlier period I conjectured (McGuire, 1967, 1969b) that this skilled-artificer concept of the researcher as forging confirmations of his or her theory in the smithy of the laboratory experiment could be corrected by moving research to natural-world field settings. However, I soon realized (McGuire, 1973c) that flight to the field simply encourages the bright young researcher to change from being a laboratory stage manager to becoming a natural world "finder" (to use a term from real estate and commerce). Good field-oriented departments end up turning out researchers with a knack for finding special natural-world settings in which a given hypothesis will come out "right" (e.g., when the group-processes prediction does not work with high school basketball teams, the researcher might try tank crews).

The perspectivist approach implies that researchers should, instead, be trained in the strategic planning of programs of research to conduct a pattern of field or laboratory (pre)studies explicitly organized, as discussed below, into a program of research designed to reveal when the hypothesis does not obtain as well as when it does, and how the relations change from setting to setting as theoretically suggested.

Ubiquity of the hypothesis-testing myth. This perspectivist critique and prescription are needed in the social and behavioral sciences because they deal with complicated and value-laden subject matter, use variables hard to manipulate, and employ willful and erratic humans as their units of observation. However, the physical scientist also needs to appreciate that the empirical confrontation is a discovery process to make explicit hidden assumptions (usually in the form of interactional hypotheses) rather than being just a testing procedure to determine if an explicit a priori hypothesis is or is not true. Imagine that Galileo, to test the hypothesis that bodies fall with an acceleration independent of their mass, winds his way wearily to the top of the Leaning Tower of Pisa, from which he drops simultaneously a ping-pong ball and a bocce ball, having predicted that their moment of impact will be seen as simultaneous by his graduate assistant Andrea Sarti, observing at ground level below. Of course, contrary to the prediction, the heavier bocce ball will impact long before the ping-pong ball floats to the ground. If the assistant then proposes rushing to the editor crying, "Stop the presses. Galileo Galilei is wrong," the maestro would laugh his long-suffering assistant to scorn with the explanation that everyone knows that the prediction is made only within the context of objects falling in a friction-free vacuum. Should the assistant protest that the "law" is usually asserted misleadingly without such qualifying phrases, he would be told that it goes without saying, because no physicist ever thinks of bodies falling in anything but a vacuum. The empirical confrontation at the Leaning Tower of Pisa would have served, not to test the theory of the mass-free acceleration of falling bodies, but to make its meaning and context clearer to the assistant, laying bare its hidden assumption that Galileo's prediction will obtain only in nonexistent friction-free vacuums. Thus the physical as well as the social scientist needs reminding that the empirical confrontation is most profitably considered, not as a critical hypothesis-testing corrective of an earlier a priori phase of creative hypothesis-generating, but rather as an a posteriori continuation of the discovery process.

STRATEGIC PLANNING OF PROGRAMS OF RESEARCH

[Adapted with permission from McGuire, 1989b.]

Perspectivism reorients thinking about empirical confrontations away from the design of individual experiments and toward the developing of programmatic series of experiments, systematically designed to explore relevant contexts and multiple explanations for the hypothesized relation and the contrary relation. Perspectivism encourages the scientist to use instinct and common sense by engaging in preliminaries like thought experiments and prestudies and making fuller use of them, not as awkward and embarrassing fumblings but as part of the main event. Perspectivism is bearish on the value of the single experiment but bullish on the potential of organized programs of research; it casts doubt on the hypothesis-testing value of empirical confrontations while emphasizing their higher contribution in continuing the discovery process (McGuire, 1994c). The rest of this chapter describes a perspectivist approach to the strategic planning of programs of research that exploits the empirical confrontation as a knowledge-discovery process rather than merely as a test of some fixed, preformulated knowledge representation. An alternative perspectivist approach to strategic planning is described in the chapter 9 research on word-ordering primacy.

The Perspectivist Agenda

Perspectivism asserts that the relation between designated variables will change from context to context and will obtain in any one context for a variety of reasons. Consequently, empirical confrontation is best used, not to test the truth of a given fixed hypothesis and a single theoretical explanation, but rather to bring out the full meaning of one's initial hypothetical insight by a program of research designed to continue the discovery process (started in the earlier conceptual confrontation) by revealing contexts in which the hypothesis is or is not adequate and the varying mix of reasons for which it obtains. Productive scientists implicitly recognize the need for programmatic exploration, but the myth that the purpose of empirical confrontation is to test fixed hypotheses reduces it to an embarrassing preliminary whose rather haphazard pursuit loses much of the information it could have revealed. Perspectivism lets this "preliminary" exploration out of the closet and puts researchers comfortably in touch with their intuitive inclinations to do such explorations, so correcting the bad science and bad faith that result from professing the myth that empirical confrontation involves using individual experiments to test a fixed a priori hypothesis and its designated theory. The next three sections describe perspectivist techniques for doing and teaching strategic planning of programmatic research on three levels of abstraction, beginning with the hypothesis on its own level of meaning, then moving to the more abstract level of theoretically accounting for the hypothesis, and then to the more concrete level of drawing specific empirical inferences from the hypothesis and its theorized explanations.

For brevity and relevance, I shall focus on the common case where the scientist arrives early at a knowledge representation in the form of a hypothesized monotonic relation between two variables, my chosen example being the hypothesis that bulimia in adolescents is positively related to how distancing their fathers had been. The perspectivist strategy for generating a program of research regards such a hypothetical insight as only the visible tip of the iceberg of one's knowledge representations whose fuller depths can be disclosed by a systematically designed program of research.

I. Strategic Planning on the Initial Inspiration's Level of Abstraction

One can begin to develop programmatic empirical research by exploiting the rich ambiguities in the initial hypothesis on its own level of abstractness. I shall consider in turn three aspects of this initial hypothetical insight that offer opportunities for discovery: meanings of each variable, expressions of the relations between them, and situational and dispositional limits within which the hypothetical relations are conjectured to obtain.

Exploring meanings of the variables. The initial hypothetical insight typically expresses a vague relation between two fuzzy variables, each inadequately representing the known and each itself inadequately represented by the label given it. One must use words when one talks – as T. S. Eliot plaintively said – perhaps even when one talks to oneself. The freeze-frame snapshot of a variable that is caught by any one label will depict the preverbalized knowledge representation from only one of many possible perspectives. Two distorting lenses intervene: The reality I am monitoring is only imperfectly depicted in my knowledge representation, and this distorted knowledge representation is only partially communicated by any one verbal label that I give to it. The first component, the *Ding-an-sich,* is (in my realist epistemology) outside the knower, but the other two components, the knowledge representation and its label, are inside the researcher and so offer the possibility that playing word games with alternative labels can be used to obtain a fuller appreciation of the underlying knowledge representation. Thus words, which began as part of the problem (because labeling aggravates the inadequacies of the knowledge representation), may become part of the solution.

In my illustrative example both dependent and independent variables, propensity to "bulimic disorders" and level of "paternal distancingness," need to be explored to recover the initial insight more fully, but for brevity's sake I shall describe verbal exploration only for the more complicated "paternal distancingness" variable. One approach to exploiting a jargon term like "paternal distancing" is to do a scholarly analysis of the literature on the topic in order to collect the variant meanings and alternative labels it has been given in past research. It is usually more cost-effective to explore one's own delusional system by playing word games such as accumulating partial synonyms for "distancingness" (hostile, uncaring, absentee, rejecting, undemonstrative, etc.) and then generating synonyms of the synonyms; a little help from one's friends or a thesaurus can enrich the list. Then one explores the limits by asking whether each of the purported synonyms in the list captures the initial insight or, if not, by identifying the nuances that make it inappropriate. Such examination may result in partitioning the synonyms into several subsets that seem to tap different subcomponents of distancingness for which separate subscores may be needed later. Another word game is to list properties (descriptors) of distancingness and organize them into a tree diagram (or into other structures) that reflects the centrality and interrelations of symptoms that make up the syndrome. Besides these connotative explorations, the meaning of paternal distancing can be pursued denotatively by listing fathers whom one judges to be at opposite poles of the distancing-parent dimension (and listing still other fathers who are intermediate in distancingness) and then abstracting, for the father located at each level, what it is in his behavior that locates him at his designated level of distancingness.

After one has used such word games to develop a working definition of distancingness (or whatever one has come to label the variable by this time), one should similarly analyze the other variable, propensity to bulimic disorders. After each variable has been analyzed separately, the partial definitions of the two should be analyzed conjointly, conjecturing how each of the proposed aspects of "distancing" would be related to each distinguished aspect of bulimic disorders. These exercises are likely to identify subscales of each variable whose relations to one another and to subscales of the other variable invite investigation, by a priori thought experiments and by empirical confrontations, perhaps in the form of a preliminary multidimensional or structural-equation analysis. These conceptual elaborations of the variable help in the next, more abstract, level of strategic planning where the researcher is called upon to generate multiple theoretical explanations for the hypothesized relation. In any individual study one has to settle for a selective operational definition of the variable, sometimes as narrow as the definition with which one started out, but the choice made after these recommended verbal explorations will be a more informed one and may include separate measures of subscales that invite exploration. Also, this exploration calls to one's attention other possible definitions to be investigated in subsequent studies in the research program.

Multimodal expression of the relation between the variables. In this Stage I of strategic planning, clarifying the initial hypothesis, a second task turns from exploring its variables to exploring the hypothesized relation between them by expressing it in verbal, pictorial, symbolic, tabular, and statistical modes for several common scaling cases. Becoming comfortable with different modes of expressing a relation grows in importance when (as in Stage III of strategic planning) one deals with more complex hypotheses of nonmonotonic, mediational, and interactional types.

Most scientists, being verbal intellectuals, probably express their hypotheses to themselves first in verbal form (though a right-brain minority may initially represent their hypotheses in graphical or diagrammatical pictorial modes in imagination or on chalkboards or scrap paper). Even within the verbal mode and for a given scaling case there are many ways of expressing the hypothesis, such as "The more distancing the adolescent's father, the more likely she or he is to develop bulimic symptoms," or "Proneness to bulimia is an increasing function of paternal distancingness." The former has the advantage of resonating with the natural course of human cognition by flowing from antecedent to consequent; the latter usefully follows mathematical convention by defining the dependent as a function of the independent variable, which suggests the logic of experimental design and statistical analysis. Facility in moving among alternative verbalizations (as in going from verbal to pictorial to tabular representations) is helpful in carrying out different aspects of empirical research. In verbalizing the hypotheses, positivity (especially in naming variables) should be maximized: "Self-esteem is negatively related to bulimia" is preferable to "Low self-esteem goes with bulimia," and "Introversion is positively related to bulimia," is preferable to "Extraversion is negatively related to bulimia." People think better with affirmational formulations (see chapter 9 in this volume).

Students should be trained to verbalize (and otherwise express) main-effect hypotheses to handle each of the three common scaling cases: (1) where both independent and dependent variables are measured continuously (on many gradations), "The more distancing the father, the more pronounced the adolescent's bulimic behavior"; (2) where the independent variable is measured dichotomously (or on only a few ordered levels) and the dependent variable continuously, "Adolescents with high-distancing fathers exhibit more pronounced bulimic behavior than do those with low-distancing fathers"; and (3) where both variables are measured dichotomously, "A greater proportion of adolescents with high-distancing fathers become bulimic than do those with low-distancing fathers." The student should be trained to word (and picture and tabularize, etc.) hypotheses precisely to convey the different implications for experimental design and statistical analysis of these different scaling cases, and to retain the same scaling case when going from one modality to another. For example, when both variables are measured dichotomously and expressed graphically in a 2 × 2 contingency table, the independent variable should go on the horizontal axis with the high level to the right, and the dependent variable on the vertical axis with the high level on top. Otherwise the pictorial depiction of this scaling case will fail to correspond to the conventional depiction of other scaling cases where positive relations go upward to the right. By training students to graph hypotheses routinely in accord with these natural tendencies their cognitive load will be lightened, their misinterpretations reduced, and their communications clearer. Through routinizing the routinizable, researcher's intellectual resources are released for grappling with the as yet unroutinized.

The student should also be trained to express the hypothesis symbolically for each of the three scaling cases. For example, when both paternal distancing (D) and offspring bulimia (B) are measured continuously, abbreviated symbolizations like $D \xrightarrow{+} B$ and $B = f^+(D)$ are convenient. Symbolic (and graphical) representations are especially useful in expressing interaction hypotheses. A student who has difficulty going directly from a verbalization of the hypothesis to a tabular expression of it that clarifies the needed statistical analyses may find that symbolic or pictorial expression of the hypothesis is a convenient intermediate step between verbal and tabular or statistical expressions. Gaining facility in expressing the hypothetical relation in these alternative modes allows the researcher to move gradually to more arcane conceptual formulations, and also to obtain a fuller insight into the meanings of a relation. Scientists vary in which modes of expression they find more provocative or more understandable; hence, gaining facility in moving from one mode of expression to others allows each investigator to translate any expression into his or her own preferred modality while keeping access to alternative modalities where needed. Besides different dispositional preferences, there are situational preferences among the modes of expression; for example, verbal expressions are particularly fertile in suggesting theoretical explanations (and linking to past research), whereas the tabular expression best guides experimental design and arraying data for appropriate statistical analysis.

I have discussed monotonic main-effect relations. Additional complexities (and therefore opportunities) enter when nonrectilinear, nonmonotonic, mediational, and interactional relations are hypothesized. Unfortunately, our current social and behavioral science measures are so crude, and our theories so imprecise, that the parameters and even the shapes of the relations are too poorly predicted for these further complexities to arise, making unnecessary (alas) their discussion here.

Conjecturing the limits of the hypothesized relation. A hypothesized relation between independent and dependent variables usually obtains more in some specifiable subpopulations or situations than in others. A third step in Stage I (strategic planning on the hypothesis's own level of concreteness) is to identify these dispositional or situational limits or interactions, along with theoretical explanations of them. In our illustrative hypothesis that bulimic tendencies increase with paternal distancingness, mention of father suggests sex dispositional interactions. For example, that father rather than parental distancingness is specified, as well as that bulimic eating disorders are reported more often for females than for males, suggests possible sex interactions: Does paternal distancingness relate to eating disorders equally in boys as in girls; is maternal distancingness also a factor; is it the distancingness of the opposite-gender parent that is most important?

As regards situational interactions, time and place circumstances typically call for thought experiments. Is the distancingness–bulimia relation (and the high incidence of bulimia itself) a recent historical development, perhaps reflecting (and largely limited to) some current and localized sociocultural situation such as growing affluence, changed family relationships, television, sexual liberation, both parents working outside the home, or a ballooning youth generation consequent upon the baby boom? And is the relation largely concentrated in certain places and social or economic strata (perhaps mainly in the upper classes in the United States and other affluent secularized societies), and if so, for what reasons? This task of identifying interaction variables, begun here in Stage I, will be approached more systematically later in Stage III of strategic planning.

II. Strategic Planning on the More Abstract, Theoretical Level

After Stage I of perspectivist strategic planning has exploited the provocativeness of the initial hypothesis on its own level of concreteness by examining its components (its variables and relation), programmatic planning moves to Stage II, the more abstract level of generating multiple theoretical explanations for the hypothesized relation. This abstract level of strategic planning calls for three undertakings, which will be described in turn: (1) generating multiple explanations for the initial hypothesis; (2) the contrary of this hypothesis asserting and generating multiple explanations for it; and (3) expressing each explanatory theory in fertile logical form.

Generating multiple explanations of the initial hypothesis.   Early in the twentieth century, logical empiricism enhanced scientists' appreciation of the utility of embedding one's hypothesis in a broader theory. Perspectivism argues further that any hypothesis should be accounted for by multiple theories (as in Platt's method of strong inference) because any one theory accounts for the hypothesized relation only partially, from just one of many possible perspectives. The student or professional researcher usually has little difficulty in generating a first explanatory theory for a hypothesis such as "The more distancing the adolescent's father, the more likely she or he is to develop bulimic disorders." Most students readily think of some theoretical explanation, usually in the form of an intervening variable that mediates the relation between the independent and dependent variables, for example, by explaining that the hypothesized relation is due to the offspring's desperate attempt to attract the distancing father's attention. The implied syllogistic argument assumes that distancingness in the father increases the offspring's efforts to attract his attention and that a way to attract father's attention is to develop a bulimic pattern of behavior.

When asked to generate second, third, and fourth explanations, students usually manage to do so, but few students volunteer more than one explanation unless explicitly asked. This hesitancy may be more emotional than intellectual and may solve itself as students become accustomed to generating multiple explanations. It may be wise to point out to the student that additional explanations are desirable, not because the first theory is inadequate, but because the initial hypothesis is so rich that multiple explanations are needed to capture its full meaning. Intellectual facility in generating additional explanations can be enhanced by training the researcher in some of the dozens of heu-ristic techniques suggested elsewhere (McGuire, 1973c, 1997b; see Table 11.1 in this volume). With suitable encouragement almost all students suggest additional theoretical explanations (e.g., the bulimic offspring's wish to make the distancing father feel guilty; the distancing father's tending to produce greater sibling rivalry; his lowering the adolescent's self-esteem, his heightening parental discord, etc.).

Explaining the contrary hypothesis.   Perspectivism's most controversial working assumption is that every hypothesis is true, that there is always some imaginable perspective from which, some context within which, the hypothesis constitutes an adequate representation of the known *Ding-an-sich* for limited purposes. That every hypothesis is true in this sense implies that the contrary of any hypothesis is also true. This epistemological position, whether or not one agrees with it, suggests a provocative creative step, namely, that whatever one's initial hypothesis, one always hypothesizes also the contrary relation between one's variables and tries to account for this opposite hypothesis by multiple explanations. Simone Weil similarly prescribed: "Method of investigation: as soon as we have thought something, try to see in what way the contrary is true." The independent and dependent variables of one's hypothesis are often related in one direction by a first mediator and in the contrary direction by another mediator, so that the net relation might go in either direction and is probably nonmonotonic over the independent variable's total range, with the dependent variable reaching its maximum level at an intermediate level of the independent variable, the maximum and other parameters of the relation depending on circumstances that affect how much variance is contributed by each of the opposed mediators (McGuire, 1968b; see chapters 1 and 3 in this volume). Here I prescribe as standard strategic practice that, after one has generated multiple explanations for one's initial hypothesis, one should stand the initial hypothesis on its head and generate multiple theories also to account for its contrary. Often the researcher's initial hypothesis is a dreadfully banal, "bubba-psychological" prediction (McGuire, 1997a, 1997b) that one's grandmother knew but which is often untrue (e.g., the selective exposure hypothesis). This affirming-the-contrary tactic has the compensation that the more trivially obvious the initial hypothesis, the more strikingly novel is the contrary relation.

Generating explanations for the contrary relation tends to be more difficult than generating theories to account for the originally hypothesized relation, but most students, if encouraged, can come up with multiple explanations of the contrary prediction that fathers' distancingness lessens the offspring's proneness to bulimia (e.g., that having a distancing father would have resulted in the offspring's developing more skill in coping with rejection, or being less interested in physical attractiveness, or becoming more peer-oriented, or depending less on across-sex gratification, etc.). While explaining the initial hypothesis the student moves with his or her ongoing conceptual flow and often accounts for a relatively obvious relation; but explaining why the contrary relation occurs usually requires accounting for a novel, counterintuitive proposition. In accounting for the initial hypothesis each additional explanation tends to come with more difficulty; but in accounting for the contrary hypothesis, generating a first theoretical explanation tends to be the hardest, with further explanations following more easily. Perhaps generating a first explanation for the contrary of one's initial hypothesis gives one confidence that it can be done, and an idea of how it is done, so that additional explanations then flow more easily. Because it tends to be more difficult to generate explanations for the contrary of one's original inspiration, one may settle for generating fewer explanations for the contrary than for the original hypothesis, perhaps in all generating four to six distinctive explanations for the original proposition and two to four to account for the contrary prediction. Usually, only a few particularly interesting explanations of each hypothesis will be selected for full follow-up in the early stages of one's empirical research program.

Formalizing the expression of the theoretical explanations.   When one has generated multiple theories to explain both hypotheses, the original and its contrary, the final step in Stage II of perspectivist strategic planning is to express each theory with clear logical formality. Theories generated to account for the types of hypotheses discussed here (which are the types usually generated by students) are of the mediational type, IV $\rightarrow$ MV $\rightarrow$ DV. Such explanations can be formalized syllogistically, the independent variable serving as the subject term of the minor premise and of the conclusion, the dependent variable serving as the predicate term of the major premise and of the conclusion, and the explanatory mediational process serving as the intervening variable that enters the two premises as the syllogism's middle term. For example, if the original hypothesis, that paternal distancingness is positively related to an offspring's bulimia proneness, is first explained in terms of the offspring's desperation to gain the father's attention, this explanatory theory can be formalized syllogistically as follows:

> *Minor premise:* "The more distancing the father, the greater is the offspring's craving for his attention."

> *Major premise:* "The greater the offspring's craving for paternal attention, the more prone he or she is to bulimia."

Conclusion (the initial hypothesis): "Therefore, the more distancing the father, the greater is the offspring's proneness to bulimia."

Some explanations have a chain of mediators and so require a series of premises that make up a polysyllogism. More rarely proffered explanations have a logical structure other than these mediational ones that can be formalized syllogistically. (Nonscientific students of the topic, from the Hellenics like Aristotle to modern philosophers like Karl Popper, are more likely to give categorical explanations such as "All men are mortal" or "No swan is black.") However, syllogistic mediational explanations constitute over 90% of theories given when sophisticated research students in my classes are asked to account for a hypothesized relation, and so for brevity I shall confine the Stage II discussion to this type of theory.

My prescription that theoretical explanations of the hypothesis be logically formalized may sound pedantic, but formalization yields at least a half-dozen dividends. (1) It allows a diagnostic check on the validity of the theory, both materially (by providing a check of whether the independent, dependent, and mediating variables are used in the same sense in both propositions in which they appear) and formally (by checking whether each variable appears in the correct premise and ascertaining that there is not an odd number of negatives among the relations). (2) Formalizing forces the researcher to clarify the explanation; for example, the explanatory mediating variable (the offspring's craving for paternal attention) may have to be rephrased and rethought (as were the independent and dependent variables in Stage I) in order to keep each premise plausible and the syllogism valid. (3) Formalization allows testing the theory for tautology by ascertaining whether the theory's middle term (the intervening variable) overlaps with either dependent or independent variable by definition; if so, the theory is simply repeating, rather than explaining, the hypothesis. (4) Formalizing allows a plausibility check on each premise, diagnostically evaluating the explanation's strong and weak links and likely limiting contexts. For example, does the minor premise that "The more distancing the father, the greater is the offspring's craving for his attention" ring true, and under what circumstances? If one can easily generate a backup mediational syllogism that accounts for each premise, then it is plausible; if one cannot, then the explanation is suspect as farfetched or as obtaining only in some rare contexts where the noncompelling premise would be plausible. (5) Formalizing helps to ascertain the independence of alternative theories by allowing a check of whether their middle (explanatory) variables are nonoverlapping. (6) An important sixth benefit of formalization is that it increases the theory's heuristic provocativeness, as described below. Hence, although logically formalizing one's theory is sometimes regarded as inimical to creativity or at best as a pedantic endgame, a postcreative polishing-up phase of knowledge construction and communication, Stage III will show that formalization is an evocative creative tool.

III. Strategic Planning on the More Concrete, Empirical Level

Stage III of perspectivist strategic planning of a research program moves the discovery process to a more concrete level by using the information implicit in the original hypothesis and expanded in Stages I and II to generate further hypotheses. Stage I reveals the fuller meanings of the initial hypothesis's variables and of the relation between them. Stage II reveals and formalizes alternative explanations that could account for the original hypothesis or for its contrary. Stage III now exploits this revealed information by using it to generate additional hypotheses. For brevity I shall limit the discussion of Stage III to describing how the theories formalized in Stage II can be used for generating mediational and interactional hypotheses, followed by a brief addendum on additional hypotheses-generating techniques using information gained in Stage I. A fuller discussion can be found in McGuire (1989b).

Mediational hypotheses. The explanatory power of the usual mediational type of theory described in the previous section resides in its identifying an intervening variable that is affected by the independent variable and in turn affects the dependent variable, thus breaking down a relatively large causal jump from independent to dependent variable into two smaller steps, a type of explanation that seems rather pitiful in its essential structure but is the type that researchers usually give. The syllogistic formalization of such mediational explanations identifies the middle term, the one appearing in both premises but not in the conclusion of the argument, as the basic explanatory concept (the intervening variable) identified by that theory. Multiple theories to explain a given hypothesis are meaningfully different only to the extent that their middle terms (the mediating, intervening variables) are nonoverlapping. For example, craving for paternal affection, wanting to punish the father, loss of self-esteem, and so on, are distinctive explanations for why paternal distancing and bulimia should be related only to the extent that their syllogistic formalization identifies middle terms that are interestingly different – for example, by provoking distinctive interaction predictions.

Syllogistic formalization of a theory highlights the middle term as explanation for the hypothesized relation. Formalizing the self-esteem explanation of our original hypothesis that paternal distancingness promotes bulimia adds two subpredictions, the minor premise that father's distancingness is negatively related to offspring's self-esteem and the major premise that self-esteem is negatively related to bulimic tendencies. In order to test the theory the experimental design should include a measure, not only of the initial independent and dependent variables, distancing and bulimia, but also of the mediational variable, self-esteem. The empirical confrontation can then provide data for determining the extent to which the initial hypothesis obtains and also on the extent to which (as estimated by covariance analysis) the hypothesized relation obtains because of the theorized self-esteem intervening variable. Separate tests of the minor and major premises diagnose the strength of each link in the theory. Further, if a significant independent-to-dependent-variable relation remains after adjusting for self-esteem, it indicates that one or more additional explanatory variables are operating. Hence, adding the mediating variable identified by a theory's formalization provides empirical feedback on five relevant hypotheses rather than just on the original one. To exploit the creative potential of the theorized mediating variable, its meaning should be explored by various word games, and its relations to dependent and independent variables should be expressed in a variety of modalities – verbal, pictorial, tabular, symbolic, and statistical – as described earlier for the initial hypothesis.

Interactional hypotheses.   Each theory generated to explain the initial hypothesis implies not only one mediational but also multiple interactional predictions. Formalizing the theory makes its mediational prediction mechanically obvious, but further creative effort is needed to generate its interactional implications. Formalizing mediational theories into minor and major premises facilitates this creative generation of interactional hypotheses because each premise serves as a launching pad that suggests numerous dispositional and situational interaction variables. One has only to ask what third variable would multiply the relation specified in either premise. For example, when paternal distancing's relation to bulimia is explained in terms of the offspring's craving for the father's attention, the minor premise that "The more distancing the father, the greater the offspring's craving to win his attention" raises the question of dispositional interactions in the form of personal characteristics that would multiply this minor-premise relation, and hence the conclusion (e.g., the offspring's chronic need affiliation, being an only child, having few nonfamily friends, etc.). This premise also suggests numerous situational inter-acting variables – for example, how nurturant the mother is, the amount of control the father has over the offspring's goal attainment, how often the father comes in contact with offspring, how often the family moved, and the centrality of eating behavior in the family's in-teractions. Adding such dispositional or situational variables to the experimental design allows investigating not only the initial hypothe-sis but also each theorized explanation of it. After using the minor premise to generate multiple dispositional and situational interaction predictions, one can then use the major premise for the same purpose. Formalization of each theoretical explanation thus provides guidance for generating numerous interaction predictions, each interesting in its own right, and testing the explanatory power of each theory and its limits, and those of the initial hypothesis.

Programmatic planning that generates formidable lists of interac-tion predictions from each theory could become an embarrassment of riches unless one selectively chooses a small, informative subset of manageable interaction variables for inclusion in the design of the early studies. Distinctiveness is one criterion of choice; although each independent explanation posits one distinctive mediating variable, several different explanations might all imply the same interaction hy-pothesis, albeit for different reasons. Hence, priority might be given to interactional variables implied by one, and only one, of the theories whose power to explain the conclusion hypothesis one wishes to ex-plore. Other criteria for selecting interaction variables are their ease of manipulation and measuring, their richness of further implications, their potential main effect, their likely power, and their unexpected-ness. Each interaction variable generated in this Stage III of strategic planning reveals contexts that affect how strongly and why the initial hypothesis obtains.

Generating other types of hypotheses to distinguish explanations. Besides using the formalized theories to suggest distinctive (1) mediational and (2) interactional hypotheses as just described, four other creative procedures can exploit the insights gained in Stages I and II of strategic planning. A third and fourth procedure use information obtained in Stage I word games employed to explore the meaning of the independent and dependent variables. (3) Verbal explorations of the independent variable typically suggest a variety of ways to manipulate it that relate the dependent variable to different degrees and for different reasons, leading to further hypotheses, which can be investigated empirically by including alternative manipulations of the independent variable in the experimental design. (4) Stage I explorations of the dependent variable usually reveal subscales that thought experiments suggest are related to the independent variable to different degrees and for different reasons, conjectures that can be investigated by using a dependent variable measure yielding separate scores for these subscales (as well as a composite overall score). These additional hypotheses about independent-variable manipulations and dependent-variable subscales are of interest in that they clarify the meanings of variables, indicate contextual limitations of the original hypotheses, and reveal theoretical reasons for which the hypothesized relation obtains.

Two more demanding discovery procedures usable in Stage III to generate further predictions focus on the relation rather than on the variables of the initial hypothesis. (5) The separate independent/dependent variable relations implied by each of various theorized mediators can be integrated to yield a single complex function over a wide range of the independent variable. To use our bulimia example, integrating just two explanations – hostility to the other sex and craving for affection – suggests that over its whole range paternal distancingness will have a nonmonotonic inverted-U relation to bulimia. (6) Alternatively, one can identify a set of variables (including independent and dependent, and multiple mediational and interactional variables assembled by the procedures above) that are relevant to the alternative theories, and one can allow these to covary naturally. Then measuring each variable at successive time intervals will allow covariance structure modeling to identify, or at least test, expected paths and directions of influence among the variables.

Briefly, strategic planning involves expanding one's appreciation of one's original insight, first (in Stage I) on its own level of abstraction by exploring the meanings of the variables in the initial hypothesis and the relation between them. Next, on a more abstract Stage II theoretical level, multiple explanations for the original hypothesis and for its contrary are generated and formalized. Then, on a more concrete Stage III level, each premise of each formalized theory is used to generate additional mediational and interactional hypotheses. By including judiciously chosen subsets of these additional variables in the experimental designs of a systematic series of empirical studies, one can map the contexts in which alternative relations obtain, the mix of reasons for which each obtains, and the extent to which further explanations are necessary.

Establishing Priorities for a Systematic Program of Research

There is a fertile contradiction between this chapter's opening description of knowledge and the type of strategic planning I have subsequently proposed. My opening discussion of the origins, functions, and nature of knowledge depicted it as reducing the overwhelming complexities of the self and environmental reality to a happy oversimplification, a manageable compromise between completely ignoring a world that is too much with us versus taking its fullness overwhelmingly into account. In contrast, the three-stage strategy for planning research programs that I have been describing in the second half of this chapter might seem to introduce many complexities and qualifications that the initial simple hypothesis had mercifully screened out. Admittedly, any experiment necessitates vast oversimplification; the difference is that the oversimplifications in the initially stated hypothesis were ill-considered, whereas the oversimplifications that emerge after Stages I, II, and III of perspectivist strategic planning can be informed choices among explicit alternatives, pursued within a program that makes the whole more than the sum of its parts.

Strategic planning has the added yield of organizing the knowledge surrounding the initial insight within a conceptual structure that allows knowledge representations to be grasped on a higher level of complexity than is possible with the scattered aspects of the initial inspiration. Good thinking calls for laborious and complicated conceptualizing. This need not be anxiety-arousing or distracting if the researcher organizes her or his conceptualizations manageably. One convenient array is a matrix whose column headings are a list of the major and minor premises of the several theories generated to explain the original hypothesis, followed by the columns for premises of the theories that explain the contrary hypothesis. The row headings of the matrix might be the different types of hypotheses (e.g., the initial main effect, followed by the mediational, and then the multiple interactional-situational and interactional-personal predictions yielded by each premise of each theory in turn). Further rows would be provided for types of independent variable manipulations and of dependent variable subscales. Entered in each cell of such a matrix would be the column independent variable's hypothesized relation to the row dependent variable.

Once one masters these techniques for handling conceptual complexity, one begins to appreciate that complexity is a source of enrichment rather than confusion, an appreciation that enhances one's morale and daring. Productive nineteenth-century scientists such as Darwin, Locke, and Faraday kept notebooks on their thoughts and observations, often with elegant cross-reference systems that helped them to face complexities without demoralization or fear of forgetting. Such use of daybooks seems to have fallen into disuse among present-day scientists, but the practice may revive on a new level of sophistication as the use of the personal computer allows for exploiting perspectivist strategic planning with more sophisticated systems for multiple indexing, reindexing, and retrieving such notes.

The need for selectivity in programming empirical research. When one proceeds from conceptual analysis to empirical confrontation, strategic planning's revelation of the richness of the initial insight is particularly likely to cause indigestion because empirical research is expensive – as we often remind granting agencies – and so any empirical confrontation must be of a restricted, highly selective scope. One way of coping is to identify criteria for assigning priorities and then chop up the rich conceptual feast concocted during the three-stage strategic planning into manageable chunks suitable for a series of cost-effective experiments. Even if resources allowed, it would be inefficient to design one grand experiment that would include a dozen or two independent, dependent, mediational, and interactional variables identified as pertinent in those three planning stages. Such a full-court press would require an enormous investment of effort before any empirical feedback would be received. Methodological difficulties that become apparent only at the end might require redoing the whole study. It is more efficient to start with a highly selective initial experiment no more complex than that typically undertaken by a conventional preperspectivist. The difference is that the perspectivist's initial study includes a subset of variables deliberately compiled as a cost-effective first study from a rich array of relevant variables identified in the three-stage strategy, rather than the usual preperspectivist accidental mélange.

Shaping the initial and subsequent studies in a research program.   Given an initial hypothesis such as that offspring bulimia is positively related to paternal distancing, the experimental design for the first study might appropriately include the initial hypothesis's independent and dependent variables (both of which would have been refined, perhaps with subscales, by the word games in Stage I of strategic planning) plus two to four additional variables, mediational or interactional, each derivable from one and only one of alternative explanatory theories identified in Stage II. In this way the first experiment will test not only the initial hypothesis but further implications of at least two alternative explanations of it.

This initial experiment can be followed conservatively by a second study focused on the same two theories but including in the design alternative interactional variables and further subscales of the measures of the independent and dependent variables. Alternatively, a more adventurous second experiment could investigate a third and fourth theory by introducing into the design some of their uniquely implied mediators, interactions, manipulations, and subscales. By the third, if not the second, experiment one should grapple also with the contrary of the initial hypothesis by introducing into the design mediating and interacting variables implied by two explanations of the contrary hypothesis, so that the research program will communicate how vastly the relation between the original variables of interest, paternal distancingness and offspring bulimia will vary and even reverse as a function of context. At this point in the research program it would become useful to tap a sufficiently wide range of paternal distancingness to allow investigating whether proneness to bulimia has a nonmonotonic, inverted U-shaped relation (see chapter 4) to distancing over its full range.

Studies subsequent to the first should be guided, not only by the a priori programmatic planning, but also by the findings in the earlier studies, for example, by the relative strengths of predicted relations in different contexts or by serendipitous main and interaction effects that emerge when dispositional characteristics, like sex, or situational circumstances, like ordering, are varied within the design simply due to sampling or counterbalancing procedures. In the initial experiments in the program it is often more efficient to use manipulations of the independent variable to answer some precise theory-derived questions, whereas later experiments in the program use naturalistic situations in which a dozen or so variables, revealed by theory and the earlier studies to be critical, are allowed to covary naturally and are measured at several time intervals so that time-series causal models can reveal complex paths of reciprocal and mediated causality, and can give some estimate of fluctuations in effect sizes.

CONCLUSIONS

Perspectivism answers Marx's good-field, no-hit sneer at philosophy by being a tool for both understanding and changing science. As an interpretive epistemology it involves theorizing about theory, which risks circularity but yields hermeneutic insights. It is a dour theory of knowledge in pointing out that the necessary representations of reality are necessarily misrepresentations fraught with errors of oversimplification, distortion, and extrapolation. It depicts knowing tragically as an undertaking that we cannot do well but cannot do without. However, perspectivism is also a happy epistemology in proposing that, although every knowledge representation is usually wrong, each is occasionally right; that although our insights are hazy, this fuzziness can be a source of enrichment and heuristic provocativeness; that although empirical confrontation cannot test hypotheses, it can perform the more important function of continuing their discovery.

Perspectivism goes beyond being a philosophy of science to being a psychology of science, both prescribing and describing how science is done. It is insidiously revolutionary in that, rather than either justifying the current modes of conducting scientific research or iconoclastically calling for rejection of current practices, perspectivism subtly invites scientists to use empirical work to do deliberatively the contextual explorations that they now do furtively while pretending to be doing hypothesis testing. Perspectivism invites the scientist to recognize and exploit the rich ambiguities of her or his initial insight rather than suppressing them, using a priori conceptual analyses to unfold in organizable fashion the richness in the initial ambiguous insight and its contrary. Further, by recognizing the higher purpose of empirical confrontation as a continuation of the discovery process rather than as simply a test of a petrified a priori hypothesis and theory, perspectivism encourages and guides the scientist into making more appropriate and powerful use of the empirical processes of science by doing with deliberate care the thought experiments and "prestudies" now done with apologetic negligence. Perspectivism encourages and guides the scientist to do what intuition and experience already incline him or her to do, instead of suppressing these fertile exploratory impulses in order to maintain the pretense of following a naive logical-empiricism program. This preserves the researcher from bad faith and bad science. To paraphrase Hopkins, it leaves the scientist with the fine delight that fathers thought, aim now known and hand at work now never wrong, feeling the role, the rise, the carol, the creation, until the winter world, with some sighs, yields its explanations.

ENVOI

My way has been a long and peregrinating one, described here with some shortcuts. It is not for everyone, perhaps not for anyone else. It may be best if each of us, with glances at paths made by travelers who have gone before, makes his or her own way; but one's own way should be taken deliberately and egosyntonically, not stumbled into by chance. The authenticity of the work may reside, not so much in its matter or form, but in its style. Style is not everything, but no style is nothing at all.

Selected References

The full versions of the publications excerpted in this book cited several thousand references, many of which were deleted as part of the abridging process for this volume, but thousands of citations remain. Rather than sacrifice a hundred pages of text to listing references for all the works cited, I have adopted a lesser-of-evils economical solution of providing full references only for the McGuire publications excerpted here. This will allow the interested reader to find, in those McGuire publications listed, full references to all the works cited in the unabridged originals. The references to my cited publications are listed chronologically, the better to indicate the historical development of my thought.

Anderson, L. R., & McGuire, W. J. (1965d). Prior reassurance of group consensus as a factor in producing resistance to persuasion. *Sociometry, 28,* 44–56.

Iyengar, S., & McGuire, W. J. (Eds.). (1993a). *Explorations in political psychology.* Durham, NC: Duke University Press.

McGuire, W. J. (1950). The relative utilization of positional associations and inter-item associations in learning series of items in sequence. Unpublished M.A. thesis, Fordham University.

   (1957). Order of presentation as a factor in "conditioning" persuasiveness. In C. I. Hovland et al., *Order of presentation in persuasion* (pp. 98–114). New Haven, CT: Yale University Press.

   (1960a). Cognitive consistency and attitude change. *Journal of Abnormal and Social Psychology, 60,* 345–353.

   (1960b). Direct and indirect persuasive effects of dissonance-producing messages. *Journal of Abnormal and Social Psychology, 60,* 354–358.

   (1960c). A syllogistic analysis of cognitive relationships. In C. I. Hovland & M. J. Rosenberg (Eds.), *Attitude organization and change* (pp. 65–111). New Haven, CT: Yale University Press.

   (1961a). The effectiveness of supportive and refutational defenses in immunizing and restoring beliefs against persuasion. *Sociometry, 24,* 184–197.

(1961b). A multiprocess model for paired-associate learning. *Journal of Experimental Psychology, 62,* 335–347.

(1961c). Some deleterious effects on a perceptual-motor skill produced by an instructional film: Massing effects, interference and anxiety. In A. A. Lumsdaine (Ed.), *Student response in programmed instruction* (pp. 177–185). Washington, DC: National Academy of Science.

(1961d). Some factors influencing the effectiveness of demonstrational films: Repetition of instruction, slow motion, distribution of showings and instructional narrations. In A. A. Lumsdaine (Ed.), *Student response in programmed instruction* (pp. 187–207). Washington, DC: National Academy of Science.

(1961e). Effects of serial position and proximity to "reward" within a demonstrational film. In A. A. Lumsdaine (Ed.), *Student response in programmed instruction* (pp. 209–216). Washington, DC: National Academy of Science.

(1961f). Interpolated motivational statements within a programmed series of instructions as a distribution of practice factor. In A. A. Lumsdaine (Ed.), *Student response in programmed instruction* (pp. 411–415). Washington, DC: National Academy of Science.

(1961g). Audience participation and audio-visual instruction: Overt-covert responding and rate of presentation. In A. A. Lumsdaine (Ed.), *Student response in programmed instruction* (pp. 417–426). Washington, DC: National Academy of Science.

(1961h). Resistance to persuasion conferred by active and passive prior refutation of the same and alternative counterarguments. *Journal of Abnormal and Social Psychology, 63,* 326–332.

McGuire, W. J., & Papageorgis, D. (1961i). The relative efficacy of various types of prior belief-defenses in producing immunity to persuasion. *Journal of Abnormal and Social Psychology, 62,* 327–337.

McGuire, W. J. (1962a). Persistence of the resistance to persuasion induced by various types of prior belief defense. *Journal of Abnormal and Social Psychology, 64,* 241–248.

(1962b). Book review of O. J. Harvey, D. E. Hunt, & H. M. Schroder, *Conceptual systems and personality organization* (New York: Wiley, 1961). In *ACPA Newsletter, 12*(2), 6–7.

(1962c). Book review of M. Sherif, & C. I. Hovland, *Social judgment.* (New Haven, CT: Yale University Press, 1961). In *Contemporary Psychology, 7,* 320–322.

McGuire, W. J., & Papageorgis, D. (1962d). Effectiveness of forewarning in developing resistance to persuasion. *Public Opinion Quarterly, 26,* 24–34.

McGuire, W. J. (1963a). Book Review of L. Doob, *Communication in Africa* (New Haven, CT: Yale University Press, 1961). In *American Anthropologist, 65,* 172–173.

(1963b). *Immunization against persuasion*. AAAS Award manuscript, August.

(1964a) Book Review of J. Brehm, & A. R. Cohen, *Explorations in cognitive dissonance* (New York: Wiley, 1962). In *American Journal of Psychology, 77*, 337–338.

(1964b). Inducing resistance to persuasion: Some contemporary approaches. In L. Berkowitz (Ed.), *Advances in experimental social psychology* (Vol. 1, pp. 191–229). New York: Academic Press.

(1965a). Discussion of W. N. Schoenfeld's "Learning theory and social psychology." In O. Klineberg & R. Christie (Eds.), *Perspectives in Social Psychology* (pp. 135–140). New York: Holt.

(1965b). Techniques pour la création de la resistance à la persuasion: La role de la menace préable à la croyance. *Bulletin du centre E. R. P., 14*, 305–315.

McGuire, W. J., & Millman, S. (1965c). Anticipatory belief lowering following forewarning of a persuasive attack. *Journal of Personality and Social Psychology, 2*, 471–480.

McGuire, W. J. (1966a). Basic research and advertising practice: A dialogue (with Paul E. J. Gerhold). In Leo Bogart (Ed.), *Psychology in media strategy* (pp. 66–88). Chicago: American Marketing Association.

(1966b). Attitudes and opinions. In P. R. Farnsworth (Ed.), *Annual Review of Psychology* (Vol. 17, pp. 475–514). Palo Alto, CA: Annual Reviews, Inc.

(1966c). Current status of cognitive consistency theories. In S. Feldman (Ed.), *Cognitive consistency* (pp. 1–46). New York: Academic Press.

(1967). Some impending reorientations in social psychology. *Journal of Experimental Social Psychology, 3*, 124–139.

(1968a). Personality and attitude change: An information-processing theory. In A. G. Greenwald (Ed.), *Psychological foundations of attitudes* (pp. 171–196). New York: Academic Press.

(1968b). Personality and susceptibility to social influence. In E. F. Borgatta & W. W. Lambert (Eds.), *Handbook of personality theory and research* (pp. 1130–1187). Chicago: Rand McNally.

(1968c). *Theories of cognitive consistency*. Chicago: Rand McNally. [W. J. McGuire is coeditor of the volume and author of three chapters.]

(1968d). Theory of the structure of human thought. In R. P. Abelson et al. (Eds.), *Theories of cognitive consistency: A sourcebook* (pp. 140–162). Chicago: Rand McNally.

(1968e). Intersections of consistency theory with other psychological theories: Résumé and response. In R. P. Abelson et al. (Eds.), *Theories of cognitive consistency: A sourcebook* (pp. 165–167, 275–297). Chicago: Rand McNally.

(1968f). Selective exposure: A summing up. In R. P. Abelson et al. (Eds.), *Theories of cognitive consistency: A sourcebook* (pp. 769–770, 797–800). Chicago: Rand McNally.

(1969a). Attitude and attitude change. In G. Lindzey & E. Aronson (Eds.), *Handbook of social psychology* (Vol. 3, pp. 136–314). Reading, MA: Addison-Wesley.

(1969b). Theory-oriented research in natural settings: The best of both worlds for social psychology. In M. Sherif & C. Sherif (Eds.), *Interdisciplinary relations in the social sciences* (pp. 21–51). Chicago: Aldine.

(1969c). Suspiciousness of experimenter's intent as an artifact in social research. In R. Rosenthal & R. Rosnow (Eds.), *Artifacts in behavioral research* (pp. 13–57). New York: Academic Press.

(1970a, February). Immunization against persuasion. *Psychology Today,* pp. 36–39, 63–65.

(1970b). Designing communications to change attitudes regarding drug abuse. In J. Wittenborn (Ed.), *Communication and drug abuse* (pp. 70–108). Springfield, IL: Thomas.

(1970c). Attitudes and their change. In *Psychology Today: An introduction.* (pp. 613–633). Del Mar, CA: CRM Books.

(1971). The guiding theories behind attitude research. In C. W. King & D. J. Tigert (Eds.), *Attitude research reaches new heights* (pp. 26–48). New York: AMA.

(1972a). Attitude change: An information-processing paradigm. In C. G. McClintock (Ed.), *Experimental social psychology* (pp. 108–141). New York: Holt, Rinehart & Winston.

(1972b). Social psychology. In P. C. Dodwell, *New horizons in psychology-2* (pp. 219–242). Middlesex, Eng.: Penguin.

(1973a). Persuasion, resistance and attitude change. In I. deSola Pool and W. Schramm (Eds.), *Handbook of communications* (pp. 216–252). Chicago: Rand McNally.

(1973b). Persuasion. In G. A. Miller (Ed.), *Communication, language, and meaning* (pp. 242–255). New York: Basic Books.

(1973c). The yin and yang of progress in social psychology: Seven koan. *Journal of Personality and Social Psychology, 26,* 446–456.

(1974a). The social psychological perspective. In G. A. Kimble, N. Garmezy, & E. Zigler (Eds.), *Principles of general psychology* (pp. 616–638). New York: Ronald Press.

(1974b). Attitude and beliefs. *Encyclopaedia Britannica, 2* (15th ed., 360–363).

(1974c). Persuasion. *Encyclopaedia Britannica, 14* (15th ed., 122–127).

(1974d). Communication-persuasion models for drug education: Experimental findings. In M. Goodstadt (Ed.), *Research on methods and pro-*

grams of drug education (pp. 1–26). Toronto: Addiction Research Foundation.

(1974e). Psychological motives and communication gratification. In J. Blumler & E. Katz (Eds.), *The uses of mass communication: Current perspectives on gratifications research* (pp. 167–196). Beverly Hills: Sage.

(1975). The concepts of attitudes and their relations to behaviors. In H. W. Sinaiko & L. A. Broedling (Eds.), *Perspectives on attitude assessment: Surveys and their alternatives* (pp. 16–40). Washington, DC: Smithsonian Institute.

McGuire, W. J., & Padawer-Singer, A. (1976a). Trait salience in the spontaneous self concept. *Journal of Personality and Social Psychology, 33,* 743–754.

McGuire, W. J. (1976b). Some internal psychological factors influencing consumer choice. *Journal of Consumer Research, 2,* 302–319.

(1976c). Historical comparisons: Testing psychological hypotheses with cross-era data. *International Journal of Psychology, 11,* 161–183.

(1976d, 20 May). Position/summary paper on televised over-the-counter drug advertising. Testimony before the FTC/FCC OTC Drug Advertising to Children Panel. Washington, DC.

(1976e). Persuasion and social control. In *American Psychological Association Master Lectures* (cassette). Washington, DC: American Psychological Association.

(1977a). Attitudes and opinions. In B. B. Wolman (Ed.), *International encyclopaedia of psychiatry, psychology, psychoanalysis, and neurology* (Vol. 2, pp. 196–201). New York: Van Nostrand, Reinhold.

(1977b). Social influence. In B. B. Wolman (Ed.), *International encyclopaedia of psychiatry, psychology, psychoanalysis, and neurology* (Vol. 10, pp. 285–289). New York: Van Nostrand, Reinhold.

(1977c). Psychological factors influencing consumer choice. In R. Ferber (Ed.), *Selected aspects of consumer behavior* (pp. 319–359). Washington, DC: U.S. Government Printing Office.

McGuire, W. J., McGuire, C. V., Child, P., & Fujioka, T. (1978a). Salience of ethnicity in the spontaneous self-concept as a function of one's ethnic distinctiveness in the social environment. *Journal of Personality and Social Psychology, 36,* 511–520.

McGuire, W. J. (1978b). An information-processing model of advertising effectiveness. In H. L. Davis & A. J. Silk (Eds.), *Behavioral and management science in marketing* (pp. 156–180). New York: Ronald (Wiley).

(1978c). Retrieving the information from the literature. In B. Lipstein & W. J. McGuire (Eds.), *Evaluating advertising* (pp. xv–xxvi). New York: Advertising Research Foundation.

438   *Selected References*

(1978d). The communication/persuasion matrix. In B. Lipstein & W. J. McGuire (Eds.), *Evaluating advertising* (pp. xxvii–xxxv). New York: Advertising Research Foundation.

McGuire, W. J., McGuire, C. V., & Winton, W. (1979a). Effects of household sex composition on the salience of one's gender in the spontaneous self-concept. *Journal of Experimental Social Psychology, 15,* 77–90.

McGuire, W. J., Fujioka, T., & McGuire, C. V. (1979b). The place of school in the child's self-concept. *Impact on Instructional Improvement, 15,* 3–10.

McGuire, W. J., & McGuire, C. V. (1980a). Salience of handedness in the spontaneous self-concept. *Perceptual and Motor Skills, 50,* 3–7.

McGuire, W. J. (1980b). Behavioral medicine, public health, and communication theories. *National Forum, 40,* 18–24.

(1980c). The development of theory in social psychology. In R. Gilmour & S. Duck (Eds.), *The development of social psychology* (pp. 53–80). London: Academic Press.

(1980d). Social psychology – postscript. In P. C. Dodwell (Ed.), *New Horizons in Psychology* (2nd ed., pp. 272–277). London: Penguin.

(1980e). The value of privacy versus the need to know. In W. C. Bier (Ed.), *Privacy: A vanishing value?* (pp. 331–347). New York: Fordham University Press.

(1980f). Communication and social influence processes. In M. P. Feldman & J. F. Orford (Eds.), *The social psychology of psychological problems* (pp. 341–365). Sussex, Eng.: Wiley.

(1980g). The communication-persuasion model and health-risk labeling. In L. A. Morris, M. Mazis, & I. Barofsky (Eds.), *Banbury Report 6: Product labeling and health risks* (pp. 99–119). Cold Spring Harbor, NY: Cold Spring Harbor Laboratories.

(1980h). William J. McGuire. In R.I. Evans (Ed.), *The making of social psychology* (pp. 171–186). New York: Gardner.

(1981a). The probabilogical model of cognitive structure and attitude change. In R. Petty, T. Ostrom, & T. Brock (Eds.), *Cognitive responses in persuasion* (pp. 291–307). Hillsdale, NJ: Erlbaum.

McGuire, W. J., & McGuire, C. V. (1981b). The spontaneous self-concept as affected by personal distinctiveness. In M. D. Lynch, A. Norem-Hebeisen, & K. Gergen (Eds.), *The self-concept* (pp. 147–171). New York: Ballinger.

McGuire, W. J. (1981c). Theoretical foundations of public communication campaigns. In R. Rice & W. Paisley (Eds.), *Public communication campaigns* (pp. 41–70). Beverly Hills, CA: Sage.

McGuire, W. J., & McGuire, C. V. (1982a). Significant others in self-space: Sex differences and developmental trends in the social self. In J. Suls (Ed.), *Social psychological perspectives on the self* (pp. 71–96). Hillsdale, NJ: Erlbaum.

McGuire, W. J. (1982b, 14 May). Putting attitude research to work in marketing practice. *Marketing News, 15*(23), 2–18.

(1982c). Conceptualizing attitudes and attitude change for nutritional research and education. In L. S. Sims & J. H. MacNeil (Chairpersons), *Attitude theory and measurement in food and nutrition research* (pp. 1–19). Proceedings of a symposium on human nutrition improvement, June 14–17, 1980. Pennsylvania State University, University Park, PA.

(1982d). New developments in psychology as they bear on context effects. *ARF Conference Report, 28* (pp. 19–20).

(1983a). A contextualist theory of knowledge: Its implications for innovation and reform in psychological research. In L. Berkowitz (Ed.), *Advances in experimental social psychology* (Vol. 16, pp. 1–47). New York: Academic Press.

(1983b). Public persuasion campaigns. In B. B. Wolman (Ed.), *Progress volume: International encyclopedia.* New York: Aesculaprium.

(1984a). Search for the self: Going beyond self-esteem and the reactive self. In R. A. Zucker, J. Aronoff, & A. I. Rabin (Eds.), *Personality and the prediction of behavior* (pp. 73–120). New York: Academic Press.

(1984b). Public communication as a strategy for inducing health-promoting behavioral change. *Preventive Medicine, 13,* 299–319.

(1984c). Perspectivism: A look back at the future. *Contemporary Social Psychology, 10* (5 & 6), 19–39.

(1985a). Attitudes and attitude change. In G. Lindzey & E. Aronson (Eds.), *Handbook of social psychology* (3rd ed., Vol. 2, pp. 233–346). New York: Random House.

(1985b). Toward social psychology's second century. In S. Koch & D. E. Leary (Eds.), *A century of psychology as science* (pp. 558–590). New York: McGraw-Hill.

(1986a). The vicissitudes of attitudes and similar representational constructs in twentieth century psychology. *European Journal of Social Psychology, 16,* 89–130.

(1986b). The myth of massive media impact: Savagings and salvagings. In G. Comstock (Ed.), *Public communication and behavior, Vol. 1* (pp. 173–257). New York: Academic Press.

(1986c). A perspectivist looks at contextualism and the future of behavioral science. In R. Rosnow and M. Georgoudi (Eds.), *Contextualism and understanding in behavioral science: Implications for research and theory* (pp. 271–301). New York: Praeger.

McGuire, W. J., McGuire, C. V., & Cheever, J. (1986d). The self in society: Effects of social contexts on the sense of self. *British Journal of Social Psychology, 25,* 259–270.

McGuire, W. J. (1986e). Author's rejoinder to reviewers' comments on "The self in society." *British Journal of Social Psychology, 25,* 275.

McGuire, W. J., & McGuire, C. V. (1986f). Differences in conceptualizing self versus conceptualizing other people as manifested in contrasting verb types used in natural speech. *Journal of Personality and Social Psychology, 51,* 1135–1143.

McGuire, W. J. (1986g). Persuasion research. *Public Relations, 4*(4), 13–16.

McGuire, W. J., & McGuire, C. V. (1987). Developmental trends and gender differences in the subjective experience of self. T. Honess & K. Yardley (Eds.), *Self and identity: Individual change and development* (pp. 134–146). London: Routledge Kegan Paul.

(1988). Content and process in the experience of self. In L. Berkowitz (Ed.), *Advances in experimental social psychology* (Vol. 21, pp. 97–144). New York: Academic Press.

McGuire, W. J. (1989a). The structure of individual attitudes and attitude systems. In A. R. Pratkanis, S. J. Breckler, & A. G. Greenwald (Eds.), *Attitude structure and function* (pp. 37–69). Hillsdale, NJ: Erlbaum.

(1989b). A perspectivist approach to the strategic planning of programmatic scientific research. In B. Gholson, W. R. Shadish, Jr., R. A. Neimeyer, & A. C. Houts (Eds.), *The psychology of science: Contributions to metascience* (pp. 214–245). New York: Cambridge University Press.

(1989c). Persuasion. In E. Barnouw (Ed.), *International encyclopedia of communications* (Vol. 3, pp. 266–270). New York: Oxford University Press.

(1989e). A mediational theory of susceptibility to social influence. In V. Gheorghiu, P. Netter, H. J. Eysenck, & R. Rosenthal (Eds.), *Suggestibility: Theory and research* (pp. 305–322). Heidelberg: Springer.

(1989f). Theoretical foundations of campaigns. In R. E. Rice and C. Atkin (Eds.), *Public communication campaigns* (2nd ed., pp. 43–65). Beverly Hills, CA: Sage.

(1990). Dynamic operations of thought systems. *American Psychologist, 45,* 504–512.

McGuire, W. J., & McGuire, C. V. (1991a). The affirmational versus negational self-concepts. In J. Strauss and G. R. Goethals (Eds.), *The self: Interdisciplinary approaches* (pp. 107–120). New York: Springer Verlag.

McGuire, W. J. (1991b). Using guiding-idea theories of the person to develop educational campaigns against drug abuse and other health-threatening behavior. *Health Education Research: Theory and Practice, 6,* 173–184 (special issue on "Theory").

McGuire, W. J., & McGuire, C. V. (1991c). The content, structure, and operation of thought systems. In R. S. Wyer, Jr., & T. K. Srull (Eds.), *Advances in social cognition* (Vol. 4, pp. 1–78). Hillsdale, NJ: Erlbaum.

McGuire, W. J. (1991d). Homage to our critics: A dialectical collaboration. In R. S. Wyer, Jr., & T. K. Srull (Eds.), *Advances in social cognition* (Vol. 4, pp. 215–266). Hillsdale, NJ: Erlbaum.

(1991e). Who's afraid of the big bad media? In A. A. Berger (Ed.), *Mass media USA: Process and effect* (2nd ed., pp. 272–280). New York: Longman.

(1992a). Possible excuses for claiming massive media effects despite the weak evidence. In S. Rothman (Ed.), *The mass media in liberal democratic societies* (pp. 121–146). New York: Paragon House.

McGuire, W. J., & McGuire, C. V. (1992b). Psychological significance of seemingly arbitrary word-order regularities: The case of kin pairs. In G. Semin & K. Fiedler (Eds.), *Language, interaction, and social cognition* (pp. 214–236). London: Sage.

(1992c). Cognitive-versus-affective positivity asymmetries in thought systems. *European Journal of Social Psychology, 22,* 571–591.

McGuire, W. J. (1992d). Designing a persuasion campaign to reduce substance abuse. In J. White, R. Ali, P. Christie, S. Cormack, M. Caughwin, J. Mendoza, & R. Sweeney (Eds.), *Drug problems in our society: Dimensions and perspectives* (pp. 168–176). Parkside, South Australia: Drug and Alcohol Services Council.

(1993b). The poly–psy relationship: Three phases of a long affair. In S. Iyengar & W. J. McGuire (Eds.), *Explorations in political psychology* (pp. 9–35). Durham, NC: Duke University Press.

(1993c). Attitudes and behavior. In S. Iyengar & W. J. McGuire (Eds.), *Explorations in political psychology* (pp. 65–69). Durham, NC: Duke University Press.

(1993d). The big one: Eagly and Chaiken's "Psychology of attitudes." *Psychological Inquiry, 4,* 370–378.

(1994a). Uses of historical data in psychology: Comments on Münsterberg (1899). *Psychological Review, 101,* 243–247.

(1994b). Using mass media communication to enhance public health. In L. Sechrest, T. E. Backer, E. M. Rogers, T. F. Campbell, & M. L. Grady (Eds.), *Effective dissemination of clinical health information. AHCPR Publication No. 95–0015* (pp. 125–151). Rockville, MD: Public Health Service, Agency for Health Care Policy and Research.

(1994c). The psychology of behavior and the behavior of psychologists. *Revista Mexicana de Análisis de la conducta (Mexican Journal of Behavior Analysis), 20, Monographic issue,* 75–100.

(1995). Transferring research findings on persuasion to improve drug-abuse prevention programs. In T. E. Backer, S. L. David, & G. Soucy (Eds.), *Reviewing the behavioral science knowledge base on technology transfer.* National Institute on Drug Abuse Research Monograph Series 155 (NIH Publication No. 95–4035, pp. 225–245). Washington, DC: National Institutes on Drug Abuse.

(1996a). The communication and attitude-change program in the 1950s at Yale. In E. E. Dennis & E. Wartella (Eds.), *American communication research: The remembered history* (pp. 39–59). Hillsdale, NJ: Erlbaum.

McGuire, W. J., & McGuire, C. V. (1996b). Enhancing self-esteem by directed thinking tasks: Cognitive and affective positivity asymmetries. *Journal of Personality and Social Psychology, 70,* 1117–1124.

McGuire, W. J. (1997a). Going beyond the banalities of bubbapsychology: A perspectivist social psychology. In A. Haslam and C. McGarty (Eds.), *The message of social psychology* (pp. 221–237). Oxford: Blackwell Publishers.

(1997b). Creative hypothesis generating in psychology: Some useful heuristics. *Annual Review of Psychology, 48,* 1–30. Palo Alto, CA: Annual Reviews.

Papageorgis, D., & McGuire, W. J. (1961j). The generality of immunity to persuasion produced by pre-exposure to weakened counter-arguments. *Journal of Abnormal and Social Psychology, 62,* 475–481.

Watts, W., & McGuire, W. J. (1964c). Persistence of induced opinion change and retention of inducing message content. *Journal of Abnormal and Social Psychology, 68,* 233–241.

Index